ADJUSTMENT WITH A HUMAN FACE

Volume I

Adjustment with a Human Face

VOLUME I
Protecting the Vulnerable and Promoting Growth

Edited by

Giovanni Andrea Cornia, Richard Jolly, and Frances Stewart

CLARENDON PRESS · OXFORD

Oxford University Press, Walton Street, Oxford OX2 6DP
Oxford New York Toronto
Delhi Bombay Calcutta Madras Karachi
Petaling Jaya Singapore Hong Kong Tokyo
Nairobi Dar es Salaam Cape Town
Melbourne Auckland
and associated companies in
Berlin Ibadan

Oxford is a trade mark of Oxford University Press

Published in the United States
by Oxford University Press, New York

First published 1987
Reprinted 1988 (twice), 1989, 1990

British Library Cataloguing in Publication Data
Adjustment with a human face.
Vol. 1: Protecting the vulnerable and promoting growth
1. Developing countries—Social conditions
2. Developing countries—Economic policy
I. Cornia, Giovanni   II. Jolly, Richard
III. Stewart, Frances
909'.097240828   HN980
ISBN 0–19–828610–4
ISBN 0–19–828609–0 (Pbk)

Library of Congress Cataloging in Publication Data
Adjustment with a human face.
Bibliography: p.   ; Includes index.
1. Child welfare.
2. Children–Economic conditions.
3. Economic policy. 4. Depressions.
I. Cornia, Giovanni Andrea.
II. Jolly, Richard.
III. Stewart, Frances.
HV713.A37 1987   362.7'042   87–11137
ISBN 0–19–828610–4 (v. 1)
ISBN 0–19–828609–0 (Pbk)

Printed and bound in
Great Britain by Courier International Ltd,
Tiptree, Essex

To the memory of Nicholas Kaldor

Foreword

James P. Grant, Executive Director, UNICEF

The care and protection of children is a practice and an ethic rooted deep in the wisdom and culture of all societies. Children are the vulnerable, at birth the tiny ones, whose very survival depends, day by day, on the food, the clothing, the warmth and shelter, as well as the love and tenderness provided. During their years of growth, guidance and nurture, comradeship, and health and education are added to these basic needs.

All this is so obvious and deep-rooted, that most people everywhere take it for granted. Indeed, in many societies and traditions, parents can be taken to court or otherwise admonished for neglect of their children. Religious teaching down the ages has reinforced this ethic, underlining the duty of parents towards their children and sometimes threatening very severe punishment on those who fail in this duty.

Over this last century, national responsibilities for child care and protection have evolved further and wider. Many countries now have legislation defining child rights and parental obligations, and many have set up social services to provide for children when their rights and obligations are neglected.

Yet internationally, concern and responsibility still lag far behind personal or national sensitivities and commitments. Public awareness and thinking too often stop at national boundaries—until a loud emergency, such as the Ethiopian famine or the Bhopal tragedy in India, jerks people into awareness by bringing home the human reality of hunger and suffering in terms which everyone can understand. Then governments act—and the finer points of responsibility become secondary to a common interest in urgent care.

At the moment, children are suffering through an acute silent emergency—the effects of recession and financial drought on already low levels of household consumption, nutrition, and basic welfare in probably two-thirds of the countries of the Third World. Young children and vulnerable groups such as pregnant women and nursing mothers are, in most countries, the major victims, with lifelong damage a common result. More sensitive national and international economic policies could avoid much of the suffering and human damage—yet so far, only limited action has been taken to protect the incomes and nutrition of the poor, and investment in the social sectors, and to make more effective use of the amounts available for the social sectors.

It is these national and international *economic* concerns which are the subject of this book. The book draws on UNICEF work over the last few years to show how children have been suffering unnecessarily through neglect of their needs in the making of economic policy, nationally and internationally. The book follows a long UNICEF tradition in putting the emphasis on what can be done—and giving examples of positive approaches in practice.

The need for applying these new approaches is urgent. Millions of children are suffering now, many of them in countries which until now have framed their economic and financial policies with little thought, if any, for the human consequences of these policies for the lives and futures of children and other vulnerable groups.

Action requires a double stimulus. To know what to do and to have the motivation to do it. We have the knowledge. Can we now extend our sense of ethic and responsibility to generate the motivation to act?

J. P. G.

Acknowledgements

This study draws on the ideas and initiatives of many groups. Within UNICEF, we would like to thank those of our colleagues who, from the beginning, have emphasized the importance of adjustment issues for the well-being of children and encouraged our work. Besides Jim Grant, who provided unfailing support, special mention should be made of Eduardo Bustelo, Denis Caillaux, Pratima Kale, and Farid Rahman for their pioneering work on these issues in Latin America, Ghana, the Philippines, and Sri Lanka. We should particularly mention the support from UNICEF's Executive Board and the special encouragement we received from certain governments, initially the governments of Canada, Netherlands, and Sweden, but subsequently from many others, from both developed and developing countries.

We should also like to thank many people in other international agencies. Staff from the International Monetary Fund, the World Bank, the Department of International Economic and Social Affairs of the United Nations, the International Labour Office, the World Food Programme, the World Health Organization, and the Pan-American Health Organization, the Economic Commission for Latin America, the Economic Commission for Africa, and others have often been consulted and have provided considerable help. Naturally none of them are responsible for the views we have developed.

A number of individuals outside the international system have given us substantial help: Sidney Dell, Reginald Green, Stephanie Griffith-Jones, Gerald Helleiner, Joan Nelson, and Hans Singer. Without their support over the last three years, this study would be much weaker.

Several helped us with a review of the first full draft on Roosevelt Island in June 1986, joined by Henry Mosley, John Williamson, Lal Jayawardena, Per Pinstrup-Andersen, and Alan Berg. We thank them all.

Special mention should also be made of the many non-governmental organizations including Oxfam, the International Coalition for Development Action, and others that, with their first-hand experience and direct involvement with the effects of economic decline and indebtedness on the poor, have provided a constant reminder of the need to provide concrete and relevant alternatives.

We also thank those who prepared the country case studies, which form a basic part of the study and which are issued separately as Volume II:

Botswana	Victoria J. Quinn, Mark S. Cohen, John Mason, Cornell University, Nutritional Surveillance Program in Eastern and Southern Africa, and B. N. Kgosidintsi, Ministry of Health, Gaborone
Brazil (São Paulo)	Roberto Macedo, University of São Paulo, Brazil

Chile	Dagmar Raczynski, CIEPLAN, Santiago
Ghana	UNICEF, Accra
Jamaica	Derick Boyd, University of the West Indies, Kingston
Peru	Leonel Figueroa, Central Bank, Lima
Philippines	UNICEF, Manila
South Korea	Sang-Mok Suh and David Williamson, Korean Development Institute, Seoul
Sri Lanka	UNICEF, Colombo
Zimbabwe	Rob Davies and David Sanders, University of Zimbabwe

The ideas in the study have also benefited by meetings. We are especially grateful to the Society for International Development, where Richard Jolly presented the Barbara Ward Lecture on 'Adjustment with a Human Face' at the 18th World Conference in 1985, and FEDESARROLLO and the government of Colombia, for organizing a seminar on these themes in Bogota in February 1986.

A particular word of thanks goes to Eva Jespersen who provided professional help in data collection and analysis, and assisted with many useful comments and editorial support.

We thank our colleagues who have helped type and retype the manuscript, and apologize to them for the long hours, the bad handwriting, and numerous changes. For this help, we shall treasure the memories and comradeship of Josephine Rajasegera, Gillian Usher, Karen Pitts, and Michelle Dufort.

May we end by underlining two points. First, there is bound to be some difference of view on many of the issues put forward. To avoid institutional and irrelevant controversies, these ideas have been put forward in the names of the authors concerned, thus making clear that the particulars of the argument and the details of every recommendation cannot be taken formally to represent the position of any of the institutions involved, or any of the individuals on whose help we have drawn. Secondly, we wish to make quite clear that our purpose is constructive. If we identify inadequacies in the past, it is to learn lessons for the future. Our hope is to seek a better outcome for the many millions of children, particularly from poorer households, who are caught up in the economic difficulties and adjustment processes in developing countries. We hope that our effort may be a modest contribution to the making of future policies that will better take their needs into account, and improve the situation of children in the years ahead.

G.A.C., R.J., and F.S.

Contents

Notes on Contributors

GIOVANNI ANDREA CORNIA is Senior Planning Officer at UNICEF. He previously worked at UNCTAD, and the Economic Studies Centre of Fiat. His writings include work on savings in developing countries, on land reform, and the impact of world recession on children.

GERALD K. HELLEINER is a Professor of Economics at the University of Toronto. His many publications include work on technology transfer and multinational corporations, North–South relations, and international finance and adjustment.

MAURICE JARAMILLO is a researcher at the International Food Policy Research Institute.

RICHARD JOLLY is Deputy Executive Director of UNICEF responsible for programmes. He was formerly Director of the Institute of Development Studies at the University of Sussex. He has written widely on development issues, focusing on education, employment, and basic needs.

RICHARD LONGHURST is a Visiting Fellow at the Institute of Development Studies at the University of Sussex. He is an agricultural economist working in the area of food and nutrition.

W. HENRY MOSLEY is Professor at the School of Hygiene and Public Health, Johns Hopkins University. He is a demographer and has made considerable contributions to analysis of the relationship between biological, social, and other factors in determining health status.

PER PINSTRUP-ANDERSEN is Professor of Food Economics and director of the Cornell Nutrition Surveillance Program. He was previously director of the Food Consumption and Nutrition Policy Program at the International Food Policy Research Institute. He has written extensively on food policy issues.

FRANCES STEWART is a Fellow of Somerville College, and Senior Research Officer at Queen Elizabeth House, Oxford. She worked at UNICEF as Special Adviser on Adjustment. She is a development economist, and has published widely on technology and development, basic needs, and international trade and monetary issues.

List of Figures

List of Tables

Abbreviations

ATI	Appropriate Technology International
CARE	Co-operative for Relief Everywhere
CFF	Compensatory Financing Facility
CIEPLAN	Corporacion Investigaciones Economicas Latino America
CPI	Consumer Price Index
CRS	Catholic Relief Services
EA	Extended Arrangement
ECLA	Economic Commission for Latin America
ESCAP	Economic and Social Commission for Asia and the Pacific
FAO	Food and Agricultural Organization
GATT	General Agreement on Tariffs and Trade
GOBI–FF	Growth monitoring, Oral rehydration therapy, Breast feeding, Immunization–Female Education, Family Spacing, Food
IFAD	International Fund for Agricultural Development
IFPRI	International Food Policy Research Institute
ILO	International Labour Office
IMF	International Monetary Fund
NGO	Non-governmental Organization
ODA	Official Development Assistance
OECD	Organization for Economic Co-operation and Development
ORS	Oral Rehydration Salts
ORT	Oral Rehydration Therapy
PAHO	Pan-American Health Organization
SAC	Structural Adjustment Credit
SAL	Structural Adjustment Loan
SBA	Stand-by Agreement
SDR	Special Drawing Rights
SPWP	Special Public Works Programme
STABEX	Stabilization of Export Earnings
UN-ACC/SCN	United Nations Administrative Co-ordinating Committee/Subcommittee on Nutrition
UN-DIESA	United Nations Department of International Economic and Social Affairs
UNDP	United Nations Development Programme
UNICEF	United Nations Children's Fund
UNRISD	United Nations Research Institute on Social Development
WEP	World Employment Programme

Definitions

Adjustment. The process of responding to (often severe) imbalances in the economy, particularly deficits in a country's balance of payment, usually by adopting measures which expand exports, reduce imports, or otherwise attract foreign exchange to a country. Often, measures to curb a government deficit by increasing government revenue or reducing expenditure are also involved. These actions involve changes in the structure of the economy.

Adjustment policy. A purposeful and coherent set of policies towards the goal of economic adjustment. Since the goal of reducing a deficit can be achieved in different ways, and over different time periods, one can speak of a short-term adjustment policy, growth-oriented adjustment policy, or, of course, an adjustment policy focused on growth and human needs, thus 'adjustment with a human face'.

Balance of payments. A systematic record of the economic transactions between a nation's residents and non-residents during a given period, usually one calendar or fiscal year. It covers the flow of real resources (including factor services, such as the services of labour and capital) across the boundaries of the domestic economy, changes in foreign assets and liabilities resulting from economic transactions, and transfer payments to and from the rest of the world. Balance of payments accounts comprise two broad categories: the *current account*, which measures merchandise trade, factor and non-factor service income, and transfer receipts and payments, and the *capital account*, which measures changes in domestic and foreign capital assets and liabilities.

Debt service. The sum of interest payments and repayments of principal on external debt. The debt service ratio is total debt service divided by exports of goods and services.

GDP (Gross Domestic Product). The total final output of goods and services produced by an economy—that is, by residents and non-residents, regardless of the allocation to domestic and foreign claims. It is calculated without making deductions for depreciation.

GNP (Gross National Product). The total domestic and foreign output claimed by residents. It comprises gross domestic product adjusted by net factor income from abroad. Factor income comprises receipts that residents receive from abroad for factor services (labour, investment, and interest) less similar payments made to non-residents abroad. It is calculated without making deductions for depreciation.

IMR (Infant Mortality Rate). Annual deaths of infants under one year of age per 1,000 live births.

LBW (Low Birth Weight). The percentage of births below 2,500 grams, which is a sensitive measure of mother's health and nutrition during pregnancy and before. The lower an infant's birth weight below 2,500 grams, the greater the infant's vulnerability to infections and other problems and the greater the risk of sickness and death.

Malnutrition. For children under five, this is most commonly measured as the percentage of children falling below the WHO standardized international measure of weight for age, with moderate malnutrition meaning less than 75 per cent of international standards, and severe malnutrition meaning less than 60 per cent. In addition to weight for age, two other commonly used measures are:

1. *Stunting*: in which height for age falls below the international standard norms, usually indicating nutritional deficiencies in an earlier period of a child's growth.

2. *Nutritional wasting*: in which a child's weight for height is below 80 per cent of the international standard norms, usually indicating current nutritional deficiencies.

ODA (Official Development Assistance). Grants and loans made on concessional financial terms from official sources, with the objective of promoting economic development and welfare. It includes the value of technical co-operation and assistance.

Stabilization. An extreme variation of adjustment, in which the emphasis is on 'stabilizing' the external and internal deficits in the short term, often by sharp reductions in the level of economic activity in the economy. Relatively little weight is given to maintaining or resolving economic growth, which in stabilization is usually treated as a longer term issue.

Terms of trade. A measure of the relative level of export prices compared with import prices. Calculated as the ratio of a country's index of export unit value to the index of import unit value, this indicator shows changes over a base year in the level of export prices as a percentage of import prices.

Introduction

Giovanni Andrea Cornia, Richard Jolly, and Frances Stewart

After three decades of remarkable progress, improvements in the welfare of children in many parts of the world began to falter in the 1970s. The rate of reduction in infant and young child mortality slowed, as did progress in raising economic welfare, schooling, and provision of other basic needs. All this followed a period since the Second World War when as much progress had been made in reducing infant and young child mortality as over the previous two thousand years—and when, for all the remaining problems, many other indicators of human welfare showed significant, if uneven, advance.

After this faltering in the 1970s, two strongly contradictory forces were set loose in the early 1980s. On the one hand, world recession bit deep into the Third World, especially into Africa, Latin America, and the Middle East. Asia was both more insulated and showed more resilience and economic dynamism, though even in Asia some countries, like the Philippines, suffered serious setbacks. But in Africa and Latin America the economic crisis has been, and still is, extremely severe. The result of these downward pressures from recession were serious set-backs to economic progress and massive deterioration in the economic circumstances of many millions of families in the developing world. Some two-thirds of developing countries registered negative or negligible growth from 1980–85, and many indicators of human welfare showed marked deterioration, including, in a number of countries, nutrition levels of the under-5s, the age group most vulnerable to permanent damage.

At the same time, more positive forces were also at work. Over the last few years, there has been a surge of action to put certain basic low-cost child protection measures into practice on a massive scale. World vaccine use for immunization against measles, polio, and four other diseases expanded three times from 1983 to 1985. Over the same period, there was a widespread increase in action to combat dehydration from childhood diarrhoea, indicated by a threefold rise in the use of oral rehydration salts. It is estimated that these two measures alone saved the lives of well over one million children a year in 1985, offsetting at least in part the downward forces of recession and economic setbacks, especially on early child survival and avoidance of disability.

Yet the coverage and focus of these positive interventions so far have been limited, and the evidence of rising malnutrition and other indicators of human deterioration shows that there is still far to go if the positive forces are to offset the downward ones over the wide range of influences which affect nutrition, welfare, and human development, as well as the basic indicators of infant and child mortality. Much more can be done, and it is the purpose of this study to suggest specific and practical ways in which the range and impact of such positive interventions can be broadened.

'Adjustment with a human face' is the name we have given to the range of economic and other policy measures which we believe are needed. 'Adjustment' indicates that for most of the developing countries, these policies must be part and parcel of the national 'adjustment' policies widely adopted to tackle the economic crises facing these countries—the acute deficits in the balance of payments and the government budget, often also rapid inflation rates and negligible or negative economic growth. 'The human face' indicates the need for the human implications of an adjustment policy to be made an integral part of adjustment policy as a whole, not to be treated as an additional welfare component. As de Larosière, Managing Director of the IMF put it:

the extent to which adjustment is compatible with growth and with an improvement in living standards depends in large part on what *form* that adjustment takes. Adjustment that takes the form of increases in exports, savings, investment and economic efficiency will clearly be more supportive of growth than that which relies on cuts in investment and in imports. Similarly, adjustment that pays attention to the health, nutrition and educational requirements of the most vulnerable groups is going to protect the human condition better than adjustment which ignores them. This means that the authorities will have to be concerned, not only with *if* they close the fiscal deficit but also with *how* they do so.

This study is a contribution to the question of 'how', drawing on UNICEF work and experience over the last four years and directed particularly to the issues of protecting human needs, especially of children and other vulnerable groups.

The origins of UNICEF's concerns with these issues go back to 1983, when UNICEF prepared a report entitled *The Impact of World Recession on Children*.[1] This presented a general framework of analysis and summarised the findings from a dozen country case studies, covering a wide diversity of the world's economies—industrial and developing, rich and poor, capitalist and socialist. The evidence presented showed that, with few exceptions, children and women of poorer families were the hardest hit by recession. The analysis also suggested that the worst was yet to come, a prediction unfortunately borne out by subsequent evidence of further deterioration, especially in Africa and Latin America. But the study also focused on the actions which could be taken, both to ameliorate the set-backs in the human situations and to restore economic

---

[1] A summary report was published in UNICEF's *State of the World's Children Report, 1984*. A fuller report and background papers were published in *World Development*, March 1984 (Oxford: Pergamon Press) and issued later as *The Impact of World Recession on Children*, edited by Richard Jolly and Giovanni Andrea Cornia.

growth and development, following a pattern which gives priority to meeting human needs, especially of vulnerable groups.

From the start, it was clear that practical advance towards adjustment with a human face would only be possible if it attracted the understanding and support of those in the mainstream of economic policy-making, both internationally and nationally. This approach received strong encouragement from several governments on UNICEF's executive board, initially the governments of Canada, the Netherlands, and Sweden, and later from a number of others. At the request of the IMF and the World Bank, a dialogue was started with these institutions in 1984 focusing both on the lead which these institutions might give and on ways for more effective collaboration with other international institutions, including non-government institutions, actively concerned with the human aspects of development. This dialogue has continued, and over the last year in particular, several of the international organizations have issued important statements on adjustment issues.

In parallel, and in some respects in advance, Third World leaders have been increasingly outspoken in the last few years on the need for alternative approaches to adjustment so as to regain the momentum of growth and development and to tackle the rising problem of debt, poverty, and social strain. These themes were especially strong in sessions of the General Assembly of the United Nations in 1985 and 1986, but have also been echoed in many other forums. In Latin America, a number of initiatives have been taken directed to the problem of critical poverty and adjustment. In Africa, the special session on African recovery and development directed particular attention to the needs of women, and to human resources in general, as a central part of policy reform for recovery. In Asia, though the crisis of adjustment has been less widespread, recognition of the need for more attention to the human dimension of adjustment has also been considerable.

The call for a more people-sensitive approach to adjustment is more than a matter of economic good sense or political expediency. Ultimately it rests on the ethic of human solidarity, of concern for others, of human response to human suffering. For all the evil and despair in the world today, there are some signs of this ethic in action: the outpouring of popular support and sympathy during the African drought, shown to the world by mass communication, made it impossible for governments to stand idly by while thousands starved.

The structure of this book is as follows. Part I reviews the latest evidence on the impact of recession and adjustment on poverty and vulnerable groups, drawing both on macro and micro evidence, focusing particularly on the period 1980–85. This part also analyses the various interactions between recession, adjustment and poverty, identifying which aspects of adjustment tend to impinge particularly on the poor and, by contrast, which aspects can serve to protect the poor and vulnerable.

International statements on growth-oriented adjustment and the protection of the vulnerable

Over the last year or so, awareness has grown, both of the human costs of economic difficulties in many developing countries and of the need for remedial action to protect the poor and vulnerable:

The Bank seeks to assist governments in identifying ways and means of mitigating adjustment costs and to modify the design of the policy and institutional measures accordingly. During the implementation of the adjustment programme, the government and the Bank need to monitor closely any negative impact of the programme on the most vulnerable sections of the population and help to develop compensatory programmes, targeted on the affected groups as required.

Source: World Bank, 1986.

Nutrition objectives for the poor (should) form an explicit part of adjustment policies and programmes of governments and member organizations, including special compensatory measures where appropriate, with a view to providing an adequate level of nutrition for vulnerable groups.

Source: The United Nations ACC Subcommittee on Nutrition, April, 1986.

The forms of adjustment that are most conducive to growth and to protection of human needs will not emerge by accident. They have to be encouraged by an appropriate set of incentives and policies. They will also require political courage.

Source: M. de Larosière, Managing Director of the IMF, July 1986.

The World Health Assembly calls on Member States to ensure, in cooperation with international financing institutions, that the health and nutritional status of the most disadvantaged social groups are protected when economic adjustment policies are designed and implemented.

Source: Thirty-ninth World Health Assembly Resolution, 16 May 1986.

Part I ends with a summary of 10 case studies on country experience, both on how the position of the poor has changed in recent years and on the nature of the adjustment policies these countries followed. National adjustment policies have, on the whole, successfully combined adjustment with poverty alleviation and nutritional protection in the Republic of Korea, Botswana and Zimbabwe. In other countries, economic developments have seriously eroded the levels of living of the poor and the nutritional standards of children. This was the case to varying extents and through different mechanisms, for each of the other seven country studies.

Part II draws on the earlier analysis and case studies to put forward a policy framework for adjustment with a human face. This covers macro, 'meso', sectoral, and micro policies, with respect to growth, production, and income generation, and in the key areas of employment, education, health, and nutrition. Chapter 6 provides an overview of the approach and a framework within which the elaboration of policy measures in later chapters can be set. Chapter 15 discusses the wider international changes needed to support the national changes of policy, and to make their implementation possible and fully effective. Chapter 16 summarizes the main conclusions on what needs to be done, and shows that in every case specific examples exist of the policies being applied in practice. There is, in other words, no great mystery about the sort of actions needed; what is needed is to apply them on a much wider scale than is being done at present.

This is not the place to elaborate further on the content of these actions. But it may help to clarify a few key points on the approach followed, especially in relation to some of the misunderstandings we have encountered in earlier phases of this work.

Why focus on adjustment rather than development? The study concentrates on adjustment policy because for most countries in Africa and Latin America at this time, adjustment policy is the dominating economic preoccupation for setting the frame and constraints within which all other economic and development issues have to be considered. Our concern is therefore with how the broader human issues of compelling and urgent importance can be *brought into* this priority exercise of economic policymaking. But we also recognize—indeed, it is a main theme of the approach proposed—that to respond adequately to human concerns, adjustment policy in developing countries will need to be oriented to structural change for sustained economic development over the longer term. In other words, the issue should not be adjustment *or* growth, but adjustment *for* growth.

Fortunately, over the last year the need for more growth-oriented adjustment policies has been widely recognized, to the point where it is now the new orthodoxy internationally and in the main industrial countries as well as in the Third World. One must note, however, that the international policies, actions, and financial flows needed to make possible this greater orientation to growth still lag far behind the shift in objectives; hence our identification in Chapter 15 of the urgent need for supportive international action.

Is adjustment policy (or the adjustment process) the main cause of the human difficulties and social set-backs, especially of vulnerable groups? No, this is *not* the position of this study. As in previous studies by UNICEF on this theme, we recognize that the primary cause of the downward economic pressures on the human situation in most of the countries affected is the overall economic situation, globally and nationally, not adjustment policy as such. Indeed, without some form of adjustment, the situation would often be far worse. It would be surprising to find otherwise in a world which has gone through the worst recession since the 1930s, and where commodity prices are lower than for 30 years. None the less, to recognize that adjustment is necessary for dealing with severe economic imbalances in an economy is not the same as accepting that *all* adjustment policies are or have been equally adequate for ensuring adjustment to a more growth-oriented pattern of development, in which the human needs of the vulnerable will be protected in the short as well as the medium to long term. Clearly, many past adjustment policies have been inadequate in these respects. And there is now a recognized need for a broader approach to adjustment. This is the special concern of this study.

Can poor developing countries afford to be concerned with human welfare when their economic resources are so constrained? This question is often asked (though usually by those well fed, not by the poor themselves!) and so deserves an answer, if only to make clear the basic logic of making human concerns a central part of economic policy-making. In fact, there are three reasons for not postponing attention to human needs. In the first place, the basic health, nutritional, and educational needs of the most vulnerable groups—the under-5s, pregnant women, and nursing mothers—are urgent and compelling. If neglected they can set back the health and welfare of the whole future generation of a country, in addition to adding to present human and economic miseries. Secondly, there is considerable evidence (summarized in Ch. 6) of the positive economic returns to interventions supporting basic nutrition, health, and education. They are in fact investment in human capital, and part therefore of strengthening the productive capacity of a country. Thirdly, human welfare and progress is the ultimate goal of all development policy. It takes a particular form of economic abstraction to believe this goal will be achieved in the long run without explicit attention to the human issues in the short run.

How does 'adjustment with a human face' relate to earlier thinking on development? In the 1950s growth maximization was the dominant philosophy of development. However, it became clear in the subsequent two decades that trickle-down from growth was often limited, and that increasing poverty, defined in terms of numbers of people below a poverty line, often accompanied growth because of deteriorating income distribution—partly due to high levels of unemployment and often to a process of growing inequality built into the political economy of national development. Consequently, emphasis was put on poverty eradication, employment, and income distribution, and subsequently on basic services and basic needs. Robert McNamara as head of the World Bank made some important speeches favouring poverty alleviation. By the end of the 1970s, the 'basic needs' approach was becoming dominant on the international scene, with support from bilateral aid donors, and major international institutions, notably the ILO and the World Bank.

However, the financial crisis that started in the 1970s and has dominated the development scene since then (together with shifts of political philosophy in some of the major donor countries) led to a complete switch in major international institutions' approach to development. Almost all policy advice was concerned with 'adjustment', and adjustment was generally tackled without regard for its distributional or poverty implications. The importance—recognized in the 'basic needs' and 'poverty alleviation' approaches of the 1970s—of paying specific attention to securing incomes and services for the low-income segments of the population was neglected if not ignored. Yet, if there was a need to take specific measures to ensure adequate resources went to the poor during economic growth, the need is much greater at a time of economic recession and financial crisis, when there is little or no growth to trickle down. And the economic returns to such policies are all the more important when resources are scarce.

The approach of 'adjustment with a human face' adds, therefore, a poverty alleviation dimension to adjustment in much the same way as 'redistribution with growth' and 'basic needs' added such a dimension to growth. It may be thought of as the 'basic needs' approach to adjustment. Because output per capita is declining in many countries, so that incomes of the poor are falling even with constant income distribution, and because the burden of adjustment policies often fall disproportionately on the poor, the need to add this dimension to adjustment—to protect the low-income during adjustment—is substantially greater than it was when growth could be assumed.

Having clarified some of the main points which the study covers, it is also important to indicate some of the issues beyond the limits of the study.

The study primarily concentrates on what can be done within the existing international economic order. For the authors as for many others, it is not difficult to imagine international economic policies and approaches which would provide a more positive and expansive environment within which developing countries could develop more dynamically. This vision lay behind the calls in the 1970s for a New International Economic Order and the many specific recommendations such as those in the Brandt Commission Report, *North-South: A Programme for Survival*. For the most part, we have spent little time exploring such policies and approaches in this document, on the grounds that many such analyses are available elsewhere and that progress towards them is, for the most part, stymied politically for the present. We have accordingly concentrated on what we believe could readily be done within the present international economic order. We spell out in Chapter 15 what changes within this order would still be desirable or necessary to make a more human approach possible. But none of this should disguise the much greater improvements in economic performance and dynamism which are needed—and which, we believe, the world could achieve—if a more fundamental range of international reforms were adopted.

Secondly, the study is largely written within an economic frame of analysis. There is indeed much more that could be said, both about the human dimensions of the pressures on people and on the social administrative means to carry new approaches into operation, especially grass-roots approaches which provide more scope for initiative and leadership by communities themselves. We believe that broader approaches to adjustment could provide more space and more support for such community initiatives and local-level action, and that the economic benefit of these would be considerable. But we feel that this document is not the right place to elaborate all that is required, especially since there is already considerable literature on these themes.

Our primary concern is to speak to those directly involved in the making of adjustment policy, whether as policy-makers and practitioners or as analysts of the process. It is this group who have the power and influence to make possible a broader approach, and it is this group, nationally and inter-nationally, who must be persuaded if broader policies are to be adopted.

We have also had in mind those who wish to grasp the main lines of the approach proposed, but not necessarily all the details: such readers should read Chapter 6 on the broad approach and Chapter 16 on the conclusions, dipping into other chapters for more evidence and elaboration as wanted. But we hope general readers will not miss the case studies in Chapter 5 since they provide a view of the different country contexts in which adjustment policies have to be pursued and of the specific human-focused actions which are or might be pursued as part of adjustment. The full case studies are being published as a separate volume.

PART I

Recession, Adjustment, and Child Welfare in the
1980s

1

Economic Decline and Human Welfare in the First Half of the 1980s

*Giovanni Andrea Cornia**

I Introduction

After nearly three decades of steady progress, child welfare sharply deteriorated in many developing countries during the first half of the 1980s. The evidence provided by the 10 country studies published in Volume II shows that the nutritional status of children has deteriorated in all but 2 of the 10 (South Korea and Zimbabwe). Although the gravity of the deterioration and its causes vary substantially from country to country, this general increase in malnutrition clearly points to a major change in long-term trends, extending far beyond that due to the drought in Africa alone. In addition, infant and/or child mortality rates—indicators which had for two decades shown a strong downward trend—showed some reversal in trend in three of the eight countries where data are available (Chile, Brazil, and Ghana), while in others a marked deceleration in the rate of improvement was observed. The decline in the health situation of children is further confirmed by the increasing incidence of communicable diseases like typhoid, hepatitis, tuberculosis, gastro-intestinal diseases, malaria, and yaws, observed in at least 4 out of the 10 countries analysed, as a result of the general deterioration of the living environment and of reduced prophylactic measures. Education has also been hit severely. With the exception of South Korea, Botswana, and Zimbabwe, in every country included in the analysis there have been declines in primary enrolment and completion rates or serious deterioration in the quality of education.

A search of available sources shows that deterioration in child welfare is evident in at least 4 other countries in Latin America, 14 in Sub-Saharan Africa, 3 in North Africa and the Middle East, but only 2 (besides Philippines and Sri Lanka, which are included among the 10 country studies), in South and East Asia, where in most cases the situation of children has continued to improve.

These alarming trends occurred at a time of—and in large part due to—deteriorating economic performance. World economic performance was poor

* This chapter has greatly benefited from the work of data analysis and the many useful suggestions of Eva Jespersen.

in the first half of the 1980s. The industrialized countries experienced a major
recession in 1981–83, and then grew slowly. The economic performance among
developing countries as a group was much worse: three-quarters of the countries in Latin America and Africa experienced declines in per capita income
from 1980–85. During the same period, some 70 countries introduced programmes of stabilization with or without IMF assistance. On average during
1980–85 there were 47 countries with IMF programmes every year, while
several others introduced adjustment programmes by themselves. In other
words, adjustment has been the predominant feature of economic policy-
making during the first half of the 1980s.

This chapter reviews the record of economic performance during 1980–85
and its links with changes in child welfare. Section II describes the major
economic developments among developed countries and how the deterioration
that occurred was transmitted in a magnified way to most developing countries.
Section III documents changes in the conditions affecting child welfare and
in indicators of child status in the 1980s, drawing on the 10 case studies and a
wider review of the evidence. The analytical fram ework relating changes in
macro-economic performance to child welfare used in the interpretation of the
data is presented in Annex I to this chapter.

II   The recession of the 1980s

1   Growth in industrial market economies

A major deceleration in economic growth occurred during the first half of the
1980s in the industrial market economies as compared with the second half of
the 1970s. With the exception of Japan, growth rates of output per capita in
the 1980s were about half, or less, of those recorded during the previous five
years (Table 1.1).

The strong recovery initiated in 1984 in the United States and in Japan
lasted for a short period, and from 1985 growth in GDP per capita has again
fallen below historical values.

While the causes of this sharp deceleration are still the subject of heated
controversy, there is agreement that the following three sets of factors played
an important role in the stagnation of industrial market economies in the 1980s
(Raj 1984).

1. *The emergence of wide differences in the rates of growth of labour productivity in
manufacturing.* Between 1971–80, this growth rate was 7.4 per cent in Japan,
4.5 per cent in Western Europe (excluding the United Kingdom) and 2.5
per cent in the United States. These trends were reflected in growing trade
imbalances between the United States on the one side and Western Europe
and Japan on the other. The large US trade deficit which emerged led first in
1971 to the devaluation of the dollar and subsequently to the replacement of
the fixed exchange rate regime with a new system of free currency floats. This

TABLE 1.1   *Developed market economies: per capita growth rates of real GDP, 1976–1986 (annual percentage change at 1975 prices)*

Country or country group	1976–80	1981–85	1981	1982	1983	1984	1985[a]	1986[b]
All developed market economies	2.7	1.6	0.9	−1.2	2.0	4.0	2.2	1.9
North America	2.3	1.4	1.2	−3.6	2.6	5.5	1.8	1.8
Western Europe	2.7	1.2	−0.1	0.3	1.5	2.3	2.3	2.4
Japan	4.1	3.3	3.1	2.5	2.6	4.5	4.0	1.8
Other[c]	1.5	1.0	2.4	−1.4	−1.8	4.5	1.1	−0.3

Source: UN-DIESA (1986).
[a] Preliminary estimates.
[b] UN Secretariat forecasts.
[c] Australia, New Zealand, and South Africa.

set the stage for the growing financial and monetary instability of the 1970s and 1980s.

2. *The sharp shocks provoked by the large increases in oil prices* in 1973–74 and 1979 caused serious payment imbalances and deflationary tendencies in oil-importing countries, both developed and developing. While recycling of oil surpluses in the mid- and later 1970s was greater than anticipated and helped maintain growth momentum in the world economy, recycling in the 1980s was not adequate to compensate for the deflationary tendencies generated by the second oil shock.

3. *The stringent monetarist policies adopted* in the United States, the United Kingdom and other industrial countries, consisting of tight restrictions on domestic monetary and credit expansion, pruning of government expenditure and ODA, and increases in the real rate of interest. These policies had strong contractionary effects both in the countries implementing them and in those linked to them through trade and financial relations. The sharp increase in interest rates, in addition, aggravated the debt crisis.

2   The transmission of the crisis from the developed to the developing countries

The sharp deceleration of growth in the industrial market economies was immediately transmitted to the developing countries through the mechanisms of trade, capital flows, and aid.

1. *The volume of world trade increased,* after nearly four years of virtual stagnation, by an estimated 9 per cent in 1984. Trade expansion, however, fell in 1985 and 1986 to 3.2 and 3 per cent, well below the rate of 5.1 per cent a year recorded during the 1976–80 period.

The 1984 upswing was the result of an unprecedented surge in import demand in the United States, while import growth in Europe and most developing countries remained modest. Up to four-fifths of the increase in world imports in 1984 was accounted for by US imports, consisting mainly of manufactured products. Indeed, 90 per cent of the expansion of world trade consisted in manufactured products.

The US trade linkages and import structure have therefore been the main determinants of the transmission of growth impulses and of the distribution of the gains during the 1984–85 upswing. Only those countries with access to the US market were able to take advantage of the expansion of the US economy. For numerous other countries, especially those exporting primary commodities to Western Europe, the benefits from this strong but short-lived expansion of world trade have been very modest. Indeed, the least developed countries' exports to Europe and the United States—mainly consisting of primary commodities—continued to decline in 1984.

2. *Commodity prices remained depressed* throughout the period under consideration. This should not come as a surprise in view of the situation described above. In addition to weak international demand, the prices of several commodities have been kept low by two other factors: the continued substitution by synthetics; and the growing 'dematerialization' of manufacturing production, which is becoming less input intensive.

A sharp decline in real dollar price indices of commodities occurred between 1980 and 1985 (Fig. 1.1). The drop has been rather uniform throughout the period, with only a modest reversal in 1983. As a result, on average, real commodity prices at the end of 1985 were substantially lower than in 1980 and their long-term decline continues unabated. The decline appears as dramatic if the comparison is carried out on the basis of the terms of trade of primary exporters.

3. *Stagnation in ODA.* After a decade (1970–80) of continuous growth, ODA flows have changed little during the last quinquennium. While world ODA increased from 31 to 36 billion dollars (in 1983 prices and exchange rates) between 1975 and 1980, its level broadly stagnated between 1980 and 1984, with sharp declines occurring in 1982 and 1983. Preliminary data show that ODA increased in 1985 by about 3–5 per cent in real terms, largely reflecting an increase in additional emergency assistance (amounting to more than $1 billion) to drought-stricken African countries south of the Sahara. ODA flows therefore have not compensated for the decline in other resource flows to developing countries which took place over the last five years.

4. *Capital flows, interest rates, and net transfer of resources.* The level and direction of net capital flows changed dramatically during the 1980–85 period. As a result of the large accumulation of debt in the 1970s and the banks' already considerable exposure, there has been a contraction in commercial banks' lending following the second oil shock. Private bank net lending to developing countries declined from $38 billion in 1980 to $15 billion in 1985 (World Bank

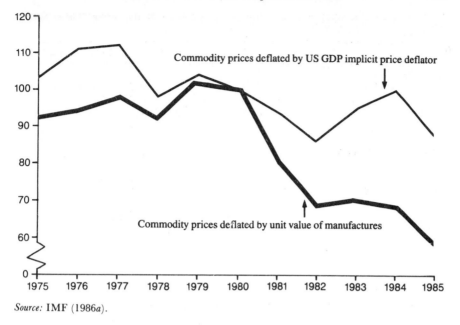

Source: IMF (1986*a*).

Fig. 1.1 Real non-fuel commodity price indexes, 1975–85 (1980 = 100)

1986*a*). At a global level there was a fundamental redirection of financial flows, with the United States becoming a magnet attracting capital flows from all over the world in order to finance its growing current account and budget deficits.

The inflow of world savings to the United States was largely triggered by the high interest rates prevailing in the American market. Nominal interest rates have been high by historical standards throughout the 1980s, with peaks of 18–20 per cent during 1980–82. The decline in nominal interest rates observed since 1981–82 has not been paralleled by a commensurate decline in real interest rates.

As a result of the increases in interest payments, stagnating ODA, and greatly reduced net inflow of capital from abroad, the capital-importing developing countries witnessed a sharp decline in the net transfer of resources during this period. In 1984 and 1985 the net transfer became negative, i.e. the developing world became a net exporter of resources to the industrial world (see Table 1.2). The situation was even more alarming considering the cases of Sub-Saharan Africa and Latin America separately.

TABLE 1.2 *Net transfer of resources to the capital-importing developing countries, 1980–1985 ($ billion)*

	1980	1981	1982	1983	1984	1985
All credits						
Net capital flow	54.2	62.5	50.8	39.7	32.0	13.0
Net interest paid	−23.6	−34.8	−50.0	−48.3	−53.9	−54.0
Net transfer	30.6	27.7	0.8	−8.6	−22.0	−41.0
Direct investment						
Net flow of investment	9.8	14.2	12.0	8.9	8.5	9.0
Net direct investment						
income	−13.7	−13.5	−13.1	−11.6	−11.3	−13.0
Net transfer	−4.0	0.7	−1.1	−2.7	−2.8	−4.0
Official grants	12.7	13.1	10.7	11.0	12.3	14.0
TOTAL	39.4	41.4	10.4	−0.3	−12.5	−31.0

Source: UN-DIESA (1986).

3 The impact on the developing economies

The asymmetric nature of international trade and financial relations is such that any change in performance in the industrialized countries is amplified in its effects on the developing economies. Consequently, the vast majority of developing countries have been very severely affected by the unsatisfactory growth of the industrial economies during the last six years and by the negative trends which have characterized the international economy.

TABLE 1.3 *Developing market economies GDP per capita growth rates, 1976–1986 (annual percentage change at 1975 prices)*

	1976–80	1981–85	1981	1982	1983	1984	1985[a]	1986[b]
All developing market economies	2.7	−1.1	−1.5	−1.7	−1.7	−0.5	−0.1	−0.3
Africa	2.4	−3.1	−5.1	−3.5	−2.5	−2.8	−1.5	−2.5
Latin America	2.9	−1.8	−1.2	−3.8	−4.9	0.8	0.1	−0.5
West Asia	−0.2	−4.4	−9.2	−0.2	−4.7	−4.1	−3.7	−2.9
South and East Asia	4.0	2.8	4.0	1.0	4.1	3.5	1.6	1.7

Source: UN-DIESA (1986).
[a] Preliminary.
[b] UN Secretariat forecasts.

As a result, an extremely severe and protracted decline occurred in the growth rate of GDP per capita for each of the four major developing regions individually and for all developing market economies together, between 1980 and 1986 (Table 1.3). While growth of GDP per capita during the 1976–80 period averaged almost 3 per cent a year, its value became negative (−1.1%

TABLE 1.4 *Number and population of developing market economies with real GDP growth at or below population growth, 1979–1985*

	Total number of countries	Population in 1985 (millions)	Number of countries affected							Population affected (1985)	
			1979	1980	1981	1982	1983	1984	1985	(millions)	(%)
All developing market economies	83	2,467	25	32	38	55	51	45	49	718	29
All excluding India	82	1,706	25	32	38	55	51	45	49	718	42
Africa	32	497	14	15	21	25	21	25	21	417	84
Latin America	23	399	6	8	12	21	19	11	18	163	41
West Asia	14	174	4	5	5	7	8	8	7	75	43
South and E. Asia	14	1 397	2	4	0	2	3	1	3	64	5
South and E. Asia excluding India	13	636	2	4	0	2	3	1	3	64	10

Source: UN-DIESA (1986).

a year) during 1981–85. Apart from Latin America (strongly influenced by the positive performance of Brazil), there was little improvement in 1984 and 1985 following the buoyant growth in the United States and the ensuing expansion in trade in manufactures. Indeed, growth performance deteriorated during those years in West and South-East Asia, while the minor improvements recorded in Africa are mainly to be attributed to the timely arrival of the rains in 1985. Preliminary data indicate that in 1986 too, output growth remained below population growth for the group as a whole, while there were little changes for the main regional aggregates.

The number of countries with growth rates of GDP per capita smaller than or equal to zero increased steadily from 25 (out of a sample of 82) in 1979 to 55 in 1982, stabilizing at around 50 in the following years (Table 1.4).

In brief, GDP per capita has been declining or stagnating for between half and two-thirds of the 82 developing market economies included in the sample, while in 1985, 718 million people, or 29 per cent of the population of the developing market economies (42 per cent excluding India) were affected by negative growth rates of GDP per capita. In Africa, 84 per cent of the population experienced a negative growth rate in GDP per capita in the same year.

The cumulative decline in GDP per capita experienced by many developing market economies over the 1980–85 period has been very large in many cases. In about a fifth of the 82 countries the cumulative decline was extremely large (greater than 20 per cent), in the next fifth it was also quite severe (10–20 per cent). Only in a little more than a quarter of the countries has there been sustained growth over 1980–85 (Table 1.5).

TABLE 1.5 *Cumulative GDP per capita growth rates, 1980–85, in a sample of 82 developing countries*

Cumulative growth rate	Latin America	West Asia	South and East Asia	Africa	Total	%
− 20% or greater	4	5	0	6	15	18
Between − 20% and − 10%	7	0	1	10	18	22
Between − 10% and 0%	7	1	1	7	16	20
Between 0% and 5%	4	3	1	3	11	13
5% or greater	1	5	10	6	22	27
No. of observations	23	14	13	32	82	100

Source: UN-DIESA (1985, 1986).

There were important geographical variations. Positive growth rates were recorded throughout the period in the South and East Asian countries, where the 1981–85 average growth rate of GDP per capita suffered only a minor decline as compared to 1976–80. There were a multiplicity of reasons behind such positive performance, including a generally low level of indebtedness and the greater self-reliance of the large economies. The sustained growth of agricultural production, the fruit of extensive investments and of rapid technical improvements over the last 10 years (in India, Pakistan, Sri Lanka, and Indonesia) and favourable agro-ecological conditions (Burma and Thailand), were also a contributing factor. A further factor was the ability of the fast-growing exporters of manufactures (South Korea, Taiwan, Hong Kong, and Singapore) to take advantage of any expansion of world trade in manufactures.

Conversely, most African and Latin American countries suffered either from high levels of indebtedness or from an excessive dependence on trade in one (or few) primary commoditie(s), and also, in some cases, from the effects of inadequate policies followed during the 1970s. In addition, in Africa, agricultural performance has been much less good, with widespread falls in output per capita; while most Latin American industry was typically less geared to competing in international markets for industrial goods than the most successful Asian countries. In these two regions, the decline in GDP per capita over 1981–85 as compared to the 1976–80 period appears to be more than twice as large as that experienced by the group of industrial market economies.

Despite this considerable diversity of experience, for developing countries as a group there was a much sharper decline in average GDP per capita from 1976–80 to 1981–85 (i.e. from 2.7 to − 1.1 per cent a year) than that recorded over the same period for the group of the developed market economies (i.e. from 2.7 to 1.6 per cent). The data support the view (Goldstein and Khan 1982, Singer 1983) that a decline in GDP per capita in the industrial countries has a multiplicative effect on the decline of export earnings and GDP per capita of developing countries as a whole. IMF estimates, for instance, suggest that a 1 per cent change in industrial country real GNP growth rate is associated on average with about a 3.5 percentage change of the same sign in the growth rate of export earnings of developing countries (de Larosière 1986).

4 *Prospects for 1987–1990 and beyond*

Growth performance in the majority of the developing countries has thus shown lasting signs of deterioration in the early 1980s. Fig. 1.2 illustrates this situation graphically. While the previous discussion has indicated that considerable variation exists among developing regions, there is widespread recognition that the economic problems of the 1980s do not merely represent a cyclical movement—however pronounced—but are indicative of a deep-seated malaise affecting important sections of the world economy, developed and developing alike.

Growth performance is expected to remain unsatisfactory over the medium term in most developing countries outside Asia (Cline 1985, Dell 1986). It is widely agreed that Latin America as a whole will have barely re-established its 1980 per capita income levels in 1990 even under optimistic assumptions

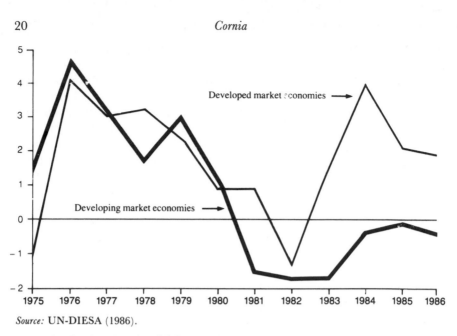

Source: UN-DIESA (1986).

Fig. 1.2   Real per capita GDP growth rates in developed and developing market economies, 1975–86

concerning capital flows, interest rates, and world trade (ECLA 1985). In view of the expected debt servicing obligations of the region, average domestic resource use in 1990 will be likely to be even lower. The depressed oil market will continue to reduce growth in many oil exporting countries, mostly in the Middle East and North Africa. For these countries too, domestic resource use per capita at the end of the decade will probably be lower than in 1980 (World Bank 1986a). The prospects of most countries in Sub-Saharan Africa deserve particular attention. The trends described in commodity prices, trade volume, and capital flows will have an extremely deleterious effect on the capacity of these countries to finance acceptable rates of growth. Even under the high-growth scenario, the World Bank (1986a) estimates that for low-income African countries GDP per capita in 1990 and 1995 will be lower than in 1973 and 1980. More than two decades of growth will have been lost, therefore, for the majority of poor African countries. Only for South and East Asia does the outlook for the next 5–10 years appear on the whole positive.

The economic problems of the first half of the 1980s are thus expected to persist for the rest of the decade and beyond unless radical measures are taken in the area of debt and capital flows and unless a strong recovery in the industrial market economies revitalizes world trade, and with it commodity prices.

Although this pessimistic scenario for the next 5–10 years continues to receive almost universal endorsement, over the last 12 months short-term growth conditions have noticeably improved. The oil price decline, the long-awaited fall in interest rates, and the awareness recently shown by the main industrial countries of the need for greater policy co-ordination may all have a positive effect on the growth of industrial market economies. The developing economies as a whole might also benefit from these changes, both directly and—in particular—indirectly through the hoped-for higher rates of growth of OECD countries. An improved performance of the world economy over the next two to three years, however, is largely dependent upon the rapid establishment of an effective mechanism for international policy co-ordination. Such a mechanism should aim at synchronizing fiscal retrenchment in the United States with more expansionary policies in countries with favourable external payment situation, ample idle capacity, and low inflation (such as West Germany and Japan), while reducing real interest rates to historically normal levels.

III Deterioration in conditions of children in the 1980s

This section examines the impact of the recessionary trends described above on the conditions of children and vulnerable groups.

The analysis is derived first from the sample of 10 developing countries, broadly representative of different regional, economic, ecological, and socio-cultural conditions, and for health and nutritional status and school achieve-ment also on the basis of a wider collection of evidence. The 10 countries in the sample are: Botswana, Ghana, and Zimbabwe in Africa; the Philippines, South Korea, and Sri Lanka in Asia; and the state of São Paulo (Brazil), Chile, Jamaica, and Peru in Latin America.

The links between economic changes and child welfare are numerous and complex. Annex I to this chapter sets out an analytic framework describing the main elements. Each case study has attempted to compile data systematically to describe how these elements have changed in recent years in the country concerned. The data are in three categories: (*a*) variables influencing the availability of resources for children, such as household income, government social expenditure, and parents' time, health, and skills (input indicators); (*b*) availability and/or use of food and key social services needed for the production of child welfare (process indicators), and (*c*) changes in child welfare, i.e. health, nutritional and educational status, and others (outcome indicators).

The evidence presented below is far from complete, particularly in the areas of health and nutrition. Available information often covers different periods, makes use of different concepts, or is derived from limited samples. From a rigorous statistical point of view this information remains fragmentary and scattered. Better data would be desirable and is indeed necessary for proper monitoring of child welfare during the adjustment process. Most of the findings in this chapter, however, consistently point in the same direction: the evidence taken as a whole indicates that serious problems have emerged during the last few years and that action is needed urgently. Waiting to take action until a more complete and rigorous data set is available would not be justified.

Tables 1.6 to 1.8 summarize the findings of the 10 country studies for the three sets of indicators. The data generally refer to the late 1970s and early 1980s period unless otherwise specified. At times the original data included in the country studies have been transformed so as to present the data in as uniform a format as possible.

(a) **Availability of resources for children ('input indicators')** With the exception of Sri Lanka, all countries included in the sample witnessed a recession of varying duration during the period under consideration. In four of them (Philippines, Ghana, Jamaica, and Peru) the cumulative decline in *GDP per capita* was 15 per cent or more, while Chile and Brazil witnessed less severe but still significant declines. Although they did experience brief recessions during that period, South Korea, Zimbabwe, and Botswana recorded overall positive growth rates of GDP per capita, while in Sri Lanka output growth per capita accelerated.

In all six countries where GDP per capita declined, *unemployment* rates rose, while in Botswana and Zimbabwe formal sector employment declined. Consistent with the sustained expansion of output, unemployment declined in Sri Lanka and, except for one year, in South Korea. With few exceptions the increases in open unemployment have been smaller than the drop in GDP, partly the result (as in Chile) of public works schemes aiming at containing the growth in the number of jobless. There were, however, other negative trends in the labour market. There is evidence of growing underemployment (Philippines, Chile, Peru, Brazil), or persistently high migration outflows preventing further deterioration on the labour market (Jamaica). There is also some disturbing evidence concerning the structure of unemployment, with a growing proportion of the unemployed belonging to the 24–45 age group, a longer average duration of unemployment, and a higher incidence of unemployment among low-income people (Chile).

With the exception of South Korea, real salaries, (i.e. money salaries deflated by the Consumer Price Index (CPI) or by the GDP deflator), have generally declined faster than the observed drop in GDP per capita. This was also the case in Sri Lanka and Zimbabwe, and possibly Botswana, where real salaries declined despite the increase in GDP per capita. Partly due to the contraction in production, this strong downward pressure on wages has been accentuated by the increase in labour force participation—particularly for women—triggered by the need to offset the drop in earnings of breadwinners. There are very few data on actual *household earnings*. However, it is implicit from the observed drop in wage rates and the rise in underemployment and unemployment that for the majority of the households in the 10 countries experiencing such developments, actual earnings have declined despite the increase in labour force participation.

Inflation (generally measured by the CPI) accelerated substantially, reaching

TABLE 1.6 *Input indicators: summary of changes for the 10-country sample*

Country	Basic period	Average GDP growth		Unemployment		Average annual growth in					Income distribution		
		Annual (%)	Cumulative (%)	Year	Rate (%)	Wages (%)	CPI (%)	Food prices (%)	Total social exp. (%)	Food subsidies (%)	Year	Gini coefficient	Bottom 40% (%)
Botswana	'80–'84	10.4	51.9	1981	7.0	...[a]	n.a.	n.a.	n.a.	n.a.	n.a.	n.a.	n.a.
Brazil, São Paulo State	'81–'84	-2.2	-9.0	1982 1984	5.8 7.1	-5.9	25.0	31.0	-8.0	n.a.	1981 1983 1984	0.565 0.584 0.576	9.70 9.00 9.20
Chile	'81–'85	-1.7	-6.8	1981 1984	10.4 15.9	-4.0	20.5	25.3	-1.0	-27.0	1981 1982	n.a. n.a.	12.8[b] 12.2
Ghana	'79–'85	-6.9	-41.4	—	n.a.	-5.1[c]	40.0	45.0	-35.0[d] -29.0[e]	n.a.	—	n.a.	n.a.
Jamaica	'78–'85	-2.3	-16.2	1972 1980 1984	23.0 26.8 25.4	-5.9[f]	n.a.	32.0[g]	-10.1	n.a.	—	n.a.	n.a.
Peru	'77–'85	-2.2	-19.8	1977 1984	5.0 10.9	-4.8[h]	83.0	n.a.	-2.1	...[i]	1971 1983	n.a. n.a.	8.20[j] 7.30[j]
Philippines	'81–'85	-3.0	-15.0	1981 1985	5.3 7.1	-5.0	20.0	20.0	1.0	n.a.	1980 1983	0.511 0.525	n.a. n.a.
South Korea	'79–'81	1.1	3.1	—	n.a.	1.3	23.0	n.a.	17.0	n.a.	1976 1980 1984	0.391 0.389 0.357	16.90 16.06 18.90
Sri Lanka	'78–'83	3.7	22.2	1978/9 1981/2	14.7 11.7	-3.7	19.0	20.0	7.0	-13.0	1978/9 1981/2	0.490 0.520	16.10 15.30
Zimbabwe	'80–'84	1.8	6.9	n.a.	n.a.	-1.0	11.2	14.5[k]	9.0[l]	2.9	—	n.a.	n.a.

[a] Wage freeze in 1982. [b] Greater Santiago only (Altimir 1984). [c] 1979–84. [d] Health, 1979–82. [e] Education, 1979–82. [f] 1983–85. [g] 1979–85. [h] Earnings, 1979–85. [i] Total elimination. [j] Bottom 50%. [k] GDP deflator and low-income CPI. [l] Health.

TABLE 1.7 *Process indicators: summary of changes for the 10-country sample*

Country	Basic period	Intake or availability of food		Access to/use of health services		Access to/use of education services	
		Change	Indicator	Change	Indicator	Change	Indicator
Botswana	'80–'84	+ve	Per capita availability of food up: 1980, 164 kg; 1982, 130 kg; 1985, 186 kg	+ve	Health facility use by vulnerable groups up; immunisations up	n.a.	n.a.
Brazil, São Paulo State	'81–'84	−ve	Per capita production of food staple down 6%	−ve	Use for emergency and curative purposes up, preventive use down	n.a.	n.a.
Chile	'81–'85	n.a.	n.a.	+ve −ve	High levels of primary health care maintained Quality of hospital cover down	−ve	PER[a] down: '81, 102.2; '84, 97.1
Ghana	'79–'85	−ve	Calorie adequacy down 88% (late '70s) to 68% ('80s)	−ve	Attendance down by 11% a year	+ve	PER constant
Jamaica	'78–'85	n.a.	n.a.	−ve	Quality of service down; charges introduced	n.a.	n.a.
Peru	'77–'85	−ve	Food production down 26% ('75–85)	n.a.	n.a.	—	PER constant
Philippines	'81–'85	−ve	Adequacy of food intake down: Feb. '84, 82%; Oct. '84, 79%	−ve	Public hospital admissions up 6% a year[b]	−ve	PER down: '81, 92% '84, 88%
South Korea	'79–'81	−ve	Daily per capita calorie intake down: '79, 2,599 '80, 2,489 '81, 2,531	+ve	Medical insurance and aid coverage up: '79, 26.4%; '81, 39.1%	+ve	Access up through tuition exemption programme for poor
Sri Lanka	'78–'83	−ve	Daily per capita calorie intake of bottom 20% down; '78/9, 1,500 '81/2, 1,370	−ve	Service standard in public facilities down	−ve	School avoidance rate for first 8 grades up: '78/9, 12.2% '81/2, 13.5%
Zimbabwe	'80–'84	n.a.	n.a.	+ve	Coverage of health care and preventive services up	+ve	PER up 20% p.a.

[a] Primary enrolment rate (6–14 years).
[b] For a sample of low-income earners in Manila.
[c] Due to growing costs of private care.

TABLE 1.8 *Outcome indicators: summary of changes for the 10-country sample*

Country	Basic period	Infant mortality rate Change	Infant mortality rate (%)	Child death rate Change	Child death rate (%)	Nutritional status Change	Nutritional status Indicator	Educational attainment Change	Educational attainment Indicator	Disease prevalence Change	Disease prevalence Indicator
Botswana	'80–84	+ve	'81, 68.0 '86, 65.0	—	n.a.	−ve	Child malnutrition up: '82, 25% '83, 30% '84, 31%	—	n.a.	—	n.a.
Brazil, Sao Paulo State	'81–'84	−ve	'82, 50.5 '83, 43.5 '84, 52.0	—	n.a.	−ve	Low birth weight incidence at São Paulo Hospital up: '80, 14.5%; '83, 16.1%	−ve	Primary school completion down: '80, 75% '83, 68%	—	n.a.
Chile	'81–'85	−ve	Decline less than trend: '81, 27.0 '84, 19.6	—	'82, 1.09 '83, 1.22 '84, 1.03	—	Pre-school malnutrition '82, 8.8% '83, 9.8% '84, 8.4%	—	n.a.	−ve	Immunizable up[a], non-immunizable down
Ghana	'79–'85	−ve	Late '70s 86.0 '80s 107.0	−ve	Late 70s 15 '80s 25–30	−ve	Pre-school malnutrition up: '80, 35.0 '84, 54.0	−ve	Primary school quality down	−ve	Persistently high morbidity, yaws and yellow fever up
Jamaica	'78–'85	—	n.a.	—	n.a.	−ve	0–4 year malnutrition up: '78, 38.3% '85, 40.8%	−ve	'O' level passing down: '78, 62% '84, 34%	—	n.a.

TABLE 1.8 (continued)

Country	Basic period	Infant mortality rate		Child death rate		Nutritional status		Educational attainment		Disease prevalence	
		Change	(%)	Change	(%)	Change	Indicator	Change	Indicator	Change	Indicator
Peru	'77–'85	—	n.a.	—	n.a.	−ve	0–6 year malnutrition up[b] '80, 41.6% '83, 68.0%	−ve	Primary school quality down, repetition and drop-outs up	−ve	Communicable diseases up ('79–'83); TBC deaths up 14%
Philippines	'81–'85	+ve	Decline less than trend: '81, 62.0 '84, 58.0	—	n.a.	−ve	Pre-school malnutrition up: '81, 17.5% '85, 22.0%	−ve	Completion rate down: '81, 67% '84, 63%	−ve	Communicable diseases up
South Korea	'79–'81	+ve	Decline less than trend: '79, 37.6 '81, 35.8	—	n.a.	+ve	Height and weight of school children up, but less than trend	—	n.a.	—	n.a.
Sri Lanka	'78–'83	+ve	Decline (on trend): '78, 37.0 '80, 34.0	—	n.a.	−ve	Severe malnutrition of children 6–60 months in rural areas up: '78/9, 6.1% '81/2, 9.4%	−ve	Literacy down among 5–14 yrs. '78/9 88% '81/2 86%	—	n.a.
Zimbabwe	'80–'81	+ve	Qualitative assessment	—	n.a.	—	Child malnutrition constant: '82 18.0–22.0%[c] '84, 16.0–25.0%	—	n.a.	+ve	Decline in incidence of disease (immunizable and non-immunizable)

[a] Typhoid, hepatitis.
[b] In south.
[c] Figures are from different surveys.

two or more digits in the early 1980s for all countries included in the sample. Although inflation started to abate towards the mid-1980s in many of the countries analysed, its damage in terms of nutritional and health status has been quite big. There is strong evidence that the effects of inflation on the poor are grossly underestimated. The index of *food prices*, or the CPI calculated on a basket of goods consumed by the poor, reveals faster rates of inflation than the CPI or the GDP price deflators, which are normally used to calculate real salaries, in five out of the six countries for which both types of information are available. Whenever this happens, the drop in the incomes of the poor is larger than indicated by the decline in real wage calculated on the basis of the average CPI.

Evidence of declines in real wages faster than in GDP per capita, and of rates of inflation for wage goods higher than the general CPI, indicates that the drop in the *real resources of the poor* has been greater than the average. This is certainly the case for the formal sector, while there is suggestive evidence that this has also occurred for most of the informal sector. For rural·areas there is some evidence (Philippines) that real wages have declined faster than average GDP per capita in both the estate and non-estate sector. In the case of estates producing export commodities whose prices fell abruptly on the world market, wages have dropped catastrophically (Negros Occidental, Philippines; estate sector of Sri Lanka). Little or no information is available about the subsistence sector, which is of major significance in Ghana, Zimbabwe, and Botswana. Data on relative *income distribution* are available for 6 of the 10 countries analysed. For all of them (Chile, South Korea, Peru, Sri Lanka, Brazil, and the Philippines) income concentration increased during the economic crisis. There is also evidence that the resumption of growth reversed this trend in Brazil and South Korea. The implications of this are examined below.

1. With declining incomes and evidence of deterioration in the relative income distribution, both the proportion and, more important, the *number of people below a given poverty line has almost certainly increased* in Ghana, the Philippines, Chile, Jamaica, Peru, and until 1984, Brazil. Only for South Korea is there evidence of declining absolute poverty. The situation is unclear in Sri Lanka, Zimbabwe, and Botswana. While little information exists on the exact magnitude of the increase in poverty, there are indications that it was sizeable. In Ghana, for instance from 1974 to 1984 the proportion in poverty is estimated to have increased from 60–65 to 70–75 and from 30–35 to 45–50 per cent for rural and urban areas respectively. In Chile, absolute poverty increased from 12 to 16 per cent between 1980 and 1982. No quantitative information is available for the other countries.

2. *Real government expenditure per capita in the social sector declined* in six of the countries (Brazil, Chile, Peru, Philippines, Ghana, Jamaica) while increasing in Zimbabwe, Botswana, Sri Lanka, and South Korea. In South Korea, government expenditure has been purposely used as a major policy instrument

to protect the poor and sustain the level of economic activity. A closer look at public health and education budgets (Brazil, Peru, Philippines) reveals in addition that during the economic crisis governments have continued to support institutions like urban hospitals and tertiary education which largely cater to upper-income families. A more detailed analysis of government expenditure trends is presented in Chapter 3.

3. *Expenditure on food subsidies or supplementary feeding declined* in the four countries for which precise data are available (Sri Lanka, Chile in 1983, Peru, and Zimbabwe in 1982–83), while there is evidence of increases in food assistance in South Korea, Jamaica, and Botswana. In the first two countries, the decline in real food subsidies and supplementary feeding is clearly associated with declining nutritional indicators.

4. Finally, some evidence exists that the *time of mothers* allocated to child care declined as women increased their participation in the labour force in order to compensate for the declining incomes of the male members of the family (Chile, Philippines, and Peru). Unless accompanied by a parallel growth in child care structures, an increase in female labour force participation may result in severe problems for the children. Indirect evidence of declines in the time allocated by parents to child care is also provided by the growing number of street- and abandoned children in Brazil and the Philippines.

(b) Availability and use of food and key social services (process indicators) In view of the observed contraction in government real expenditure per capita in social services (except in Botswana, Sri Lanka, and South Korea), and in the absence of consistent and generalized attempts to reorient public resources towards more equitable and low-cost social programmes, it is not surprising to discover a widespread contraction in service availability, rapidly escalating user costs, and a general deterioration in the quality of the services delivered in most of the countries. Not all of them, however, remained passive in the face of the general contraction in public resources. In the Philippines the authorities adopted a number of specific responses (cash benefits for medical care, development of herbal medicine, food discount projects, etc.). The serious underfunding of these programmes, however, as well as their urban and middle-class bias, did not allow them to constitute serious buffers. In Jamaica, a Food Aid Programme addressed to all vulnerable groups reached only 20 per cent of the intended beneficiaries during its first six months of operation. In other countries the decline in government social expenditure and household incomes has not been accompanied by measures capable of counterbalancing the decline in supply and use of essential services and goods, with the following results.

1. *Declines in food intake* (or availability) have occurred, either on average or for the bottom 20 to 40 per cent of the population, in Sri Lanka, Brazil, Peru, Philippines, and Ghana. In Sri Lanka, per capita daily calorie consumption of the bottom 20 per cent of the population declined from 1,500 in 1978 to

1,370 in 1982, while in Ghana estimated food availability as a percentage of requirements declined from the late 1970s to early 1980s from 88 to 68 per cent. Informed observers point to the same trend for Jamaica. Average food availability declined in Botswana between 1980 and 1982 because of drought conditions, but increased over the next three years. A similar pattern was observed in Zimbabwe. In Chile, the sharp decline in average daily per capita consumption of the bottom 60 per cent of the population observed between 1969 and 1978 probably continued in the 1980s given the sharp drop in family incomes. Even in South Korea there was a small but noticeable decline (5 per cent) in average calorie intake per capita in 1980, a year in which GDP per capita fell by almost 8 per cent. Food intake improved again with the resumption of growth.

2. *Changes in the health sector.* The situation is more complex in the health sector, where the extension of services might, on balance, have suffered proportionately less. On the one hand there are indications of closure of health facilities for budgetary reasons (Jamaica), of reduced immunization coverage and of increases in hospital consultations for curative purposes (São Paulo, Brazil) and of growing health costs for both public and private medical care (Philippines, Jamaica, and Zimbabwe). There is also evidence that in Ghana the sharp reduction in staffing and rising costs provoked an 11 per cent decline per year in health unit attendance between 1979 and 1984. On the other hand, South Korea increased medical insurance and aid coverage (from 26 to 39 per cent) rapidly, while in Zimbabwe and Botswana there has been a fast expansion in the provision and use of preventive health services. In Chile, highly effective maternal and child health services were extended despite the reduction of health expenditure per capita.

3. *In the education sector* the decline in service availability, and particularly in actual service coverage, between 1979 and 1985 is very clear. With the usual exception of South Korea, where a pre-existing programme of tuition exemption for the children of the poor was expanded during the recession of 1979–81, and of Zimbabwe, where primary enrolment expanded, in all other countries analysed there is evidence of declining primary school enrolment rates (Philippines, Chile, Sri Lanka), increasing drop-out rates (Brazil, Peru, Sri Lanka) and of massive losses of qualified teachers (Ghana and Jamaica). In Ghana, for instance, more than 4,000 fully qualified teachers left the school system between 1977 and 1981. In Jamaica, poor parents have often deferred sending their children to school as a result of the growing cost of private and often public education. No data are available for Botswana.

(c) **Child survival and welfare ('outcome indicators')** The severity of the deterioration observed for the inputs and process indicators has been reflected in noticeable and often severe losses of child welfare, as indicated below.

1. *Infant mortality and child deaths.* Infant mortality rate (IMR) data (i.e. rate

of deaths of infants in their first year) are available for 8 of the 10 countries analysed. In Sri Lanka, Botswana and South Korea—i.e. countries which experienced either no or only mild recessions—infant mortality continued to decline, although in South Korea the decline was slower than the trend. Although quantitative evidence is not available, infant mortality is widely believed to have declined in Zimbabwe due to the rapid expansion of key health services like child immunization and oral rehydration. In the Philippines and Chile, IMR continued its decline but at a substantially slower pace. In the Philippines, for instance, IMR declined 2 percentage points a year over the 1975–80 period, while between 1981–85—a period of marked economic deterioration—IMR declined on average by only 1 percentage point. In Brazil and particularly in Ghana, IMR increased substantially. In São Paulo, Brazil, the steep increase of IMR in 1984 may well be a reflection of the nation-wide increase in infant mortality between 1982 and 1984 as well as of the declining vaccination coverage and worsening nutritional conditions in the state itself. No yearly IMR data were available for Jamaica and Peru.

Only two studies present data on the *child death rate (CDR)* (i.e. rate of death among children aged between one and five years). In Ghana the CDR showed a sharp increase between the late 1970s and the early 1980s. In Chile there was a clear reversal in 1983, when the CDR rose 12 per cent over the previous year following interruption of certain nutrition and health programmes; it resumed its decline in 1984 but still remained above trend.

A search of the literature for countries other than the 10 included in the sample indicates that in Latin America the IMR increased for the whole of Brazil and Uruguay. In *Brazil* it increased from 65 to 73 per thousand (12 per cent) between 1982 and 1984, after a long period of sustained decline. While the rise in infant mortality was most pronounced in the North and North-East, it also affected the richer South and South-East regions (Becker and Lechtig 1986a). A commensurate increase was observed in *Uruguay,* where IMR increased between 1983 and 1985 from 28.6 to 31.8 per thousand. Post-neonatal mortality accounted for all of the increase (Terra and Hopenhaym 1986). Circumstantial evidence of increases in infant mortality is also reported by field workers for the 1981–86 period for *Bolivia.* In *Costa Rica,* infant mortality stagnated (at low level) during the crisis (World Bank 1986c).

It is however in *Sub-Saharan Africa* that increases in infant and child mortality are expected to be the strongest owing to the combined effect of drought and of prolonged economic plight. While recent IMR data are completely absent, there are strong indications that the number of deaths—particularly among the very young and the very old—increased substantially in 1984, and 1985 and might still have been above average in 1986 in several countries of the region.

In *South, South-East,* and *East Asia*—i.e. regions which enjoyed uninterrupted growth during the 1980s—infant and child mortality rates are on the decline in most of the countries for which data are available. However, IMR increased sharply in crisis areas such as *Negros Occidental* (Philippines) between 1983 and 1985 (UNICEF-Philippines 1985). In *Burma*, IMR increased over the 1981–82 period but fell in 1983–84. However, in 1984 it was still above 1980 levels (UNICEF-Burma 1986).

2. *Malnutrition.* All countries included in this study contain some information about nutritional status. With the exception of South Korea and Zimbabwe, there are indications that *malnutrition has been on the increase* in every country. It should be pointed out, however, that the duration, extent, and causes of such deterioration vary substantially from country to country. In Ghana and Peru, for instance, the deterioration appears as very pronounced (around 50 per cent) while in the other countries the increases *vis-à-vis* previous levels range between 10 and 25 per cent. The duration of such worsening also varies, with continuous deterioration over several years in countries such as the Philippines and Ghana, while in others, such as Chile, the worsening is of more recent origin and not clearly established. In addition, while in practically all cases economic decline and inadequate policies were the main cause, in Botswana, Ghana, and Peru climatic factors compounded these negative factors. It is likely, however, that with the exception of Botswana, the main forces behind the observed increase in malnutrition were of an economic nature.

Detailed information shows that despite sustained growth during the 1978–83 period, Sri Lanka witnessed a rapid increase (from about 6.1 per cent to 9.4 per cent) in nutritional wasting among children of 6–60 months of age in rural areas. Deterioration was also evident in the 6–23-month-old children in the estate sector. In the Philippines the percentage of children with a weight for age below 75 per cent of the expected value increased from 17.5 to 22 per cent in a few years. An increase from 38.3 to 40.8 per cent in first-, second-, and third-degree malnourished children (Gomez classification) was observed in Jamaica, where the number of hospitalizations for malnutrition and malnutrition-enteritis increased 13 per cent a year between 1978 and 1985. In Chile the downward trend in the incidence of malnutrition (measured by weight for age) among pre-school children was reversed in 1983 when a 10 per cent increase was observed. Despite a decline in 1984, preliminary data show another increase in 1985 for children below two years of age. In São Paulo there is evidence that the proportion of low birth weight babies delivered at two main city hospitals increased by about 10 per cent between 1980 and 1983. In Botswana the increase in child malnutrition rose by only 3 percentage points, from 28 to 31 per cent, despite a seven year drought and a short but severe recession, thanks to the introduction of public work, drought relief, and child feeding programmes.

In Ghana and Peru the deterioration was acute. In Ghana the proportion of pre-school children with weight for age below the third percentile of the reference population increased from about 34 to about 52 per cent between 1980 and 1983. Only a small improvement followed in 1984. Although available data cover only the southern part of the country, the incidence of first-, second-, and third-degree malnutrition rose in Peru from 42 to 68 per cent of child population. Third-degree malnutrition, in particular, increased from 0.8 to 3.0 per cent in only three years.

The conclusion that the nutritional status of children is deteriorating in many developing countries outside Asia finds strong support from the evidence provided by a variety of other sources including local surveys, donor's reports, government documents, special studies, etc. As the information presented is far from providing an exhaustive account, it is likely it may underestimate the full extent of the deterioration in Africa, Latin America, and the Middle East.

In Latin America there are numerous indications of increases in malnutrition in various parts of the region. Low birth weight increased in the *North-East of Brazil* from 10.2 in 1982 to 15.3 per cent in 1984 (Dias *et al.* 1986). While the recession and ensuing adjustment were found to be the primary causes of the increase in low birth weight prevalence, the impact of the recession might not have affected nutrition so strongly had it not been for a prior drought. These findings are confirmed indirectly by a recent World Bank study (1986*c*) on the impact of the depression in Latin America, which reports for the same country a higher prevalence of anaemia among poorer families in 1985 as compared with 1973–74. In *Uruguay,* the number of malnourished children admitted to the National Nutritional Programme almost doubled between 1982 and 1984 (Terra and Hopenhaym 1986). In *Bolivia* the nutritional status of children admitted to the main hospital of Cochabamba showed a marked deterioration between 1980 and 1983. While in 1980, 45 per cent of these children were affected by some form of malnutrition, the proportion increased to 56 per cent in 1983. In addition, three surveys carried out between 1983 and 1984 to assess the nutritional status of children showed an increase in the proportion of children at risk (Morales-Anaya 1985). A compilation of UNICEF data on prevalence of low birth weight babies indicates that increases have occurred between 1979 and 1982 in *Barbados,* from 10 to 16 per cent, and *Jamaica,* from 10 to 12 per cent. For *Mexico,* a study by Dieguez (1985) indicates that in 1984 half of low income households suffered from insufficient caloric and protein intake. Although there are no baseline data with which to compare this figure, there is a strong perception that the situation deteriorated in recent years. Indeed, the cost of a calorie in relation to the minimum salary increased on average between 1982 and 1986 by 65 per cent, with peaks of 130 per cent in the case of bread, while there were absolute cuts in the food intake of the poor in Mexico in 1983 (World Bank 1986*c*).

Data for *Sub-Saharan Africa* indicate that a sharp deterioration has occurred in all countries for which data are available, whether affected by drought or not. To start with, Catholic Relief Service monthly data on weight for age indicate that over the 1981–85 period malnutrition among children aged 6–42 months increased by various degrees in *Madagascar, Rwanda, Lesotho,* and *Burundi* (UNICEF 1985*a*). In *Zambia* the percentage incidence of malnutrition as a cause of mortality for the age bracket 1–14 years increased from 27 to 43 per cent between 1978 and 1982 (UNICEF-Zambia 1986). In *Kenya* child malnutrition went up from 24 to 28 per cent between 1977 and 1982 (UNICEF-Kenya 1984). UNICEF data on the prevalence of low birth weight indicates that increases of various proportions have occurred in *Guinea-Bissau, Rwanda, Tanzania, Zaire,* and *Cameroon* (UNICEF 1986). Scattered health data indicate furthermore that since 1980 there has been a drastic increase in the incidence of malaria, respiratory infections, diarrhoea and meningitis in *Niger* (UNICEF 1985a). In *Zambia* the surge in gastro-intestinal diseases observed recently has been associated with drought and a rapid growth of squatters (UNICEF-Zambia 1986).

Limited data are available for *North Africa and the Middle East*, which was hit by a very severe recession in the early 1980s. In *Morocco* there was a strong decline in average calorie intake between 1980 and 1984 (FAO 1986). Increasing prevalence of low birth weight is reported by UNICEF in *Iraq* for the years 1979–82. Finally, in a community-based programme for children in a low-income area in *Jordan* there has been a noticeable increase in malnutrition (measured by weight for age) between 1981 and 1985, which may reflect a deterioration in living conditions (UNICEF-UDD 1986).

In South, South-East, and East Asia, while children's nutritional problems are often still of extreme gravity, there are only a few indications of recent deterioration in nutritional status. For instance the prevalence of low birth weight babies increased from 9 to 11 per cent in *Malaysia*, and 21 to 27 per cent in *Sri Lanka* between 1979 and 1982 (UNICEF 1986). However, in several other cases (such as Thailand), there are strong indications of declines in the incidence of all forms of malnutrition during the 1980s.

3. *Morbidity data* on disease prevalence and incidence are notoriously difficult to come by and not easy to interpret. While the deterioration in mortality and, particularly, nutritional status in themselves provide a clear indication of deteriorating health status, additional indications are available for Ghana, where high levels of overall morbidity and the resurgence of diseases like yaws and yellow fever, which had previously been eradicated, have been observed. Similarly, an increase is evident in the incidence of communicable (Philippines) and non-immunizable (Chile) diseases. In Chile, typhoid fever and hepatitis have been on the increase, possibly because of cuts in government expenditure on drinking water and environmental sanitation. In Peru increasing deaths due to tuberculosis have been reported, together with a sharp increase in the number of cases of hepatitis, gastro-intestinal diseases, and typhoid fever.

4. *Educational attainment.* The reductions in enrolment rates noted were translated into lower levels of educational attainments. In Sri Lanka, for instance, there is evidence of a decline in literacy (from 88 to 86 per cent) for children aged 6–14 years between 1978/79 and 1981/82. Similarly, in the Philippines school completion rates fell from 67 to 63 per cent between 1981 and 1984.

Increases in school drop-out, failure rates, and declines in cohort survival (Sri Lanka, Ghana, Peru, Brazil) point to worsening educational attainments in periods of economic hardship. In several of these countries there are also indications of an overall decline in the quality of education (Peru, Jamaica, Ghana).

There is also some additional evidence of deterioration in the area of education in countries other than those included in the sample. In *Latin America,* enrolment rates for 3 to 19 years of age fell sharply in *Barbados* between 1982 and 1984 (Ministry of Labour 1985). In *Bolivia* a sharp increase (from 2.2 to 8.5 per cent) in school desertion rate was noted between 1980 and 1983 for the children enrolled in primary school (Morales-Anaya 1985). In *Mexico,* the decline in incomes has been accompanied by a reduction in private school enrolment (World Bank 1986c).

In *Africa,* there are also indications of deterioration in the area of education. When school fees were increased in 1982 in Bendel State of *Nigeria,* primary school enrolment decreased from 90 to 60 per cent over the following 18 months. While no data on current enrolment are available in *Zaire,* the dismissal in 1984 of 7,000 teachers from the public school system for budgetary reasons does not augur well for primary education in that country (UNICEF 1985a).

IV Conclusions

The preceding discussion shows that the growing economic imbalances and, in particular, the decline in household incomes and/or government expenditure experienced in the 1980s by 70 per cent of the developing countries in Latin America, Africa, and the Middle East have led to a widespread and sharp reversal in the trend toward the improvement in standards of child health, nutrition, and education. The evidence provided by the 10 country studies of Volume II and by a search of the literature shows that deterioration in child welfare has occurred in at least 8 countries in Latin America, 16 in Sub-Saharan Africa, 3 in North Africa and the Middle East and 4 in South and East Asia (although the situation of children in most South-East Asian countries continued to improve in most cases).

Evidence of deterioration is clearest in the area of nutrition and education, for both of which worsening conditions were evident in 8 of the 10 countries included in the sample. A more general—if still incomplete—count of changes in nutritional status shows some kind of deterioration in at least 27 countries. The increase or slower decline in infant and child mortality and morbidity was less generalized. However, in the 10 countries analysed, only in South Korea, Zimbabwe, and Sri Lanka did mortality unambiguously improve at historical rates.

The extent and severity of the deterioration in child welfare is much clearer in 1986 than could be judged from the evidence available in 1983, when

UNICEF undertook a previous assessment. After six consecutive years of decline or stagnation, the capacity of many individuals, households and governments to resist crisis has significantly weakened, while the effect of years of poor nutrition, less accessible health care, and declining educational opportunities has accumulated to the point at which permanent damage has already been done to the physical and mental capacity of much of the future labour force. Although margins for catching up exist in many of the countries affected, it will be increasingly difficult and costly to remove the damage represented by child stunting and growing illiteracy as well as by the accumulated deterioration of the physical conditions of hospitals, clinics, schools, and of the environment at large. Unless there are radical and immediate policy changes, the prediction that 'the worst is yet to come' is as valid as ever.

The evidence shows that while adverse climatic changes, particularly in 1983–84 and in Africa, have been important compounding factors, in almost every case deterioration in child welfare resulted in large part from the economic decline of the 1980s and from the lack of appropriate policies aimed at protecting the children.

Annex I   An analytical framework relating social and economic conditions and the state of children

1   The framework

Measuring and analysing changes in child welfare requires agreement on an analytical framework describing the most important causal linkages between those social, economic, and biological factors which influence child survival and development. As Mosley and Chen (1984) and UNICEF-Tanzania (1985) have shown recently, the two predominant approaches to research on child survival and development—i.e. the social science approach and the medical science approach—can now be integrated in a single meaningful framework capable of illustrating the complex chain of causes leading to deterioration in child welfare.

The framework presented here, illustrated graphically in Fig. 1.3, takes broad inspiration from the works quoted above. A typical developing country context the *immediate causes* of infant or child death are disease, injury, dietary deficiencies, and maternal and delivery factors, i.e. factors mostly reflecting biological processes. A clear understanding of the actions necessary to prevent such losses of child welfare requires investigation beyond the level of these immediate causes to *their* causes—i.e. the causes of dietary deficiencies, injury, disease and negative maternal and delivery factors. The processes linking the immediate causes to the *underlying causes* are illustrated in Fig. 1.3.

Similar considerations apply in the five other kinds of deterioration in child welfare encircled in Fig. 1.3 i.e. malnutrition, disease, disability, abandonment and delinquency, and declining school achievements. Although the underlying causes of losses in child welfare are numerous and highly interrelated, they are

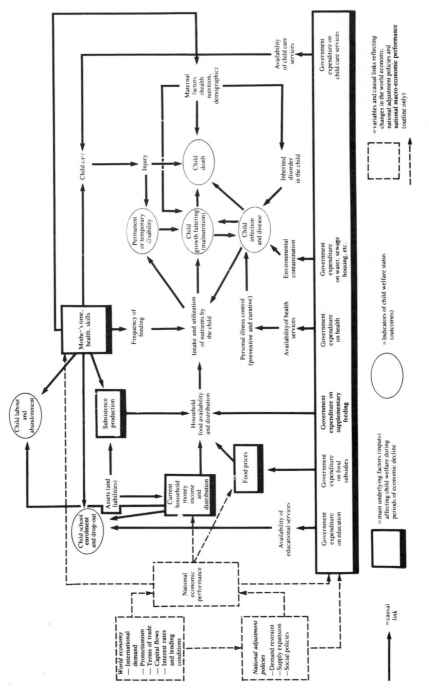

Fig. 1.3 An analytical framework linking changes in selected economic determinants and changes in selected indicators of child welfare

normally grouped in three sets representing different kinds of resources for the 'production' of child welfare:

1. *Real resources in cash or kind at the household level*. Three main variables influence the level of resources, i.e. subsistence production, money incomes (whether from wage or self-employment or from transfers), and the rate of inflation, particularly for food. Such resources are used for the satisfaction of consumption needs in the area of food, housing, clothing, transport, and, to an extent, health, water and sanitation, education and child care.

2. *Government expenditure* on health, education, child care, water and environmental sanitation, supplementary feeding, and food subsidies. Although private expenditure in these areas is far from negligible in most developing countries, social services are mainly supported by the government.

3. *Family and community characteristics*. Three elements that strongly influence the 'production' of child welfare within the household (and to a lesser extent the community) are the time, health, and skills (typically measured by the educational level) of the parents, and in particular of the mother. For fathers, the correlation between their health and educational level and that of their children is largely mediated by the relation between education and income. The health, time, and skills of mothers, in contrast, operate directly on the immediate cause of child welfare. Because of the biological link between mother and child during pregnancy and lactation, the mother's health, nutrition, and reproductive behaviour very strongly influence the health and survival of the child. Similarly the mother's level of education can affect child welfare by enhancing child feeding, rearing, and hygienic practices, and by allowing a better use of the resources existing within the family or the community. Finally the 'production' of a healthy child also requires the mother's time for pre-natal health-care visits, food preparation, bringing the child to the clinic, child hygiene, and sickness care.

Generally speaking, all three sets of variables illustrated above change during periods of recession and indiscriminate economic adjustment. Money incomes, government expenditure, food prices, and mother's time and health respond quickly to changes in economic aggregates. Subsistence production, on the other hand, is influenced more by structural variables (land quality and concentration, access to inputs, and climatic factors) than by fluctuations in the monetized sector of the economy. The current level of mothers' education is generally unaffected by short economic crisis, but might be negatively influenced (relapse in illiteracy) for those women with a minimum level of literacy if economic hardship is protracted for several years. Mothers' health and time use, in contrast, change markedly during periods of economic hardship. Some structural determinants of child welfare—such as cultural and social values influencing health practices, sex bias, etc—are omitted from the framework as they are expected to vary only imperceptibly, if at all, even during periods of pronounced economic fluctuations. For them a *ceteris paribus* assumption is generally appropriate. The five main determinants identified in Fig. 1.3 affect child welfare with different intensity and at different speed, depending on the indicator of welfare selected. In general, it would be expected that the crisis shows its effects first in terms of increasing child labour and school drop-outs, while more acute forms of social stress like malnutrition and morbidity and, eventually, mortality become evident only after severe and cumulative declines have occurred. The impact of economic decline might not be felt for some time (or, in fewer cases, at all), particularly in those countries with some capacity to resist crises and where appropriate counterbalancing policies are adopted.

A decline in GDP (whether due to recession and/or adjustment) is associated with a decline in average real incomes. This drop in incomes will be shared by each category, unless there are significant distributional shifts. The distribution of a fall in GDP among socio-occupational groups varies according to the structure and degree of monetization of the economy, the nature of the shocks leading to the recession, the relative price changes triggered by stabilization measures, the existence of buffering mechanisms (transfer payments), etc. Broad generalization on how income distribution changes with recession is therefore difficult (Addison and Demery 1985, Helleiner 1985*a*). While the poor in the little-monetized subsistence sector of the economy may not be overly affected by general economic decline, experience shows that those at the bottom or near the bottom of the income distribution in the monetized sector of the economy tend to suffer disproportionately. Indeed, because of the increase in excess labour supply that occurs in most developing country labour markets, recession tends to depress minimum wages in excess of the drop in employment and GDP (Tokman 1986, PREALC 1985*a*). Self-employment incomes in the informal sector often follow this trend as in many developing countries the latter generally produces non-tradeables (mostly services) the demand for which is largely a function of the level of income in the formal sector (see Ch. 4), while the number of people seeking a livelihood in this sector rises as formal sector employment falls.

Confronted with sharp declines in current money incomes of the employed family members, households can temporarily maintain previous levels of consumption by reducing their savings rate, by liquidating their assets, by expanding the family labour supply, and by running into debt. These responses, however, are less frequently available to very poor households, for whom a drop in purchasing power is often reflected in substantial reduction in food expenditure. For those households spending 60–80 per cent of their incomes on food, a 10 per cent drop in income may result in a 6–8 per cent reduction in food expenditure.

As shown in Fig. 1.3 food availability at the household level is also strongly influenced by food prices. Ample evidence exists that over the last decade food prices have increased faster than the average inflation rate in many developing countries (see Table 1.7). This is particularly the case during periods of adjustment, when pressures to reduce food subsidies, to increase food producer prices, and (for food-importing countries) to devalue currency lead to increases in food consumer prices. Price elasticities of demand for food are quite high (Pinstrup-Andersen 1986*a*), and increases in food prices cause much larger percentage reductions in demand among the poor (who spend a higher share of their incomes on food) than among the rich.

Food availability at the household level is also strongly influenced by direct food distribution (food rations, supplementary feeding, etc.) whose positive nutritional and income transfer effect have long been recognized (World Bank

1986*b*). During periods of recession and budgetary austerity, however, this form of food supplementation tends to be reduced or eliminated.

As a result of the three factors (decline in money incomes, rapid increases in food prices, and declining food subsidies), food expenditure declines almost by the same amount as the drop in real income. Similar responses occur with respect to other important non-food health items (drugs, water, etc.).

Such large declines in real expenditure on food do not necessarily imply large changes in the intake of calories, as households substitute cheaper food with the same caloric content for more expensive food. Using cross-sectional aggregate data from 30 countries, Behrman and Deolalikar (1986), for instance, found that average food expenditure decreases 8 per cent for every 10 per cent decline in income, but caloric intake decreases only 3 per cent. However, while middle- and low-income households can maintain their nutrient intake almost unchanged through such process of substitution, this opportunity is certainly not available to the ultra-poor (Lipton 1983*a*), i.e. those who have already exhausted the possibility of substitution and who with 80 per cent of their incomes already spent on food do not manage to satisfy 80 per cent of their minimum caloric requirements. For these people—already without enough calories for an active working life, or, worse, without enough calories to prevent stunted growth and serious health risks—declining incomes, rising food prices, and elimination of food subsidies do result in dangerous declines in food intake and in dietary deficiencies. The World Bank (1986*a*) estimates that there were respectively 730 and 340 million people in this condition in 1980. Empirical evidence drawn from longitudinal studies on Sri Lanka and Chile (Shan 1986 Raczinsky in vol. ii, ch. 3) confirms the hypothesis that statistically significant declines in calorie consumption were observed for population groups whose real incomes had declined substantially.

Insufficient intake of nutrients, and/or inadequate utilization, eventually leading to growth faltering among children can be triggered by factors which have nothing or little to do with food availability at the household level.

First, it is well known that various forms of infection, or more generally, of pathogenic invasion (diarrhoea and other intestinal affections, worm infestation, acute respiratory infections, and communicable diseases) either depress the appetite (particularly in the under-5s) and therefore reduce food intake, or—as in the case of diarrhoea—provoke serious losses of nutrients. In both cases the net effect is an increase in malnutrition. The extent of pathogenic invasion or infection (see Fig. 1.3) depends largely on the level of environmental contamination and on personal disease control factors, both preventive and curative. Apart from climatic and geological considerations, environmental contamination depends to a very large extent on expenditure—both capital and recurrent—in sectors like potable water supply, sanitation, sewage, public housing, and others. Often, during periods of protracted economic decline, government and private expenditure on such items contract (see Ch. 3). Capital expenditure, and expenditure on maintenance and supervision in particular, are key areas where financial retrenchment often takes place. As a result water pumps fall into disrepair, water sources become contaminated, garbage disposal deteriorates, and drainage of the sewage system becomes more erratic.

The ability of individuals to take preventive and curative health actions for themselves and their children depends on the availability of health services—generally, but not exclusively, provided by the state. In this case, too, protracted recession and budgetary austerity tend to depress government expenditure, with negative effects in terms of service availability and ultimately of morbidity, malnutrition, and in extreme cases mortality.

Secondly, it is clearly established that the mother's time, health, skills, and reproductive behaviour affect a child's mortality, growth, and development, school attendance and performance, and adjustment in later life. (Caldwell 1981, Zerilin and Manzoor 1985). As noted earlier, the level of education and skills of the mother do not generally change much because of economic decline even of a prolonged duration. The recession does however affect the level of education and skills of future mothers, as young girls are normally the first to be withdrawn from school in order to save on school fees and books or because they are needed to work in the fields, to take care of younger siblings, or to perform various domestic tasks in the absence of their mothers who have increased their labour supply to compensate for the decline in incomes of the heads of the household. While the increased participation of women in the labour force may partially offset the income decline of the head of the household, their absence from home can substantially reduce the time dedicated to child care and food preparation. It is possible that women try to compensate for the increase in the number of hours worked outside the household by reducing the time devoted to rest and social activities (Leslie *et al.* 1986). Time-use studies (Popkin 1980), however, show that the number of hours available to women for such activities is generally quite limited— between 1 and 3 hours—so that the women's capacity to substitute work for leisure is rather limited particularly for very poor households.

Community and governmental services in child care centres provide a substitute for the mother's child care and food preparation. But in those cases where government and community structures are lacking, it is possible that the frequency of feeding (i.e. the number of meals a day) and child care in general decline with an increase in the mother's work outside home, which can have an adverse effect on child nutritional status, particularly at an early age, and may also lead to increased risk of injury. Increasing claims on the mother's time, coupled with declining incomes and cuts in government expenditure on education, tend also to produce negative effects on child abandonment, child labour, and school drop-out rates, particularly among girls.

Lastly, child nutritional status and mortality rate are directly influenced by the mother's nutritional and health status and reproductive behaviour. An increase in maternal malnutrition due to insufficient food intake, overwork, and inadequate pre-natal care, all events related to increasing economic hardship, is immediately transmitted to the foetus, who suffers from growth faltering while still *in utero*. This in turn produces an increase in the number of still births and of low birth weights. The surge in the proportion of low-birth-weight babies generally observed during periods of severe stress is therefore a clear signal of deteriorating maternal and child conditions.

The other maternal factors (age, parity, and spacing) influencing the risk of death and health status of the child are not known to vary according to the various phases of the economic cycle, and depend on more structural variables like female literacy, socio-cultural values, and urbanization. There seems to be some evidence, however, at least, for some Latin American countries (Foxley and Raczinski, 1984 Becker and Lechtig 1986*b*), that fertility tends to decline (or to decline faster than the trend) during periods of economic depression. As the births so avoided are generally high-risk ones (generally with high parity and at close intervals), such decline in fertility triggers—*ceteris paribus*—a more than proportional decline in infant mortality and malnutrition (low birth weights). Similar phenomena have been observed clearly during war years and famines, while there is clear evidence—at least in poor agrarian societies— that the cycle of procreation is strongly influenced by seasonal fluctuations in food availability at the household level (Chambers 1979). If fertility decline is associated with economic decline, the system tends to be self-correcting and to offset, partially or totally, possible increases in low birth weight and in infant and child mortality during periods of economic decline by reducing the number of 'at risk' births.

The foregoing discussion indicates that the channels through which economic decline affects child status are diverse, numerous and complex. A substantial reduction in nutrient intake or worsening of its utilization is initially associated with changes in body heat and energy expenditure, particularly when dealing with small reductions in intake of nutrients (Sukhatme 1982). Declines in body weight, worsening health status, and eventually increasing risk of death follow for great reductions in nutrient intake and utilization. Some authors (Payne 1986) seem to doubt the meaning and health implications of an eventual loss in body weight (except of course in the case of sudden collapses of food entitlements, as during famines) by arguing that the organism responds to changes in the outside world—levels of disease, food supply, etc.—by adapting its size, weight, blood constituents, and so on to the external environment. However, Mosley and Chen (1984), among others, have clearly demonstrated that death risk consistently increases in exponential fashion with the decline in weight for age (as a proportion of the median) for each interval of observation. The relationship is particularly strong when the drop in weight for age is sudden, not permitting gradual, long-term adaptations of the organism to a lower level of food availability. In concrete terms this finding indicates that increases in 'moderate' malnutrition lead to a higher risk of death.

2 *Application of the analytical framework to past data*

The previous section presented an analytical framework that can be used for the interpretation of the effects of economic decline—whether due to external shocks, domestic factors, or adjustment policies—on the welfare of children. For a review of the empirical findings on these relationships and for the literature on the determinants of health and nutritional status of children the reader is referred to such surveys as UN-DIESA (1983), Preston (1980), and Cornia (1984*a*).

This section provides concrete illustration of the functioning of some of the crucial relations identified in the analytical framework (see Fig. 1.3).
(a) The 'food price–household food availability–nutrient intake– nutritional status–mortality' link McCord *et al.* (1980) provide a clear-

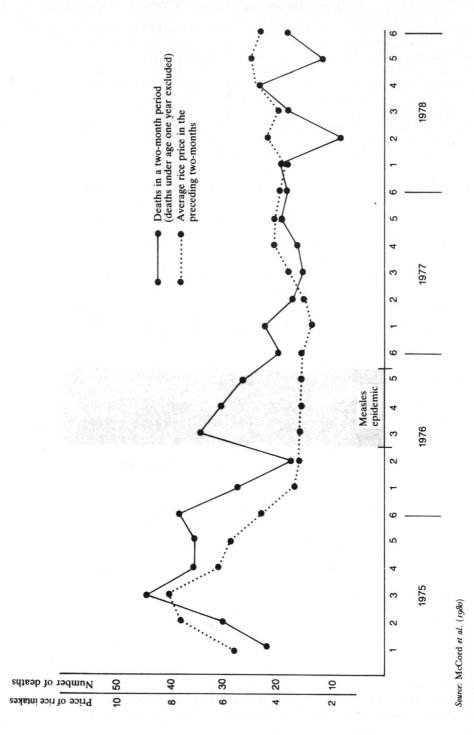

Source: McCord et al. (1980)

Fig. 1.4 Deaths and price of rice in Companiganj Thana, 1975–1978.

cut illustration (see Fig. 1.4) of how sharp increases in food prices (accompanied by stagnant money wages) led—with only a two-month lag— to sudden increases in death rates.

In 1974 and 1975 floods in Bangladesh and poor harvest in India led to a general rise in the price of staple food (rice and wheat) throughout the region ... the price of rice and wheat more than doubled. The average price of these foods in 1975 were Tk. 6.60 per seer ($0.46/kg) for rice and tk. 5.00 per seer ($0.37/kg) for wheat flower. The daily wage rate never rose above Tk. 10.00 taka per day, so that it was not possible to meet the minimum calorie needs of a family even if work was available everyday of the year, which of course, it is not ... As would be expected, the crude death rate rose more than 50 per cent and the increased deaths were concentrated among the poor, the very young and the very old. Deaths due to malnutrition, diarrhoea and tuberculosis accounted for almost all the excess mortality ... The number of deaths observed in the next four years correlates quite well with the price of rice. Excess death in 1976 reflect a combination of measles epidemic and residual malnutrition ... Economic improvement and consequent improved availability of food were associated with 70 per cent reductions of deaths due to malnutrition and diarrhoea among landless and marginal families (McCord *et al.* 1980, pp. 1–2)

Regression analysis shows that the price of rice in the preceding two months and a dummy variable for measles epidemics are positively correlated with the death rate. Their parameters are statistically significant at a level of probability of over 99 per cent.

(b) The 'incomes–food availability–nutrient intake–nutritional status–mortality' link Becker and Lechtig (1986*a*) report a substantial

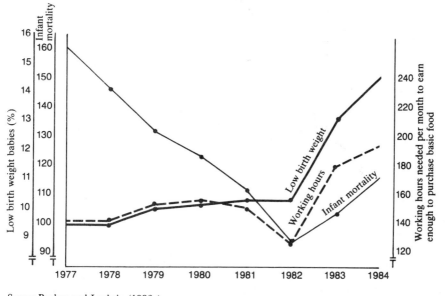

Source: Becker and Lechtig (1986*a*).

Fig. 1.5 Poverty, low birth-weight prevalence and infant mortality in the North-East of Brazil 1977–1984

decrease in infant mortality rates (i.e. from 160 to 93 per thousand) for the North-East of Brazil during 1977–82 (see Fig. 1.5). The prevalence of low-birth weight babies increased slightly, from 9.4 to 10.2 per cent. During this period the number of hours of one minimum wage required to purchase basic food for one person oscillated between 130 and 160. (In 1959 the same number was 65.) However, due to the sharp fall in wages and salaries, households' food-purchasing power was seriously reduced during 1982–84. The number of hours of one minimum wage required to purchase basic food increased abruptly, to 210 in 1983 and 240 in 1984. As a result the prevalence of low-birth-weight babies soared to 15.3 per cent in 1984. This growing trend in prevalence in low-birth-weight babies and the decline in food purchasing power triggered in turn a sharp increase in infant mortality, which rose from 93 to 116 per thousand between 1982 and 1984.

(c) The 'food subsidies–food availability–food intake–nutrition' link
Anthropometric and consumption surveys, supported by food balance-sheet data, suggest that nutritional status improved between 1976 and 1979 in Sri Lanka. Part of this improvement was attributed to a rice ration programme covering almost 50 per cent of the population. However, the situation started to change from January 1979 when the rice ration programme was restricted to the low-income groups. In September 1979 a food stamp scheme with a fixed value in stamps replaced the ration programme. The introduction of the food stamp scheme resulted in a clear reduction in the quantity of food obtainable, owing to the sharp increases in the prices of basic foods following the removal of the subsidies in early 1980. The price index for the food items increased from 107.9 in 1979 to 212.6 in 1981 and 233.4 in 1982. The improvement in incomes of the upper income groups enabled them to cope with the restriction of the ration in 1979 and the price increase in 1980. In contrast, stagnant or declining real incomes of the lower deciles together with the rapid erosion of the value of the food stamps did not permit them to acquire the same quantity of food as before even if they substituted cheaper calories from rice for flour and bread. The daily per capita calorie consumption of the bottom two deciles declined from 1,500 in 1978/79 to 1,405 in 1980/81 and 1,370 in 1981/82 (see Fig. 1.6). The nutritional impact is shown by a statistically significant increase in wasting, i.e. in the proportion of children of 6–60 months with a weight for height less than 80 per cent of the reference population (Shan 1984). A comparison of 1975/76 and 1981/82 data shows almost 50 per cent increase in wasting for the rural areas, while deteriorations were observed also for the 6–23-month group in the estate sector.

(d) The 'availability of health services–personal illness control–disease–infant mortality' link In Volume II of this book Macedo presents monthly infant mortality data for the state of São Paulo for 1980 to 1984, a period characterized by unusual declines in GDP and consumption per capita. The data presented (see Fig. 1.7) show a declining trend until the beginning of 1984, when the infant mortality rate increased sharply (almost 50 per cent) in only a few months. Even after the subsequent decline the infant mortality rate remained above trend. The main reason behind this tremendous increase was a measles outbreak in mid-1984. The effects of the outbreak, however, were magnified by a decline in measles immunization coverage in 1984. In addition,

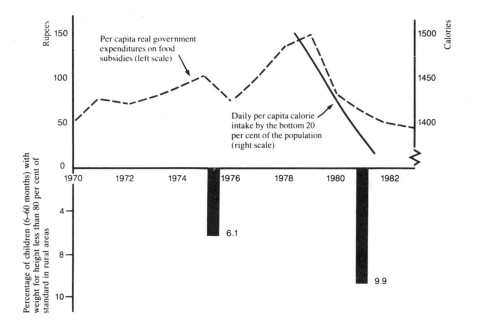

Source: UNICEF-Sri Lanka (1985).

Fig. 1.6 Per capita real government expenditures on food subsidies, calorie intake by the bottom 20 per cent of the population, and child malnutrition in Sri Lanka, 1970–82

the state secretary of health, among others, affirmed that the impact on infant mortality would not have been so evident were it not for the weakened nutritional and health status of many of the children as a consequence of three or four years of recession.

(e) The 'unemployment–income–food and prenatal care availability for the mother–perinatal mortality' link In a classic analysis of the relation between economic instability and foetal, infant, and maternal mortality in the United States, Brenner (1973) found that the deviations from the long-term trend in such health status variables as perinatal, neonatal, and infant mortality were positively correlated with the unemployment rate, with time-lags varying between 1 and 3 to 5 years (see Fig. 1.8). The author suggests that different mechanisms are at work in the case of perinatal versus neonatal mortality. In the case of perinatal mortality, the rate was affected largely through changes in the mother's condition. Unemployment (and the ensuing loss of income) and other factors related to economic fluctuation (as loss of medical insurance, for instance) negatively affected access to pre-natal care, as well as the mother's physical or emotional health due to diet alterations, hypertension, and the use of alcohol or tranquillizers.

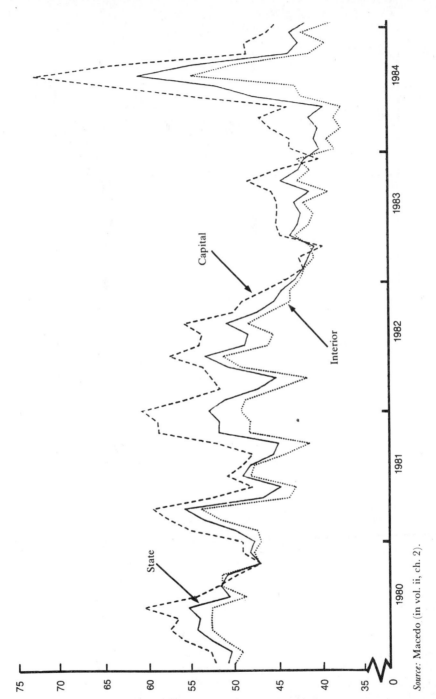

Source: Macedo (in vol. ii, ch. 2).

Fig. 1.7 Sao Paulo: Infant mortality rates, 1980–1984 (seasonally adjusted).

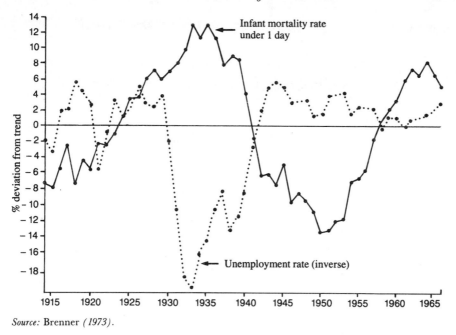

Source: Brenner *(1973)*.

Fig. 1.8　Infant mortality rate and unemployment rate in the United States, 1915–67.

2

Adjustment Policies 1980–1985: Effects on Child Welfare

*Giovanni Andrea Cornia**

I Introduction

The economic difficulties of the 1980s led to a phenomenal increase in the number of countries undertaking stabilization and adjustment programmes, with or without IMF assistance. While there is no doubt that the external shocks, together with the consequences of domestic policies followed in the 1970s, were the main factors responsible for the negative trends in growth performance and child welfare, and that without some form of adjustment the situation might have been far worse, it is important to examine developments associated with the adjustment policies adopted during the 1980s in order to assess the need for and possibility of alternatives.

'Adjustment' policies describe all policies designed to reduce the basic imbalances in the economy, both on external accounts and in domestic resource use. It is helpful to distinguish *stabilization* policies from other types of *adjustment* policies. Stabilization policies consist in reducing imbalances in the external accounts and the domestic budget by cutting down on expenditure (by the government and by firms and households), and reducing credit creation and the budget deficit. Stabilization policies are therefore deflationary, and tend to have rapid effects on the balance of trade through a reduction in imports. Other adjustment policies are designed to change the structure of the economy (i.e. achieve *structural adjustment*), so as to improve the balance of trade and the efficiency of the economy over the medium term. The intention of these adjustment policies is to expand the supply of tradables, increasing both exports and import-substitutes. IMF policies are—as we shall see—mainly, but not exclusively, stabilization policies, while the World Bank Structural Adjustment Loans (SAL) are designed to secure adjustment over the medium term.

This chapter considers the effects of prevailing adjustment policies on *growth*, *distributive equity* and *poverty*, and *child welfare*. The focus is on the policies associated with IMF programmes. World Bank SALs and Structural Adjustment Credits (SACs) have covered fewer countries, and have always been

* The work of data compilation and the many useful suggestions of Eva Jespersen are gratefully acknowledged.

associated with IMF agreements (IMF programmes have been in effect in all cases where SALs or SACs have been introduced, except in the case of Burundi, where an IMF programme followed shortly after the SAC). In addition to summarizing the experience reported in the 10 case studies and reviewing previous findings, the chapter considers some results which would be expected on the basis of economic theory and presents some empirical data on the relation between the programmes, per capita growth rates, investment levels, and current account balances in developing countries for the years 1980–85.

II Adjustment and stabilization efforts in the 1980s

For the vast majority of developing countries, the first half of the 1980s has been the most difficult period since the Great Depression. In particular, the abrupt cutting off of the supply of external finance left many countries with current account deficits they could not finance.

Under such circumstances, in many countries stabilization programmes were introduced as a matter of urgency to avoid the disruptions which could have followed uncontrolled payment crises. Many countries initiated such a process with the assistance of the IMF. Others, particularly those which could mobilize sufficient international finance independently, or those facing less severe crises, introduced adjustment packages on their own account. As a partial indication of the breadth of this phenomenon, Table 2.1 presents data on the number of countries initiating programmes with IMF assistance. During the 1970s this number averaged about 10 per year, increasing to 28 in 1980, 31 in 1981, 19 in 1982, 33 in 1983, 20 in 1984, and about 26 in 1985. On average, every year from 1980 to 1985 there were 47 countries with IMF programmes. The number of countries attempting to adjust would be even larger if those adjusting without IMF assistance were included. From 1980 to 1986, 21 countries have had SALs or SACs with the World Bank; $4.5 billion was allocated to these programmes over the period 1980–85, compared with a cumulative net flow of $30.3 billion from the Fund over this period. The vast majority of the developing countries have been affected by the adjustment process during the period under examination. Stabilization and adjustment has therefore become a predominant feature of policy-making of the first half of the 1980s.

The adjustment efforts of the 1980s occurred within a climate of rapidly declining external finance, as shown in Chapter 1. This situation certainly influenced the overall stance of the programmes in the 1980s.

III Nature of prevailing adjustment programmes

Any country facing a major and non-transitory imbalance in external accounts has to adjust, either automatically—through direct income and monetary effects—or through the introduction of orderly policies which regulate this

TABLE 2.1   *Net flow of IMF lending to the capital-importing developing countries,
1980–1985 ($ billion)*

	1980	1981	1982	1983	1984	1985
Regular facilities (higher conditionality)	2.3	5.7	4.2	8.8	4.3	1.1
Credit tranche drawings	1.5	3.3	1.9	4.0	1.2	1.0
Extended facility drawings	0.7	2.4	2.3	4.9	3.2	0.0
Special facilities (low conditionality)	1.2	—	1.4	2.2	−0.2	−0.8
Buffer stock financing	—	—	0.1	0.3	—	−0.2
Compensatory financing	0.3	0.6	1.7	2.1	—	−0.3
Oil facility	−0.7	−0.7	−0.4	−0.1	—	—
Trust fund	1.6	0.1	—	—	−0.2	−0.3
TOTAL	3.4	5.7	5.7	11.1	4.2	0.2
Characteristics of higher conditionality lending agreements						
Number initiated	28	31	19	33	20	26
Average length (months)	20	23	14	18	14	16
Number of countries with programmes in effect for more than one month	44	49	45	54	45	42

Sources: UN-DIESA (1986) and IMF *Annual Reports.*
Note: Values are net flows in SDRs converted to dollars at yearly average exchange rates. Figures
may not total because of rounding.

process in a way that is compatible, as far as possible, with the achievement
of other specific policy objectives. As this is the unavoidable reality of adjustment, the relevant question is how to design an adjustment package which
will minimize the costs involved in this process while best meeting priority
objectives. Prevailing adjustment policies generally tackle this problem by a
combination of the following three sets of policies:

1. *Expenditure-reducing policies* aiming at curtailing demand (domestic resource
use). These policies are the conventional tools of demand management. As
demand for both exportables and imports falls, the trade balance improves
because imports are reduced and domestically produced goods are freed for
export. Whenever domestic demand is in excess of full employment level,
expenditure reduction is essential. However, in all cases in which domestic
demand is at or below full employment level, expenditure-reducing policies
tend to achieve short-run equilibrium in the external balance at the expense
of the internal balance, i.e. at the cost of lower output, employment, capacity
utilization, and incomes in the domestic economy. While the output of
tradeables may not decline (although in certain cases it may) since the decline
in domestic demand may be offset by rising exports, in most cases output in
the non-tradeable sector (construction, services) *will* decline. Demand man-

agement policies generally include tighter money supply and reduced credit ceilings, curtailment of the public sector deficit, wage control, or more general policies aimed at restricting real incomes.

2. *Expenditure-switching policies*, aiming at shifting productive resources (labour and capital) from the non-tradeable to the tradeable goods sector and from consumption to investment. This is normally achieved through the manipulation of the relative prices of tradeable versus non-tradeable goods which is expected, in turn, to divert productive resources from the latter to the former sector where they can produce for export or substitute for imports. Simultaneously, as a result of the changes, there will be a shift in domestic demand away from imports to domestically produced tradeables and to non-tradeables. With complete switching the decline in output in non-tradeables will be fully offset by the increase in output in tradeables. Total output will be maintained while re-establishing the external balance. Complete switching, however, implies perfect factor mobility which in real life is limited by technical factors, as existing capital (and to some extent labour) are often sector or activity specific and cannot easily be transferred in the short run. Substantial investment may therefore be required to facilitate this process of conversion and to create new capacity in the tradeable sector employing resources formerly used in the non-tradeable sector. Expenditure-switching policies typically include policies in the areas of exchange rate devaluation, trade interventions (export subsidies, import controls, tariffs, etc.), taxes, product pricing, and policies to enhance factor mobility.

3. *Institutional and policy reforms*, such as trade liberalization, reduced role of the state in the economy, fiscal reform, privatization, reform of the financial markets, reduced exchange controls, price reform, etc. These reforms, strongly promoted in recent years by the World Bank and the IMF, can broadly be characterized as market-oriented and outward-oriented, and are believed to speed up development by increasing overall efficiency, by improving incentives and production responses to market signals, and by stimulating savings, investments, and exports. The liberalization of financial markets, for instance, is believed to increase savings, discriminate against non-profitable investments, and promote the adoption of production techniques more in line with a country's factor endowment. World Bank SALs and SACs fall into this category, being directed towards institutional and policy reforms.

This classification of adjustment policies into three separate categories is not completely satisfactory, as a few policies—pricing policies, for instance—tend to have both demand and supply effects. The distinction is of use, however, in illustrating the predominant features of a given package.

The three sets of policies differ in terms of the *time-lags* with which they have their effects on the real economy. On the one hand demand restraint (expenditure-reducing) policies tend to have a rather immediate impact on spending levels. In practice, decisions to reduce government expenditure may be slow in taking effect, as actual expenditure continues for some time to reflect previous spending decisions. Similarly, changes in the *composition of spending*, responding to changes in relative prices, will also occur in relatively little time. On the other hand, the time-lags between the adoption of expenditure switching policies and actual changes in the *structure of production* (particularly when this requires investment in conversion and expansion of productive capacity) are generally longer.

Some other characteristics of Fund programmes need to be mentioned here since they have growth and distributive implications. They are:

1. *Short time horizon.* The IMF-supported Stand-by-Agreements (SBAs), for instance, have in general a duration of 12–18 months, while the Extended Arrangements (EAs) have a duration of 36 months. Short-term programmes prevail, however. Out of the 191 stabilization programmes (161 SBAs and 30 EAs) begun or ending between 1980 and 1985 with IMF assistance, 56 per cent had a duration of one year or less. It is not uncommon to see countries initiating—and at times breaking off—three to four stabilization programmes during the period, for example, Kenya, Liberia, Zaire, Costa Rica, Jamaica, and Morocco.

2. *The predominance of macro-economic* as compared with meso, sectoral, and targeted policies.

3. *The little consideration given to effects on income distribution or on particular social groups.* While recognizing that the implementation of stabilization programmes has distributive implications, the official view is that apportioning the cost of adjustment within society is entirely a matter of political choices to be left to national governments. However, recently the IMF has agreed to explore the distributional implications of alternative policies at the request of governments (de Larosière 1986).

4. *Monitoring of the adjustment process* is carried out on the basis of a limited set of performance criteria (rate of increase of money supply, budget deficit as a proportion of GNP, amount of bank credit to the economy, etc.), with little or no attention to the performance of the real economy or welfare variables like the income of the poor or the rate of malnutrition.

IV   Effects on child welfare

Stabilization policies have numerous, diverse, and complex effects on the welfare of children. For clarity of exposition it is useful to analyse direct and indirect effects separately. The indirect effects are mediated through the overall functioning of the economy and result from changes, often of different signs, induced by various policy instruments which form part of the same package. These *indirect effects* are best assessed through an analysis of the effects of adjustment on growth, relative income distribution, and the incidence of absolute poverty. There are other *direct effects* of stabilization, however, that may influence the well-being of children quite independently from what happens to the overall growth rate and income distribution of the economy. For example, in a society where many of the poor are net food buyers, a sudden and sharp rise in food prices—which could be triggered by higher producer prices, by reduction of subsidies, or in certain cases by devaluation—can have disastrous effects, lasting months or even years, on the nutritional and health status of the very young, the very old, and the poor (see Ch. 1, Annex I) quite independently of the positive results that supply responses, changes in relative prices, or higher investment may produce. For the most part, analysis of adjustment has been concerned only with macro-economic aggregates. In view of the recent deterioration in child welfare, however, it is necessary also to examine the direct effects on vulnerable groups. A brief review of some of the direct effects is presented after the analysis of the effects of stabilization on growth, income distribution, and poverty which follows.

V Indirect effects

1 Method of analysis

Two broad methodological approaches are available for assessing the effects of adjustment programmes, i.e. the theoretical and the empirical approach.

Following the first approach, partial equilibrium analysis can be used to determine the results expected a priori from the introduction of specific policies like exchange rate devaluation, wage control, or others, which are frequently part of a stabilization programme. While this approach has a certain validity in a few straightforward cases, its applicability is limited by the existence of different theoretical models, arriving at diverging conclusions, to explain the same phenomenon. The greatest limitation however derives from the difficulties in assessing a priori the overall effect of a package, when this is made up of different policy instruments. Various policy instruments may affect either growth or distribution or poverty, in a variety of often conflicting ways and over different time periods. It is normally difficult therefore to be precise, a priori, about the net outcome of an overall package. A partial solution to this—adopted in this chapter—consists in grouping the various policy instruments into the three broad categories presented above and inferring the effects of a programme on the basis of its *composition*, i.e. on the relative dominance of policy instruments in the different categories. With this perspective, the choice of the balance of instruments becomes a crucial issue. Although operating through different channels, *expenditure reducing* (demand restraint) policies tend to produce converging results. Both a reduction in fiscal deficit and the enforcement of a wage freeze, for instance, depress the level of aggregate demand although in the first round the first may result in higher unemployment while the second in lower real wages (with less unemployment). The second-round and longer-term effects are, of course, more difficult to trace. *Expenditure switching* policies, on the other hand, are generally intended to increase the volume of goods and services supplied by the domestic economy at any given level of domestic demand. Even if their supply effects generally become apparent only after a certain time, most of these policies aim at sustaining or expanding the level of domestic economic activity. However, some of these policies have contractionary as well as expansionary effects (most obviously in the case of devaluation), and it is not always clear what the net effect will be. The third group of policies identified in the previous section (institutional and policy reform) are also meant to stimulate the efficiency and level of medium-term growth.

Clearly, the 'policy composition' of an adjustment package will need to vary with the magnitude, origin (internal or external), and likely duration of the external payment imbalance, and the country's level of indebtedness. The amount of net financing that can be expected and the socio-political environment are also factors influencing the choice of policy instruments. Whatever the resulting composition of the policy package, its expected results might be assessed on the basis of the relative dominance of the three sets of policies.

Empirical analysis has also been widely used to assess the effects of stabilization policies. An extensive discussion of such an approach can be found in Goldstein (1986). Three methods have generally been employed. The first, the 'counterfactual' approach, most often regarded as the most appropriate, consists in comparison of the effects of alternative policy packages (the one actually implemented, for instance, and the one proposed by others) by means of simulations using econometric models reconstructing both policy and outcome variables and the causal processes linking them. This approach, however, runs into a number of difficulties, the most important of which is that econometric modelling—despite significant advances—is still very much in its infancy, particularly in the case of developing countries. Models presently available are far from capturing the complexity of the economic relations involved. Moreover, each model itself normally makes use of implicit assumptions which themselves help determine the findings. For the time being, therefore, it is not possible following this approach to come to any definitive conclusions. Second, cross-country analysis can be used to examine how growth, or income distribution, or inflation, etc. have been affected by an adjustment programme taken as a whole. The effects on any given variable for countries undertaking stabilization may be compared with the values of the same variables for those countries not undergoing adjustment. The use of this 'control group', to some extent permits elimination of the bias of global economic trends (like recession) which are due to non-programme factors. Two types of analyses are normally done. One is the *policy-on/policy-off* approach by which the value of any given variable is examined in programme and non-programme observations. The other consists in *before–after* analysis, by which the value of a given variable is compared before and after the inception of a stabilization programme. The advantage of the empirical approach is that it focuses on concrete experiences of countries with programmes. Furthermore, it allows evaluation of the effects of a policy *package*, and not only of individual policies. This approach, however, is largely a 'black box' one. Moreover, there are serious problems connected with the 'control' observations, since it would be expected that countries *not* undergoing stabilization would exhibit different characteristics from those that are. As causation is not proven, its results can only be used as evidence of the association between a given policy package and a given outcome.

2 *Effects on growth performance*

(a) **Past investigations** The specific impacts of adjustment programmes, and in particular of IMF-assisted programmes, have long been the object of a heated debate. The temperature of this debate heightened in the 1980s when the number of programmes increased sharply.

Broadly, the critics argue that prevailing adjustment policies, goals, and objectives are in conflict with the pursuance of growth, and pay little attention to the distributive implications. The critique contends that the payment deficits experienced by many developing countries are 'structural' in nature, often associated with the importation of capital goods needed to provide an industrial base and eventually develop the country. External shocks (oil prices, interest rates, etc.) aggravate external deficits. Trying to correct such deficits would amount to retarding the development effort itself, leaving the poorer countries in a worsened condition of dependence. The solution, hence, does not lie in the monetary contraction which is usually part of the traditional programmes (Dell 1983). Rather, it lies in long-term financing and in the rectification of the causes of the external imbalances by means of measures affecting the real economy. From this perspective, traditional adjustment is seen as a recession-inducing, growth-retarding practice. In addition, some of the critics argue that, at least in the Latin American case, adjustment programmes have consistently depressed the share of wages out of total income (Pastor 1986).

To counter this critique, several economists both within and outside the IMF have produced a series of empirical studies documenting that at least during the 1960s and 1970s

in broad terms, programme countries recorded significant reductions in their external deficits while they exhibited only marginal changes in their growth rates of real GDP and consumption—changes that were not significantly different from those experienced by non-oil developing countries in general. Thus, considering the group of programme countries in the aggregate, the costs associated with the external adjustment effort appear to have been less severe than has sometimes been suggested by participants in the controversy on Fund conditionality (Donovan 1982, p. 197).

This, in a nutshell, summarizes the main positions which emerged from the debate and experience in the 1970s. Recently, several studies have appeared (Ground 1985, Zulu and Nsouli 1985, Goldstein 1986, Khan and Knight 1985) covering the 1980s as well as the 1970s. A conclusive analysis of the performance

of adjustment policies during the 1980s—a period characterized by greater shocks and declining bank lending since 1982—is, however, still not available.
(b) Assessing the effects on growth: a theoretical approach Following the approach described in Section 1, the analysis of the growth effects of the prevailing adjustment programmes proceeds by examining individually the effects on growth of each of the three set of policies identified above. (A recent IMF paper (Khan and Knight 1985) is of assistance in this attempt.)

1. *Concerning the growth effects of demand restraint policies*, it appears that both fiscal and monetary policies tend to affect negatively the growth rate of output, either through reduced levels of aggregate demand or through reduced investment activities, or both. Fiscal policies—such as a reduction in government recurrent expenditure or an increase in taxation not accompanied by a commensurate increase in outlay—are a priori expected to have a negative multiplier effect on the level of aggregate demand and, through it, on output. Besides influencing demand, fiscal policy can influence the growth of output through the effects of cuts in public investment on the level of private investment. Although there is considerable uncertainty as to whether public sector investment raises or reduces private investment, it appears that state investment in infrastructure and the provision of public goods has an enhancing effect on private capital formation. Therefore, beside depressing short-term output growth through aggregate demand effects, any cut in public investment in infrastructure will probably have a depressing effect on the level of private investment and thus negatively affect the long-term growth rate of the economy.

Restrictive monetary policies, resulting in a reduction in the growth of domestic credit and/or money supply, tend to affect growth mainly through a decline in domestic investment activity. In this case also there is a short-term negative aggregate demand effect as well as a negative longer-term effect due to reduced capital formation. Considerable empirical evidence exists of the effect of contractionary monetary policies. In a review of the available evidence, Khan and Knight (1985), while noting that the size of this effect varied substantially from country to country, conclude that

the studies reviewed generally indicate that, while the size of the effect varied, tighter monetary and credit policies would result in a fall in the growth rate in the first year after they were implemented. Furthermore, if monetary and credit restraint took the form of a reduction of the flow of credit to the private sector, the empirical evidence showed that private capital formation and possibly the long-run rate of growth would be adversely affected (p. 24).

In other words, demand restraint policies seem to have a depressing short-term, and possibly medium-term, effect on GDP growth.

2. *Evidence of the growth effects of supply expansion policies* is more mixed. Changes (usually increases) in producer prices have been shown to have positive effects on the rate of growth. These effects, however, take some time to materialize because of technical factors related to the process of production. Higher

producer prices in agriculture, for instance, cannot trigger an instantaneous reaction even where the possibility of expanding production exists, as it normally takes at least the time of a vegetative cycle before any increase in production arrives on the market. The most complete and recent empirical evidence on aggregate supply responses in agriculture (Scandizzo 1984), for instance, indicates that price supply elasticities have rather low value, i.e. in the range of 0.1–0.3 for the short run and 0.3–0.5 for the long run. In general, the supply–expansion component of adjustment programmes (generally involving some restructuring) takes time and investment, and is therefore conditional upon the availability of fresh finance.

The effects of exchange rate and interest rate policies are more uncertain and depend on the concrete country circumstances. Currency realignments are often necessary to revitalize competitiveness in those sectors where unutilized domestic potential exists or to bring parallel market and official prices together. However, devaluation is not a universal solution. For countries exporting primary commodities with high price and low income elasticities of demand, and importing food, fuel, and equipment, i.e. goods with a low price and high income elasticities of demand, a devaluation would be likely to have a negative or no effect on export earnings (Tokman 1986), although it might be helpful in improving the financial position of marketing bodies and in reducing large divergencies between official and parallel market prices. In addition Khan and Knight (1985) found that '... as a general rule, devaluation will be contractionary ... if the initial trade deficit is large' (p. 16). The effects of devaluation would tend to be deleterious should all developing countries producing the same primary commodities with low demand elasticities devalue successively, triggering a global increase in their export volume. For instance, Godfrey (1985) has shown that '... more than 60 per cent of Sub-Saharan Africa's agricultural export earnings appear to come from commodities for which price elasticity of demand is such that an increase in export volume would reduce export earnings' (p. 178). More generally, Khan and Knight (1985) note that '... the growth effects of exchange rate changes depends crucially on such issues as the extent and duration of the real exchange rate change, the structure of production, and the response of trade flows to relative price changes' (p. 17).

The evidence is even weaker on the effects of interest rate policies on growth. It is argued that higher interest rates will increase savings and investment, and will improve the efficiency of resource allocation by 'unifying' financial markets (Khan and Knight 1985). However, the evidence of positive effects on the aggregate level of savings (as against their distribution) is weak, while higher interest rates may have negative effects of investment. But higher real interest rates might help to reduce capital flight by making financial investment in domestic currency more attractive. Capital flight, however, is often influenced by political and psychological factors as much as relative rates of interest. In summary, the effects of higher real interest rates on savings is quite small, implying that very sizeable variations in nominal interest rates would be necessary in order to increase the saving rate. In addition, higher domestic savings do not necessarily lead to higher rates of capital formation, although there could be some positive effects on the allocation and efficiency of investment.

In conclusion it appears that supply–expansion policies, particularly those focusing on the creation of new capacity, might have medium-term growth-inducing effects provided time and investment finance are available. Some of these policies, however, have uncertain effects.

3. *The growth effects of institutional and policy reforms* are unclear. While such measures are no doubt appropriate in many cases, Helleiner (1985*b*) notes that the medium-term effects of applying such market-oriented institutional and strategic reforms as part of an adjustment package are highly uncertain. More generally, there are serious doubts about the primacy of any particular form of economic organization as such from the perspective of economic and social efficiency. As far as non-economic aspects are concerned, the choice of the economic institutions and policy mix is essentially political and should be of no concern to external creditors so long as a viable external balance is achieved (Bacha 1985).

These three sets of policies therefore have different effects on short-term growth: the first tends to be negative in effect except in cases when excessive demand (at full employment level) is fuelling inflation; the direct effects of the other categories are more ambiguous. If effective in restructuring the economy towards exportables and import substitutes, switching policies may have indirect positive effects by removing the need for further stabilization and thus permitting resumed investment and growth, or 'business as usual'.

As these three sets of policies have quite different effects in terms of growth, any attempt to analyse the growth effects of an overall adjustment package cannot ignore the issue of its composition (or 'policy mix'). A recent paper (IMF 1986*b*) permits an analysis of the policy composition of 78 Fund-supported adjustment programmes undertaken from 1980 to 1984. From the review it appears that *demand restraint policies* were implemented in almost all the countries analysed. Limits on credit expansion were applied in 99 per cent of the cases, restraint on central government expenditure in 91 per cent, wage restraint in 60 per cent, and reduction in the budget deficit as percentage of GDP in 83 per cent. Potentially growth-stimulating *supply expansion policies* were, in contrast, adopted less frequently. Pricing policies were introduced in about 40 per cent of the 78 cases analysed, exchange rate policies in 54 per cent, interest rate reform in 27 per cent, and development or restructuring of a sector in 65 per cent.

Given this policy mix, it appears therefore that prevailing adjustment programmes tend to be predominantly deflationary, certainly in the short run and possibly also in the medium run. This tendency is exacerbated by the time-lags necessary before supply expansion policies start producing their effects.

The deflationery mix of prevailing policies is partly due to scarcity of finance. Finance for adjustment provided to developing countries by the commercial banks and by the IMF is declining and its distribution is becoming increasingly skewed (Killick 1985). Further reduction in availability of resources is projected, so that there will be limits to what investment and restructuring can be undertaken. In this context, external balance will be largely achieved by demand contraction.

(c) Assessing the effects on growth: an examination of 1980–1985 data Previous empirical analysis of the effects of stabilization on growth was mainly based on data covering the 1960s and 1970s. Reichman and Stillson (1978), looking at the effects of IMF programmes on growth in both developed and developing countries over the 1963–72 period, found that of the 70 cases examined, growth rates increased in the first programme year in 33 countries, decreased in 28 countries, and showed practically no change in 9 countries. Their research comes to findings similar to those of Donovan (1982) noted above, i.e. significant balance of payments improvements accompanied by unimportant changes in inflation and mixed effects on growth. More recently, Killick (1984), analysing 1974–79 data, comes to the conclusion that, overall, IMF programmes[1] have not generally had strong deflationary effects but there are indications that negative growth effects were stronger in the most recent years' (p. 265).

No analysis so far has covered the first half of the 1980s, a period characterized by a sharp recession, a rapid increase in the number of countries undergoing stabilization, and a staggering decline in capital flows to developing countries. In an attempt to fill this vacuum, an analysis of the growth effects of stabilization programmes has been carried out for the years 1980–85. Of the 71 countries with IMF-assisted programmes in 1980–85, 16 countries have been eliminated from the sample and 4 African countries are only included in part, due to lack of data. (See Annex I to this chapter for a full list of countries; Annex II provides fuller details of the findings.) The remaining countries in the sample have been grouped into four regions, i.e. Asia, Latin America, Africa, and Developing Europe. The following variables were compiled for each year between 1980 and 1985:

(a) GDP per capita growth rate in real terms;
(b) year-to-year change in the GDP per capita growth rate;
(c) year-to-year change in the level of gross investment in real terms;
(d) year-to-year change in the balance of payment on current account.

For each variable, values in the first programme year were analysed, where the 'first programme year' is defined as the first year in which a stabilization programme runs for six months or more. In several cases a country had a series of first programme years as a series of SBAs or EAs succeeded each other with little or no interruption. Changes in the growth rate of GDP per capita between ± 0.4 per cent have been considered to represent a non-significant change, while in the case of investment and balance of payment the threshold was fixed at ± 1.0 per cent. The results are reviewed below.

1. *Current growth*. Table 2.2 presents the number of positive and negative (or insignificant) growth rates of GDP per capita for each year over the 1980–85 period for countries with an ongoing IMF-assisted programme. For Latin

TABLE 2.2 *Number of years with positive and negative per capita growth rates of GDP in countries with IMF-assisted programmes, 1980–1985*

	Africa	Latin America	Asia	Developing Europe	Total
Positive growth	27	17	19	8	71
Negative or insignificant growth	65	42	4	4	115

Source: See Table 2.2a in Annex II.
Note: 'Insignificant' = ± 0.4%.

America and Africa the proportion of negative rates is very high. As noted earlier, in general Asia did better than the other developing continents. The data from Developing Europe are not representative as they include observations from only three countries (Cyprus, Yugoslavia, and Turkey).

In this period, therefore, countries undergoing adjustment programmes had a high probability of experiencing a negative growth rate of GDP per capita in the year immediately following the programme. This might not be indicative of a deflationary bias in prevailing programmes, but rather of the economic problems leading the countries to request the assistance of the Fund.

To provide further light on the situation, analysis was carried out of the changes occurring in the growth rate of GDP per capita during the first programme year. No improvement or deterioration in the rate of growth would be indicative of the inability of the policies to achieve the objective of correcting the external imbalance while sustaining growth.

Table 2.3 shows that in 71 out of 124 cases, the growth rate of GDP per capita either stagnated or declined. In addition, out of the 53 cases for which an improvement was recorded, the growth rate of GDP per capita remained negative or insignificant in 22 cases. Of the three large regions, Africa shows

TABLE 2.3 *Changes in per capita growth rate of GDP in the first year of IMF-assisted programmes, 1980–1985*

	Africa	Latin America	Asia	Developing Europe	Total
Positive changes	31	14	6	2	53
Negative or insignificant changes	33	21	11	6	71

Source: See Table 2.3A in Annex II.
Note: 'Insignificant' = ± 0.4%.

the best ratio of improvements versus deteriorations, while Asia and Latin America both show 60 per cent or more experiencing deterioration.

The data presented above and in Annex II indicate that the proportion of countries showing a decline or stagnation in the first programme year has increased, although modestly, from about 52 per cent found by Reichman and Stillson (1978) for the years 1963–72 to 57 per cent for the years 1980–85. In a large number of cases adjustment programmes are not able to bring about improvement in the external balance while at the same time sustaining short-term growth.

2. *Medium-term growth.* In view of the extremely frequent programmes under-taken at short intervals by many developing countries in the 1980–85 period, it has not been possible to carry out an analysis of the effects of adjustment policies on the medium-term growth of GDP per capita on a sufficiently large sample of countries. In most cases the beginning of a new programme was 'interfering' with medium-term effects of a previous programme, therefore making it impossible to separate the medium-term effects of an old programme from the short-term effects of a new one. To help form an opinion on the medium-term effects of stabilization policies on growth performance, an analy-sis was carried out of the year-to-year changes in investment levels in real terms between 1980 and 1983 (the latest year for which information on investments was available).

TABLE 2.4 *Changes in real investment levels for countries with IMF-assisted programmes, 1980–1983*

	Africa	Latin America	Asia	Developing Europe	Total
Positive changes	29	17	9	3	58
Negative or insignificant changes	42	23	9	6	80

Source: See Table 2.4A in Annex II.
Note: 'Insignificant' = ± 1.0%.

Table 2.4 shows that real investment over the period 1980–83 declined or stagnated in nearly 60 per cent of countries where IMF programmes were in effect. This was the case in all regions except Asia. There were however big variations over time and regions (see Table 2.4A in Annex II). A drop or an insignificant change in investment level in programme countries seems to have been the rule in 1981–83 particularly in Africa, where investment declined in two-thirds of the cases both in 1981 and in 1983 (15 out of 22 cases in 1981, and 10 out of 15 cases in 1983).

To a very large extent these data confirm the finding that the programmes in the early 1980s, and particularly in the crisis years of 1981–82, have tended to emphasize reduced use of domestic resources and have not introduced elements of structural adjustment and investment expansion. The decline in investment occurred among a large proportion of countries over these years. In 1982, 63 per cent of countries for which data exist experienced a decline in investment level, among developing countries (UNCTAD 1985). Investment ratios fell in 32 of the 45 developing countries. For developing market economies as a whole the investment ratio fell from 24.6 per cent in 1982 to 22.7 per cent in 1984, while GDP was also generally stagnant or declining. This decline in investment has reduced medium-term growth prospects.

The trends noted above cannot be divorced from developments in the debt situation. Countries with large debt servicing obligations have to adjust perennially to a continuous external shock represented by the massive transfer or resources necessary for the servicing of interest and amortization on the accumulated debt (Dell 1986). Table 2.5 shows the proportion of GNP which has been transferred abroad in major debtor countries, largely in the form of

TABLE 2.5 *Domestic savings, net factor payment and national savings in selected countries, 1984 (as percentage of GNP)*

	Domestic savings	Net factor payments	National savings
Argentina	21.6	−8.8	12.8
Brazil	23.2	−5.4	17.8
Cameroon*a*	25.2	−5.3	19.7
Chile	14.1	−10.3	3.7
Colombia	18.3	−1.8	16.6
Ecuador	25.2	−8.0	17.1
Kenya	20.2	−2.7	17.5
Korea, Republic of	30.3	−3.5	26.8
Malaysia	33.8	−6.8	26.9
Mexico	30.6	−6.1	24.5
Peru	21.9	−6.9	15.0
Philippines	20.7	−3.7	17.1
Venezuela	30.9	−6.0	24.9
Zambia*a*	13.5	−7.2	6.2

Source: Dell (1986).
*a*1983.

interest payments on the debt. Such a large reduction in national savings sharply reduces the potential for capital accumulation and growth, while exerting a negative influence on the current level of imports and, through them, on current growth.

3. *Balance of payments on current account.* It appears that, on balance, programme countries have been relatively successful in bringing about positive changes in their current account balance for 1980–84. (See Table 2.6 and Table 2.6A in Annex II.) More than half the programme countries have improved their external accounts. These improvements were much more

marked in the years 1982 and 1983, i.e. precisely the years in which investment expenditure, GDP per capita and growth rates were falling. There is therefore a strong suggestion that '... the surest way to improve the current account by

TABLE 2.6 *Changes (year-to-year) in current account balance in 54 countries with IMF-assisted programmes, 1980–1984 (in current SDR prices)*

	Africa	Latin America	Asia	Developing Europe	Total
Positive change	44	23	10	8	85
Negative or insignificant change	30	25	10	2	67

Source: See Table 2.6A in Annex II.
Note: 'Insignificant' = ± 1.0%.

economic contraction is to limit import-intensive capital formation. A vicious circle appears—cutting investment to improve the current account in the short run makes potential foreign exchange shortfalls more severe in the future. Many economies are on this self-destructive tread mill' (Taylor 1986, p. 2).

An additional element strongly supporting the view that the improvement in the current account is the result of import (and output) contraction rather than export (and output) expansion is offered by the analysis of trade accounts over the period 1981–85. According to Goldstein (1986), the volume of imports to programme countries declined every year between 1980 and 1983, most noticeably in 1983 with a fall of 7.7 per cent. As Fig. 2.1 shows, for instance, of the 16 indebted countries plotted, 13 reduced their deficit or improved their surplus position (to service the debt) by sharply reducing their imports. In this process only two countries (Brazil and Mexico) managed to expand their exports. Conversely South Korea, and to an extent Turkey, managed to reduce their trade deficit by substantially expanding both imports and, even more rapidly, exports. Needless to say, both countries experienced high growth of GDP per capita during the same period.

3 Effects on distributive equity

While it is difficult to assess the effects on growth of adjustment policies, the situation is even more complex—both from a theoretical and empirical point of view—when examining the effects of such policies on relative income distribution. To start with, most theorizing about income distribution has focused on the question of functional distribution of income. In practice, however, many developing countries include large informal and/or non-monetized sectors, for which the usual concepts of functional income distribution lack applicability. Data on the size distribution of income (by individuals or households) or on distribution by socio-economic groups, i.e. information giving a

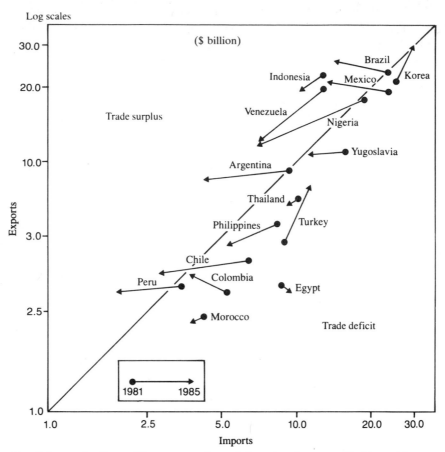

Log scales

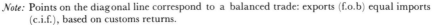

Note: Points on the diagonal line correspond to a balanced trade: exports (f.o.b) equal imports
      (c.i.f.), based on customs returns.

Source: GATT Secretariat Press Release, March 1986.

Fig. 2.1   Development in the merchandise trade and sixteen indebted countries: 1985
                compared with 1981

reasonably accurate idea of the effects of stabilization on relative income
distribution, are seldom available.

  Country situations, economic structures, and social stratification, furthermore, vary substantially from place to place. Analysis of the distributive effects
of stabilization should distinguish households at least according to major socio-
economic categories, i.e.: wage earners (in both urban and rural areas); self
employed; small and subsistence farmers; rentiers and capitalists; and destitutes. Different adjustment policies differently affect these various socio-
economic groups. Wage restraint policies, for instance, cause some hardship to
those engaged in the formal sector, but it is not necessarily true that these
are the most disadvantaged group and that therefore income inequality will

increase. This might be the case in countries where the share of modern-sector wages in GDP is high, but not where modern-sector wage earners are an economic élite. In very poor, highly rural countries, in particular, a major distributive preoccupation should be the improvement of rural–urban terms of trade and not the relative income distribution within the modern sector (Johnson and Salop 1980).

As a general rule, in order to form an opinion on the changes in income distribution following the introduction of stabilization policies, it will be useful to monitor at least the following variables: agricultural terms of trade, wage rates, food prices, change in aggregate demand, and of course the type, targeting, and size of public expenditure. Conclusions about the changes in income distribution following from stabilization will therefore depend on changes in such variables, as well as on the relative importance of the socio-economic groups identified above.

Due to the great variety of country circumstances and adjustment packages, it is difficult to arrive at any general *ex ante* conclusion about the distributive impact of adjustment policies, although it is clear that effectively implemented programmes are unlikely to be distributionally neutral and can cause severe deteriorations for given population groups (see later). However, it is easier to come to some more specific conclusions for some groups of economies, like for instance the highly monetized economies of Latin America which have an important wage sector, an equally large informal sector, a very small subsistence sector, and important cash crop activities.

The literature reviewing the *ex post* evidence does not come to consistent conclusions. Foxley (1981), examining the impact of monetarist stabilization programmes introduced in four Latin American countries, shows that in all cases real wages fell, while unemployment and income inequality rose in two. Recent studies by the Inter-American Development Bank (1985) and PREALC (Tokman 1986) come to similar conclusions, while a review of the adjustment performance of 18 Latin American countries between 1965 and 1981 (Pastor 1986) finds that IMF programmes were significantly and consistently associated with declines in the wage share. However, a study by Altimir (1984) analysing the joint effects of the economic crisis and adjustment measures in five Central and South American countries over the 1979–82 period generally finds little variation in the shape of relative income distribution. The study notes, furthermore, that household income distribution by size does not appear to be a sensitive measure of changes taking place in the relative position of household groups.

Killick (1984), after reviewing some of the evidence, concludes that '[IMF] programmes are likely to have rather complex effects on income distribution and are unlikely to have any systematic tendency either to increase or reduce income concentration' (p. 265). Analogous conclusions are arrived at from a theoretical perspective by Addison and Demery (1985) and Helleiner (1985a). The IMF (1986b) review quoted above notes that the available evidence provides no basis to contend that Fund-supported adjustment programmes lead to significantly worse relative income distributions compared to any practical alternative.

One may therefore tentatively conclude, in the absence of a comprehensive empirical analysis of the issue, that the available evidence suggests that while IMF programmes are not distributionally neutral, they do not appear to have had a systematic tendency to worsen income distribution significantly, except in Latin American countries.

4 *The overall effect on poverty levels*

While practically all analyses of adjustment focus on the effects on growth and relative income distribution (and on balance of payments and inflation), most of them do not assess their effects in terms of overall poverty rates. Yet *this is actually the crucial issue*, far more important than assessing often insignificant changes in the relative income distribution. A massive increase in poverty can occur in the absence of growing income inequality if output declines substantially—as in Costa Rica, where poverty rates increased between 1979 and 1982 from 17 to 29 per cent owing to the sharp GDP decline following the introduction of severe adjustment policies (Altimir 1984). The evidence provided in Sections b and c suggests that prevailing programmes have a deflationary content reducing the incomes of the poor, as well as incomes of most other members of society. These effects are sometimes compounded by deterioration in income distribution. It seems correct to conclude that, overall, prevailing adjustment programmes tend to increase aggregate poverty, or in other words the number of people—and of children—living below the poverty line. This does not mean, of course, that every programme has had an adverse effect on poverty levels. Rather, that on average, this tendency prevails, particularly when demand restraint policies predominate.

V Direct effects

Besides the overall effect on poverty that an adjustment package tends to have, some of its specific components have a direct and unambiguous impact on particular socio-economic groups, at least in the short term. Because of the nature of the deprivations they might cause (death, brain-damaging and growth-retarding malnutrition, permanent disease-caused impairment, etc.), these effects are of a long-term nature and cannot be dismissed as part of the short-term belt-tightening necessary for growth restoration. For example, a growing amount of evidence indicates that:

1. Indiscriminate *cuts in government health expenditure*, often part of an adjustment programme, lead to declines in the health status of the population. Macedo (in vol. ii, ch. 2) documents delays in the implementation of the Expanded Programme of Immunization in São Paulo State (Brazil) that led

to an outbreak of deadly communicable diseases among children, while the case study on Ghana (vol. ii, ch. 4) illustrates the sharp deterioration in indicators such as incidence of infectious diseases and disease-specific mortality rates following cuts in primary health care expenditure.

2. A radical *reduction in real food subsidies* in Sri Lanka, while diverting resources to investment activities as part of a new adjustment package, led to an increase in third-degree malnutrition among the children of the poorest (vol. ii, ch. 9). Similarly Raczynski (vol. ii, ch. 3) indicates that in Chile in 1983 the cancellation of a budget-financed child-feeding programme, part of an overall attempt to reduce the fiscal deficit, led to a statistically significant nation-wide increase in child mortality. The latter resumed its downward decline as soon as the programme was reintroduced.

3. *Sharp increases in food prices*, resulting from rises in producer prices or from devaluation, unless accompanied by compensatory measures can cause malnutrition to rise among those around or below the poverty line. In The Gambia, for instance, child malnutrition increased when a Fund–Bank supported adjustment programme led to an increase in food prices without accompanying buffering measures (UNICEF–The Gambia 1985). In general, sharp increases in relative prices of food can have devastating effects on poor households who are net food buyers.

4. *Fiscal policies* typically implemented as part of orthodox adjustment are *often regressive*. As noted by IMF (1986*b*), 76 per cent of the programmes supported by IMF between 1980 and 1983 included increases in indirect taxes and 46 per cent in tariffs, fees and charges, as against 13 per cent involving increases in personal, corporate and property taxes.

All in all, the aggregate tendency of prevailing adjustment policies to have poverty-inducing effects together with the negative influence of specific policies give rise to serious concern about the influence of such policies on human conditions, especially for vulnerable groups and particularly in the initial period of a programme, i.e. during the time necessary for supply–expansion policies to start yielding some results. This concern is heightened by the fact that for many countries the need to adjust seems to be a continuous one in the 1980s, as external conditions remain highly unfavourable.

VI Conclusions

The analysis above has shown that among IMF-assisted countries improvements in current account balance were recorded in 56 per cent of countries in the 1980s, but in almost 60 per cent of these countries growth deteriorated or did not improve in the first programme year, and real investment levels also declined or stagnated between 1980 and 1983 in almost 60 per cent of countries with Fund-assisted programmes. With falling output and, at best, mixed evidence about changes in income distribution in many developing countries, the number of people in poverty in many 'adjusting countries' increased. It is

Cornia

not possible, methodologically, to attribute precise causal responsibility for this deterioration in human conditions. In many cases, the pernicious effects of world recession, declining capital flows, and high interest rates, as well as local weather conditions, have represented a major obstacle to the functioning of such policies.

However, the evidence of the 1980s points to the inability of the current approach to adjustment to sustain short- and medium-term growth while bringing about improvements in the external balance in the prevailing international environment. The observed drop in investment levels appears particularly alarming as it tends to mortgage not only current but also future growth. Thus, if one of the primary objective of adjustment policies is the promotion of growth and trade, this objective is not being fulfilled in many cases. A continuation of the same approach would be likely have a further depressing effect on growth.

Alternatives must be found. The urgency of finding new solutions is especially pressing when considering the poverty-inducing effects that the current approach tends to have, and the direct negative effects that some macro-economic policies have on the health and nutritional status of the poorest, and of children in particular, unless they are accompanied by compensatory measures. Ignoring the needs of the poor is not only unethical, it is also inefficient. As the Managing Director of the IMF has recently stated '... It is hard to visualise how viable external position can be achieved if large segments of the work force lack the vocational skills—or even worse, the basic nutritional and health standards—to produce goods that are competitive in world markets' (de Larosière 1986, p. 6).

A new approach to adjustment will have to address the problem of how a viable external position can be achieved while sustaining output growth and protecting the minimum human needs of the population. Encouraging signs in this direction have already started to emerge. During the Annual Meeting of the Fund and the World Bank in Seoul, October 1985, US Treasury Secretary James Baker stressed the need for *growth-oriented* adjustment in developing countries and underscored the need for increased lending by multilateral development banks and commercial banks in support of the policy efforts. Similarly, the need for a *human face* of adjustment is being increasingly recognized as a fundamental element of the new approach by a growing number of institutions and individuals.

The development of such an alternative approach to adjustment forms the substance of the second part of this volume.

Annex I   Countries with IMF programmes 1980–1985

Included in the sample	Included in part*	Not included in the sample*
AFRICA		
Egypt	Central African Republic	Congo
Ethiopia	Mauritania	Equatorial Guinea
Gabon	Mauritius	Gambia, The
Ghana	Rwanda	Guinea
Ivory Coast		South Africa
Kenya		
Liberia		
Madagascar		
Malawi		
Mali		
Morocco		
Niger		
Senegal		
Sierra Leone		
Somalia		
Sudan		
Tanzania		
Togo		
Uganda		
Zaire		
Zambia		
Zimbabwe		
LATIN AMERICA		
Argentina		Belize
Barbados		Dominica
Bolivia		Grenada
Brazil		
Chile		
Costa Rica		
Dominican Republic		
Ecuador		
El Salvador		
Guatemala		
Guyana		
Haiti		
Honduras		
Jamaica		
Mexico		
Panama		
Peru		
Uruguay		

Included in the sample	Included in part*	Not included in the sample*
Uruguay		

ASIA

Bangladesh		China, People's
Burma		Republic
India		Laos, People's Repub-
Korea, Republic of		lic
Pakistan		Nepal
Philippines		Solomon Islands
Sri Lanka		Western Samoa
Thailand		

DEVELOPING EUROPE

Cyprus		Hungary
Turkey		Portugal
Yugoslavia		Romania

* Countries were excluded from the sample, or only included in part, due to lack of data.

Annex II

TABLE 2.2A   *Number of years with positive and negative per capita growth rates of GDP in countries with IMF-assisted programmes, 1980–1985*

	1980	1981	1982	1983	1984	1985	Total	%
Africa								
Positive growth	5	6	3	4	2	7	27	29
Negative or insignificant growth	8	13	13	9	15	7	5	71
Latin America								
Positive growth	4	2	1	3	6	1	17	29
Negative or insignificant growth	6	5	7	11	5	8	42	71
Asia								
Positive growth	2	7	3	3	2	2	19	83
Negative or insignificant growth	2	0	0	1	0	1	4	17
Developing Europe								
Positive growth	1	3	1	1	2	0	8	67
Negative or insignificant growth	1	0	1	1	0	1	4	33
All countries								
Positive growth	12	18	8	11	12	10	71	38
Negative or insignificant growth	17	18	21	22	20	17	115	62

Sources: UN-DIESA (1985, 1986), IMF *Annual Reports*, 1979–85, and *IMF Surveys*.
Note: 'Insignificant' growth = ±0.4%.

TABLE 2.3A   *Number of changes in per capita growth rate of GDP in the first year of IMF-assisted programmes, 1980–1985*

	1980	1981	1982	1983	1984	1985	Total	%
Africa								
Positive changes	4	6	3	7	4	7	31	48
Negative or insignificant changes	4	8	4	5	8	4	33	52
Latin America								
Positive changes	0	1	1	8	4	0	14	40
Negative or insignificant changes	7	2	3	4	1	4	21	60
Asia								
Positive changes	0	3	0	2	0	1	6	36
Negative or insignificant changes	3	2	2	1	2	1	11	64
Developing Europe								
Positive changes	0	0	0	0	2	0	2	25
Negative or insignificant changes	2	2	0	1	0	1	6	75
All countries								
Positive changes	4	10	4	17	10	8	53	43
Negative or insignificant changes	16	14	9	11	11	10	71	57

Sources: UN-DIESA (1985, 1986), IMF *Annual Reports*, 1979–85, and *IMF Surveys*.
Note: 'Insignificant' = ± 0.4%.

TABLE 2.4Λ   *Changes in real investment levels for countries with IMF-assisted programmes, 1980–1983*

	1980	1981	1982	1983	Total	%
Africa						
Positive changes	10	7	7	5	29	40
Negative or insignificant changes	6	15	11	10	42	60
Latin America						
Positive changes	6	3	1	6	17	42
Negative or insignificant changes	4	4	7	8	23	58
Asia						
Positive changes	1	3	2	3	9	50
Negative or insignificant changes	3	4	1	1	9	50
Developing Europe						
Positive changes	1	1	0	1	3	33
Negative or insignificant changes	1	2	2	1	6	67
All countries						
Positive changes	18	14	10	15	58	42
Negative or insignificant changes	14	25	21	20	80	58

Sources: UN-DIESA (1985, 1986), IMF *Annual Reports*, 1979–85, and *IMF Surveys*.
Note: 'Insignificant' = ± 1.0%.

TABLE 2.6A *Changes (year to year) in current account balance in 54 countries with IMF-assisted programmes (in current SDR prices)*

	1980	1981	1982	1983	1984	Total	%
Africa							
Positive changes	7	12	9	10	6	44	60
Negative or insignificant changes	9	9	6	1	5	30	40
Latin America							
Positive changes	2	3	6	9	3	23	48
Negative or insignificant changes	8	4	2	5	6	25	52
Asia							
Positive changes	1	2	2	3	2	10	50
Negative or insignificant changes	3	5	1	1	0	10	50
Developing Europe							
Positive changes	1	3	2	1	1	8	80
Negative or insignificant changes	1	0	0	1	0	2	20
All countries							
Positive changes	11	20	19	23	12	85	56
Negative or insignificant changes	21	18	9	8	11	67	44

Sources: IMF, Balance of Payments Statistics, vol. 36, 37: 1–5.UN-DIESA (1985, 1986), IMF *Annual Reports*, 1979–85, and *IMF Surveys.*
Note: 'Insignificant' = ± 1.0%.

3

The Impact on Government Expenditure

Per Pinstrup-Andersen, Maurice Jaramillo, and Frances Stewart

Adjustment policies frequently involve cut-backs in government expenditure.
From 1980 to 1984, real government expenditure per capita fell in over half
the countries of the developing world, with a greater proportion declining
among countries with adjustment policies than among those without. Vulnerable groups are particularly affected by changes in government expenditure
on basic health and education services and on food subsidies. This chapter
reviews developments in these areas in the 1980s. Section I looks at health and
education and Section II at food subsidies.

I The crisis and basic health and education services*

In many countries, the economic crisis of the 1980s has had a devastating
effect on the basic health and educational services available to the most
vulnerable, reducing existing services in both quality and quantity, and preventing progress towards extension of services to the whole population. Some
countries, however, have managed to protect their basic services during the
period. Here we explore the effects of the crisis on health and education services
in more detail. First, the main developments are summarized, then a more
detailed analysis follows of how countries have reacted to government expenditure cuts.

1 The impact on health and education

Graphic illustration of the deterioration in basic health and education services
is shown by some country examples: in Ghana, where prolonged crisis resulted
in a cut of health expenditure per capita to 1982/83 of 80 per cent of the 1974
level, a project to immunize against yellow fever met only 50 per cent of its
target, and all project vehicles were withdrawn because of shortage of fuel.
Lack of expenditure on maintenance meant that in the Accra region, in mid-
1983, 20 out of 57 refrigerators were not functioning (UNICEF-Ghana 1984).
In Mozambique the drugs and equipment needed to maintain the primary
health care infrastructure cannot be maintained because of shortages of foreign
exchange. In Zaire, as a result of budget cuts, 7,000 teachers were taken off

* This section has benefited greatly from research assistance from Albino Barrera.

TABLE 3.1   *Annual percentage change in per capita expenditure on health and education, 1973–79 and 1979–83 (at constant prices)*

	Number of countries in sample	1973–79	1979–83	% of countries decelerating
Africa	10	+ 3.5	− 0.1	60
Latin America	14	+ 4.2	+ 2.3	80
Middle East	2	+ 11.7	− 7.2	100
South and South-East Asia	10	+ 10.2	+ 7.2	80

Source: IMF (1986*e*).
Note: Figures are regional averages weighted by 1979 expenditure on health and education.

the government payroll in 1984. In Ethiopia, even in the primary schools of Addis Ababa a textbook is shared by at least four students.

The negative effects of the financial crisis on basic services are not confined to direct cuts in expenditure in these services. The collapse of the transport system that has occurred in many parts of Africa—following lack of maintenance to roads and vehicles and higher fuel prices—has adversely affected supplies for the rural health system. 'High oil costs, scarcities and restricted imports have adverse effects not only on installation, but also on maintenance of services. When paraffin runs out, the refrigerators in village dispensaries can no longer protect vaccines from deterioration and water pumps fall idle' (UNICEF 1981).

The visibly deteriorating conditions of basic services in many countries are due to the compounded effects of the general financial crisis together with specific cuts in health and education expenditures.

There were reductions in government expenditure on health and education per capita in many countries in the 1980s, with a marked deceleration in growth in expenditure per capita on average in Africa, Latin America, and the Middle East.

In Latin America, from 1980 to 1984, expenditure on health per capita fell in 14 countries (61 per cent of the countries for which there are data). For most countries, data are only available for 1979–83. For these years, per capita expenditure on health fell in 7 out of the 15 countries in Africa where there are data, in 3 out of 7 countries in the Middle East, and in 4 out of 12 countries in South and East Asia (Table 3.2).

There were cuts in education expenditure per capita in a third of the countries for which there are data in Africa, in 10 countries (nearly 60 per cent) in Latin America, and in two countries each in the Middle East and in Asia. Unfortunately, the data do not extend to all countries, nor are they up-to-date, stopping in many cases in 1982. The comparison between the more recent and comprehensive data from the World Health Organization (WHO)

TABLE 3.2 *Percentage changes in per capita GDP and government expenditures in sample of developing countries, 1980–85 and 1979–83*

	Africa		Latin America		Middle East		Asia	
GDP per capita, 1980–85 (1980–84)								
Declining	13	(39)	18	(33)	4	(5)	2	(7)
Increasing	5	(9)	5	(7)	2	(5)	8	(24)
Percentage declining	72	(81)	78	(83)	67	(50)	20	(23)
Government expenditure (total) per capita 1979–83								
Declining	9		6		4		2	
Increasing	6		10		2		9	
Percentage declining	60		38		67		18	
Government expenditure (consumption) per capita 1980–84								
Declining	18		16		4		3	
Increasing	15		7		6		9	
Percentage declining	55		70		40		25	
Share of health and education in total government expenditures 1979–83								
Declining	7		11		2		4	
Increasing	8		4		5		8	
Percentage declining	47		73		29		33	
Expenditure per capita on health 1979–83								
Declining	7		14*	[8]	3		4	
Increasing	8		9*	[8]	4		8	
Percentage declining	47		61	[50]	43		33	
Expenditure per capita on education 1979–83								
Declining	5		10		2		2	
Increasing	10		7		5		10	
Declining percentage	33		59		29		17	

Sources: IMF (1985), WHO (1986), UN-DIESA (1986).
* WHO data 1980–84.
[] IMF data 1979–83.
() Data for 1980–84.

for Latin America and the 1979–83 data suggests that the latter understate the extent of the cuts. The WHO data for 1980–84 show 14 countries out of 23 suffering declining expenditure on health while the 1979–83 data show 8 countries out of 16 experiencing cuts.

(a) **Most severely affected countries** Table 3.3 lists the countries (of those for which there are data), which suffered the most substantial cuts in expenditure in health and education in the 1980s. Nineteen of the 22 countries experienced declining GDP per capita. However, among those most severely affected by cuts, the cuts in health expenditure per capita exceeded the rate of decline of GDP in all countries except two—in a number of cases, by a considerable margin. Thus, while countries which cut expenditure on health and education were on average those experiencing worse economic conditions (as measured by decline in GDP per capita) than those which increased social sector expenditures, the evidence clearly shows that there was room for choice about the direction and extent of changing social expenditure. Some countries increased their expenditures on health and expenditure while experiencing declines in GDP per capita (e.g. Kenya, Kuwait, Zambia, Mexico), while others cut health and education much more proportionately than the fall in per capita income.

TABLE 3.3 *Countries with the most severe cuts in per capita GDP and health and education expenditures (annual percentage change)*

	Health	Education	GDP
Africa	1979–83	1979–83	1980–85
Ghana	− 15.8[a]	− 9.5[a]	− 4.4
Malawi	− 9.8[a]	+ 7.0[a]	− 1.0
Sudan	− 9.5	− 16.8[a]	− 2.6
Togo	− 7.5	+ 3.3	− 3.7
Liberia	− 6.9	− 0.6	− 7.1
Mauritius	− 6.6	− 7.7	
Tunisia	− 6.4[a]	− 16.6[a]	+ 1.4
Latin America	1980–84[b]	1979–83[c]	1980–84[b]
Bolivia	− 77.7[d]	− 14.1	− 27.5
Guatemala	− 58.3	n.a.	− 14.8
Dominican Republic	− 46.5	− 4.1	+ 1.8
Surinam	− 44.2[e]	n.a.	n.a.
El Salvador	− 32.4	− 8.1	− 25.6
Chile	− 23.8	+ 0.7[a]	− 6.7
Barbados	− 21.3	n.a.	− 5.0
Jamaica	− 18.5	− 24.1[f]	− 5.6
Costa Rica	− 16.5	− 16.5[a]	− 12.3
Honduras	− 15.2	n.a.	− 11.5
Argentina	− 13.9	− 8.9[a]	− 13.9
Uruguay	− 13.4	− 6.1[a]	− 12.0
South and East Asia	1979–83	1979–83	1980–83
Sri Lanka	− 12.9[a]	+ 1.6[a]	+ 2.5
Philippines	− 1.3[a]	+ 0.8[a]	− 2.7
Middle East			
Israel	− 3.8[a]	− 0.4[a]	− 0.1
Jordan	− 3.1[a]	+ 2.3[a]	+ 1.3

Source: As Table 3.2.
Note: The list extends only to countries for which data are available. Full data are only available for 15 countries in Africa (out of a possible 38).
[a]1979–82   [b]Cumulative.   [c]Per annum.   [d]To 1982.   [e]To 1983.   [f]Cumulative 1980–85.

The relationship between GDP per capita and expenditure on social sectors per capita is the outcome of (*a*) the share of government expenditure in GDP; and (*b*) the share of health and education in government expenditure.

In this respect, the experience of Africa in the 1980s contrasted with that of Latin America. In Africa, the share of government expenditure in GDP *declined* for a little over half the countries for which data are available, but the share of health and education in government expenditure increased in a little over half the countries. In contrast, in Latin America the share of government expenditure in GDP *rose* in nearly three-quarters of the countries, but the proportion of countries that cut the share going to health and education was much higher than in Africa (nearly three-quarters). The net effect was that the decline in GDP led to more cuts in social sector expenditures in Latin America than in Africa. Expenditure per capita on education fell in 59 per cent of the countries in Latin America, compared with 33 per cent of the countries in Africa; and on health by 61 per cent of the countries in Latin America and 47 per cent of the countries in Africa (Table 3.2).

2 Patterns of expenditure cuts

(a) **Sectoral expenditure** When aggregate government expenditure is falling in real terms, sectors may be *highly protected* (HP), i.e. actually experience an increase in real expenditure during cuts, *protected* (P), i.e. when expenditure on the sector is cut by a smaller percentage than the aggregate percentage cut, or *vulnerable* (V), i.e. experience an expenditure cut greater than the aggregate percentage cut. Table 3.4 shows how different sectors fared during expenditure cuts from 1979–83. There was considerable variation in individual country behaviour. The priorities given to different sectors during cuts are shown in Table 3.5.

Cuts in government expenditure tended to fall most on economic services and least on defence, with education and health being in an intermediate position. Taking all developing countries, both health and education did better (rose or were cut less) than aggregate expenditure in more than half the cases. African countries protected the education sector most whereas in Latin America this was the most vulnerable sector. In contrast, health expenditure was especially vulnerable in Africa and most protected in Latin America. Asia exhibits the same pattern as Africa with even greater protection for the education sector and more vulnerability for health.

An analysis of expenditure cuts in the 1970s (Hicks and Kubisch 1984) found that social sector expenditure and defence were relatively protected, and the worst cuts fell on economic expenditures. The results presented here are more ambiguous with respect to expenditure on health and education, which taking all countries together were cut more than total expenditure in around 40 per cent of the cases, but highly protected in around 33 per cent. The 1970s experience that the greatest cuts were borne by economic services and the least by defence was repeated in the 1980s.

(b) **Expenditure cuts by type** The heaviest cuts fell on capital expenditure: in three-quarters of the cases (Table 3.6) capital expenditure was cut

Andersen, Jaramillo, and Stewart

TABLE 3.4 *Government expenditure cuts by sector, 1979–83 (percentage of cases in each category)*

	All ($N=57$)	Africa ($N=16$)	Asia ($N=8$)	Europe ($N=6$)	Middle East ($N=7$)	Latin America ($N=20$)
General public services						
Vulnerable	40	38	25	33	43	45
Protected	23	25	25	17	14	25
Highly protected	37	31	50	50	43	30
Defence						
Vulnerable	25	44	38	0	29	32
Protected	36	19	25	67	29	26
Highly Protected	39	38	38	33	43	42
Education						
Vulnerable	46	38	25	50	29	65
Protected	22	25	50	25	29	5
Highly protected	33	38	25	25	43	30
Health						
Vulnerable	40	56	63	0	33	26
Protected	25	25	13	25	17	32
Highly protected	36	19	25	75	50	42
Economic services[a]						
Vulnerable	66	53	75	100	71	58
Protected	13	20	0	0	0	21
Highly protected	22	27	25	0	29	21

Source: IMF (1985).
Note: 'vulnerable' = percentage decline more than aggregate expenditure; 'protected' = percentage decline less than aggregate expenditure; 'highly protected' = percentage increase during cuts in aggregate expenditure.
Totals may not add to 100 because of rounding.
[a] Includes expenditure on agriculture, forestry; and fishing, mining; manufacturing; construction; utilities; and transport.

34
35

proportionately more than total expenditure, a significantly higher proportion than any other category of expenditure. The high proportion of heavy cuts in capital expenditure occurred in every region, and in Africa, Latin America and the Middle East the proportion of countries in which capital expenditure was especially vulnerable was greater than for all other types of expenditure. In Asia and Europe, however, these cuts were equalled or exceeded by cuts on subsidies. Subsidies were the second most vulnerable type of expenditure for developing countries as a whole, being cut more than total expenditure in over half the cases. However, they were more protected in Africa (where in over 40 per cent of cases they *increased* during expenditure falls). Wage payments were cut more than total expenditure in the lowest proportion of cases for all countries (less than one-third). In Africa, Asia and Europe wage payments

TABLE 3.5 *Priorities during expenditure cuts, 1979–83 (percentage of cases in each category)*

All countries		Africa		Latin America	
MOST VULNERABLE SECTORS					
Economic services	66	Health	56	Education	65
Education	46	Economic services	53	Economic services	58
General public		Defence	44	General public	
services	40	Education	38	services	45
Health	40	General public		Defence	32
Defence	25	services	38	Heallth	26
LEAST VULNERABLE SECTORS (HIGHLY PROTECTED)					
Defence	39	Education	38	Health	42
General public		Defence	38	Defence	42
services	37	General public		Education	30
Health	36	services	31	General public	
Education	33	Economic services	27	services	30
Economic services	22	Health	19	Economics	21

Source: IMF (1985).

increased during expenditure cuts in over 40 per cent of the cases. Among Latin American countries only one-quarter of the countries increased their expenditures on wages during cuts, but another half cut them less than total expenditures. The purchase of goods was highly protected in a higher proportion of all cases than any other type of expenditure. While this finding applied to Latin America, Africa was a definite exception, with purchase of goods being the second most vulnerable item there, and the second least highly protected.

To summarize, capital expenditure was most cut, followed by subsidies; wages were most protected, followed by purchase of goods.

(c) Capital expenditure by sector The sector suffering most during cuts in capital expenditure was economic services, which was cut more than the total capital expenditure in two-thirds of cases, and increased during general cuts in only 13 per cent of the cases (Table 3.7). For all countries, capital expenditure in the health and education sectors suffered relatively less than other sectors, being cut less or increased during cuts in over 60 per cent of general expenditure reductions. In Africa, capital expenditure on education was protected more than health during cuts, and in Latin America the health sector was protected more than education. However, this took place in a context in which capital expenditure as a whole was typically cut more than proportionately to government expenditure as a whole. The especially harsh treatment of capital expenditure in the economic sector, coming on top of the

TABLE 3.6   *Expenditure cuts by type, 1979–83 (percentage of cases in each category)*

	All	Africa	Asia	Europe	Middle East	Latin America
Capital expenditures	(35)	(8)	(5)	(2)	(7)	(13)
Vulnerable	74	75	60	100	71	77
Protected	9	13	20	0	0	8
Highly protected	17	13	20	0	29	15
Goods	(51)	(14)	(8)	(5)	(7)	(17)
Vulnerable	43	64	75	0	14	35
Protected	20	21	0	40	29	18
Highly protected	37	14	25	60	57	47
Wages	(46)	(12)	(7)	(4)	(7)	(16)
Vulnerable	30	42	14	25	43	25
Protected	35	17	43	25	29	50
Highly protected	35	42	43	50	29	25
Subsidies	(51)	(14)	(8)	(5)	(7)	(17)
Vulnerable	53	36	63	100	57	47
Protected	18	21	13	0	29	18
Highly protected	29	43	25	0	14	35

Source: IMF (1985).
Note: Totals may not add to 100 because of rounding. Numbers in parentheses are number of cases in each category.

specially harsh treatment of capital expenditure in the total, suggests that activities related to economic growth were particularly hard hit by government expenditure cuts during this period.

3   Conclusion on health and education

Expenditure per capita on health and education fell sharply in a large number of countries in Africa and Latin America in the early 1980s, while growth rates decelerated almost everywhere. Comprehensive data are only available up to 1982/83, but evidence from WHO and our country studies suggests that even more countries experienced cuts in more recent years. Previous analysis of expenditure on the effects on social service expenditure during expenditure cuts (Hicks and Kubish 1984) tended to mask this clear negative impact by focusing primarily on shares of social sector expenditure in total government expenditure rather than on real levels of expenditure per capita.

The falls in expenditure per capita on health and education were more widespread in Latin America than Africa, as a higher proportion of Latin American countries reduced the share of expenditure going to these sectors. Typically, Latin American countries cut education more, while African countries cut health more.

TABLE 3.7   *Cuts in government capital expenditures by sectors, 1979–83 (percentage in each category)*

	All	Africa	Asia	Europe	Middle East	Latin America
General public services	(63)	(16)	(9)	(7)	(7)	(24)
Vulnerable	44	63	44	43	29	38
Protected	21	13	11	0	29	33
Highly protected	35	25	44	57	43	29
Defence	(22)	(6)	(2)	(1)	(5)	(8)
Vulnerable	55	67	0	100	40	63
Protected	9	17	0	0	0	13
Highly protected	36	17	100	0	60	25
Education	(62)	(17)	(9)	(5)	(7)	(24)
Vulnerable	39	24	56	60	29	42
Protected	18	18	22	0	0	25
Highly protected	44	59	22	40	71	33
Health	(61)	(16)	(9)	(5)	(7)	(24)
Vulnerable	39	44	67	20	29	33
Protected	20	25	11	0	14	25
Highly protected	41	31	22	80	57	42
Economic services	(61)	(16)	(9)	(5)	(7)	(24)
Vulnerable	66	69	56	60	71	67
Protected	21	31	22	0	0	25
Highly protected	13	0	22	40	29	8

Source: IMF (1985).

In general, capital expenditure was cut most and wage payments were most protected during expenditure cuts.

Access of vulnerable groups to basic health and educational services can be viewed as the outcome of a chain of events linking per capita GDP to basic services (Fig. 3.1). The many links in this chain show that there is no inevitability about the connection between declining GDP per capita and declining services. At each stage of the chain the effects may be countered or magnified. Empirical evidence summarized above has shown that some countries have made choices which have magnified the effects, while others have protected the services of vulnerable groups. For example, Kenya suffered a decline in per capita GDP in the 1980s (of 1 per cent a year) but government expenditure rose (1979–82) by over 2 per cent a year, and the share of health and education in total government expenditure also rose leading to an annual rise in health and education expenditure per head of over 5 per cent between 1979 and 1982. Conversely, in Bolivia the effects of falling GDP were magnified with public expenditure per capita falling twice as fast as GDP and the share of education and health in government expenditure also falling, so that a yearly 6 per cent fall in GDP per capita was translated into an annual fall of over 17

Andersen, Jaramillo, and Stewart

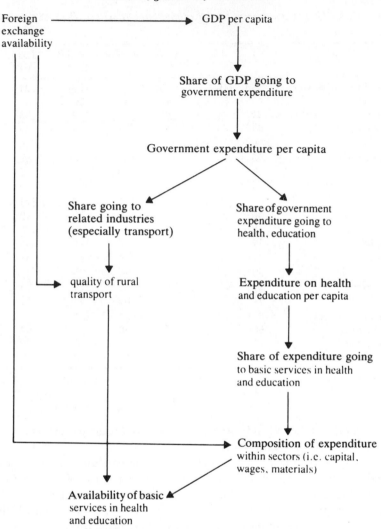

Fig. 3.1 Links between economic crisis and basic services

per cent in per capita expenditure on health and education. The health and education sector expenditure figures do not end the chain—it is further important to explore how this expenditure is distributed between different types of services. In the Philippines, for example, government expenditure supporting four modern hospitals specializing in heart, kidney and lung diseases is five times as great as total expenditure on primary health care. In Zimbabwe, the share of primary education in total educational expenditure and the share of primary health care in total health sector expenditure increased in the 1980s, indicating the potential for restructuring within the sectors. However, data do not permit systematic analysis of this intrasectoral distribution for most countries.

Almost invariably, the worst-affected countries in health and education have been those which have magnified the effects of GDP decline. One fundamental requirement in order to protect the vulnerable is to reverse the decline in GDP per capita: but some countries have succeeded in extending the services of the vulnerable during economic stagnation by making choices at each stage of the chain which would protect the basic services. Later chapters on sectoral choices illustrate how this may be done, and also show that it need not involve high costs, or very substantial shifts in resources.

II Government expenditures on explicit food subsidies in selected countries, 1980–1985*

Subsidies aimed at maintaining low food prices for consumers form a significant share of government expenditures in a number of developing countries. Besides their contribution to government deficits, these subsidies are often perceived to entail economic costs because they introduce price distortions into the economy. For these reasons, macro-economic adjustment programmes frequently include attempts to reduce government expenditures on consumer food subsidies. Thus, capping or reducing food subsidies was part of about one-third of 94 adjustment programmes supported by the IMF during recent years (IMF 1986c).

No global estimates of government expenditures on food subsidies are available. Furthermore, many countries do not report such expenditures as a separate item in available statistical documents. Because of the difficulties of access to the necessary data, little is known about changes in the magnitude of food subsidy expenditures over time. Here an attempt is made to provide such information for 10 countries for which basic data could be obtained. The selection of the countries to be included was based exclusively on whether data could be obtained within the time-frame for the analysis. Since countries with large subsidy expenditures are more likely to report the relevant data, the sample is heavily biased towards these countries, and is therefore likely to account for a relatively large share of global expenditures on food subsidies. Trends in subsidy expenditures observed in the 10 countries may therefore well reflect global trends.

The subsidy programmes in the 10 countries are described elsewhere (Pinstrup-Andersen 1987), and only a brief description is provided here. The programmes in Bangladesh, India, and Pakistan provide rations of wheat and/or rice to households through ration or 'fair price' shops at subsidized prices. In Bangladesh, the programme is primarily urban and certain rural

* Assistance from Raisuddin Ahmed, Harold Alderman, Neville Edirisinghe, P.S. George, Shubh Kumar, and Nora Lustig in obtaining data for this section is gratefully acknowledged.

areas are excluded from the Pakistan programme. The programmes are generally not targeted on the basis of household incomes.

The programmes in Brazil and Morocco consist of untargeted price subsidies for wheat. An untargeted wheat price subsidy programme is also found in Egypt along with subsidized rations of a number of other commodities. While the wheat subsidy is totally untargeted in Egypt, a small proportion of households (less than 10 per cent) is excluded from receiving the rations of other commodities on the basis of farm size and residence. The Colombian food stamp programme is the only truly targeted one among the 10. This programme, which was discontinued in 1982, was targeted on areas with high rates of poverty and malnutrition, and on pre-scholars and pregnant and lactating women within such areas. The programme was connected with primary health care.

The Mexican programme provides an untargeted price subsidy for tortilla, a commonly consumed processed maize food. This programme is biased towards urban consumers because most rural consumers make their own tortillas from maize flour which is not subsidized. The Sri Lanka programme consists of food stamps made available to about one-half of the population. This programme is biased in favour of lower-income households. Finally, the Zambian programme provides untargeted price subsidies for maize through the public marketing boards.

The magnitudes of food subsidy expenditures for the latest year for which data could be obtained in the 10 countries are shown in Table 3.8. With an

TABLE 3.8   *Government expenditures on food subsidies in selected countries*

	Latest year available	In US dollars			In national currency	
		Current ($million)	Current ($/capita)	Deflated cost index (1980 = 100)	Current	Deflated (1980 = 100)
Bangladesh	1985	89.30	0.91	92	217	124
Brazil	1985	323.19	2.38	19	2,964	31
Colombia	1982[a]	2.41	0.09	71	113	71
Egypt[b]	1985	2,933.51	60.48	142	185	95
Egypt[c]	1985	1,337.80	27.58	71	185	95
India	1985	691.24	0.92	71	145	93
Mexico	1984	1,110.50	14.46	73	670	99
Morocco	1985	277.48	11.75	68	227	140
Pakistan	1985	145.53	1.51	34	71	50
Sri Lanka	1985	68.44	4.32	42	89	51
Zambia	1982	17.01	2.82	38	52	41

Source: Pinstrup-Andersen (1987).
[a] Discontinued in 1982.
[b] Using official exchange rate.
[c] Using free market exchange rate.

expenditure of almost $3,000 million (at official exchange rates) or $1,338 million (at free market exchange rates) during 1985, Egypt spends more on food subsidies than any other developing country. Other countries with large subsidy expenditures include Mexico (primarily for maize and tortilla), India (ration shops for staple grains), and Brazil (wheat).

Subsidy expenditures in current values of national currencies increased in 7 of the 10 countries during the period 1980–85. The increase was particularly large in Brazil, Mexico, Morocco, Bangladesh, and Egypt (Table 3.8). However, much of the increase was due to inflation, and only two countries (Bangladesh and Morocco) show larger deflated food subsidy expenditures in 1985 than in 1980 (Table 3.8). There has been a clear downward trend in the deflated cost of food subsidies in some countries, notably Sri Lanka, Brazil, and Zambia, while other countries, such as Mexico, Bangladesh, and Morocco, show large fluctuations with no apparent trend.

At deflated dollar values all countries, except Egypt at official exchange rates, show decreasing trends during the first half of the 1980s. The cuts are severe in some countries, such as Brazil where the subsidy costs in 1985 were only 19 per cent of the costs in 1980 (Table 3.8). In other countries (e.g. Pakistan, Zambia, and Sri Lanka), food subsidies expressed in constant dollars dropped to between one-half and one-third of the 1980 levels during the five-year period. The dollar costs are obviously influenced by changes in the exchange rates, and in some countries a large proportion of the decreases (e.g. Brazil and Mexico) is explained by large devaluations during the period.

Annual per capita expenditures vary considerably among the study countries from a high of $28 in Egypt (using the free market exchange rate) to 9 cents in Colombia (Table 3.8). Except for Bangladesh and Egypt if the official exchange rate is used, all study countries show a decrease in per capita expenditures in current as well as deflated dollars. The decreases in the deflated per capita expenditures are shown in Fig. 3.2.

Thus, if the 10 countries are representative of the global situation, it may be concluded that government food subsidy expenditures have increased less than the domestic inflation and also less than the combined effect of inflation and devaluation against the dollar.

There is also strong evidence that government expenditures on food subsidies have increased less than other government expenditures. Thus, except for Morocco, all the study countries show a decrease in the proportion of the total government budget spent on food subsidies (Table 3.9). Decreases of 50 per cent or more are found in several of the countries—e.g. Brazil, Pakistan, Sri Lanka, and Zambia. Some countries, such as Sri Lanka and Zambia show a continuous year-by-year decline while other countries show an increase in some years.

These changed are reflected in decreases in food subsidies as a percentage of GDP (Table 3.9). Thus, in Sri Lanka, the cost of the food stamp scheme dropped from more than 3 per cent of GDP in 1980 to about 1 per cent in

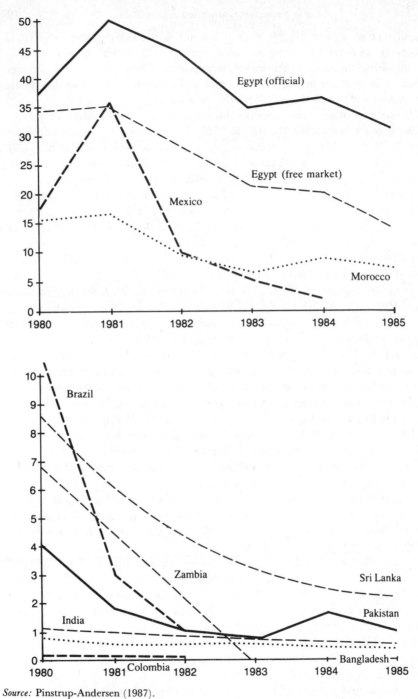

Source: Pinstrup-Andersen (1987).

Fig. 3.2 Per capita government expenditures on food subsidies, 1980–1985 (in 1980 US dollars)

1985. Drops of similar magnitudes were observed for Pakistan, Brazil and Zambia, while increases were estimated for Morocco and Bangladesh.

Based on the evidence above from 10 countries it appears that there has been a general decrease in government expenditure on food subsidies during the period 1980–85 both in real terms and as a share of total government budgets and GDP.

While changes in the magnitude of food subsidy expenditures may provide some guidelines for changes in the benefits derived by the poor, a number of additional factors, including other factors affecting food prices and the degree and aim of targeting and efficiency of the subsidy programme, influence the impact of a given subsidy expenditure on the welfare of the poor. These factors vary across countries and over time, and cuts in food subsidy expenditure need not result in negative welfare effects for the poor if appropriate changes are made in the subsidy scheme. Thus it is important to analyse both changes in the magnitude of subsidies and changes in the design and implementation of the subsidy schemes, particularly those related to targeting and efficiency. While a detailed analysis of the factors associated with changes in food subsidy expenditures in the 10 countries is beyond the scope of this chapter (such analysis is provided in Pinstrup–Andersen 1987), a few observations may be useful.

The observed decreases in the real value of government expenditures on food subsidies are not in the main due to explicit policy action aimed at subsidy programmes. Devaulations of national currencies and falling import prices of subsidized goods—e.g., wheat, rice, and sugar—have contributed to falling subsidy costs in dollars in many countries with little or no explicit policy action toward food subsidies. World rice prices fell from about $500/metric tonnes (MT) in 1980 to about $350/MT in 1985. Wheat prices fell during the same period from about $170/MT to about $100/MT. The largest relative price decrease occurred for sugar, which fell from about $60/MT to $8/MT. Deflating prices by the US cost of living index, with the 1980 index as 100, the indices for 1985 were 55 for rice, 58 for wheat, and 13 for sugar. With this US-based index, the real price decreases for rice and wheat were larger than the real decreases in subsidy expenditures for 6 of the 10 countries (Table 3.8).

The subsidy represents a wedge introduced between the price at which the government imports or procures food plus marketing costs and the price at which it is made available to consumers. Thus, if governments acquired the food at the going international prices, our findings imply that the decreases in those prices fully account for the decrease in subsidy costs in those six countries, leaving considerable room for increasing real benefits to consumers along with decreasing government costs. Thus, although this analysis does not provide estimates of changes in benefits, it appears that consumer benefits may not have been reduced at the same rate as the cost reductions. In fact, the cost reductions did not preclude increases in consumer benefits in more than half of the countries studied.

TABLE 3.9   *Government expenditures on food subsidies as percentage of total government expenditure and GDP*

	Food subsidies as percentage of total government expenditure			Food subsidies as percentage of GDP		
	1980 (%)	Latest year available	(%)	1980 (%)	Latest year available	(%)
Bangladesh	5.74	1985	3.78	0.58	1985	0.63
Brazil	5.56	1985	1.65	0.51	1985	0.16
Colombia	0.06	1982	0.04	0.01	1982	0.01
Egypt	16.44	1984	15.58	7.16	1985	6.64
India	3.53	1985	2.19	0.46	1985	0.36
Mexico	3.71	1984	2.59	0.65	1984	0.63
Morocco	5.02	1985	7.91	1.75	1985	2.33
Pakistan	7.93	1985	4.11	1.37	1985	0.48
Sri Lanka	7.22	1985	2.77	3.13	1985	1.16
Zambia	2.82	1982	1.21	0.99	1982	0.44

Source: Pinstrup-Andersen (1987).

However, changes in international prices may not be reflected in changes in domestic food prices in the event of devaluation or increases in domestic price incentives for local farmers, both of which occurred in a number of cases in the 1980s. Many developing countries increased domestic food prices during the period 1980–85 to reduce implicit price subsidies and provide stronger incentives to producers. In those countries, the earlier reasoning does not apply and it is possible that reductions in consumer benefits may have equalled or exceeded savings in explicit subsidy costs because domestic and international prices moved in different directions.

In four countries—Brazil, Pakistan, Sri Lanka, and Zambia—the savings in food subsidy costs exceeded international price decreases. Decreases in consumer benefits are likely to have occurred in these countries. Evidence from other sources show large decreases in consumer benefits in Sri Lanka (Edirisinghe 1986, Shan 1986).

Explicit policy measures were taken to reduce subsidies in Colombia and Sri Lanka. In Colombia, a food stamp programme which had been in effect since 1976 was discontinued in 1982 and a long-standing untargeted ration scheme in Sri Lanka was targeted in 1977 and converted to a targeted food stamp programme in 1979. Cost savings were obtained initially from targeting to only one-half of the population and subsequently by maintaining a constant nominal value of the food stamps in the face of rapidly increasing prices.

None of the 10 countries have succeeded in effectively increasing the degree of targeting of food subsidies to the absolute poor since 1980. Furthermore, there are no indications that the efficiency of the subsidy programmes has improved. Thus, except for the gains associated with the effect of falling real government procurement prices it appears that the declines in the real cost of explicit food subsidies have resulted in similar declines in the real incomes of poor consumers. This is a rather disturbing conclusion, and it is of paramount importance that any future cuts in the real value of explicit food subsidies over and above savings from lower procurement prices be accompanied by improved targeting and/or efficiency to ensure that the poorest population groups are not negatively affected. This is particularly important at a time when prices paid to the producer are being increased, and implicit food subsidies to the consumer reduced, in many countries.

4

Adjustment at the Household Level: Potentials and Limitations of Survival Strategies

Giovanni Andrea Cornia

I Introduction

The earlier chapters have analysed the most important effects of recession and adjustment policies on selected macro-economic indicators and on specific indicators of child welfare. The argument was largely conducted in aggregate terms, with limited analysis of responses to economic decline at the household level. This chapter analyses the effects of economic decline on household strategies and the informal sector, which can play a positive role during the adjustment process. This will permit a better understanding of the processes at work and help to formulate policies to favour disadvantaged groups.

For the majority of low-income households (whether part of the informal sector or not), adjustment entails a variety of adaptations—known as survival strategies—in the creation and use of resources (labour force participation, migration, consumption, etc.). These survival strategies are often attributed with the potential for reducing welfare losses during periods of decline. There is a need therefore to examine these household-level responses in greater detail with the purpose of ascertaining (*a*) the extent to which these grass-roots adjustments effectively buffer the poor and the vulnerable during crisis periods, and (*b*) the kind of policy support required to strengthen such survival mechanisms.

II The informal sector and its relationship with the formal sector

Despite substantial research over the last 10–15 years (Hart 1973, Sethuraman 1976), considerable controversy still exists about the role of the informal sector as an important source of growth. Furthermore, most analysis has examined the role of the informal sector during periods of overall economic expansion. Little is known of its behaviour during periods of protracted recession.

Even a cursory examination of the literature (Oshima 1971, Sethuraman 1981) indicates that at least in parts of the informal sector there is an autonomous and efficient capacity for generating growth in the income of the poor. It would seem imperative therefore to assign to the sector a more important role during periods of rigorous adjustment when employment and income generation in the formal sector generally decline. However, the measures proposed to develop the informal sector cannot be abstracted from the linkages between the sector and its formal counterpart. The nature of such linkages is certainly a matter of utmost importance for policy formulation (Tokman 1978). If, for instance, the informal–formal sector relation is one of subordination and dependence, with the formal sector siphoning off the productivity gains of the informal sector through various mechanisms (price determination, oligopolistic market control, differential wages, etc.), then the informal sector would hardly be in a position to retain its surplus, accumulate capital, and trigger a process of evolutionary growth (Moser 1978, Wellings and Sutcliffe 1984). In this case policies to support the informal sector would have a negligible impact on the incomes of the poor, so that it would be pointless to isolate the informal sector as a target and suggest policies for employment promotion and income generation. Opposite conclusions are arrived at if a benign informal–formal sector relationship is assumed, with either important exchanges of goods and services between the two sectors (Hart 1970), or with the informal sector seen as an autonomous, self-contained part of the economy (ILO 1972), in which its surplus is reinvested within the sector.

A conceptual framework for the analysis of recent evidence is presented in Fig. 4.1. The informal sector is assumed to be composed of three major subsectors characterized by different degrees of integration with the formal sector. They are:

1. *Small-scale subcontracting*, consisting in the production of intermediate goods for the formal sector. In the short–medium run its rate of expansion is clearly dependent on the rate of growth of the formal sector.

2. *Small-scale manufacturing*—producing consumer goods for the domestic market which are generally purchased by low- and middle-income households from both the formal and informal sectors. Not infrequently the goods produced compete with those of the formal sector. In this case, elements favouring the informal sector are its low wages and earnings, the smallness of certain markets (unreachable for the formal sector), and locational advantage. Shifts in consumer preferences towards 'modern goods' or trends in cost efficiency, may, however, lead to the loss of some of its markets. The rate of expansion of this part of the informal sector therefore partly depends on the growth of the formal sector and on its relative competitiveness. As a large part of informal sector production is purchased by its members, its rate of expansion is also influenced by its endogenous capacity to accumulate and grow.

3. *Retail trade, small-scale transport, and personal services* (repairs, domestic services, tailoring, barbers, etc.) purchased by low- and middle-income people. Little competition exists with the formal sector, which is almost completely absent from these industries. The rate of expansion of this subsector depends on the level of demand in the formal and the informal sector.

Within this framework, the formal sector is seen as a supplier of goods

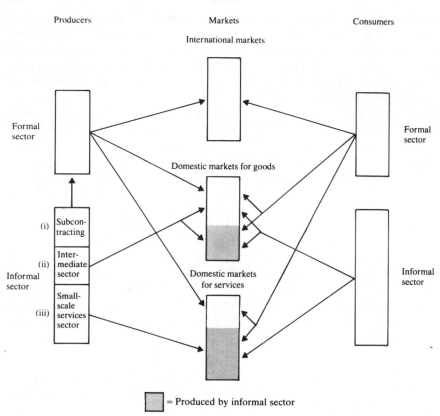

Fig. 4.1   Relationship between the formal and the informal sector

and modern services (financial, insurance, transport, etc.) to the foreign and domestic markets. The formal sector purchases goods and services from the foreign market as well as from both formal and informal domestic sectors. With Tokman (1978, p. 1071), it can therefore be concluded that 'The informal sector should neither be seen as a completely integrated nor as an autonomous sector, but rather as one with significant links with the rest of the economy, while simultaneously it also presents a considerable degree of self-containment'.

During periods of recession and rigorous adjustment owing to losses of external markets or to domestic deflation, employment (and, in most cases, wages) in the formal sector decline while its supply of goods falls. The level of aggregate demand declines, and the demand for intermediate and final goods and services produced by the informal sector declines accordingly. The relation of integration with the formal sector, in this case, turns out to be deleterious as the effects of the crisis are immediately transmitted to the informal sector. Policies in support of activities like subcontracting, petty trade, and personal services, for instance, would have only limited effects, as a constant or growing number of job-seekers would have to share a shrinking market. There are parts of the informal sector, however, that can generate more income, jobs, and output even during periods of overall contraction of the economy. To start with, the small-scale manufacturing sector competes with the formal sector in several markets (processed foods, clothing, simple metal products, etc.). During the adjustment process those losing their jobs in the formal sector (and perhaps others) enter the informal sector (Tokman 1986). In view of the completely unregulated nature of the informal sector labour market this is immediately translated into reduction of its earnings, wages, and product prices (and, typically, a deterioration in the formal/informal sector terms of trade). Hence, in those sectors where the formal and informal sector compete with each other there may be price-induced substitution of formal by informal sector goods which may be reinforced by a switch in consumption to low-income goods produced in the informal sector, as household incomes fall. This substitution may not affect the aggregate level of output, but it may have positive distributional implications, and may increase the labour intensity of production. Adjustment policies should therefore be designed to facilitate and support this process of substitution.

Secondly, as seen above, a considerable portion of the informal sector, producing both goods and services, is to a very large extent self-contained. That is, informal sector households work for each other and buy each others' products. In many developing countries the sector as a whole occupies between 50 and 70 per cent of the urban population (Mazumdar 1976, ILO-JASPA 1984). The level of output and earnings in the sector could therefore be increased by enhancing its *supply potential* and *internal exchange*. Supply capacity however, is typically severely constrained by insufficient access to financing, inputs, foreign exchange, technical training, physical infrastructure, etc. Policies aimed at removing such constraints could generate very positive results in terms of employment, output, and income distribution during periods of decline in the overall economy. In addition, because of the lower capital intensity and higher productive efficiency of the informal sector, the costs in terms of investment finance, foreign exchange, and intermediate inputs would be substantially smaller than for similar policies for the formal sector.

III Survival strategies at the household and community level

This section attempts to systematize some of the evidence on how low-income households—often from the informal or formal sector, but also destitutes, openly unemployed, small farmers, etc.—have reacted to the sharp declines in available resources observed during the last six or seven years in many developing countries. Despite the contributions to the economic and sociological literature of the last 10 years (Duque and Pastrana 1973, Safilios-Rothschild 1980, Saenz and Di Paula 1981, Raczynski and Serrano 1985) and despite the general flourishing of 'village' and 'poverty' studies, little is known on the mechanisms and strategies allowing poor people to survive under conditions of extreme deprivation. Even less is known on the adaptations made in recent years in those countries where the army of the poor has been swollen by the ranks of those forced out of the formal sector by dramatic falls in production and employment.

The analysis that follows is based on the fragmentary information available. Broadly, survival strategies can be grouped in three categories, i.e. strategies for the creation of resources; strategies for improving the use of existing resources; and extended family and migration strategies.

1 Strategies aiming at the generation of resources

The purpose of these strategies is to try to maintain the level of *current income* enjoyed by the household or at least to contain its fall within acceptable limits. Facing declines in the real wage or employment level or other income-earning potential of those family members occupied productively, the household reacts in a number of ways:

1. *Increasing the supply of labour to the economy.* Evidence of such an increase is shown by increasing rates of participation in the labour force or can be inferred from the increase in the size of the informal sector. Circumstantial evidence obtained through interviews, special studies, etc. also provides some indications of this phenomenon. In Costa Rica, for example, the labour force participation rate rose between 1979 and 1982 from 50.5 to 51.2 per cent, while the urban informal and rural traditional sectors grew substantially. A disaggregation of participation rates shows that the increase in labour supply was concentrated among women head of households, men over 50 non-head of households, and to a somewhat less important extent, women non-head of households (PREALC 1985*b*). Simiarly, in Brazil women's labour force participation increased from 37.9 to 39.8 per cent during the crisis year 1983–84 while men's participation rates stagnated (PREALC 1985*a*). Evidence of increasing women's activity rates is reported for Chile and Uruguay by Leslie *et al.* (1986), while the country study on the Philippines (vol. ii, ch. 7) shows that labour force participation increased from 60 to 64 per cent between 1982 and 1984. The increase was paticularly large for women (from 43.7 to 48.3 per cent).

Circumstantial evidence of increasing activity rates also exists for Chile (Raczynski and Serrano 1985), where a series of interviews with women from low-income households in Greater Santiago reveals that during the years of the crisis (1980–84) all women belonging to such households had engaged in some form of highly unstable and mostly part-time market production.

Households have been observed to engage in quasi-legal or completely illicit activities such as beer-brewing, smuggling, prostitution, and drug cultivation and trafficking in conditions of extreme deprivation. The situation of unskilled landless women left behind by their men who migrated in search of work has been found to be extremely precarious. With no assets or skills these women crucially depend on their husbands' remittances for their and their children's survival, and they are often forced to turn to begging or prostitution. These trends have been noticed in countries as different as India (Mies 1984), Peru (Karp-Toledo 1983), and several African countries (May and Stichter 1984).

PREALC (1985*a*) gives ample evidence of the increasing relative size of the informal sector for countries as different as Argentina, Brazil, the Dominican Republic, and Venezuela. For Latin America as a whole the informal sector grew from 29 to 32 per cent of the non-agricultural active population between 1980 and 2985 (Tokman 1986). Similar indications are available for Sub-Saharan Africa, for which Gozo and Aboagye (1985) report that informal sector employment grew from 44 to 52 per cent between 1974 and 1980. The increase is partly a response to declining formal sector opportunities and partly evidence of increased household labour supply.

It appears, therefore, that economic crisis has increasingly drawn members of the 'non-primary' labour force into market production. In the case of women this intensifies the demand on their time and could limit their ability to spend a minimum amount of time on health and nutrition-related activities. Where extended-family arrangements are not available this can have a nutritionally adverse impact on the welfare of children. Therefore, increases in activity rates of women should be accompanied by a commensurate increase in child care services (whether state-provided or community-based) or by improvements in time-saving household equipment (Popkin 1980, Franklin and de Valdés 1985).

2. *Increasing self-production.* Faced with sharply declining incomes and increasingly difficult employment prospects, households at times withdraw from market production and increase self-production (or subsistence production). This trend has been observed most often in food production, shelter construction and some services (child care, health, etc.). Opportunities for growing one's own food are generally greater in rural than urban areas. But increasing farming of small, family plots is reported even for the relatively dense city of Santiago (Raczynski and Serrano 1985). There is also some evidence of increasing small plots and family gardens in the periphery of São Paulo (Rios 1984, Macedo in vol. ii, ch. 2). In African towns increased self-production of food is generally a significant possibility. In Burkina Faso, for instance, the government has strongly encouraged the urban population to cultivate family and collective plots. Interventions along these lines have long been recommended (UNICEF 1982, WHO/UNICEF 1985), and should receive particular attention during periods of recession and adjustment owing to their cost efficiency and to their potential nutritional benefits. The provision of seeds, simple implements, and technical assistance can substantially increase the production of nutritious and high value-added vegetables, groundnuts, fruits, and so on from small plots and thus improve the nutritional status of family members.

Another area where increases of self-production have been observed is that of child health and care. In Latin America, for instance, various *clubes de madres* set up simple child care centres managed by the mothers themselves who alternate in weekly shifts. In this way a substantial amount of mothers' time is freed for productive and other purposes. If some technical assistance and resources are made available (by NGOs, donors, government agencies) such programmes can become valid entry points for education about nutrition, diarrhoea control, breast-feeding, etc., all aiming at empowering the mothers and, at the same time, transferring some health care activities to the family level. A crucial precondition for the success of these activities was found to be a high level of community participation and the existence of local leadership.

For Peru evidence also exists (Karp-Toledo 1983) of the rediscovery, during periods of growing economic hardship, of traditional forms of mutual help in the form of *voluntary labour exchange* for the construction of a house, harvesting, etc. Increased labour exchange was found to be a general strategy to survive and break away from the vicious circle of poverty among small farmers of the southern part of Sri Lanka (Wickramaarachchi 1984). When the share of modern inputs needed for the completion of the projects was kept within reasonable margins, these attempts at mobilizing idle labour resources through communal forms of labour exchange met with considerable success. In the Indian city of Hyderabad considerable capital investment has been created by poor families in the form of self-help housing. With 9,000 houses self-built, approximately 80 million rupees ($6 million) in housing stock was developed from family resources and labour (Cousins and Goydre 1979).

3. *Changing assets–liability position.* Increasing indebtedness in the form of consumer debt at neighbourhood stores is quite common even in periods of less acute deprivation (Raczynski and Serrano 1985). While such stores generally charge high prices, their sales on credit can help sustain a poor household's consumption level for limited periods. However, in South Asia, where credit networks are controlled by money-lenders charging exorbitant rates of interest, going into debt is often the first step towards permanent poverty. Wickramaarachchi (1984, p. 27) mentions, for instance, that in the southern province of Sri Lanka, to borrow 2,760 rupees for essential consumption for three months a family has to pay 1,656 rupees in interest, corresponding to an annual interest rate of about 250 per cent. Consumer and production credit therefore needs to be made available on different conditions. Some examples of alternative credit schemes are provided in Chapter 10.

All authors agree that the sale of assets is a strategy to which recourse is made only under extreme circumstances. This is particularly true in the case of productive assets (tools, cattle, land, machinery): not only does their sale reduce the future productive (and subsistence) capacity of the household, but it frequently generates only a fraction of the original market value as, typically, many households are forced to sell at the same time. Cutler (1984), analysing

1982–83 data on Ethiopia, suggests that one useful indicator of approaching crisis is an increased volume of sales of assets, livestock in particular.

4. *Increasing the flow of income transfers.* Public transfer programmes are usually small or non-existent. However, a recent World Bank study (Kaufman and Lindauer 1984) shows that private transfers—usually within the family—can be substantial. Data on income in the low-income areas of Santa Ana in El Salvador in 1976 show that private income transfers accounted for 11 per cent of total household income among low-income households. About one-third of all families received some transfer income during the survey month. For these families, income transfers accounted for about 40 per cent of the total household income, while 60 per cent of all female-headed families received some such support as compared to less than 25 per cent for male-headed families.

The income transfers tended to have progressive effects on income distribution within each extended family, as the transfer income was directed towards basic needs expenditure and the income of the net givers of transfer income was substantially higher than that of recipients. However, the risk-pooling ability and the level of income transfers within each extended family is always limited by the family's overall income and wealth. Public programmes transferring income (in cash or in food, for instance) are therefore necessary to sustain the livelihood of the poorest families, particularly during periods of recession and adjustment when income transfers from the extended family are bound to decline. The cases of South Korea and Botswana (vol. ii) provide examples of such public income transfers.

Analysing the crisis years of 1980–85 in Chile, Raczynski (vol. ii, ch. 3), finds substantially increased use of the official aid network, even when this entails a certain social stigma (like being certified as in a condition of extreme poverty) and if qualifying for public assistance entails a substantial opportunity cost (for transport, fees for obtaining various certificates, etc.). Despite these problems, she shows that in Chile public income transfers (unemployment benefit, municipal subsidy, supplementary feeding, and school lunches) became very important for the survival of low-income households during the years of recession and adjustment.

Not all developing countries, however, have at their disposal either a well-established and comprehensive public assistance infrastructure or significant funds to provide, as in the case of Chile. Therefore, while the redistributive role of the state should be promoted, in many circumstances extended-family and informal networks will remain the main source of income transfers and short-term credit for poor households. Mutual aid and co-operation—like borrowing small amounts of food or money, sharing food, fuel, etc., small gifts of food and other goods, exchange of services, and moral support—can help survival during difficult periods up to a point. In economic terms, this dense network of exchanges *does* increase the overall value of goods and services available to a poor community while improving their distribution. It should be clear, however, that the poorer the community and the less the solidarity,

the lesser the changes of this strategy to contain the decline in people's livelihood and the greater the need for outside intervention.

2 *Strategies for improving the efficiency of existing resources*

These strategies aim at moderating the decline in levels of material consumption and family welfare (as measured, for instance, by calorie intake
per capita) in the wake of generally declining resources. The difficulty in
maintaining income levels (despite the strategies aiming at creating resources)
by necessity make these 'consumption strategies' play a fundamental role in
buffering the poor and the children during periods of adjustment. Among
them the following can be distinguished:

1. *Changes in purchasing habits.* Raczynski and Serrano (1985) note that when
family incomes became scarce and more unstable, families in Chile tended to
abandon the monthly wholesale purchase of less perishable food items (sugar,
tea, flour, cooking oil, etc.). The crisis forced households to purchase these
goods more frequently, in smaller quantities, and at substantially higher prices
in small neighbourhood stores. A reduction in household purchasing power
thus occurs. Macedo (vol. ii, ch. 2) presents examples for São Paulo, Brazil of
how the communities and the local authorities have tried to offset such a
negative trend. Facing rapidly growing food prices, households were encouraged by the authorities to make greater use of the Central Wholesale Market
where prices were as much as 40 per cent lower than average retail prices.
According to government reports, in the areas where it operates the programme
covers 10 per cent of the population, mostly lower-middle class. The poorest,
however, continue to face difficulties of access because of their location. Communities have also organized themselves—with government support—for the
collective purchase of 12 basic items at controlled prices. To solve the distance
problem, goods are transported to the various neighbourhoods and sold locally.
The government estimates that about 400,000 people were covered by such
activities. In a similar scheme, groups of about 20 families bought a basic list
of products (rice, beans, oil, cassava, potatoes, etc.) at fixed wholesale prices
from 'food network' stores. An interesting experience along these lines is
reported for Peru (see below). The main essence of all these private and public
efforts is to *reduce the cost of basic food items*. While securing an adequate food
supply at prices that are stable and accessible to all households, and in
particular to the low-income and destitute ones, should be the main concern
of a national food policy, these examples show that real family welfare can be
substantially protected by grass-roots efforts aimed at cutting commercial
margins. As such, these efforts ought to receive full policy and organisational
support.

2. *Changes in food preparation habits.* Huaman (n.d.), UNICEF-Peru (1985),
Lafosse (1984), and Van der Linde (1984) report on the experience of the
comedores populares which have developed in Lima since 1980 as a response to

a seriously aggravating economic situation. In this scheme a group of 15–50 households jointly carries out the bulk purchase of food and prepares and cooks it on specially equipped premises. Meals, however, are consumed at home. The food preparation is done by the women of participating households, who alternate in daily shifts every four to five days. Each family pays according to the number of meals requested. The *comedores populares* receive a certain amount of food assistance from local and international agencies, mostly in the form of rice, cooking oil, kitchen equipment, etc. The scheme, however, is to a large extent self-financed, and there are *comedores* which operate without assistance. The number of *comedores* is estimated by UNICEF-Peru (1985) at over 300 and by Lafosse (1984, p. 26) at 635.

The economic rationale behind the *comedores populares* is quite simple: the meals prepared there are substantially cheaper and nutritionally more balanced that those prepared at home, for the following reasons. First, the donated food (which would be much more difficult to distribute without such a structure) lowers the cost of the meals by an estimated 30 per cent. Secondly, bulk procurement of food allows for substantial reductions in the unit costs. Thirdly, there are economies of scale in cooking, particularly on expensive items like fuel and cooking oil. The scheme has two additional advantages. First, it frees a substantial amount of women's time for generating income and child-care. Secondly, extremely poor households are either temporarily exempted from paying for the meals or are given the meals on credit. In this way the *comedores populares* become instruments of income redistribution in favour of the poor.

Changes in processing technologies can also maintain or even increase food intake. Women in rural Ghana, for instance, have developed new techniques for gutting and brining fish where texture was otherwise unacceptable (Timberlake 1985). This simple breakthrough resulted in widespread consumption of triggerfish, a cheap source of local protein.

3. *Changes in overall consumption patterns.* When the possibility of maintaining previous consumption levels by one of the strategies described above has been exhausted, households have no other choice but to modify their overall consumption patterns. Apart from households below or near the absolute poverty line, this procees need not entail costs in terms of nutritional status. Raczynski (vol. ii) found for Chile that, as expected, some of the non-basic items (clothing, other consumer durables, leisure, relatively expensive foods, etc.) were eliminated first. These were followed by cuts in more basic expenditure items such as water charges, fuel, rent, and, among foods, protein-rich items (milk, eggs, fish, etc.). The last to be reduced was expenditure on basic staples (bread, rice, and noodles) and children's education (see below).

4. *Changes in dietary patterns.* Poor households, which spend between 60 and 80 per cent of their incomes on food, are forced, first to increase the proportion of food expenditure in total expenditure; secondly, to concentrate their food expenditure almost exclusively on calories; and thirdly, to substitute cheap for expensive source of calories. This series of concomitant substitutions can be

triggered by sharp fluctuations in the relative prices of food (Pinstrup-Andersen 1985), as well as by falling income, or in rural areas by shifts from food crop to cash production to expand the export sector. This process of substitution in consumption is quite an efficient mechanism for sustaining nutrient intake even in the face of sharp income drops or price hikes (Behrman 1986). However, it cannot be of help for those already consuming the cheapest nutrients, particularly in insufficient quantities. Evidence provided in Volume II for Chile, Sri Lanka, and South Korea shows that after a long series of such adaptations a decline in per capita calorie intake takes place. A wealth of other evidence points in the same direction. Deterioration in diet quality and composition was found in both urban and rural areas of the Peruvian provinces of Arequipa, Puno, and Cuzco during 1983, due to severe economic decline and drought (Karp-Toledo 1983). Raczynski and Serrano (1985) report that in half of the poor households interviewed in the Greater Santiago area, by 1983 the decline in income had led to insufficient and unbalanced diets. Commenting on the effects of food price rises in Sub-Saharan Africa, Green and Singer (1984, p. 297), note that '... the increase in the cost of staples worsens the existing widespread calorie deficiencies, with especially negative effects on children. The shift is both to less balanced diets and less food.'

While nutrition education can improve the capacity of poor households to make better use of their resources to some extent, appropriate pricing and distribution policies and food subsidies can have a far greater impact in protecting the poor. The price of those 'foods of the poor' with high nutritional values, for instance, could be either subsidized or regulated (Perrin and Scobie 1981, Mateus 1983). Chapter 13 dealing with nutritional interventions discusses these policies in detail.

5. *Changes in intrahousehold food distribution.* Evidence on this issue is extremely weak. Circumstantial evidence (Raczynski and Serrano 1985) suggests that in Chile women of poor households would experience more than commensurate declines in food intake during periods of declining food availability. More investigation is necessary to clarify this, but it is plausible that in societies characterized by sex bias in the family allocation of food and health care (Chen *et al.* 1981), a decline in food availability could be distributed in an increasingly inegalitarian way, with women and young girls suffering disproportionately. There are, however, examples of appropriate targeting of scarce or declining food resources on the weakest group at the household and village (Haque *et al.* 1975) and national level (Jolly 1985).

3 Extended family and migration strategies

These strategies change the composition and location of the household to increase its income earning potential or change the ratio between its needs and resources. Among them one may note:

1. *Changes in the household composition and organization.* As part of the general strategy by which poor families vary their structure and composition in their attempt to adapt to growing imbalances between resources and needs (Tienda 1978), poor households have responded to the crisis by incorporating new members with the purpose of sharing living costs or by 'farming out' some of their children to better-off families (Safilios-Rothschild 1980). Adults previously living alone were incorporated into other households in periods of growing income deficits in Chile (Raczynski and Serrano 1985, pp. 209–12), Peru (Karp-Toledo 1983), and Brazil (Rios 1984). In the last case there is also evidence of concentration of several families in one household. The studies quoted confirm that this 'extension' of the household is generally accompanied by an increase in the number of people economically active. The growth in the size of the household—which finds its justification in the existence of economies of scale in consumption and in the pooling of some services—is consistent with findings showing that among the poor, the small households are the poorest (Mohan and Hartline 1984).

Other kinds of changes in household structure are inspired by the desire to reduce household size (and with it expenditure), and to provide some of its members with a better environment during periods of economic hardship. This is the case when one or more children are sent to live with better-off relatives or friends who take charge of their subsistence (Safilios-Rothschild 1980, Raczynski and Serrano 1985).

2. *Migration* is also one of the strategies followed by poor families faced by increasingly difficult living and working prospects. As in the case sale of assets, recourse to migration occurs generally under conditions of severe deprivation. In analysing households' responses to the 1983/84 drought in Ethiopia for instance, Cutler (1984) distinguishes three types of migration. The first is temporary labour-seeking migration of non-heads of households. In many countries such migration often becomes of long duration (May and Stichter 1984), and has a series of positive (remittances) and negative effects on the women and children left behind. Youssef and Hetler (1984) note, however, that in many countries (Mali, Ghana, Brazil, Togo, Nigeria, etc.), out-migration of men has forcibly made the woman the major, if not the sole, supporter of rural households. The number of women-headed households relying on insufficient and unstable remittances has grown. This situation is worse in those societies where women's access to assets, credit, land, etc. is restricted. The second type consists of relief-seeking migration of the head of the household, while the third—normally occurring only under conditions of extreme deprivation—entails the migration of the whole family. Such strategies mostly consist in households migrating from rural to urban areas or within the rural areas. Urban to rural and intra-urban flows are much less frequent, but in societies where farm land is abundant and accessible, increasingly difficult conditions in urban areas can lead some city dwellers to return to subsistence farming. Some evidence, for instance, seems to indicate that the recent sharp fall in

urban earnings in Accra and Dar es Salaam have provoked a return flow of migration to rural areas.

IV   A policy perspective for informal and survival strategies

The analysis had illustrated the various strategies adopted by poor households as a response to the economic ills caused by recession and adjustment. Many, if not most, of these strategies are not new, and have been adopted, often throughout their lives, by many of the poor. It is obvious, however, that households will increasingly have recourse to them during periods of overall economic decline. Under such circumstances some of these strategies can play a very important role as buffering mechanisms. There is a risk, however, in representing such strategies as an inexpensive, *laissez-faire* solution to the problems of the poor faced with a deteriorating economic environment, with their existence used as an excuse for policy inaction. Not only do they generally only partially offset the effects of economic decline but most have diminishing returns (e.g. assets can only be sold once), and thus cannot provide continued help in the face of protracted decline in incomes and living conditions. There is a need therefore to assess the efficiency and equity of these survival mechanisms and the extent to which policy support can improve their effectiveness.

While each situation should be considered as a separate case, previous discussion shows that these survival strategies can, broadly speaking, be divided into three categories in terms of their relative efficiency in protecting the poor.

1. *Survival strategies with negative, doubtful, or only temporary positive effects.* Certain survival strategies, like engaging in illicit activities (smuggling and the drug trade), have negative economic (and other) effects on society as a whole, even if they may bring some immediate benefit to the persons adopting them. As such, they should not be encouraged or supported. However, in certain cases, some of the less illicit activites, including smuggling of consumer goods and even non-exploitative child labour, may have to be tolerated or regulated as their suppression would leave some households without any source of sustenance. Some labour market strategies might also have an overall negative effect although they may solve the problems of some individuals. For instance, the increase of labour supply to the wage sector during periods of falling earnings tends to depress the wage rate and may even decrease the overall wage bill as a growing number of job-seekers compete for a stagnant number of jobs. Similar conclusions were drawn in Section 3 concerning strategies of self-employment in those activities depending on the level of demand originating from the formal sector of the economy. The sale of productive assets, often taking place under conditions of distress, or the contraction of new debt are strategies that in general bring only temporary relief while making future subsistence more problematic. The results of migration are uncertain. While in periods of expansion, rural–urban, interregional, and international migration may be a reflection of labour mobility leading to higher household

incomes, during periods of economic decline the recourse to migration is likely to produce dubious results in terms of overcrowding the informal-sector labour market and urban overcrowding. For those left behind in the countryside there will also be problems, such as an increase in the number of women-headed households, lack of agricultural manpower, etc. It is possible, however, that some forms of rural resettlement can prove viable solutions to localized rural crisis.

This group of survival strategies with rather limited or negative value for poor households taken as a whole should not be the target of policy support or encouragement, although some of these responses will have to be tolerated and regulated. In certain cases, a more active policy involvement may be necessary to offset particularly negative household responses. For instance, growing child abandonment or an increasingly skewed intrahousehold food distribution will require government action in the areas of child care and social communication.

2. *Survival strategies trying to compensate for inadequate or non-existent government policies.* These strategies generally have positive, if limited, results. The same and better results could be achieved through the implementation of appropriate government policies. For instance, strategies aimed at reducing consumer prices of basic items through collective wholesale purchases would have no reason to exist if the foods of the poor (and a few other items) were subsidized, or if retail prices of the same goods were subject to government control. The same considerations are valid when considering those poor people's strategies aimed at increasing their reliance on income transfers from the extended family and on informal aid networks, or at modifying the composition of the household by incorporating relatives. A government income transfer scheme would have stronger and more systematic distributional effects than these survival mechanisms. Policy support for this group of strategies should be extended selectively. In some cases (consumer co-operatives, for instance) the results can be impressive while in others the benefits that can realistically be expected are less. In every case, more comprehensive government intervention would be desirable.

3. *Survival strategies with strong potential for protecting the poor and the children during periods of economic decline.* These include strategies aimed at increasing productivity and employment in that part of the informal sector which competes with the formal sector or which has an autonomous capacity to grow through its internal market. Because of the high efficiency of production of the informal sector (low capital and high value added per worker, low foreign exchange ratio, etc.), the provision of resources and policy support for these activities can have positive employment, income, and distributional results. Examples of such policy support are given in Chapter 10. Supporting self-help activities through appropriate policies in food production, shelter construction, child care, and social services would also yield positive results. Many examples provided in this volume show that standards of living and child nutritional

status can be effectively protected by mobilizing the productive and organizational potential of poor communities. Policy support in this area can be very efficient. Small amounts of external resources, some training and technical assistance, and a favourable environment can substantially increase non-market production and the availability of community-based services. If properly supported, these survival strategies can play a major role as a complement or even as a substitute for official government intervention particularly in very poor communities. Examples of such policy support can be found in Chapters 10, 11, and 13. Policy support for the extension of communal efforts to substitute for part of household activities could probably also help in food preparation and child health and care, for example, where communal activities have been shown to yield positive results. In most cases the promotion of this group of survival strategies requires an increasing role to be played by the local communities and greater communal activity in both production and consumption. Community participation, local entrepreneurship, and leadership are the key to the success of such initiatives, which deserve full policy support.

In conclusion, policy support should unreservedly be extended to those survival strategies emphasizing the growth of employment and productivity of small-scale, informal sector manufacturing; support to communities for self-production and exhange of food, shelter, and community-based services; and increasing communal efforts in basic needs. Because of the comparative efficiency of this group of survival strategies, policy support would be likely to produce better results than where support is exclusively concentrated on the formal sector. Other survival policies illustrated above should receive only selective support or be subject to regulation. All in all, while it is difficult to generalize, support for survival strategies should be seen as a complement to and not as a substitute for efficient and equitable macro-economic policies and sustained growth in the formal sector of the economy.

5

Country Experience with Adjustment

Giovanni Andrea Cornia and Frances Stewart

I Introduction

Investigation into the complex relationships between economic development
and the health and welfare of vulnerable groups requires in-depth analysis of
particular countries. Ten country studies were undertaken, three in Africa—
Botswana, Ghana, and Zimbabwe; three in Asia—the Philippines, South
Korea, and Sri Lanka; and four in South America—São Paulo in Brazil, Peru,
Chile, and Jamaica.

In addition to geography, these countries represent a wide variety of experience with respect to economic developments and to the human dimension. All
countries had some problems in the 1970s—partly due to the oil price rise of
1973–74 and its aftermath—but most had managed largely to overcome them
and experienced sustained growth in the 1970s. For Ghana and Jamaica,
however, the problems of the 1980s represented a prolongation of economic
crisis and stagnation which had lasted for much of the 1970s. Each of the 10
countries has been adversely affected by the world recession in the 1980s. All
suffered from some combination of the syndrome of difficulties that occurred
on a world-wide basis in the 1980s—accumulated debt, high interest rates,
collapse of lending, and stagnating world markets. However, their experience
with respect to commodity prices has differed, with Botswana and South
Korea being, for different reasons, affected less than the others. Each country
developed major imbalances in the 1980s. The precise cause varied, as will be
clear from the discussion below. The three countries in Africa have each been
subject, in varying degree, to drought, as well as to problems of economic
origin.

The countries' starting point at the end of the 1970s differed with respect
to the human dimension as well as economic circumstances. Sri Lanka, Chile,
and also Jamaica had high achievements on health, nutrition, and education
in the 1970s, despite rather poor economic performance. The Philippines was
an intermediate case, with good achievements on education but strong and
rising inequalities both in primary income and in the distribution of social
expenditure. South Korea had very strong economic performance and fairly
good achievements on the human dimension, especially education. In contrast,
Brazil and Peru had greatly neglected the basic needs of the low-income, and

had experienced a rapid, élitist pattern of growth. Ghana's good achievements on health and education in earlier periods had been eroded during the 1970s. Zimbabwe had suffered from racial inequalities imposed by the white regime.

The case studies, which are contained in Volume II, describe and analyse economic developments in the 1980s, the adjustment experience, and the impact on the vulnerable, especially women and children. Summaries of the experience of each country are presented below. Although most of the studies briefly describe the historical backdrop against which the most recent developments have taken place, attention is focused on the experience of the late 1970s and 1980s.

II Summary of country experience

1 *Botswana* (1980–1984)

Botswana enjoyed a very rapid rate of growth in the 1970s, largely based on minerals, especially on rapid growth in the production and export of diamonds. In the 1980s, Botswana experienced two types of shock: first and of much less importance, a temporary hiccup in the diamond market in 1981 led to the emergence of a trade deficit, but diamond exports resumed rapid growth from 1983. Secondly, there was acute and prolonged drought from 1982, which still has not ended.

The government adopted orthodox stabilization policies in response to the first shock: government expenditure was restrained, monetary policy was tightened, and a wage freeze was introduced. These policies attracted short-run capital and stabilized imports. Meanwhile, the international diamond market recovered, a new diamond mine was opened, and rapid growth in exports and GDP was resumed. The trade deficit was rapidly eliminated. The diamond-induced crisis was short-lived and its effects were hardly felt by the most vulnerable, who are in the urban informal sector and the rural areas and are only indirectly affected by the diamond economy.

The drought was much more prolonged and of much greater direct relevance to vulnerable groups, who were simultaneously threatened by loss of income and reduced food availability. This especially affected the rural population who form 80 per cent of the population, although agriculture accounts for only 8.5 per cent of GDP.

The Botswana government introduced comprehensive and substantial drought relief measures. They included: (*a*) A labour-based relief programme which provides employment on infrastructural projects. The objective is to replace 50 per cent of the income lost due to crop failure. In 1985/86 it is estimated that 74,000 workers were covered, with replacement of 37 per cent of income loss due to crop failure. (*b*) Human water relief: funds are made available to help repair water systems and transport emergency water supplies when local sources dry up. (*c*) Arable agricultural relief and recovery programmes with assistance to small farmers to clear land, and provide inputs, including the provision of free seeds. (*d*) Livestock relief and recovery programmes to assist in vaccination and feed, and provide a guaranteed market for cattle. (*e*) Supplementary feeding programmes for primary school children, under 5s (for all children in the rural areas and the most malnourished in urban areas), pregnant and lactating women, and tuberculosis patients. In 1985/86 there were 678,000 beneficiaries, or 62 per cent of Botswana's population.

The 1982–86 Drought Relief Programme appears to have been successful in preventing a major rise in hunger and malnutrition. Malnutrition has been contained, with a rise from 25 to 31 per cent in the number of children below 80 per cent of the Gomez standard over the period, despite a five-year drought which in other countries provoked mass starvation. Although crop production in 1985 was substantially below the 1980 and 1981 level, food availability had increased significantly.

The government allocated $21 million to drought relief in 1985/86 (i.e. $18 per capita), or 2 per cent of GDP. The donors' contribution amounted to another $21 million. The government's budget for drought relief was equivalent to 17 per cent of development expenditures.

An integral and essential part of the drought relief effort is the nutritional surveillance and early warning system which provides information ranging from rainfall to nutritional status of children and health, permitting timely identification of problems and appropriate interventions.

The Botswana system of drought relief is designed to meet nutritional needs which arise through loss of household income. Although in Botswana, as indeed often elsewhere, this loss arises from drought, the system would be equally applicable to other causes of rising poverty and malnutrition among vulnerable groups, including losses arising from recession and the process of adjustment. Botswana's ability to meet the emerging food gaps is partly a result of the prosperity of the diamond industry, which greatly increases import and revenue capacity. However, the total cost of the programmes, which cover over 70 per cent of the population, is nevertheless within the capacity of other countries which are less fortunate in their main primary product.

2 *São Paulo, Brazil* (1981–1984)

The second oil shock, the increase in international interest rates, and the decline in commercial lending brought to an end a long period of uninterrupted growth in Brazil. In 1980, both trade and current account balances deteriorated sharply. Adjustment started at the end of 1980, while an adjustment programme with IMF assistance was agreed upon in early 1983. The policies implemented between 1981 and 1985 included a series of devaluations. High interest rates were maintained, taxes were raised, and government expenditure reduced. A restrictive wage policy was introduced. Additional incentives to exports and restrictions on imports were established, while new impulse was given to import substitution in the oil, non-ferrous metals, chemical, and other sectors. The most important goal of the package, i.e. the creation of a large surplus in the trade balance to service huge interest payments on the foreign debt, was achieved, mostly through import restraint. However in 1984 and 1985 a substantial increase in exports, in the wake of the recovery in the United States, also contributed to the trade surplus.

As a result of these policies GDP, and to a greater extent GNP per capita, fell between 1981 and 1983. Growth was resumed in 1984 and 1985, but real wages continued declining until the second half of 1985. Unemployment increased between 1981 and 1984 (with some exceptions in 1982) in the six major metropolitan areas of the country, including São Paulo. The urban informal sector increased by 1.8 million between 1981 and 1983, a clear sign of growing underemployment. There was an overall decline in mean income, particularly during 1981–83, while the losses suffered by the poorer groups were the greatest. Income concentration therefore increased between 1981 and 1983, starting to decline again in 1984 with the beginning of the recovery. Because of the measures promoting the production of sugar-cane alcohol and the promotion of export crops, food production per capita decreased sharply during 1981–84, and food prices increased more rapidly than the cost of living index.

Altogether, macro balances were re-established quite rapidly but at a considerable social cost, particularly for the poorest section of society. In addition, this achievement was threatened by the surge of inflation (400 per cent) and the drop in investment levels due to the transfer abroad of a large portion of the investible surplus (equal in 1983 to 5.7 per of GDP and to about a third of national savings). The inflation problem was attacked through a *plan cruzado* introduced in February 1986, which was successful for a short period, but inflationary pressures remained strong. The need to create new capacity conflicts, however, with debt servicing obligations.

The institutional response to the social problems created by the adjustment process in Brazil, and in São Paulo State in particular, has been grossly inadequate. Only exceptionally has the federal government (which frames the main policies and controls most budgetary resources) tried to do something to alleviate the social impact of the recession. Measures include: (*a*) a special Fund for Social Investment (Finsocial) to undertake programmes in the areas of food and nutrition, health, housing for the poor, etc; (*b*) a subsidy to those families facing problems with their monthly mortgage payments; and (*c*) a rent control scheme for residential housing. However, these measures were not part of an organic plan for alleviating the impact of the crisis and were seriously flawed in terms of their scope, administration, efficacy, and—above all—distributive equity.

At the level of the state and city of São Paulo, various measures were taken to mitigate the negative effects of the crisis. Several schemes were started to reduce the cost of food, soup kitchens were established, and incentives to vegetable gardening were provided. However, as the chronic scarcity of budgetary resources of state and local governments was worsened by the recession, the scope of these interventions grew increasingly limited in comparison with the needs created by the crisis.

The inadequacy of the institutional response is also reflected in the trends in social expenditure from 1981–85. At the federal level there were reductions in the health care programme, while state social expenditure in São Paulo dropped substantially both relative to other budget items and in absolute terms, particularly in education. The share of health and education in total expenditure grew only in the city of São Paulo, leading to constant and even growing levels of expenditure despite the fall of the total budget.

These measures did not provide efficient protection to the poor against the rigours of the adjustment process. In São Paulo State, the infant mortality rate, which had steadily declined over 1981–83, increased sharply in 1984 because of a measles epidemic, the effects of which were magnified by the worsened nutritional status of many children. Over the 1983–84 period infant mortality rates rose for Brazil as a whole and also for the richer states of the South and South-East. In addition, the incidence of low birth weights recorded in the main hospitals in São Paulo increased between 1980 and 1983. There was a sharp increase in the number of curative and emergency consultations, as opposed to visits for preventive purposes, in hospital attendance by children in the city of Santo Andre. The number of emergency consultations grew even faster, confirming a picture of worsening child health. Data from the school system show even more pronounced deterioration, with increases in the rates of failure and drop-out observed in all São Paulo's departments between 1981 and 1984. Child abandonment and delinquency also increased and are often referred to as one of the most negative consequences of the crisis.

The 1981–85 Brazilian adjustment experience can therefore be considered quite successful in re-establishing external balance, stabilizing the growth of foreign debt, and re-establishing positive growth of GDP in 1984 and 1985. Serious doubts persist, however, on the sustainability of this, in view of the negative effect on investment of the continuous diversion of a large part of the investible surplus to the service of the debt. From a social point of view the adjustment experience can be considered a failure as macro-economic policies were formulated without any consideration for their human impact and as the social measures implemented to mitigate the impact of such policies were limited in scope, poorly administered, and to a large extent distributionally regressive.

3 *Chile* (1981–1985)

Despite the persistence of high levels of unemployment, GDP per capita in Chile grew at an impressive average rate of 6.5 per cent a year during 1977–81. This achievement was facilitated by the substantial increase in foreign lending to the country (foreign debt grew during the same period from $5.2 to 15.5 billion) and by the sustained growth of world trade in the second half of the 1970s. During these years, the Chilean economy underwent major transformations in the areas of foreign trade and market orientation. All non-tariff barriers were eliminated, while import duties were reduced to 10 per cent; capital markets were liberalized and state enterprises privatized. This resulted in a ballooning of imports and widening trade gap, financed by massive borrowing from abroad. The world recession which began in 1981 found an economy much more vulnerable to external influences than in earlier years.

The external shock suffered in 1981/82 was considerable. Terms of trade deteriorated by 26 per cent between 1978 and 1982, while interest payments on the foreign debt grew fourfold in this period. As a result, the current account deficit almost quadrupled from 1980 to 1981, the year in which foreign lending dropped by 80 per cent.

To deal with this situation, the government introduced a package of monetary and fiscal measures aiming at reducing aggregate demand and imports by deflating the domestic economy. It is widely held that this package aggravated the effects of the external shock and that a more gradualistic and selective approach would have been more appropriate. Following the introduction of the package, output growth per capita slowed in 1981, falling in 1982 (− 15.5 per cent) and 1983 (− 2.2 per cent). An improvement in 1984 (3.9 per cent) was quickly reversed in 1985 (0.5 per cent). By 1985 GDP per capita was below both its 1980 and 1970 level.

The impact on households, and particularly on the poorest, was extremely severe. Open unemployment increased from 11.1 per cent in 1981 to 20.8 per cent in 1983 and to 17.7 per cent in 1984. Formal sector salaries declined by 10 per cent while inflation rose again—particularly for the goods purchased by the poor. For the Greater Santiago area, the income share of the bottom 40 per cent of the population declined between 1981 and 1982, while overall government expenditure was reduced.

Despite the economic deterioration and increase in poverty, there was not a major decline in child welfare over this period, while in certain sectors progress continued. Chile has had a strong historic commitment to the health and education of children. During this period, government social policy was purposely geared to moderating the effects of the recession and of adjustment on some of the weakest groups, the under-6s and pregnant and lactating mothers in particular. The major components of social policy were a series of public work schemes, which in 1983 occupied 13 per cent of the total labour force; subsidies to under-8s and pregnant women in conditions of extreme poverty; nutritional surveillance and supplementation programmes, for all under-6s; a nutritional rehabilitation programme for severely malnourished under-2s; and primary school feeding programmes. Social expenditure on these programmes increased despite the aggregate drop in government expenditure. Overall expenditure on health and education also declined.

On the whole, these programmes, particularly those focusing on integrated and targeted interventions in the areas of maternal and child health and nutrition, have been successful in protecting the poor from some of the adverse effects of recession and adjustment. The infant mortality rate continued its impressive decline (although at a slower rate), as did the incidence of immunizable diseases. Data on the incidence of malnutrition among pre-school children showed a continuous decline until 1983, when an increase of about 10 per cent was recorded. In 1984 the trend resumed its decline, although 1985 data show that malnutrition increased again for the under-2s. Particularly during the last two or three years, the extent of this broad success has been tempered by several signs of deterioration. Child mortality (ages 1–4) increased substantially in 1983 although it declined again in 1984, while in the same year the proportion of malnourished pregnant women rose as compared with 1982. Also, an official survey carried out in a low-income area of Greater Santiago shows that malnutrition among school-age children increased from 4.6 to 15.8 per cent between 1980 and 1983, while typhoid fever and hepatitis— diseases reflecting overall changes in environmental sanitation—show increased incidence during the 1981–84 period.

In conclusion, it appears that while serious doubts exist about the efficiency of the macro-economic stabilization measures adopted in 1981, the Chilean experience demonstrates that it is possible to protect the health and nutritional status of the most vulnerable groups in society (pre-school children and pregnant women) through highly targeted and integrated programmes. Ironically, the success of such programmes is underlined by the increases in the indices of malnutrition among children and pregnant women and of child mortality in 1983, a year in which such programmes suffered a contraction for budgetary reasons. In more general terms, however, the data of the last two years seem to question the feasibility of indefinitely sustaining the health and nutritional status of the population through highly targeted measures in a context of economic stagnation and growing poverty.

4 *Ghana* (1979–1985)

Ghana experienced a period of prolonged stagnation from the latter half of the 1960s until the 1980s. Per capita income fell by one-third from 1974 to 1982. A dramatic fall in production of the main export crop, cocoa, a severe deterioration in the terms of trade, and a near collapse of foreign aid and capital inflow sharply reduced import capacity. Food production did not keep pace with population. Inflation accelerated reaching three digits in the early 1980s. The economic stagnation was the combined effect of poor economic management and severely adverse external circumstances. From 1982–1984, this was compounded by acute drought.

The prolonged economic stagnation had large negative effects on the health and nutrition of many Ghanaians. By 1982 total food availability was only 68 per cent of minimum basic calorie requirements (with Chad, the lowest in Africa). Real incomes among low-income households fell until they were grossly inadequate to meet minimum food needs.

The social sectors were undermined by the collapse of tax revenue that accompanied the economic collapse and the massive exodus of trained manpower. By 1983 tax revenue had fallen to about 5 per cent of GDP, from 17 per cent 10 years earlier. In the health sector real expenditure per capita declined almost 80 per cent. Attendance at hospitals and health clinics dropped by about one-third between 1979 and 1984.

Worsening health and nutrition has resulted, especially among children. The infant mortality rate, which had fallen to about 80 per 1,000 in the mid-1970s, was around 100 in 1980 and had risen to 110–20 in 1983–84. All evidence points to a big deterioration in nutrition standards: the proportion of children whose weight for age was below the third percentile of the Harvard standard increased from 35 per cent in 1980 to 47 per cent in 1983 (with some small fall in 1984).

The households most acutely affected by the crisis were low-income urban households. In the rural areas, the position of small farmers in the Northern and Upper Regions is especially precarious; their health and welfare is markedly worse than elsewhere, according to every indicator. Within each category, children and lactating and nursing mothers are the worst affected.

In 1983 the government introduced a comprehensive package of economic policy reforms, backed by stand-by arrangements and compensatory finance from the Fund, the World Bank, and others. The Economic Recovery Programme has produced a remarkable turn-around in policies, towards improving the macro balances and rehabilitating parts of the economy. Despite some adverse circumstances, including the drought and the repatriation of about one million Ghanaians from Nigeria, it is already showing substantial achievements. Growth of per capita incomes has been positive during the last three years, while the inflation rate has been reduced to below 15 per cent a year. Foreign aid and capital inflows are starting to pick up and there has been a reduction in debt arrears. But debt service obligations are rising sharply and will be over 50 per cent of exports from 1985 to 1987.

While the recovery programme was designed primarily to deal with *economic* variables and targets, the government has initiated some programmes in the social sectors, recognizing the need to rehabilitate the social sectors and protect and restore human health and nutrition. The government is actively supporting the development of a comprehensive Human Recovery Programme.

Broadly, there are three elements to such a programme: action to protect the nutritional status of vulnerable groups and ensure food security; action to rehabilitate and restructure the social sectors; and action to introduce new low-cost interventions in health and nutrition (often cutting across sectors) to extend to Ghanaian children the benefits of the Child Survival and Development Revolution.

In the area of food security and food entitlements, the long-run aim is to secure sufficient growth in incomes and food availability so that low-income groups may meet their own nutritional needs. In the short run, the big nutritional gap requires emergency interim action, which might include: (*a*) measures to restore food production, especially among small farmers making food crops (including subsistence crops) a priority, along with export crops, for inputs, extension, and research; (*b*) targeted feeding programmes for children, and lactating and pregnant women, in deprived areas; (*c*) food-for-work schemes in the rural and urban areas to provide additional employment and help rehabilitate infrastructure, especially water, sanitation, and refuse disposal services; and (*d*) support of small-scale activities.

In the social sectors, action is needed to increase the availability of essential recurrent inputs, such as drugs, school books, and basic spare parts; to rehabilitate capital equipment, using community action and food-for-work schemes; and to help halt the outflow of personnel by restoring working conditions.

Specific additional measures—including immunization and diarrhoea control—are necessary to strengthen the health support, especially for children and pregnant and lactating women. These measures are a vital complement to additional food in improving and monitoring basic nutrition.

The prolonged recession produced a collapse in major sources of funding including a dwindling of community action and support, a near-evaporation of the tax base, and a diminution of foreign capital inflows to a very low level. Reversing these downward trends represents potential for financing the recovery programme. Restructuring of expenditures within the social sectors by redirecting resources from less important areas would also contribute to financing the programme.

Community action is a vital element, not only for the resources it potentially offers in labour, organization, and materials but also for the mobilization of a self-reliant commitment to meeting the whole community's most basic needs. To support such action, the establishment of a fund to provide financial support for projects initiated and partly financed by the village or urban community is suggested.

5 *Jamaica* (1978–1985)

Jamaica has experienced prolonged economic decline since the early 1970s. GDP per capita fell over 30 per cent from 1972 to 1980. Although it rose from 1981–83, it has since fallen back to the 1980 level. One major cause of the economic problems was the weak performance of bauxite and alumina exports, which accounted for 60–70 per cent of exports over most of the period.

In the 1970s, the government of Michael Manley and the People's National Party had a strong commitment to maintaining real wages and employment and protecting vulnerable groups. But this was not sustainable, in view of the economic decline and the large imbalances emerging. Government expenditure rose to 40 per cent of GDP in 1980–81, the budget deficit was 17 per cent of GDP, while the current account deficit was over $200 million. The Manley government was reluctant to undertake the stringent stabilization measures required by the IMF, but unable to find finance to manage without the Fund. A succession of agreements with the Fund from 1977 were suspended because of failures on performance criteria, culminating in the 1980 'IMF' election won by the Jamaica Labour Party headed by Edward Seaga. The Seaga government found it much easier to reach agreement with the Fund, in the absence of philosophical and political differences, and a rather relaxed stand-by agreement was concluded in 1981. The foreign exchange problem was eased by inflow of official capital, but exports continued to decline and the fiscal and current account deficits to mount. Consequently, at the beginning of 1984, the government concluded a strongly deflationary agreement with the Fund, including a large devaluation and restrictions on government expenditure and credit. This led to an improvement in the budget deficit (with a rise in revenue and a fall in expenditure), and a fall in GDP per capita in 1984 and 1985. The trade deficit showed an improvement compared with 1981 to 1983, but was still substantially bigger than from 1977–79.

In the 1970s vulnerable groups suffered from falling real incomes and high unemployment, but were partially protected by government expenditure on the social sectors, food subsidies, price controls, and employment schemes. In the 1980s, downward pressure on real wages has been worsened by reduced price controls and subsidies, and the impact of the large devaluations on imported foods (which include the basic cereals consumed by the poor). Unemployment has remained very high, at 26 per cent overall in 1984, with over 50 per cent among the 14–24 age group, and over 66 per cent among women of this age.

For 1984, it was estimated that a five-person household with two wage-earners spending 75 per cent of their income on food would be able to buy only 50 per cent of a minimum basket of goods, that would meet dietary requirements at an acceptable level. The prices of the minimum basket increased by 45 per cent from October 1984 to March 1986, with a higher increase for basic imported cereals, cornmeal, flour, and rice. From September 1983 to July 1985 the increase in the minimum wage did not keep pace with the price of the minimum basket. The government introduced a Food Aid Programme in July 1984 designed to protect the vulnerable. The target—school children, pregnant and nursing women, infants, the elderly, and very poor people—covers half the population. The scheme is not adequate in benefits per recipient to meet needs and has been subject to administrative problems.

The deflationary policies led to a decline in real government expenditure of 29 per cent (1981/82–1985/86). Social sector expenditure was cut by more, with the share of total expenditure going to the social services falling from 31 per cent to 24 per cent over the same period. Education expenditure per head of the population aged 0–14 declined by 40 per cent, and per capita health expenditure by 33 per cent. There were large cuts in expenditure on water and housing. The expenditure cuts have led to declining real incomes of staff, shortages of recurrent inputs, and neglect of repair and maintenance. Some schools have been closed down and hospitals and health clinics downgraded. Some charges have been introduced for health services.

National nutrition surveys show declining levels of nutrition among children. The proportion of children showing some signs of malnutrition rose from 38 per cent in 1978 to 41 per cent in 1985. This decline was experienced in both rural and urban areas. The trend is confirmed by evidence of admission to the island's major children's hospital, with the number of children admitted suffering from malnutrition more than doubling from 1978 to 1985 and a threefold rise in the number suffering from malnutrition-related gastro-enteritis. The sharpest increases occurred in 1984 and 1985.

The experience of Jamaica in the 1970s showed the difficulty of sustaining social services and real incomes and employment in the medium term in the face of acute economic problems. In the 1980s, tough stabilization programmes have caused declining incomes and rising food prices and have cut deeply into social services. Vulnerable groups, which comprise as much as half the population, have suffered most. The deterioration is indicated by evidence of rising malnutrition among children. While the stabilization programmes of the 1980s have had heavy social costs, they have not so far provided the basis for economic prosperity. Taking the 1980s as a whole, the imbalances—both external and internal—have been worse than in the Manley years, and incomes per capita have been declining in the years since 1983.

6 *Peru* (1977–1985)

Over the 1977–85 period there was a significant change in development policies in Peru. From 1969, import-substitution, land reform, and increased involvement in the economic sphere represented the major policy thrusts. During 1969–75 output per capita increased on average at 3.2 per cent per annum. However in 1976 and 1977 growth slowed considerably, while the balance of payments deteriorated. The policy stance shifted towards a more orthodox approach. Two packages inspired by this general view were introduced with the assistance of the IMF: in 1977/78 and again in 1982/84.

The 1977/78 package was intended to reduce aggregate demand drastically, through a sharp contraction in the budget deficit, wage adjustments below the rate of inflation, and monetary restrictions. The budget deficit was reduced through cuts in public sector salaries, investment, and food subsidies, and increases in tariffs and charges. Measures aimed to expand the supply of tradeables included devaluation and establishing positive real interest rates. Measures were taken to increase the role of the market, including trade liberalization and privatization of state enterprises.

This adjustment package led to a marked contraction of GDP per capita in 1978 and to a significant rise in inflation. After an improvement in output growth and external accounts in 1979 and 1980, the situation started deteriorating again in 1981, partly because of the sharp increase in international interest rates, the slow-down of world trade, and the 1983 drought.

By 1985 GDP per capita had fallen to the level of the 1960s, with a cumulative decline over the 1977–85 period close to 20 per cent. Meanwhile inflation had escalated from 30 per cent in 1977 to 160 per cent in 1985, while debt servicing obligations had reached 140 per cent of export earnings in 1985. Open unemployment increased from 5 to 10 per cent between 1977 and 1984, while underemployment grew from 48 to 54 per cent. Formal sector wages showed a continuous decline throughout the period. At the end of 1985, they were equal to 64 per cent of their 1979 level and to 44 per cent of that of 1973. Rural incomes probably deteriorated because of declines in output and relative prices. An already highly skewed income distribution deteriorated further.

Social policy did not shelter the poor from the hardship caused by the economic decline. Total social expenditure dropped from an observed 26 per cent of total expenditure over the 1968–76 period to 18 per cent over the 1977–85 period. The health share was roughly constant, but expenditure remained heavily concentrated in urban areas. The share of education fell from an average of 20 per cent in 1968–76 to 12 per cent over 1977–84, with expenditure on university education growing from 35 to 43 per cent between 1977 and 1983. Food and fuel subsidies were completely eliminated. While eliminating substantial wastage—a considerable part of the subsidy benefited the urban middle class—the lack of any cushioning measures for low-income households led to a negative impact on the urban poor.

Despite the lack of data on IMR and other social indicators, there is agreement that the human cost of recession and adjustment has been high. Average food availability per capita declined by 26 per cent, while there are indications that child malnutrition sharply increased in the southern part of the country between 1980 and 1983. The incidence of several communicable diseases increased, as did the number of deaths due to tuberculosis. Although primary enrolment rates did not decline, over 1977–83 there was an increase in the rates of repetition and drop-out, together with a widespread decline in the quality of education. In summary, the policy approach followed during the 1977–85 period proved highly inefficient from both an economic and social point of view.

In July 1985 the newly elected government introduced more expansionary policies aimed at reactivating domestic production and introducing important elements of redistribution in favour of low-income households. Salary increases above inflation were granted, particularly at the bottom of the pay scale, with the purpose of expanding demand and, through it, output and capacity utilization. To keep inflation under control, the government sharply reduced the interest rate (in parallel with the decline in inflation) and guaranteed a stable exchange rate for essential inputs, while prices have temporarily been frozen. Credit, fiscal, and pricing policies were used both to sustain key production sectors (like agriculture, non-traditional exports, and the informal sector) and to trigger a redistribution of income in favour of the rural and urban marginal population. Public works schemes have also been organized. In order to secure the foreign exchange and credit needed for the success of this strategy, payments on foreign public debt has been limited to 10 per cent of export earnings, while restrictions were temporarily imposed on capital exports and profit repatriation.

Social expenditure is projected to increase and be restructured in favour of underserved areas and towards low-cost basic services with extensive coverage like immunization, essential drugs, food supplementation, and primary education.

While it is certainly too soon to assess the performance of the new package, and while many questions remain about its future viability, it is worth noting that during its first 12 months the employment situation in Lima eased while real wages increased and output grew at an estimated 4 per cent. Furthermore, inflation was sharply reduced, and the fiscal deficit remained under control. Overall growth in 1986 is estimated to be 8 per cent, a major change in performance compared with previous years.

7   *The Philippines* (1981–1985)

The Philippines economy has been subject to the common economic shocks that have confronted so many countries—the two oil price increases in the 1970s, high interest rates, the world economic recession, and deteriorating terms of trade in the 1980s. Again like many other countries, the Philippines 'adjusted' to the first oil shock mainly by borrowing, and so was faced by escalating debt service obligations in the 1980s, which by 1984 took nearly 42 per cent of total government expenditure. External and internal imbalances grew to unsustainable proportions. By 1982, the current account deficit was 8.1 per cent of GNP, the budget deficit had risen to 4.3 per cent of GNP, and the inflation rate was over 10 per cent. These developments, together with evaporation of confidence for political reasons following Benigno Aquino's assassination, led to capital flight and rapid depletion of international reserves.

Deflationary stabilization measures were initiated in 1983, and in December 1984 the government reached agreement with the IMF. The programme included restrictions on government expenditures and increases in taxation,

controls on credit creation, and reforms in the areas of tariffs, public investment, and energy.

The stabilization efforts were successful in terms of the conventional balances: the current account deficit has almost been eliminated, following very
severe falls in imports (of 19 per cent in 1984 and 16 per cent in 1985); the
budget deficit was reduced by 60 per cent; and the inflation rate was reduced
to 5 per cent. But the achievement was at the expense of growth, employment,
and real incomes. GNP per capita fell to its 1975 level. Employment fell in
every sector except services. The unemployment rate rose. Real earnings have
fallen very substantially for every category of worker and in every industry—
by 46 per cent on average for all urban wage and salary earners from 1982 to
1985, and by 48 per cent among own-account workers; in the rural areas the
fall was 31 per cent for wage and salary workers and 41 per cent for own-
account workers.

These developments occurred in a society which already was highly unequal
with considerable poverty. The Gini coefficient was around 0.5 in 1980 and
rose further in the 1980s. The highest incidence of poverty is to be found in
the rural areas, where about three-quarters of the poorest groups (bottom 30
per cent of the income distribution) are located. Low-income rural households
include small farmers, tenants, labourers, and small fishermen. The urban
poor are concentrated in Manila, mainly working in the informal sector.
Declining real wages and employment opportunities in the 1980s meant that
an increasing number of households fell below a poverty threshold. On average,
in the third quarter of 1985, real wages of wage and salary earners were one-
quarter of the World Bank estimates of a poverty threshold for a six-person
household, while rural wages were 22 per cent of the minimum.

Inequalities in income distribution are paralleled by inequitable distribution
of public resources. In the health sector, for example, government subsidies to
private hospitals for heart, kidney, and lung diseases, which cater to upper-
income groups, were five times as great as the total allocation for primary
health care.

The stabilization efforts involved cuts in government expenditure, which
fell overall by 17 per cent per capita between 1979 and 1984. Education
expenditure per capita in 1984 was 30 per cent below the 1979 level, and
health and community amenities fell by one-third.

The human impact of these developments was shown by rising rates of
malnutrition—(the proportion of seriously underweight under-5s rose from 17
per cent in 1982 to 22 per cent in 1985); by a slow-down in the fall in infant
mortality rates, and a sharp rise in infant mortality in the worst-affected region
of Negros; reduced prevalence of contraceptives and a deceleration in the
slow-down in the crude birth rate; a deterioration in the quality and access to
elementary education, with falling participation, retention, and cohort survival
rates, and an increase in repetition rates; and an increase in street children
begging, stealing, and scavenging for a living; and a rise in the crime rate.

Both the extent and incidence of poverty and the weakness of the Philippines economy is in large part due to the development strategy adopted in the 1970s, which favoured industry over agriculture, and large scale over small scale. The terms of trade and effective protection were strongly biased against agriculture. There was a large gap between urban and rural incomes, with income per worker in industry estimated to be over five times that in agriculture in 1983. Adjustment policies to protect the vulnerable require a reversal in this long-term development strategy.

The elements of a strategy of adjustment with a human face in the Philippine context include: (*a*) replacement of stabilization by an expansionary adjustment process; (*b*) renegotiation of debt servicing so that development objectives are no longer subordinated to debt servicing obligations; (*c*) adoption of a long-term development strategy to favour agricultural development and the rural sector, which requires removal of the strong biases in past government policy against the agricultural sector. This strategy is a necessary aspect of tackling poverty given the concentration of poverty in the rural areas; (*d*) enhancing the impact of the social services, by reallocation within them to meet priority needs, focusing on low-cost, community-based interventions; (*e*) enforcing environmental laws; and (*f*) closer surveillance and monitoring of the impact of adjustment programmes.

8   South Korea (1979–1981)

After a 15-year period of uninterrupted growth during which output expanded at an average rate of 9.9 per cent a year, in 1979 the South Korean economy started facing severe growth and balance of payment problems. Already by the end of 1978 export volume was stagnating, while the oil price increases of the late 1970s raised the country's oil bill from $2.3 billion in 1978 to $5.8 billion in 1980, an increase equal to almost 6 per cent of GNP. The stagnation of world trade between 1980 and 1983 further reduced the growth potential of the South Korean economy.

The sharp deterioration of the external sector was aggravated by the assassination in October 1979 of President Park, which created a climate of social unrest and political uncertainty, and by a 22 per cent drop in agricultural production in 1980 owing to adverse weather.

As a result of these combined adversities, by mid-1979 the South Korean economy went into recession. Seasonally adjusted GNP declined during the last two quarters of 1979 and continued declining throughout 1980. Recovery began in 1981. However, the increase in non-agricultural GNP was only 3 per cent, far lower than in the past. Between 1979 and 1981 the current account balance recorded deficits of $4.1, 5.3, and 4.6 billion, while the consumer price index increased during the same period to levels oscillating between 20 and 30 per cent.

Even this relatively short recession produced visible effects in terms of social welfare. Although far from severe, such effects represented a clear early warning of far greater deterioration which could have occurred if the crisis had not been well managed. Per capita real income declined by about 10 per cent between 1979 and 1981. In addition, relative income distribution showed clear signs of deterioration. As a result, average calorie and protein intake declined by 4.4 per cent and 3.5 per cent respectively in 1980, while between 1979 and 1981 the weight and height of children of 5, 9, and 12 years of age grew at lower rates than previously.

The stabilization–adjustment package introduced in late 1980 avoided further deterioration in social welfare. Four major policy thrusts were at its centre: (*a*) promoting price stability through tight monetary and fiscal measures and incomes policy; (*b*) promoting economic and import liberalization and allowing market principles to play a larger role in the economy; (*c*) encouraging structural adjustment towards technology-intensive sectors; and (*d*) preserving and, where possible, improving social welfare in the face of the recession and of the adjustments just described.

Within the social sector, the response to the crisis consisted in the introduction of new programmes and a sharp acceleration of old ones. Among them: (*a*) In 1979 a medical assistance programme was organized for the lowest income groups. Their members were entitled to receive medical care (particularly maternal and child care) which they otherwise would have been unable to afford. The scheme (covering 8 per cent of the population in 1984) is completely free for those unable to work (the aged, chronically sick, etc.) while the programme pays 50 per cent of hospital costs and all out-patient expenses for low-income people able to work. (*b*) Health insurance coverage was extended significantly, i.e. from 10.5 per cent of the population in 1978 to 29.5 per cent in 1981. By the end of 1984, 41.3 per cent of the population were covered. (*c*) Public works programmes were organized as a countercyclical measure to provide employment to the poor during crisis periods. Expenditure on such programmes jumped from 15 billion won in 1978 to 34 billion in 1979, declining to 13 billion in 1982 as recovery progressed. In 1980 the employment creation effect of the programme was estimated at 9.4 million man-days. (*d*) Direct income transfers were made available to those unable to work, who could not benefit from expanded employment opportunities. In-kind assistance was made available to the poor in the form of cereals, cash assistance for fuel, and tuition exemption for their children. In 1982 about 2 million persons received benefits from this programme. (*e*) Public expenditure on education grew throughout the 1979–84 period. Similar increases occurred in public expenditure housing.

The policy package was broadly successful in achieving its goals. Inflation declined rapidly, GNP growth and income distribution improved, and the current account deficit narrowed substantially. In terms of social welfare, the measures have been successful on a double account. First, by rapidly restoring growth and improving income distribution they have avoided a further diffusion of poverty and its persistence over time. Secondly, by deliberately sheltering the poor, the vulnerable, and the children from the recession, they have mitigated—or completely prevented—its negative effects. Indeed, the percentage of absolutely poor and the infant mortality rate continued to decline at historical rates during the years of the recession.

The South Korean experience shows that the adverse social impact of the world recession can be reduced through deliberate policy measures taken by the country concerned, and that such measures can successfully be combined with adjustment measures designed to restructure the economy and restore economic growth.

9   Sri Lanka (1978–1983)

From independence (and before), Sri Lanka was strongly committed to developing a welfare state. Policies included a sizeable and universal food subsidy, and free and universal health and education services. As a result performance on basic needs was outstanding in relation to per capita income. But from the late 1950s Sri Lanka experienced slow growth, chronic balance of payments problems, and rising unemployment.

The new government introduced major policy changes from November 1977, designed to transform the economy to an outward orientation with a much greater role for the market. Policy reforms included devaluation and import liberalization, reduced public sector monopolies, and improved producer prices for farmers. Following the reforms, the rate of growth accelerated to 4.7 per cent a year (1978–84), compared with 2.9 per cent a year in the period 1970–77. Investment rose as a share of GDP. However, domestic savings remained sluggish and much of the investment was foreign-financed. Employment rose and the unemployment rate fell by half, although unemployment remains high among the young and more educated. The inflation rate accelerated. The increased rate of growth of output was shared by all sectors of the economy. Domestic (non-plantation) agriculture grew by 5 per cent annually, and Sir Lanka came close to self-sufficiency in rice production after having been a heavy importer. There was not much structural change: the industrial sector remained small, some of industry was eliminated by competition from imports, and there was no significant growth of maufactured exports.

Income distribution, however, deteriorated. Real wages in the organized sector fell for all categories when deflated by an appropriate price index. Real wages fell (although by less) in most parts of the informal sector, but probably not in paddy cultivation or in construction. The lower deciles fared worst: the share in income of the lowest 40 per cent of spending units fell from 19.3 per cent in 1973 to 15.3 per cent in 1981/82. In 1979 the government restricted the food subsidy and then replaced it by targeted food stamps. These did not retain their real value with the rise in food prices that ensued. The targeting was not altogether successful in confining benefits to lower-income groups because of widespread underdeclaration of income.

There is evidence that while the infant mortality rate has continued declining, the combined effects of falling real wages, rising food prices, and the food stamp system have led to increases in the already high rates of malnutrition. Comparing 1980/82 with 1974/75 the extent of stunting decreased, but wasting increased for all age groups in the rural areas. The bottom 30 per cent of the income distribution have had an uninterrupted decline in their calorie consumption since 1969/70. The top 50 per cent have improved their intake over the period as a whole. Per capita consumption of rice, wheat flour, bread, sugar, and coconuts all fell among the lowest 20 per cent of the population between 1978/79 and 1981/82, while per capita consumption increased among the top 60 per cent.

Expenditure on the social sectors as a whole fell from 33 per cent of the budget in 1977 to 22 per cent in 1983, this fall being largely due to the decline in expenditure on the food subsidy. Real per capita expenditure remained roughly constant, with a rise in capital expenditure and a fall in recurrent. Both the health and education sectors have suffered from shortage of finance for repairs and maintenance, and for inputs such as drugs and school-books. Falling real incomes have led to low morale and staff shortages in the public sector. In health, doctors have been permitted to combine public with private practice, which has led to a decline in the quality of public sector care. There has been a big rise in drug expenditure since the monopoly of the State Pharmaceutical Corporation was ended. There has been some switch away from expenditure on basic services. In education, the share of tertiary education has risen (from 7 to 16 per cent of the education budget, 1977–83), and in health, patient care (curative) services have risen from 62 to 74 per cent. The 1970s as a whole saw a rise in primary education and an increase in literacy, but from 1979 to 1981 it appears that there was some fall off in both.

In the Sri Lankan case, adjustment policies have been associated with an increase in economic growth, reduced unemployment, and an improved external position. However, inflation accelerated and the budget remained in deficit. The policies, together with changes in the food subsidy, have also been associated with declining real wages and rising malnutrition in the rural areas. Some of the progress achieved in increasing participation in education in the 1970s seem to have been halted, and possibly reversed. In the health sector, there has been rising investment in new buildings and sophisticated equipment, but morale and possibly standards in basic health services have fallen with restricted recurrent expenditures and increasing private practice. In the 1950s and 1960s, Sri Lanka was spectacularly successful in meeting human needs. With very low per capita income, literacy was high, and life expectancy near developed country levels. This achievement is being undermined by the policy changes of recent years.

10 Zimbabwe (1980–1984)

At the time of Independence in April 1980, Zimbabwe inherited a typical underdeveloped economy further distorted by racial inequalities. For several years previously, GDP per capita had fallen because of trade sanctions and—later—the disruptions caused by the War of Liberation, among other factors.

After Independence the government embarked on a series of major long-term reforms to correct the distortions inherited from the previous regime and to stimulate the economy. Both education and health received strong support while being reoriented in favour of the lower-income strata. As the land question was central to the liberation struggle, a major land resettlement programme for the landless was launched with the assistance of international donors, while significant efforts were subsequently undertaken to improve the productivity of small farmers by enhancing their access to credit, inputs, technical assistance, and marketing facilities. At the macro-economic level the economy was stimulated by the removal of sanctions, large wage increases, and a good agricultural season. GDP per capita for 1980–81 grew at an average annual rate of 9 per cent, real wages increased by 27 per cent in real terms, and formal sector employment grew by 5 per cent after five years of continuous decline.

The rapid expansion of the economy and of public expenditure produced growing strains on the current account and budget deficits. The situation might have remained manageable if two powerful exogenous shocks had not affected the economy towards the end of 1981. First, an extremely severe drought, lasting from 1981/82 until the end of 1984, which depressed export earnings and rural incomes and led to considerable imports of foods. Secondly, the world recession negatively affected the demand for Zimbabwean exports. In 1982, the country entered into a severe recession which was aggravated by the drought. Both fiscal and current account deficits increased substantially in 1982 and 1983.

In 1982 and 1983, the government introduced a series of adjustment measures comprising wage increases smaller than inflation, a reduction in subsidies and an increase in administered prices, devaluation of the Zimbabwean dollar and temporary suspension of profit and dividend remittances, ceilings on government and domestic credit expansion, and an increase in interest rates. This restrictionary package has to be viewed against the very strong expansionary policies adopted at Independence.

Most of the programmes launched after Independence in the areas of health, nutrition, education, water, and support for small farmers were sustained, or expanded, or suffered minor modifications during the period of the drought and adjustment. In addition, a major drought relief programme was launched in 1982/83 and further expanded in 1983/84. Free health care was maintained for those earning less than 150 Zimbabwean dollars a month (although inflation reduced the number of eligible beneficiaries), while the immunization and diarrhoeal disease control programmes rapidly expanded. A children's supplementary feeding programme was instituted, providing a daily energy-rich meal to undernourished children in rural areas. At the peak of the drought the scheme provided food to over a quarter of a million children. Similarly, efforts were sustained in the education sector, where communities were increasingly called on to contribute inputs in kind and labour.

While external assistance played an important role, government social expenditure expanded to support these efforts. Health expenditure, for instance, increased by no less than 70 per cent in real terms between 1980 and 1982. While it declined by 9 per cent in 1983 it increased again by 13 per cent in 1984, stabilizing in 1985. The fantastic increase of the first two years was thus not reversed by the recession and adjustment programme. A growing proportion of this expenditure was devoted to preventive as opposed to curative services.

Thanks to these measures the economic costs of recession, adjustment and drought were not translated into substantial human costs. Real salaries fell between 1982 and 1984, cancelling out the gains of the previous two years and there was a reduction of about 20 per cent in the real value of food subsidies between 1981 and 1984, while the low-income Consumer Price Index increased by 23 per cent a year in 1983 and 1984. But despite these severe economic costs, it appears that the infant mortality rate has declined continuously since Independence while scattered evidence suggests that there has probably been no significant change in the prevalence of undernutrition amongst rural children (Davis and Sanders in vol. ii, ch. 10) despite an extremely severe drought and the decline in household incomes observed in 1982–84. Primary school enrolment has continued to rise at a rapid rate.

In 1984 a timid recovery began that grew stronger in 1985: the drought finally ended and there was a substantial increase in production (and marketed output) of small farmers.

In conclusion, while some questions remain about the viability of the present macro-economic balances, the Zimbabwean experience shows that despite passing on some of the economic cost of adjustment to households, particularly in the formal sector, the adjustment package adopted managed to sustain continued improvements in the well-being of children, while some of the long-term reforms initiated after Independence contributed to a resumption of growth after two to three years.

III Adjustment lessons

In view of the variety of situations presented above, it is not easy to summarize the adjustment experiences of the 10 countries. Nevertheless there seem to be a few general lessons worth distilling:

1. *The shocks to which the majority of the countries had to adjust were of an exogenous nature,* i.e. the results of changes in either the international environment or in

climatic conditions, both factors beyond the control of national authorities. Most countries faced deterioration in terms of trade either because of the fall in export prices (bauxite in Jamaica, copper for Chile and Peru, sugar in the Philippines, etc.) or because of increases in import prices (oil for South Korea, Brazil, and Zimbabwe). Changes in the international financial market (epitomized by the rise in interest rates and decline in lending) affected all of them, and in particular those such as the Latin American nations with large debts.

Drought was also an important factor causing economic decline in Zimbabwe (1982–84), Ghana (1982–84), Botswana (1980–85), and parts of Peru (1983).

Domestic policies were an important contributory factor in a number of countries (most notably, Ghana, 1974–83; Peru, 1977–85; Chile, 1981–85; and the Philippines, 1981–85). However, the crisis most of these countries had to face was predominantly of an exogenous nature. This important conclusion requires full consideration by the international community in considering adjustment programmes and the amount of financial support to be provided.

2. *Adjustment is necessary.* Whatever the nature of the shock affecting the economy, countries have to adjust to a changing environment. Failure to do so normally entails huge losses of output and human welfare. In South Korea, timely introduction (in 1980) of a growth-oriented package combining elements of structural adjustment and protection of the vulnerable permitted resumption of growth and social progress after a recession which, because of the policies adopted, lasted only 18 months. In Ghana, on the contrary, postponement of needed economic adjustments was an important factor contributing to the continuous decline observed between 1974 and 1983.

The issue, therefore, is not whether to adjust or not, but how.

3. *Growth oriented approaches with structural adjustment have been adopted successfully.* While several of the 10 countries analysed followed predominantly contractionary policies others adopted more growth-oriented approaches incorporating elements of structural adjustment, and in some cases of human protection (Table 5.1). South Korea, Botswana (1983–85), Zimbabwe, and Peru (1985–86) managed to combine structural adjustment, economic growth, and protection of the human dimension, although Zimbabwe's economy might require further adjustment, while the results of the recent Peruvian experiment are not fully established. These countries avoided the dismal combination of depressed output and deterioration in health and nutritional status of children which is to be found in Ghana (1974–82), Peru (1977–85), Jamaica (1981–85), and the Philippines.

4. *Growth-oriented adjustment is necessary but not sufficient* to protect vulnerable groups. Countries like Brazil and Sri Lanka managed either to sustain growth or to resume it shortly after the introduction of appropriate macro-economic policies. The lack of a coherent and adequate effort to protect vulnerable groups during the adjustment process, however, meant that some deterioration

T A B L E 5.1   *Typology of the adjustment experience of the 10-country sample*

Social policy	Macro-economic policy		
	No adjustment policy	Predominantly contractionary	Predominantly growth-oriented and structural
Vulnerable protected	Jamaica ('72–'80)	Botswana ('81–'82), Chile ('81–'85)	South Korea ('81–'83), Zimbabwe ('80–'85), Botswana ('83–'85), Peru ('85–'86)
Vulnerable not well protected	Ghana ('74–'82)	Peru ('75–'85), Philippines ('81–'85), Jamaica ('81–'85)	Brazil ('81–'85), Sri Lanka ('78–'84), Ghana ('83–'85)

in human conditions was evident in these two countries despite sustained growth in resources.

5. *In the short–medium term, the well-being of children and other vulnerable groups can be protected and even improved with the adoption of appropriate targeted programmes*, even during periods of economic decline. However, there are limits to what this approach can achieve in the medium–long run, when growth becomes essential.

In Chile, for instance, highly targeted health and nutritional programmes focusing on pre-school children and pregnant and lactating women succeeded in achieving a continuous decline in infant and child mortality and malnutrition in the first part of the 1980s, despite a severe drop in output and growing unemployment. Since 1983–84, however, there have been increasing signs of growing malnutrition and even increases in child mortality (in 1983) as targeted interventions may no longer be sufficient to offset the decline in household resources caused by macro-economic developments.

Clearly, richer, better administered, and more equity-oriented countries can benefit from this approach for longer periods of time than resource-starved and poorly managed countries. Nonetheless, in the latter countries too there is scope for promoting some key programmes in favour of the poor by reorienting the use of existing resources.

6. *Most programmes aimed at protecting the poor are relatively inexpensive* in terms of total government expenditure and GDP. At the peak of the drought in 1984, the Drought Relief Programme in Zimbabwe barely absorbed 2 per cent of total government expenditure, while the public work programmes implemented during the recession of 1979 in South Korea took less than 1 per cent of government expenditure. The extremely successful nutrition and

rehabilitation programmes in Chile involved only a small fraction of government expenditure.

7. *Foreign finance is important* in facilitating a smooth programme of adjustment. While the availability of medium–long term finance in sufficient amount allows the investment necessary for structural adjustment, as in the case of Ghana between 1983–85, external assistance (often to meet foreign exchange costs of imported inputs) for specific programmes designed to protect the poor also proved an important element for the successful protection of human conditions. Eighteen per cent of the successful Expanded Programme of Immunization in Zimbabwe (in 1983), and half the cost of the Drought Relief Programme in Botswana was met by external donors.

The country experience therefore shows that more positive alternatives *are* possible. Reduced output and declining standards of health and nutrition need not accompany adjustment. The country stories provide powerful insight into the sort of programmes that are likely to ensure positive achievement, i.e. adjustment with a human face. These policies and programmes are analysed in depth in Part II.

PART II

An Alternative Approach: Growth-oriented
Adjustment with a Human Face

6

An Overview of the Alternative Approach

Giovanni Andrea Cornia, Richard Jolly, and Frances Stewart

I Introduction

The first part of this book has shown the inadequacy of conventional approaches to adjustment from the perspective of protecting the vulnerable and promoting growth. In many countries, the position of the poor has worsened during adjustments, with deterioration in nutrition levels and educational achievements of children. Moreover, investment rates have frequently also slowed or fallen. With reduced expenditure on both human and physical resources, the prospects for economic growth in the medium term have worsened. It is clear that alternative adjustment packages are needed.

Alternative adjustment packages—which protect the human condition while restoring economic growth, or 'adjustment with a human face'—*are* possible. Some countries have managed to avoid many of the negative effects typically associated with adjustment and succeeded in maintaining and even improving standards of health and nutrition, resuming growth after only a short time. Developments in these countries provide some important insights into how to achieve a satisfactory alternative. This chapter builds on these insights to provide an overview of the major elements involved in adjustment with a human face, each of which is then developed in more depth in a subsequent chapter.

II Adjustment with a human face: the objective

The objective of the alternative approach is to combine adjustment with protection of the vulnerable and the restoration of economic growth. The two aspects of the objective are closely related, though not the same. An emphasis on growth is far from sufficient to ensure the protection of the vulnerable in the long run, and may often involve even greater pressures on them in the short run. In the short run, it is possible to protect the vulnerable without economic growth by careful policy interventions targeted towards the poor and needy. But prolonged economic stagnation undermines the possibility of sustaining the position of the poor, as the experience of Ghana, Jamaica, and Chile indicate. Consequently the restoration of economic growth in the medium term must be a critically important part of achieving adjustment with a human face. Moreover, the health, nutrition, and education of a nation's children is one of the most important determinants of its economical potential, so protecting the vulnerable is also essential for promoting growth in the short as well as the medium and long term.

In the early 1980s, the dominant emphasis of adjustment packages was on securing a sustainable balance of payments position and non-inflationary domestic conditions. It was too readily assumed that the achievement of sustainable balance, on both external and domestic fronts, would be both necessary and sufficient for the restoration of economic growth, while the fate of vulnerable groups was considered to be a matter for national governments to deal with in their own way and not an issue of adjustment policy. Experience has shown that none of these assumptions can any longer be accepted without question, and there have been many calls for a broader approach to adjustment.

1. *Growth-oriented adjustment.* The evidence of declining per capita income and cuts in investment rates shows that the conventional approach to adjustment has not restored growth as expected. It is now widely accepted that for economic growth additional policies and in many cases more finance will be needed. In the autumn of 1985 US Secretary of State James Baker led an initiative to emphasize more growth-oriented adjustment, in contrast to the prevailing approach to adjustment, and this initiative has been taken up by the major financial institutions.

2. *The human dimension.* There is a more urgent need to incorporate the well-being of vulnerable groups into the objectives of adjustment policy. The evidence summarized in Chapter 1 shows how standards of health and nutrition may be undermined unless a specific attempt is made to protect the vulnerable during adjustment. Growth alone is not sufficient, as the example of Brazil in the 1970s and 1980s and Sri Lanka in the 1980s has indicated. To ensure that low-income and vulnerable groups, and especially children, do not suffer permanent damage, protection of their basic living standards has to become an explicit objective of adjustment, and programmes must be devised and monitored on this account. This objective should be formally incorporated in international statements of adjustment policy and in the agreements with every individual country which endorses the objective.

3. *Requirements of satisfactory adjustment.* The characteristics of desirable adjustment need to be considered carefully from two perspectives. First, experience of the 1980s has shown that many countries have 'adjusted' by adopting stabilization measures. The reduction of imbalances—external and internal—can and has been achieved by reducing expenditure, output, and imports, so that a low-level equilibrium is achieved, associated with a decline in GDP, investment, and employment, and decreasing capacity utilization. But although the imbalances have been eliminated, the ensuing economic situation is in no way satisfactory. Satisfactory adjustment involves restructuring the

economy so that major imbalances are eliminated *at a desirable level of output, investment, and human needs protection*, with the economy in shape for future growth and sustained development.

Secondly, it must be stressed that adjustment must take place in the industrialized countries and in the international system as well as in the developing economies. External imbalances in an economy arise from the interaction between it and the world economy. Major national imbalances may emerge from changes in the world economy, without any deterioration in domestic economic management. This might occur with a fall in commodity prices, a rise in interest rates, a fall in the market for manufactures, or a decline in capital inflows. If large changes of this sort occur—as of course they all did in the 1980s—and if they show no signs of reversal, national economies do have to adjust to them. But viewed from the perspective of international economic management, the appropriate adjustment may not be (certainly not entirely) in the national economies where the major and unsustainable imbalances emerge, but in the international conditions which gave rise to them—i.e. in the factors determining the world level of demand, commodity prices, interest rates, capital flows, etc. The extent of adjustment needed at the national level then depends on how far international conditions change. The magnitude of national adjustment necessary may be very different from the magnitude desirable.

The deterioration in world economic conditions over the last decade has been substantial, and it seems likely that this deterioration will not be reversed—in the short to medium term—to any substantial extent. It follows that countries do have to adjust to these conditions. Although the bulk of this book is concerned with exploring better forms of *national* adjustment in the developing countries, the need for adjustment in *international* conditions is of paramount importance because for many countries the extent of adjustment required under present conditions is clearly excessive, and for some may not be possible without intolerable sacrifice—sacrifice not only of human and social conditions, but also of democracy. For, in the words of Brazil's President Sarney, 'A debt paid in poverty is an account paid in democracy'.

Chapter 15 briefly explores mechanisms for reforming international conditions, especially those which would permit a broader approach to adjustment. More of the book is devoted to national adjustment because developing economies have no alternative but to adjust, one way or another; unfortunately, there is little to compel appropriate changes in international conditions, in spite of the very great human—and economic—gains that could result.

III Major elements in adjustment with a human face

The first essential element is for *explicit acceptance of the objective* by national and international decision-makers, with the determination to apply the principles that follow consistently at all levels of decision-making.

The objective has implications for large areas of policy—in particular for the nature and timing of macro adjustments, and consequently for external finance, for meso policies, for the design of sectoral interventions, for compensatory policies, and for the process of monitoring adjustment and development. The needs, possibilities, and policies will vary with country circumstances. The main elements are summarized below: interpretation will vary between countries, with different countries needing to emphasize different elements.

Six distinct elements are involved:

1. *Macro policies which are more expansionary*, with the objective of sustaining levels of output, investment, and the satisfaction of human needs, over the adjustment period, and gradually moving to acceleration of development. This typically implies a different *timing* of adjustment, with more gradual correction of imbalances. This in turn requires more medium-term external finance than for adjustment packages designed to achieve very short-term results.

2. *Meso policies designed to help fulfill priorities in meeting the needs of vulnerable groups and promoting economic growth*, in the context of limited resources, must be adopted. These include policies towards taxation, government expenditure, aid, credit, foreign exchange, and asset distribution, which together help determine the distribution of incomes and of resources. The resource constraint which always faced developing countries is greatly tightened by the requirements of adjustment. It follows that there is a correspondingly greater need to improve the allocation of resources. Therefore *prioritizing, selectivity, redistribution*, and *restructuring* are essential aspects of achieving adjustments with a human face. Priorities include those expenditures and activities which help maintain the incomes of the poor and contribute to the production and delivery of the basic goods and services they need, as well investments and other inputs which are essential for growth.

3. *Sectoral policies to achieve restructuring in the productive sector* within any aggregate level of resource availability. This involves promoting opportunities, resources, and productivity in the small-scale sector, both in agriculture and in industry and services.

4. *Policies designed to increase the equity and efficiency of the social sector* by redirecting effort and resources from high-cost areas which do not contribute to basic needs towards low-cost basic services, and by improving the targeting of interventions. Active support for a new range of initiatives which mobilize people for health and education, and for greater community action in such areas as housing, water, and sanitation, will often need to be part of this.

5. *Compensatory programmes* to protect the basic living standards, health, and nutrition of the low-income during adjustment, before restructuring of production and economic growth have raised output and incomes sufficiently to enable the most vulnerable to meet minimum acceptable standards. The appropriate design for compensatory programmes depends on country cir-

cumstances: two major elements are emergency public works employment schemes to sustain incomes through employment, and nutrition interventions, encompassing targeted food subsidies and direct feeding for the most vulnerable.

6. *Monitoring* of the living standards, health, and nutrition of the vulnerable during adjustment. Such monitoring needs to be on a regular basis (quarterly for some items, as with much economic data), and processed speedily so that progress can be assessed and the design of programmes modified accordingly. Monitoring of the human dimension should be given at least as much weight as monitoring monetary variables has in current approaches to adjustment.

These are the six main elements. The actual package must depend on country circumstances. It will differ according to the economic structure and potential of the economy, financial options, the characteristics of the vulnerable groups in society, and administrative structures and potential. There can be no single package appropriate for every circumstance—indeed, quite the contrary, there are likely to be differences in every concrete case. An eclectic approach is necessary with respect to policy interventions at each level—macro, meso, and sectoral—and to institutional structures.

Earlier approaches to adjustment, such as those adopted under the auspices of the IMF, have contained three distinct categories of policy—those related to demand, supply-side policies, and more general institutional reforms. In general, they have concentrated mainly on the macro balances, leaving the meso implications to 'fall-out' from the existing system. The human face approach to adjustment also focuses on the aggregate macro balances in the economy, but it includes meso policies as an integral part of adjustment policies. This is essential if the vulnerable are to be protected and growth promoted in a highly resource-constrained situation. As with macro policies, meso policies also affect demand and supply—in this case demand and supply for priority resource uses in both the private and the public sector. Institutional reform also has a role—in particular reforms in institutional structures to facilitate measures to improve the position of the vulnerable, including the development and guidance of community initiatives, and more generally increased participation, especially of women, which is essential to raising incomes and improving services for the vulnerable.

Each of the six elements, which together provide the basis for adjustment with a human face, is discussed in considerable detail—and with examples taken from actual experience—in the remainder of this book. The rest of this section provides further introductory discussion of the six elements as a general background.

1   Macro policies, finance, and timing

To achieve genuine adjustment rather than stabilization implies a more expansionary path. Deflation of domestic demand should be limited to the amount needed to release resources for exports and to produce import substitutes, and where relevant, to reduce inflationary pressures on the domestic economy. But the main aim must be to expand production rather than to depress investment and consumption. Maintaining investment is essential to restore medium-term economic growth, and to maintain levels of output and employment. In general, such an adjustment path implies that adjustment in the external and internal balances takes place over the medium term (i.e. three to five years) rather than in a very short time (12 to 18 months is the typical duration of most IMF agreements).

In most cases, the more medium-term perspective would require more external financial support, with a greater element of medium-term finance than stabilization packages with more short-term perspective. Greater financial support may be secured by increasing current inflows of public and private capital, or by reducing current outflows on debt servicing. National governments themselves have some control over these flows. International support is also required in many cases as will be discussed further below. Alternative macro-policies are discussed in Chapter 7.

2   Meso policies

Meso policies are designed to maintain the basic standards of the poor and sustain conditions for growth, during resource constraint, by improving equity and efficiency of resource use. This requires that available resources are allocated on a *priority* basis to those sectors and activities with the highest potential for growth and poverty eradication. Credit, expenditure, taxation, pricing policies, aid, tariffs, etc, should be applied with *selectivity* to ensure achievement of priorities. The need for prioritizing and selectivity and the use of meso policies are discussed in greater detail in Chapter 8.

Restructuring may take place between and within sectors, both in production and government expenditure. Some elements of conventional packages—e.g. devaluation and changing producer prices—are concerned with restructuring production between sectors (towards tradeables generally and agriculture in particular). These policies may contribute to both adjustment and economic growth. But by themselves they are not likely to protect the vulnerable—indeed, in certain cases they may worsen the situation of the poor. For this, appropriate policies are needed to achieve restructuring within sectors.

There is very major potential for restructuring within public expenditure in most countries. This includes reallocating expenditures between sectors—notably from defence to the social sectors. In 1983, the proportion of central government expenditure taken by defence among low and lower-middle income countries, according to World Bank estimates, varied from 4.2 per cent (Sierra Leone) to 34.8 per cent (Pakistan), while the proportion spent on health varied from 1.0 per cent (Pakistan) to 22.5 per cent (Costa Rica); and on education from 1.9 per cent (India, but most educational expenditure in India occurs at state level) to 26.9 per cent (Bolivia). These very large variations indicate the potential for restructuring. So far, as shown in Chapter 3, government expenditure cuts have tended to be focused relatively more on economic services, while both defence and the social sectors have been relatively protected. As with production, restructuring of government expenditure must be accompanied by sectoral policies to ensure that the vulnerable benefit.

3 Sectoral policies: restructuring in the productive sector

To protect the vulnerable, special policies are needed to restructure towards activities which extend employment and raise the incomes of low-income households. These include programmes to help expand output and incomes of small-scale farmers and to assist small-scale enterprises in manufacturing and services to acquire credit and to improve their technology. Women play a dominant role in small-scale farming in Africa, and are particularly significant as entrepreneurs and as employees in the urban informal sector in most countries. To reach the most vulnerable, it is therefore essential to make special efforts to incorporate women fully into programme design and execution. Programmes for supporting small farmers are discussed in Chapter 9. The potential and policy needs for raising productivity and incomes in the informal sector are considered in Chapter 10.

4 Policies for increasing the equity and efficiency of the social sector

There is strong potential for reallocation within sectors, towards basic services and from high-cost to low-cost interventions. Basic services typically receive less than half the total allocation, and sometimes only a small fraction of the total. Both Zimbabwe and South Korea succeeded in improving basic services during recession and adjustment by shifting expenditures towards basic services within the social sectors, and towards the social sectors in the budget as a whole. Low-cost interventions can greatly improve health, while involving only small additional expenditures in relation to the total. Oral rehydration therapy (ORT) for example, substitutes for much more expensive intravenous techniques. Basic medicines for the whole population of Tanzania were provided for only 30 cents a person (Ch. 11).

The design of social sector interventions to achieve the required restructuring are discussed in general in Chapter 8, while more detailed proposals for the health sector are discussed in Chapter 11, and for the education sector in Chapter 12.

5   Compensatory programmes

The sharp cuts in incomes of the vulnerable together with the rises in food
prices that often accompany recession and adjustment can lead to an emergency situation for the most vulnerable in which some babies and children will
die, and permanent damage may be done to the mental and physical capacity
of a generation of children. Programmes to restore growth and to help small
farmers and enterprises in the informal sector will help the vulnerable over
time, but in the short term more fast-acting measures may be needed. These
include emergency employment works which can sustain incomes from employment, while also helping to rehabilitate and extend social and economic
infrastructure. Public works have been highly successful in maintaining
minimum incomes in many parts of the world. Their role is discussed in detail
in Chapter 10.

Nutrition interventions are also essential where there are high and rising
rates of malnutrition and where the macro adjustment measures are likely to
increase the price of food. Measures include targeted food subsidies, health
support, and direct feeding of the most vulnerable—especially the under-5s
and pregnant and lactating women. The various nutrition interventions which
may be appropriate are described in Chapter 13.

During recession and adjustment, as poor households find themselves under
pressure on several fronts—declining employment opportunities and wages,
rising food prices, and diminishing standards of social service—the level of
living of the family, and especially of children, increasingly depends on measures taken within the household to protect basic standards. The 'coping
mechanisms' are numerous and varied. They are discussed in general in
Chapter 4 and described in more detail for Chile in Volume II, Chapter 3.
Although ultimately the strength of these mechanisms depends on the nature of
the household and of informal social networks, there is much the government can
do to assist and strengthen them. Some possible policies are discussed in
Chapter 4.

6   Monitoring

Monitoring of what is happening to the incomes, nutrition, and health of the
low-income population is essential both to assess progress and to help identify
policy needs. Both Botswana and Chile, which have introduced systematic
programmes to support nutritional standards, have a well-established system
of monitoring. In Botswana, for example, this monitoring occurs on a monthly
basis, and information is available broken down by region and locality to assist
in the design of programmes. This means that deficiencies can be readily
identified and action taken. In most countries, statistics of the social dimension
are notoriously inadequate, being collected sporadically and processed after
considerable delay. Systematic and timely data collection is essential if the

human dimension is to be incorporated into adjustment policy and programme monitoring. Relevant aspects include nutritional levels among children, proportion of low birth weight infants, and incomes of low-income households. Information on these matters should form a routine part of statistical requests by international financial agencies, and an integral aspect of programme monitoring. Issues of statistics and monitoring are discussed in Chapter 14.

IV Political and administrative dynamics

A major emphasis of adjustment with a human face is *restructuring*—i.e. the reallocation of resources to priority needs. This is clearly essential if the resources going to the vulnerable are to be protected and even increased at a time when resources are limited. By its nature restructuring will tend to come up against political and bureaucratic obstacles, as it involves removing resources from some uses in order to relocate them in priority areas. In the medium term, most parts of society will gain as economic growth is resumed, and as the full participation of the whole population generates more social and political stability. But it is true that short-term opposition—both political and bureaucratic—may well occur. Considerable political determination and courage is therefore necessary for full realization of the objective in the ways outlined above. In some societies, minor improvements in resource allocation may be all that is possible. But in others, especially those societies with a long tradition of meeting the needs of the most vulnerable and protecting them from excessive fluctuations, and those that have recently become democracies and are determined to maintain their political progress and to realize the full support of the population, major advances are possible.

Two elements would strengthen governments' ability and determination to achieve adjustment with a human face. On the one hand, *community participation* can play a critical role—in helping to formulate policy, in providing the administrative mechanisms for aspects of the programme, such as community feeding schemes, construction and rehabilitation of social capital at the community level, and income raising schemes (see proposals in the Ghana country study in vol. ii, ch. 4), and in providing resources of labour and food to pay for some basic services. In making full use of the local community's potential, the programmes will not only raise resources and increase the relevance of policies, but will also provide strong political support for adjustment with a human face which will help counter potential opposition of other interests. On the other hand, *the international community* can also play a crucial supporting role by providing additional resources for governments which adopt policies that protect the vulnerable and promote growth, and by being prepared to reallocate their own existing commitments to these ends.

V   The international dimension

Some aspects of the changes needed internationally to support adjustment with
a human face have been touched on above. These policies fall into three broad
categories.

1. *Policies that make the world environment more friendly towards the Third World*
and consequently ease the adjustment problem by reducing the extent of
adjustment developing countries have to undertake and also making the
necessary adjustment easier to secure. Policies include those that help ensure
rapid and sustained levels of world demand; those that extend markets for
developing countries, through reduced protectionism and subsidization of
developed countries' exports of primary products; reductions of interest rates
and consequently of debt servicing obligations; and policies to increase net
resource flows (public and private) to developing countries. Net resource
flows may be raised by increasing bilateral and multilateral resource flows in
aggregate, and by agreed reductions of the debt servicing obligation, some
write-off of the debt, or stretching out of servicing (e.g. through debt capping).

2. *Buffer mechanisms.* If all these measures were put into effect, there would
be a very substantial improvement in the international environment, reducing
the need for additional measures. But realistically it is unlikely that a total
transformation will be achieved, and even with an improvement in trend,
fluctuations are likely. There is a need therefore to devise buffer mechanisms, at
an international level, which would automatically compensate poor countries
when adverse international circumstances force excessive short-term adjustment and cause worsening conditions among the vulnerable. Such measures
would be designed to prevent a repetition of the events observed today and
recorded in this book. The measures could include increased financial compensation for commodity price fluctuations (an extended Compensatory
Finance facility through the IMF, or extension of the Lomé STABEX
arrangements), or automatic debt relief, or increased SDRs for countries
experiencing worsening human indicators following international developments. These buffer mechanisms would be triggered by evidence of rising
malnutrition or worsening in other human indicators related to deteriorating
economic conditions. The 1986 IMF agreement with Mexico, is an important
innovation in this direction, involving triggering devices to secure an increase
in resource flows if the oil price or the growth rate falls below a certain level.
For a 'human face' approach, an extension of this is required to generate
additional financial support if *human* conditions deteriorate.

3. *Special additional support.* Within any international framework encompassing overall conditions, trigger mechanisms, and buffer facilities, there is a
need to provide special support for countries following 'human face' policies,
and to change conditionality and modalities of adjustment negotiations generally to encourage and facilitate the adoption of this approach. Such policies
would include increasing the magnitude of aid flows for these countries, per-

mitting generous debt restructuring, extending a greater proportion of financial support on a medium-term basis, and agreeing to reallocate capital flows to help meet the priorities.

Conditionality needs to include the objective of restoring growth and protecting the vulnerable in the formulation of programmes and in monitoring, with a longer-term perspective, to permit the more gradual adjustment proposed. The modalities of formulating and negotiating adjustment packages need to be changed so that those concerned with the vulnerable and with economic growth are centrally involved on both sides—both at the national level (involving social sector and planning ministries as well as ministries of finance and the central bank), and at the international level, where agencies concerned with the human dimension should be involved as well as those concerned with growth and with finance.

These changes in conditionality and modalities are needed generally, for all countries—not only those actively following adjustment with a human face— to encourage the protection of the human dimension.

The international dimension is discussed further in Chapter 15.

VI Production not welfare

The case for adjustment with a human face is of course compelling from a humanitarian perspective. When millions are affected by famine, there is moral outrage and action across the world; a similar attitude must surely prevail when the cause is economic, and the effects, although less dramatic, include rising infant deaths, mounting suffering, and permanent damage among millions. But the case for this set of policies may be made in basic *economic* terms. There are economic justifications for each of the policy changes proposed, with abundant empirical evidence of their reality.

1. Many studies have shown that small farms have higher land productivity than large (e.g. Berry and Cline 1979, and review in Ch. 9). Given the opportunity, some small farmers adopt new varieties as quickly and sometimes earlier and more intensively than large (Hayami 1981, Barker and Herdt 1984).

2. Evidence from Africa and Latin America shows that small-scale enterprises have social rates of return far in excess of large firms in many industries (see Table 10.5).

3. Benefit–cost ratios of more than 1.5 are common in public works schemes (see Table 10.2)

4. Poor levels of nutrition are strongly associated with poor worker productivity (see reviews of Rao Maturu 1979, and Scrimshaw 1986).

5. Many studies have shown that adults stunted as a result of child malnutrition have lower productivity in physical work than normal adults (Scrimshaw 1986).

6. The output of farmers with four or more years' education has been shown

to be up to 25 per cent more than farmers with no education (World Bank 1980, Table 5.3). In general, primary education shows high rates of return, much higher than secondary and university education, and higher than much physical capital investment. Psacharopoulos (1985) estimates the average social rates of return as 26 per cent in Latin America, and slightly higher in Asia and Africa.

7. At a macro level, countries with more literate populations have shown higher growth rates (McGranahan *et al.* 1985, World Bank 1980).

8. A near-universal conclusion of empirical investigation is that female education increases standards of nutrition, reduces infant mortality, and rates of fertility (see Barerra 1986).

VII   Time paths of adjustment and incomes of the poor

Different approaches to adjustment involve different time-paths in the behaviour of average consumption per head, and of the consumption levels of the vulnerable. These are shown stylistically in Figs. 6.1, 6.2, and 6.3.

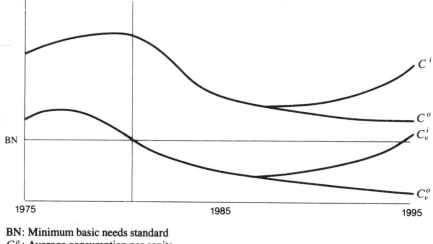

BN: Minimum basic needs standard
C^o: Average consumption per capita
C_v^o: Average consumption per capita of bottom 40%
C^i: Average consumption per capita if external conditions improve
C_v^i: Average consumption per capita of bottom 40% if external conditions improve

Fig. 6.1   Paths of average per capita consumption and average per capita consumption of bottom 40 per cent when no adjustment measures are taken

There are, of course, many possible variations in the decline in income and consumption per capita. In Fig. 6.1, $C^o v$ shows a sharp fall followed by unmitigated long-term decline, on the assumption that no 'adjustment' measures are taken, nationally or internationally, and that domestic inadequacies of policy are so severe that without major corrections, the downward path of production and per capita consumption is likely to continue. The Ghana experience of the 1970s and early 1980s followed this pattern. In other cases, as $C'v$, there may be some hopes of future upturn if external conditions improve.

Note that there is a certain arbitrariness about the precise basic needs minimum line, and also about the magnitudes of the movement in per capita consumption levels. So the precise numbers falling below the minimum and for how long, cannot be determined. But the *direction* of change is known.

There are, of course, many possible trends in C_v. Fig. 6.1 shows the most favourable of the likely options (in the absence of special action) where the consumption of the vulnerable (e.g. the bottom 40 per cent of the population) moves pro rata with per capita consumption for the whole country, implying unchanged household income shares for the bottom strata of the population. If, in contrast, economic stagnation impinges particularly on the vulnerable, their average consumption levels would decline even more than shown.

1   The impact of adjustment policy

Conventional adjustment policies of the type widely adopted in the early 1980s will have further impact on the living standards of the population. Usually this impact will involve some conscious reduction of consumption in the short run in the hope of restoring balances, investment, and growth in the longer run.

This is shown in Fig. 6.2 as the curve C^x_v—involving a further reduction in consumption in the short period, and, after a time, some return to growth of income and consumption. This addition to growth will result, in principle, both from restructuring the economy and from an extra inflow of funds from abroad. In practice, as shown in Part I, neither in theory nor in practice is it clear that orthodox policies generally have lead to such a restoration in growth.

Fig. 6.2 illustrates a more growth-oriented adjustment path—C^g_v, corresponding to the emerging consensus about the need for conscious concern with promoting economic growth in the process of adjustment. In this case the consumption levels of the poor fall during the initial adjustment period, as with the previous approach to adjustment, but start to rise, eventually quite rapidly, as growth is resumed.

With the growth-oriented approach as with the orthodox approach, average per capita consumption of the poor may fall below a basic needs minimum for some time. Consequently, in countries following this path without special action to protect the basic needs of the vulnerable, there may be increasing numbers of people (and/or increasing levels of deficiency per capita among the poor) whose basic food, health, and education needs are unmet, and who are increasingly less able to support the process of economic revival and participate in its achievement. In economic parlance, there will be dis-investment in human capital, affecting both the shorter and longer run. In the

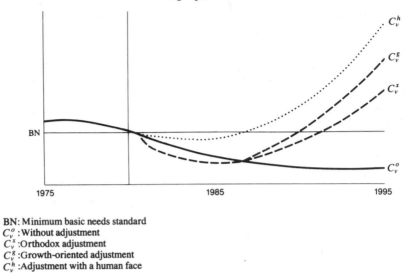

BN: Minimum basic needs standard
C_v^o : Without adjustment
C_v^x : Orthodox adjustment
C_v^g : Growth-oriented adjustment
C_v^h : Adjustment with a human face

Fig. 6.2   Paths of average per capita consumption of bottom 40% under different adjustment policies

short run, low levels of nutrition and probably increased incidence of illness will have direct negative effects on productivity and output, especially in the small-scale agricultural sector and the urban informal sector. The longer-run effects will be even more serious, especially for the under-5s, who will suffer permanent damage to their mental and physical capacities.

2   Adjustment with a human face

Adjustment with a human face combines the basic elements of adjustment with protection of the vulnerable and promotion of growth. It aims to see the entire population meet its basic needs for nutrition, health, and education. This is shown on Fig. 6.2 as C_v^h, which describes adjustment where special measures are taken to protect the basic needs of the vulnerable throughout the adjustment period. Consumption needs of the vulnerable would be kept as near as possible at the minimum basic needs level until economic growth permits it to rise.

By providing for the basic needs of the poor, adjustment with a human face would add to the growth potential of the economy because of the positive economic returns associated with the policies summarized in the previous section. The high economic returns to human investment mean that in the longer run the growth rate with such a strategy would be *at least as high* as with growth-oriented adjustment. And if the human face policies are financed by reallocating expenditures from low-priority consumption items (private and public), then the growth rate will be higher than with growth-oriented adjustment. The phasing of these additions to growth will vary, however, since some human investments have a wider range in the time pattern of their effects than normal investments. Some can have very short-term effects, as, for example, productivity increases following nutritional improvements among workers; others will have long delayed effects, as in the case of the benefits to the future labour force of current improvements in child nutrition and primary education; while improved conditions and incentives for small farmers and urban producers may show benefits to growth in the medium term.

Consequently, there are a considerable number of possible patterns of growth. Some alternatives are depicted on Fig. 6.3. Growth-oriented investment is shown as C^g_v. Adjustment with a human face, where growth picks up more quickly and increases faster than growth-oriented adjustment, is shown as C^h_v (1). This might describe the South Korean case. The curve $C^h_v(2)$ shows adjustment with a human face where growth effects of human investments are delayed, but eventually lead to more rapid growth than growth-oriented adjustment alone. And $C^h_v(3)$ shows adjustment with a human face that protects the human dimension during the adjustment period and achieves the same growth rate as growth-oriented adjustment, but with some delay.

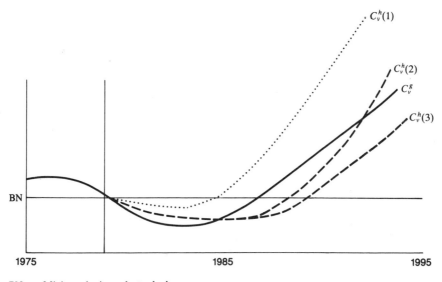

BN   : Minimum basic needs standards
C^g_v : Growth-oriented adjustment
$C^h_v(1)$: Adjustment with a human face
$C^h_v(2)$: Adjustment with a human face, delayed growth effects
$C^h_v(3)$: Adjustment with a human face, delayed growth effects, sacrificing some short term investment

Fig. 6.3 Paths of average per capita consumption of bottom 40% under growth-oriented adjustment and alternative options of adjustment with a human face

Obviously each of these curves is an abstraction representing different possibilities. And it must be emphasized that they are abstractions from which many other factors, economic, political, and social, are excluded. But by showing the time-patterns of growth and incomes in relation to basic human needs, they may help to illustrate the importance of conscious concern with the needs of the vulnerable in the short run and the general benefits to growth which can flow from this in the longer term.

Alternative Macro Policies, Meso Policies, and Vulnerable Groups

Frances Stewart

I Introduction

Macro policies are those policies directed at the macro aggregates in the economy. They include, for example, the money supply, the budget surplus/deficit, the level of government expenditure—in fact, all the variables that form part of most IMF adjustment packages. The earlier analysis of the impact of recession and adjustment policies on vulnerable groups showed how important macro policies are in influencing the conditions of vulnerable groups, in both the short and the medium term. Consequently, an essential element in any strategy for adjustment with a human face is to ensure that, at the very least, the macro policies do not, through their negative effects on vulnerable groups, undermine other human face policies being introduced, and, at best, contribute directly to the improvement of the conditions of vulnerable groups.

This chapter considers how a human face approach will affect the design of macro policies. It should be emphasized that the aim is to develop organizing principles, not detailed programmes, because the latter must depend on the specific circumstances prevailing when a country programme is designed.

Macro policies have both an immediate direct impact on vulnerable groups (e.g., by altering the level of employment and/or food prices), and also a longer term effect as a result of the impact on the pattern and rate of growth of the economy.

As shown in the general discussion on how recession and adjustment have affected vulnerable groups, and in the case studies exploring that impact in particular countries, there are three major ways in which vulnerable groups may be affected by macro policies.

1. Through the impact on incomes of low-income households: by affecting wage and employment trends in the formal sector and, more indirectly, opportunities for informal sector income-earning opportunities. Macro policies affect rural incomes primarily through their effects on the terms of trade of the agricultural sector.

2. By affecting the availability and price of major items of consumption of low-income households, especially *food*.

3. Through the impact on levels of government expenditure relating to vulnerable groups, especially in the social sectors.

Analysis of the impact of conventional policy packages on vulnerable groups has shown that in the short run these have often been associated with negative impacts on each of the three elements, although causal responsibility as between the economic difficulties which necessitated the adjustment and the adjustment policies themselves is not clear. Real incomes and employment, especially in the urban area, have typically been depressed during the adjustment process, food prices have risen and government expenditure on the social services has often been cut. However, in some cases, rural incomes have risen, at least relatively, as agricultural prices were raised.

Moreover, as shown in Chapter 2 many countries with conventional adjustment packages have continued to experience declining incomes. There is no evidence that the policies adopted have promoted economic growth and some evidence that growth may have been reduced with falling investment rates.

It is because of such negative impacts that it is necessary to introduce explicit policies to protect vulnerable groups during adjustment. In addition to specific micro policies, adjustment with a human face requires alternative macro and meso policies which explicitly recognize the need to sustain the standards of the most vulnerable in society.

II   Growth-oriented adjustment

The objective of protecting vulnerable groups during adjustment implies protecting the vulnerable *immediately* the policies are introduced, not waiting until general economic growth is resumed. But such protection is unlikely to be sustainable in the face of prolonged decline in per capita incomes—of the dimension, for example, that has been experienced in many parts of Sub-Saharan Africa throughout this decade. Consequently, a critical element in adjustment with a human dimension is halting the decline in per capita income. Yet as shown earlier, many adjustment programmes in recent years have been associated with continued decline in per capita incomes. In the medium term, the ability to improve the conditions of the vulnerable on a sustained basis generally requires a resumption of economic growth. For countries where conditions of the most vulnerable are very deficient—for example in Ghana, where only 30 per cent of the population have any access to health services, where sanitation and water facilities cover less than half the population, and where incomes of poor households are grossly inadequate to meet minimum food needs—bringing the conditions of the poor up to tolerable levels will only be possible if economic growth is restored.

Economic growth may improve the conditions of the vulnerable through the three mechanisms described above:

1. *By improving employment and wage levels* in the formal sector, and indirectly earnings opportunities in the informal sector which provides intermediate

goods and services for use by the formal sector and supplies consumer goods and services to wage-earners in the formal sector; and by increasing peasant incomes.

2. *By improving supplies of food.* Economic growth is generally associated with improved supplies of food and other basic wage goods, and less rapid rises in their prices. In countries with a large agricultural sector, growth in domestic food production is likely to form an important aspect of achieving aggregate growth. Where countries rely heavily on food imports, improved economic growth will increase the capacity to import food (as in Botswana, see vol. ii ch. 1). In either case, improved supplies will help to moderate price inflation.

3. *By increasing taxable capacity* and consequently government's ability to provide basic health and educational services.

Deteriorating per capita incomes tend—unless offsetting measures are taken—to have adverse effects on all three mechanisms. Consequently, *adjustment with growth is an important aspect of adjustment with a human face.* The recent advocacy of growth-oriented adjustment, inititated by Secretary of the US Treasury James Baker and now being explored by the major financial institutions, is therefore a very important aspect of achieving adjustment with a human face.

However, it is apparent from examining the mechanisms connecting economic growth with the welfare of vulnerable groups that while growth is conducive to improved welfare of the poorest, this improvement in welfare does not necessarily or automatically follow from accelerated growth. Capital-intensive patterns of growth in the industrial sector associated with slow employment growth and deteriorating urban income distribution, or agricultural growth which is based on inappropriate mechanization and is associated with increasing inequality of rural income distribution, lead to growth with minimal trickle-down, and little or no improvement in the condition of the poor. Agricultural growth consisting of expanding non-food cash crops may mean that growth is accompanied by falling food supplies and rising food prices, as in the recent history of Brazil. Expanding tax capacity may be accompanied by little change in expenditure on the basic services of the poor. Consequently, while growth-oriented adjustment is, typically, a necessary condition for achieving adjustment with a human dimension, it is not sufficient. Even with a broadly appropriate pattern of growth, it may be necessary to take explicit action to ensure that the growth is equitable, and that the vulnerable participate, not only in terms of employment and household incomes but also in their access to social services. Therefore, the policies of adjustment with a human face need to be designed to achieve both growth-oriented adjustment and to include specific actions directed towards human needs. Sectoral policies and specific measures focused on the poor will be needed.

III External finance

It is obvious that, in general, a higher level of external finance would make it easier for countries to secure growth-oriented adjustment with a human face. More external finance reduces the need for short-term disabsorption, permitting structural adjustment to take place over the medium term without increasing short-term unemployment. More external finance also eases the need for downward adjustment of investment, government expenditure, and consumption.

The acute economic and social problems of the 1980s have arisen in part because of the collapse of international lending. In both Africa and Latin America, the large amount of *net lending* in the 1970s was replaced by a *net outflow* of funds in the 1980s as interest payments exceeded lending. The changing pattern in the net transfer of funds is dramatically indicated by the following figures (IMF 1986*b*, Table 33):

Net annual transfer* (*$ billion*)

	1977/78	1984/85
Africa	+ 8.6	− 5.4
Latin America	+ 4.9	− 39.0

* Calculated as current account balance less interest payments.

To achieve the objective in a way that is both comprehensive (i.e. across many countries) and sustained will certainly be easier with, and may require, a reversal of this financial squeeze. In some poor countries, resumed growth may not be possible without substantially more external finance to pay for essential intermediate inputs. Analysis of recent experience of both Tanzania and Zambia suggests this to be the case in these countries. As the Baker plan recognized, extra finance is an essential element in securing growth-oriented adjustment. The need to protect vulnerable groups provides a further urgent reason for more finance (see Ch. 15).

However, while extra finance is highly desirable—especially to secure growth—this does not mean that countries can do nothing to achieve adjustment with a human face until there is a major change in the financial commitments of developed countries. Countries can affect their own financial situation by their own actions; and within a given financial limitation, they can greatly improve their achievements by the policies they adopt.

Country policy towards financial flows

The net transfer of external finance received by a country consists in the following net balance:

Positive	*Negative*
+ Gross lending (private and public)	− Amortization
+ Gross grant aid	− Interest payments

Governments have some control over each of these items, a control which varies with the particular circumstances of the country. For example:

1. *Countries with good credit rating may choose to increase their gross borrowing.* This was the policy adopted by Brazil in the 1970s permitting investments in large import-substitution projects, which had results in improving the trade balance in the 1980s. Similarly, South Korea chose to borrow both in the 1970s and 1980s, which allowed adjustment to take place with less deflation and unemployment than in the absence of borrowing. In the 1970s some countries borrowed in order to avoid making necessary adjustments. This may protect vulnerable groups in the short run, but unless the adverse shock is rapidly reversed it will lead to more problems in the medium term, since countries will then be faced with *two* problems: the initial adjustment problem *and* a debt problem arising from the borrowing. This is what happened to some countries in the 1970s. This strategy obviously is not being advocated here. Rather, the objective is to borrow to permit adjustment to take place more slowly and less painfully, with less deflation and unemployment than in the absence of borrowing. This type of slower adjustment not only makes it easier to protect the vulnerable during adjustment but also to promote medium-term growth, since levels of investment can be maintained. The choice of greater external borrowing and less deflation is only an option for those countries which have not seen their credit ratings reduced to near zero, following the accumulation of debts combined with ineffective adjustment.

2. *Countries with a large debt have some choice over rates of amortization and interest,* which they may exercise unilaterally (e.g. the recent experience of Peru) or by negotiation (the recent experience of Mexico). Rescheduling of amortization, in particular, offers a changing time-profile of net financial flows, which potentially extends to most of the seriously affected countries. Especially if combined with some debt relief, it could considerably improve countries' access to external resources. For example, a major rescheduling would greatly improve Ghana's medium-term prospects, while without such rescheduling debt service obligations may reach over 60 per cent of export earnings. The study of the Philippines also suggests that policies towards debt are an important element in determining options. To some extent, the debt rescheduling option depends on agreement from creditor countries. However, far-sighted creditors should be prepared to accept a rescheduling which offers a high probability of restoring economic viability and therefore long-term repayment capacity. More generally, international mechanisms relating debt relief to country needs should be adopted—with special attention paid to the relationship between debt repayment schedules and the health and nutrition of vulnerable groups. Nyerere asked 'must we starve our children to pay our debts?' The aim—at a country level and an international one—must be to devise policies which avoid this. International debt relief mechanisms are discussed further in Chapter 15.

3. *Aid flows are likely to be greater if a country shows a determination to adopt policies*

which protect vulnerable groups. The Ghana study suggested an additional annual cost of $65 million per annum for a more human-oriented adjustment programme. It seems likely that donors would finance some of this extra cost, for the human, economic, and political advantages that would follow. In Botswana, aid donors have met 50 per cent of the costs of drought relief measures.

For these reasons, it seems that the finance limitation should *not* be treated as immutable—either from the perspective of individual countries, or from that of international aggregates.

An important feature of adjustment which combines growth and the protection of human welfare compared with previous adjustment strategies is the difference in the *time perspective*. Both growth and the human dimension require that there should be lesser immediate sacrifices to secure adjustment (i.e lesser reduction in growth-related activities and in the provision of basic needs), so that the short-term adjustment in imbalances (balance of payments and budget) would be smaller, but the medium-term achievements would be greater. Full achievement of this preferred time perspective typically requires more short-term external finance. But if the financial constraint is not relaxed, there are policies which could greatly contribute to the objective within any existing financial limitation. These are discussed in the next section.

IV Alternative macro policies

The assumption of a given external financial constraint in the short term makes the options more limited. But reallocation of resources and incomes within a given total can improve the fulfilment of priority targets, and may in certain circumstances even ensure *better* achievement than with more resources but less attempt to direct resources to priority areas. This was indicated, for example, by the successful achievements—on basic needs as well as the war effort—in Britain during the Second World War. Consequently, in times of strict resource constraints, macro policies must be designed to ensure that the major priorities for protecting vulnerable groups and promoting growth are met despite the resource limitations. The precise activities to be included in each of the priority areas will vary according to the circumstances, but some generalizations are possible.

In the growth priority, investment is the most obvious item, including investment in infrastructure and in 'productive' sectors, and also in human capital. Some intermediate inputs are also essential for growth. Not all investment is equally productive, and some investments are actually unproductive. So the growth priority includes only those investments with a positive social rate of return.

The human dimension priority covers all expenditures related to the income-earning capacity of very poor households, to the basic health, education, and sanitation services they receive, and to their nutritional status.

The precise dividing line between priorities is bound to be a bit arbitrary, and to be subject to much political debate. But the extremes (top priority, bottom priority) will usually be easy to determine. Even though it is unlikely that any country will come to universal consensus on priorities or execute any agreement on priorities comprehensively and without exceptions, the attempt to plan according to priorities will improve resource allocation from the perspective of protecting the human dimension compared with normal decision-making.

Macro policy packages generally take the form of target values for selected priority instruments—e.g. exchange rate, tax levels, budget deficit, credit creation. Adjustment with a human face has implications for the selection of instruments, targets, and performance criteria. Moreover, these macro variables can be associated with a variety of sectoral or micro implications—e.g. the same tax burden expressed as a proportion of GDP may fall on direct or indirect taxes, on the rich or poor, on industry or agriculture. These will be called 'meso' implications, to distinguish them from macro aggregates or micro projects. Generally, conventional adjustment packages take a broadly neutral view of meso implications, allowing them to occur as determined by the normal workings of the system. Adjustment which combines growth and the human dimension, in contrast, is predominantly concerned with the meso implications, in order to ensure that the objectives are met to a maximum extent possible in the context of a given macro policy package.

There are, then, three types of policy interventions which help to achieve the objective of growth-oriented adjustment with a human dimension:

1. *Policies determining the levels of macro variables,* which are directed at influencing macro aggregates in the economy. These include levels of taxation and government expenditure, credit creation, the exchange rate, etc. They are intended to influence the level of national income, the rate of inflation, the external balance. These are the variables normally defined as forming part of the macro policy package.

2. *Meso policies, or policies that influence the allocation of income and resources,* within a given macro policy package. These concern the distributional and allocational impact of particular macro variables (e.g. the distribution of government expenditure, or of taxation).

3. *Policy reforms and institutional changes likely to improve the performance* of given macro and meso policies (e.g. by increasing female participation).

1 Macro policy variables

The choice of instruments, the targets chosen, and the selected performance criteria need to take both growth and human objectives and priorities into account. The appropriate policy package will vary according to country circumstances, and therefore cannot be laid down here. However, some general points need to be made.

1. *Minimizing deflation.* Adjustment with a human face would try to minimize deflationary adjustment—i.e. adjustment achieved by compressing domestic expenditures more than the amount likely to be absorbed by production of additional exports. The approach would aim to minimize this type of deflation because it is a significant source of adverse developments for vulnerable groups and for growth (through rising unemployment, reduced incomes, reduced government expenditures, and depressed investment).

Deflation of domestic expenditure is typically designed to achieve three objectives: first, to reduce domestic absorption so that more resources may be devoted to exports and/or import substitutes, which is essential to improve the external trade balance. For large changes in the trade balance, such domestic disabsorption is essential. Where an improved balance may be achieved by *increasing supply* instead of depressing demand, it is clearly preferable. Usually, additional supply requires investment in new capacity and is therefore only possible in the medium term. But in economies with much unused capacity this can be a short-term policy which does not require deflation. Typically, however, there may not be much excess capacity of a kind which can immediately be used to produce extra exports or import substitutes. Hence disabsorption may be necessary to release resources for improving the external balance. But in many countries, there is little short-term flexibility in domestic resource use. In the short run, resources cannot be transferred, for example, from producing maize for domestic consumption to producing coffee for export, or from building clinics to textile exports. Rapid and low-cost resource switching is only possible, on any scale, for countries with highly flexible economies, which generally means economies with well-developed manufacturing sectors. For others, investment and therefore time is necessary. It follows that the short-run potential of using domestic disabsorption or deflation to achieve the resource switch and improved external balance is limited in many economies.

The second objective of deflation is to depress domestic consumption and investment so as to reduce imports. This can be very effective in improving the external balance quickly. It has occurred in Jamaica since 1983, for example, and Botswana in 1980–81. But it is costly in terms of the human face objective since it typically hurts vulnerable groups and depresses investment. Moreover, it produces only a temporary improvement in the external balance, which will be reversed once the deflation stops. However, in the absence of sufficient bridging finance, it may be necessary to attain temporary improvement while more medium-term measures to improve the capacity to produce exports and/or import substitutes have time to take effect. But great care is needed to ensure that the short-term deflation does not *impede* the medium-term efforts by reducing human and physical capital.

The third objective of deflationary policies is to reduce the inflation rate. In some cases, controls on credit creation have been advocated even were the external balance is satisfactory, in order to control inflation. On balance, adjustment with a human face would put less weight on inflation control as an objective in its own right, and only give it substantial importance where the inflation itself is clearly threatening the vulnerable.

It follows from this discussion that domestic disabsorption (or deflation) may have a role to play, but the approach would aim to minimize that role, and would seek bridging finance in order to do so. Typically, then, macro policies to protect the vulnerable might be associated with higher budget deficits (or slower reduction in deficits) than is the case in the more orthodox packages.

While limitation of external resources may necessitate some deflation in the short run, some countries have succeeded in combining adjustment with economic growth, with only short periods of rising unemployment, showing that appropriate policies can reduce this deflationary element. The experience of Brazil and South Korea both illustrate the possibilities. By adopting import-substitution policies in major sectors, by expanding sectors (e.g. construction) with low import coefficients, and by promoting exports, improvement in the trade balance was achieved without massive underemployment of domestic resources. It will be more difficult to achieve this in countries with more rigid structures, and especially those highly dependent on primary exports, but even in these contexts there is normally some possibility of changing the structure of output so as to reduce the necessity for deflation. Consequently the approach would be likely to be associated with less strict targets on budgetary balance and credit creation.

2. *Levels of taxation and public expenditure.* The approach is likely to require higher levels of government expenditure, and taxes. The level of taxation and government expenditure may vary considerably consistent with any particular target budget balance. Some priorities are almost invariably in the public sector (e.g. primary health care, primary education, sanitation, economic infrastructure); some of a type which are generally in the private sector (small-scale farming and industry) but may need public expenditure on supporting infrastructure and services; and some may be in either sector (e.g. drug production, transport). For quintessentially public sector activities, priority achievement may require a higher level of expenditure (by central, regional, or local government) accompanied by higher revenue from taxation or charges to finance it. Higher taxation is normally necessary where taxation and public expenditure have fallen to very low levels both absolutely and as a proportion of GDP, as in Ghana in 1983 when government expenditure had fallen to less than 5 per cent of GDP. Higher levels of revenue may be achieved by improving the efficiency of tax collection as well as by extending taxation and increasing tax rates. There is great variation across countries in the proportion of GDP accounted for by taxation and other sources of government revenue. Among developing countries Ghana's low of 5 per cent represented the bottom of the range, while ratios of around 30 per cent are found in a few countries (e.g. Egypt, Yugoslavia, Trinidad and Tobago).

3. *Systematic consideration of impact on vulnerable groups.* Adjustment with a human face requires that the impact on vulnerable groups be explicitly considered for *each* policy instrument, including policies towards privatization and the role of the public sector, the exchange rate, etc. This perspective would often mean more gradual transition to avoid sudden large distributional changes. In general, explicit consideration of the implications for vulnerable groups would be likely to alter the chosen policy mix and the pace of adjustment.

4. *Compensatory measures.* Where policy instruments can be shown seriously to hurt vulnerable groups, they should only be introduced if accompanied by compensatory action. These compensatory measures should be regarded as an intrinsic part of the policy package, and their costs be included as costs of the package. For example, devaluation and raised producer prices for the agricultural sector often lead to higher food prices and reduced real incomes for low-income households and for agricultural labourers. Where such changes seriously hurt vulnerable groups they should only be introduced if accompanied by compensatory changes in incomes or food subsidies for the low-income. Where such compensation is not possible alternative policies, e.g., export subsidies, import taxes, multiple exchange rates, should be considered.

Monitoring macro performance. Programme monitoring and performance criteria should include the welfare of vulnerable groups (e.g. as measured by nutritional indicators, and real incomes of those below the poverty line) as well as growth-related indicators (e.g. levels of investment and growth in GDP).

2   Meso policies: priorities and selectivity

Macro aggregates, such as the budget deficit and levels of public expenditure, have direct implications for the achievement of our objectives. But any given macro aggregate—e.g. budgetary balance, or GNP level—may be associated with many different levels of achievement with respect to the two priority areas, as shown by the fact that some low-income economies manage to attain higher levels of basic services for the most vulnerable than some high-income societies: contrast, for example, the achievements of Sri Lanka and of Brazil. While the normal adjustment package has targets for macro variables but is not concerned with the allocation of these items to priority and non-priority areas, in the human face approach the effects on resource and income distribution as between priority and non-priority areas is critical.

Consequently, whatever the policy package, the macro policies must be married with their consequence for distribution of resources between priorities, and meso policies must be designed so that the two together (the macro policies and the meso consequences) protect vulnerable groups during adjustment.

To illuminate the position, macro targets may be thought of as dictating the speed of a wheel (rotations per second). The consequences of this rotation for the rest of the system will depend on the size and number of cogs on that wheel and other wheels linked to it. While timing the speed of rotation may be broadly determined by external finance, the meso consequences can be greatly altered by altering the dimension and number of associated cogs and wheels. The approach may be summarized as *combining macro instruments with selectivity.*

In practical terms, this approach means that all expenditures/incomes affected by macro policies and relevant to the achievement on growth and the human dimension be divided into priority and non-priority elements. A three-fold classification is suggested:

1. *Priority I*: activities/resources/expenditures/incomes essential for the achievement of growth and the protection of the human needs of low-income groups
2. *Priority II*: intermediate items
3. *Priority III*: activities, etc., definitely not related to the above

Precise categorization into these three priorities will always be problematic. In the first place, the objective of protecting vulnerable groups is multi-dimensional (e.g. it includes incomes, nutrition, education). Some expenditures may be of high priority in terms of one dimension, but not others—e.g. employment in the defence industries, which may help generate incomes among the poor, but the resulting output may be a low priority in human face terms. Secondly, within each dimension, whether an item is priority or not must depend on the political context and may often be a matter of judgement. For example, while nutrition may be a priority, food may not be the major obstacle to improved nutrition in a particular context. Thirdly, the precise dividing line between the three catagories is bound to be arbitrary. This is one reason why an intermediate category (II) has been proposed—this would include all 'ambiguous' items. The aim would be to realize as much of category II as possible. Some of the problems involved in selecting priorities and fulfilling them are discussed at much greater length in Chapter 8.

Despite the problems of categorization, it is nevertheless possible to divide incomes, expenditures, etc. roughly into three categories. Some types of expenditure or income are obviously not of top priority for meeting the needs of vulnerable groups (e.g. luxury consumption items), while others would certainly be somewhere in the top priority (e.g. vaccines). A completely watertight and acceptable categorization of all items will never be possible. However, a rough ordering can greatly improve achievement of the objective in a resource-constrained setting.

The aim of any strategy devoted to achieving growth and protecting the vulnerable would be to achieve 100 per cent of the Priority I activities; as many of the Priority II as is possible; and, until all I and II are achieved, as few of Priority III as possible. Each policy instrument would be used to achieve this objective. Economies vary in the instruments they have, and therefore how this approach would be interpreted in practice. However, all governments have some instruments influencing the allocation of activities and the achievement of priorities. In a human face approach these instruments would be used explicitly to achieve the objectives of protecting the vulnerable and promoting growth. How this would operate will become clearer in a brief consideration of particular policies.

V   Meso policies

Each meso policy is concerned with improving the impact of a given macro variable on the allocation of resources and/or the distribution of income so as better to achieve the priorities. Some of the policies achieve this primarily by affecting the availability (supply) of goods and services; and some more indirectly by affecting income distribution and consequently demand.

Supply variables include decisions on the allocation of public expenditure, of aid, and the distribution of credit. Policies affecting *demand* include policies towards taxation and subsidies and towards incomes. Price controls and policies towards import tariffs may affect both supply and demand.

··

POLICY INSTRUMENT	OBJECTIVE : to secure priorities in:
	Supply
Public expenditure allocation	Supply of public goods
Aid allocation	
Distribution of credit	Supply of goods from private sector
Import allocation	
Producer price controls	
	Demand
Indirect taxes and subsidies	Demand for consumer goods from private sector (level and distribution)
Direct personal taxes	
Consumer price controls	
Tariffs; exchange rate	
Incomes/wages policy	
Public works	
Land reform	

Fig. 7.1. Policy instruments available to ensure allocation of resources to priority objectives

Fig. 7.1 summarizes the array of instruments available to ensure priorities The actual range of policy instruments varies with the country. For example, controls (e.g. over imports, or investment, or prices) are used in some economies, but not elsewhere. It is apparent from Fig. 7.1 (which is by no means a complete description of policy options) that there are an abundance of policy instruments—more instruments than objectives. Even economies with minimal controls exercise direct control over allocation of public expenditure and donors' aid. Every economy uses direct and indirect taxes, and most have some subsidies, which together help achieve priorities in consumption. The human face approach requires that collectively the available policy instruments be used to secure the stated priorities. Generally this would be attainable with full use of existing policy instruments and would not require additional ones.

The same priorities may be achieved by different policy instruments (e.g. use of the price system or allocation by controls). In a particular case, the preferred instruments must depend on which instruments are available, how effective they are likely to be, political preferences, and constraints. Constraints—political or administrative—may make it necessary to use a combination of policies, rather than (as in the theoretical ideal) a single policy instrument for each objective.

A brief discussion of individual policies will help to explain how they may promote the achievement of the selected priorities.

1   Policies to influence supply

Several policy instruments may be adopted to influence supply.

1. *Public expenditure.* Every government has direct control over allocation of public expenditure. In principle, prioritizing public expenditure—permitting all I and a minimum of III—is straightforward. Selectivity in public expenditure may involve both intersectoral and intrasectoral allocations. In the former category, defence may be reduced and social sector expenditure or food subsidies increased, for example. As an example in the latter category, tertiary education may be cut and primary education expanded. However, a good deal of social sector expenditure and food subsidies are of a non-priority nature—i.e. they go towards non-priority types of expenditure, consumed mainly by middle-income groups (e.g. some hospitals). Consequently, re-allocating between sectors may not help achieve priorities unless the intrasectoral allocations are also improved. The prime focus must be on meeting the specific needs of vulnerable groups (e.g. expansion of primary health care). Reallocation towards meeting these needs could be achieved by reallocation towards basic health care from within the health sector, or from other parts of the public sector, or from private expenditures.

Selectivity may also involve choices with respect to type of expenditure (e.g. recurrent versus capital; purchased inputs versus wages) so as best to meet priority objectives. Each of these allocations offers considerable potential for improving achievements on growth and the human dimension, within any macro constraints. In practice, of course, there will be bureaucratic and political obstacles to complete rationalization of priorities along these lines. These may limit improved allocation but are unlikely entirely to prevent it.

2. *Aid finance.* Like public expenditure (with which it typically overlaps), discretionary project-by-project decisions are the rule in aid, giving rise to opportunities to be selective. Selectivity needs the active co-operation of aid donors, as well as initiative by the government. Moreover, the political and bureaucratic problems are likely to be at least as great as with public expenditure. Past decisions—already incorporated in half-built roads or hospitals,

for example—are particularly difficult to change, and may account for a large proportion of current aid-flows. However, the potential for achieving priorities by reallocation within aid can be great. For example, an ILO mission in Tanzania found that additional finance for priority imports, equivalent to 10 per cent of total imports, could be secured by cutting back on non-priority aid projects and switching half the amount saved to general import finance (ILO/JASPA 1982).

The choice of priorities to promote growth and the human dimension is likely to accord with the objectives of many aid donors. Together aid finance and the public sector usually account for over half the investment decisions, and often over three-quarters—so that the administrative tool for exercising priorities over much of investment exists, even in non-planned economies. In principle, the priorities could be translated into 'social values' and 'social cost-benefit' analysis, thus reconciling them with a more economistic approach to project evaluation and public expenditure decisions.

3. *Private sector supply* may be affected by credit policy, producer price policies, and other controls (e.g. over import allocation, or investment decisions) where these exist.

4. *Credit policy*. The government can require that credit is allocated only to priority areas. This was an important feature of Killick's proposed alternative package for Kenya (see Killick *et al.* 1984). In Zimbabwe, an increasing proportion of agricultural credit has been given to the small farmers. Credit is an essential aspect of schemes to promote small-scale industrial activities (see Ch. 10). However, the availability of foreign finance can bypass domestic allocations, so that the policy would need to be supplemented with a review of the allocation of foreign finance to ensure consistency with priorities.

5. *Producer prices*. Many governments offer floor (and/or ceiling) producer prices for major agricultural commodities. Assuming that conditions exist to make these prices effective (i.e. absence of a blackmarket, prompt payment of producers by the marketing authorities, availability of consumer and producer goods for purchase by agricultural producers at reasonable prices), producer prices are a powerful mechanism for influencing the agricultural terms of trade and the relative incentive to produce food as against other cash crops. Producer prices affect priority objectives by helping determine the incomes of rural producers and the availability of food. They may simultaneously help the rural vulnerable (unless they are subsistence producers, or landless labourers) and hurt the urban vulnerable (as food consumers). Careful analysis is therefore needed to determine appropriate policies. Rising food prices contribute to the long-term food supply objective and also to maintaining incomes of small farmers, while hurting low-income urban households and landless labourers. In the short term, special measures will be needed (e.g. food stamps) to protect these groups when producer prices of food are increased. The country studies illustrate some of the consequences of changes in producer prices in different contexts. In the Philippines, the collapsed sugar price due to external develop-

ments was the major source of problems for the vulnerable sugar workers in the estates of Negros Occidental. In Ghana, the increased cocoa price—which formed an important part of the adjustment programme—has contributed to the recovery of cocoa production and exports (helping the growth objective), but price increases have not been extended to the crops produced by the poorest farmers in the north, so that the most vulnerable groups have not benefited. However, in Zimbabwe, high producer prices for grain have assisted small farmers and have also led to an expansion of grain production which has resulted in a food surplus in the country and has helped stabilize urban prices. The policy has thus been in accordance with priorities of growth and human needs.

2   Policies to influence demand and real incomes

A number of policies may be employed to influence demand and real incomes:

1. *Taxation.* As discussed earlier, protection of vulnerable groups would normally be helped by higher *levels* of taxation and expenditure. Within any total, the tax incidence may be used to further the objective. *Direct* taxes influence the distribution of disposable income with progressive taxation reducing the disposable income of upper income groups, a Priority III item. But the extent of this effect is normally limited by administrative and political constraints. *Indirect* taxes and subsidies offer more potential: indirect taxes on luxury consumption items may reduce the disposable income of upper-income groups and consumption on low-priority goods and services, while subsidies on basic goods and services consumed by the poor increase the real incomes of the vulnerable and encourage a switch in consumption to priority items.

2. *Consumer price controls.* Some economies have a full array of price controls, but these are often ineffective when there are large imbalances between demand at official prices and supply, as is typical during economic crises. In such a context, consumer price controls may therefore not be effective in achieving priority objectives. But where price controls are supported by adequate supplies, they may be used to ensure stable prices of basic commodities for low-income urban households. The conventional adjustment package often requires dismantling of some or all price controls. The approach suggested here would be to reduce the number of controls to a small number on key basic commodities, and to support control on these key prices by policies to generate adequate supplies. In fact, price control policies might better be considered as supply policies for key basic commodities, with any price increment being a symptom of failure of supply. The key commodities should normally include a basic staple food, a basic fuel, soap and basic drugs.

3. *Import controls and tariffs.* Import controls and tariffs can affect patterns of demand and supply. The lowest priority items should be subject to very high tariffs, or banned, while controls and tariffs should be reduced on priority items. As far as *intermediate* products are concerned (viz. parts, raw materials,

etc.), the priority to be attached to the item depends on the priority of the final product. In economic crisis, this may involve reducing or even eliminating supplies to some industries.

4. *Wages and employment policy* directly influence the incomes of employees. Adjustment packages often reduce real wages and employment in the public sector. Such policies generally contribute to the stabilization objective by simultaneously improving the public sector balance (through reducing government expenditure) and reducing incomes and consumption, and therefore imports. Whether some adjustment of this type is necessary depends on the macro balances in the economy. The effects of such policies on vulnerable groups depend on whether the government sector is relatively a high-wage or low-wage employer, and how the policies are administered. Real wages can be reduced selectively so as to protect those on the minimum. If incomes of vulnerable groups would be seriously affected by reduced government employment, then reduction, if essential, should be phased in gradually, and compensatory employment provided as far as possible in the form of public works and promotion of small-scale enterprises.

5. *Land reform* (and other forms of asset redistribution), contributes to the ability of low-income groups to raise their incomes as well as generally improving the efficiency of resource use. In some contexts it can be of critical importance to maintaining and raising incomes of the rural poor.

This brief (and incomplete) review of meso policies shows that governments have many instruments which could be used to attain the priorities that form an intrinsic part of protecting the human dimension and promoting growth in a resource-constrained context. These are not new policy instruments, but instruments already in use, generally without systematic regard for their consequences for vulnerable groups and for growth. To some extent, this is a consequence of the politics of decision-making, especially in crisis. But to some extent, it is due to the lack of a systematic approach to attaining priorities.

3   Policy reforms and institutional changes

These are changes designed to improve the design of adjustment policies from a human dimension perspective, and to make any given set of policies more effective in reaching vulnerable groups. They involve changes in *national mechanisms* associated with developing adjustment packages, and increased *empowerment* and *participation* of vulnerable groups.

1. *National mechanisms.* Traditionally, the Ministry of Finance has taken the lead role in the formation of adjustment policies and in negotiations with international institutions. Inevitably, this gives major priority to stabilization aspects of the package, since these are the priority concerns of finance ministries. Extending the objective beyond stabilization to growth and welfare of vulnerable groups requires that those parts of government concerned with these

issues (development of planning ministries and the social sector ministries) form an integral part of the team which develops adjustment policies.

This requires that they are brought into the process of policy formation and consultation with international institutions at the initial stages, and not at a late stage when most decisions have already been made. The precise mechanism for achieving this will vary according to country circumstances: interministerial committees or task forces, reporting to the President or Prime Minister, offer possible mechanisms. Similarly, international institutions concerned with development and the human dimension need to be incorporated into decision-making on adjustment.

2. *Empowerment and participation* of vulnerable groups, especially women, helps to secure the political commitment to get the policies introduced and effectively implemented; to improve the design of policies so that they correspond to the needs and conditions of the people to whom they are directed; and to improve the efficiency of the policies in terms of their objectives. It has been established, for example, that public works schemes are more efficient and have better distributional effect when local people are involved in their design (see Ch. 10).

Changes which assist in this empowerment and participation include:

(*a*) developing institutions to assist in organization of the landless, women's groups, urban poor, etc. (the Grameen Bank and SEWA—see Ch. 10—are examples);

(*b*) providing financial support to community efforts;

(*c*) building requirements for consultation and participation into project design.

Some of these issues are discussed further in Chapter 8 on the design of sectoral interventions. The need for changes in mechanisms, however, extends beyond sectoral issues to mechanisms covering the design and implementation of macro and meso policies.

VI Conclusions

Giving clear priority to protection of vulnerable groups both in the short and medium run has important implications for the design of adjustment policies. In general, it requires a less deflationary approach to adjustment and more access to finance, secured either by borrowing more or deferring payments on existing debts. In choosing macro policies, the implication of each policy for vulnerable groups should be explicitly considered and the effects on vulnerable groups be systematically incorporated into the process of monitoring achievements. In order to maximize achievements where the use of resources are constrained, expenditures and incomes should be grouped into priorities, and all policy instruments aimed to achieve the chosen priorities within a given resource constraint.

This approach to adjustment has implications for national mechanisms to develop policy packages—those whose first concern is with vulnerable groups and with growth must be integrally incorporated into the process of policy formation. It also requires measures to increase the empowerment and participation of vulnerable groups.

In the studies of country experience, three countries adopted a combination of macro and meso policies which protected vulnerable groups during shocks and succeeded in restoring economic growth after only a short interruption. These were Botswana, South Korea, and Zimbabwe. The three countries followed quite conventional but relatively expansionary macro policies, while the needs of the poor were protected by measures to sustain their incomes and to reallocate resources to basic health and education, and nutrition interventions for the most vulnerable. Botswana placed great emphasis on employment creation through public works to help restore incomes lost by drought. South Korea also made use of public works to maintain incomes during economic recession. In Zimbabwe, credit, marketing and supplies favoured the small-scale farmers, whose marketed production in consequence surged from 10 per cent of the total in 1980 to 38 per cent in 1985. The most comprehensive direct nutrition support was provided by Botswana. Both South Korea and Zimbabwe increased the share of education and health in government expenditure and the share of basic services in total social sector expenditure. In Zimbabwe, for example, total government expenditure increased by over 60 per cent in real terms from 1980 to 1984; the share of education and health in the total rose from 22 to 27 per cent, while the share of defence in recurrent expenditure fell from 44 to 28 per cent. Preventive medicine rose from 7.6 per cent to 14 per cent in total health expenditure, and the share of primary education in total educational expenditure nearly doubled from 32 to 58 per cent.

In each country, the government adopted a selective approach which combined meso policies favouring the vulnerable with more conventional macro policies. Their experience shows it is possible to adopt adjustment policies which succeed in protecting the vulnerable while restoring growth.

8

Social Policy-making: Restructuring, Targeting Efficiency

Giovanni Andrea Cornia*

I Introduction and premiss

This chapter discusses some general principles that might be of assistance in the formulation of social policies during periods of adjustment. More concrete and detailed applications of these principles are presented in the five chapters dealing with policy-making on health, education, support to the income of the rural and urban poor, and nutrition. A general discussion, however, provides a better understanding of the main thrust of an alternative approach to social sector policy-making during periods of adjustment.

To start with, a major objective of public policy during adjustment periods should consist in enhancing the *redistributive role* of the state, compensating not only for structural inequalities in the distribution of assets, incomes, and opportunities but also for the heavy burden of adjustment borne by the poor. One way to enhance this role consists in expanding the supply of basic goods and services to the poor during a period of general contraction of the economy. The provision of goods and services in the areas of health, education, and nutrition, in particular, has been shown to have positive redistributive effects (Selowsky 1979, Meerman 1979). Another approach consists in the creation of *buffering mechanisms* protecting the poor from the hardships provoked by recession and the implementation of severe stabilization measures. Under such circumstances special provisions need to be made, like instituting labour-intensive public works schemes, subsidizing certain items, suspending the payment of given charges, etc.—often only for limited periods of time.

Secondly, the *relation between economic and social sector policies* during periods of adjustment should receive closer scrutiny. In many cases these two sets of policies are regarded as independent one from the other. Economic policies tend to be given priority, while the formulation of social policy generally takes place within a pre-established macro-economic framework which does not pay much attention to distributive and welfare issues. This situation is often

---

* Sections II. 2 on community financing and III. 3 on targeting were prepared by Frances Stewart.

responsible for the failure of adjustment policies to generate adequate social support.

The separation between economic and social policies should be rejected. Economic policies do influence human welfare and that of children in particular, as shown in earlier chapters. Social policies also influence economic performance. Reduction in health care expenditure and in nutritional support for the poor, for instance, represent a typical case of disinvestment in human resources with adverse effects on nutritional levels and short- and long-term production prospects.

Social policy-making should therefore not be seen as an appendix to, but as an integral part of, the overall process of policy-making during adjustment. Economic decisions concerning resource allocation, pricing, expenditure cuts, etc., should be assessed in terms of their potential effects on human ecology. So far this has not occurred too often. In Brazil, for instance, the substitution of oil imports by alcohol extracted from sugar-cane had a negative impact on average calorie intake. To produce 50 litres of alcohol for car engines, one ton of sugar-cane is needed, which in turn requires land equivalent to the amount needed to grow food for 200 people. The continued expansion of agricultural land used for growing sugar-cane or export crops forced a drop in the cultivation of basic foods for domestic consumption, leading to growing shortfalls in calorie intake (UNICEF-Brazil 1984). Equally, decisions concerning the social sector must be considered in terms of their support for restoring and sustaining growth. In other words, there is a need to formulate these two sets of policies in an integrated fashion.

The need for integration between social and economic policies becomes even more evident when considering the *time-lags* with which various types of policies produce their effects. As argued in Chapter 2, while macro-economic demand-restraint policies have an *immediate* depressing effect on output, employment, and incomes, supply-expansion policies require *a few years* at least before they start producing increases in output. Many households may therefore face long periods of deprivation, possibly with irreversible effects on small children and other vulnerable groups. There is a need to bridge this gap. Appropriate social policies, such as instituting income-generating schemes and nutritional support, do have immediate positive effects that can offset the immediate negative effect of demand-restraint policies.

Thirdly, the articulation of social policies should receive closer scrutiny. First, there is a need for *social group analysis* in developing social sector policies. While some social policies aim at the whole population, certain specific socio-economic or age/sex groups are affected by recession and adjustment far more severely than average. As such they should be the target of specific policy support. Besides allowing identification of those in need, such an approach is fundamental for the design of appropriate targeting. Secondly social policy should not be limited to the provision of health and education services. As the experience of the 10 country studies shows, interventions in these two sectors alone cannot guarantee acceptable standards of living for poor children and their households. Food subsidies, income transfers, income generation, support to small-scale productive activities were applied—if temporarily—in Zimbabwe, Botswana, Peru, South Korea, and Chile. In particular, the need for increased interventions in the area of food and nutrition was recognized in the majority of the countries analysed. *During periods of recession and adjustment the scope of social policy must be widened.*

Directly or indirectly all policies towards the social sectors have implications for the *efficiency, equity,* and *level of resources* of the sectors. Broadly, policies can be grouped in two categories, those aiming at sustaining the flow of resources to the social sector, and those aiming at improving the efficiency and equity of use of such resources.

II Sustaining the flow of resources for adjustment in the social sector

This section examines the available policy options for maintaining, and when feasible expanding, the flow of resources to the social sector during periods of adjustment.

1 Sustaining budgetary allocations to the social sector

Budgetary resources are known to be limited in most developing countries. The evidence provided in Chapters 1 and 3 indicates that in the early 1980s, total government expenditure has been declining in about half of the developing countries for which information is available. However, except in cases like that of Ghana where the decline in GDP, tax base, government revenue, and total expenditure was so pronounced as to make any attempt to sustain any particular kind of outlay illusory, there almost invariably is scope for maintaining real levels of social sector expenditure. Whether the latter will decline or increase is largely a matter of political choice. In Sri Lanka, for instance, in 1985 food subsidies received an allocation of 1,700 million rupees, while it was reckoned that the minimum needed to reach all the eligible was of the order of 2,500–3,000 million rupees. It was argued that lack of resources did not permit a rise in the allocation to the required level. During the same year, however, the national airline received a subsidy of 1,000 million rupees.

There are also examples where social expenditure has increased during general recession and adjustment. Jolly and Cornia (1984), for instance, provide evidence of how real social expenditures were increased in South Korea during the 1979–81 recession. In Burkina Faso real per capita expenditure on health was increased between 1980 and 1983 by 3.6 per cent a year despite a sharp drop in GDP per capita and total government expenditure per capita. On the occasion of the budget speech in January 1986, the President of Indonesia announced that, despite a 50 per cent cut in the overall development

budget owing to sharp declines in oil and gas revenue, none of the Child
Survival Development activities would suffer any reduction, while the funds
allocated to immunization were actually increased (Antara News Agency, 7
January 1986). For many countries there is also evidence that in the second
half of the 1970s (Hicks and Kubisch 1983) and between 1979 and 1983 (see
Ch. 3) the social sector was 'relatively protected' from budgetary cuts as social
expenditure declined more slowly than total expenditure.

In a number of cases, the flow of budgetary resources to the social sector
has been sustained through the imposition of *ad hoc* taxes, the revenue of which
was specifically to be used for social objectives. In Brazil, for instance, one of
the federal government responses to the crises was the creation of the Fund for
Social Investment (Finsocial) in May 1982. Finsocial was fed by an additional
0.5 per cent tax on sales and a 5 per cent surcharge on corporate income tax,
and was designed to finance programmes in the areas of food and nutrition,
housing for the poor, health, education, and support to small farming. In 1982,
Finsocial collected resources of approximately $300 million, while in 1984 the
level reached almost $1 billion. While the sales tax feeding Finsocial is likely
to be regressive, the degree of progressivity of the expenditure has not yet been
evaluated. Whatever its shortcomings, the Finsocial experience proves that
considerable resources for the social sector can be mobilized in a relatively
short period of time. More thorough utilization of the fiscal instrument (both in
direct and indirect taxation) could generate important resources for sustaining
priority expenditure in the social sector. This is true even in low-income
economies. Increases in taxes on beer and cigarettes would allow many countries in Africa to finance a good part of the local cost of primary health care.

There is a clear case therefore for arguing for a sustained flow of public
resources to the social sector. The degree of persuasiveness of the argument
could be greatly increased in particular cases if the request for funds was
accompanied by specific indications about their use. There is a case also for
arguing for a selective application of budgetary cuts when total government
expenditure declines. As the examples given above indicate, these cuts should
be targeted so as to avoid impinging on the basic services of the most vulnerable.

2   Introducing or increasing user charges

User charges were found to account for between 10 and 15 per cent of total
government health expenditure for 1977 to 1983 for the 17 countries for which
information was compiled by the World Bank (de Ferranti 1984). De Ferranti
and others estimate that even under the most optimistic assumptions, this share
is not likely to surpass 20–25 per cent of total government expenditure over
the next 5–10 years. At the same time, the share of private health expenditure
in total health expenditure, including water expenditure, averages around 50
per cent, with peaks of 80 per cent and over. Thus, households already devote
a substantial amount of their resources to health care and other services, with

only a small fraction of this private expenditure going to the public sector, normally to pay for health workers and drugs. A similar picture would emerge with respect to user charges in education, water, and other social sectors.

During recent years there has been an increasing tendency to present user charges as a possible way of alleviating the resource constraint provoked by the economic decline of the 1980s (de Ferranti 1984). Indeed the country studies provide evidence of rising charges in sectors such as health, water, education, and other.

However, the potentially regressive nature of user charges should be emphasized, as in many developing countries the need for health care, education, etc. rarely coincides with the ability to pay for it. Raising charges in these sectors will have an adverse effect on vulnerable groups in three ways: *firstly*, it may lead to lesser use of services by vulnerable people. As noted earlier, Bendel State in southern Nigeria, for instance, after the reintroduction of school fees, primary school enrolment dropped from 90 to 60 per cent during an 18-month period ending in 1984 (UNICEF 1985a). *Secondly*, experience in the health sector shows that the introduction of fees tends to discourage the utilization of preventive services in particular (pre-natal care, immunization, etc.), for which patients may not see an immediate relevance. Preventive services, however, have been shown to be much more cost-efficient than curative methods, and also to prevent some adult health problems in childhood (Lechtig *et al.* 1980). By reducing the use of preventive services, greater economic costs (for curative services) or welfare losses (death, illness, etc.) will be borne in the future. *Thirdly*, for those who continue to use the service, the introduction of a charge will have a negative income effect which may adversely affect the household's ability to meet other basic needs (e.g. purchase food). Raising charges during a period of economic recession has an even more marked effect as households' incomes decline and their ability to rely on private health, sanitation, education, and other social services is substantially eroded. For instance, the study of the Philippines (vol. ii, ch. 7) documents that in 1984/85 there was a sharp increase in attendance at public clinics as the soaring cost of private care and declines in incomes made private services no longer accessible to many low-income households.

The various social sectors, however, comprise different types of services, some clearly geared to the needs of the poor, others catering to the needs of the middle and upper class. While primary education, disease control programmes, and basic curative services are part of a *basic needs* basket and are therefore not well suited for the introduction of charges, the same cannot be said about university education and elective cosmetic surgery (which could be designated as 'high-income' services). For the latter group, some form of cost recovery would be advisable in most developing countries. A report from the World Bank (1984), for instance, suggests that for most countries it would be efficient and equitable to shift a greater share of the cost of higher education to those who benefit from it. There is also a third, *intermediate*, category, including most curative health services, secondary education, and others. For them selective cost recovery based on an income criterion might be desirable.

It is also important to distinguish between *nominal* and *substantial* user charges. The former are principally intended to deter unnecessary use of services and are not expected to generate large revenues. Their main purpose is to promote a more efficient use of resources. In the case of health services, for instance, too little time is often spent on essential services because valuable staff and supplies are overburdened with treating lower priority cases. Substantial charges, in contrast, aim at recouping a much larger part of the cost borne by the public administration.

In conclusion, while a case-by-case approach is warranted, the preceding discussion suggests that: (*a*) cost recovery is not generally to be recommended (either for the poor or for the rich) for that group of public services that meet basic needs, including primary education, public health and preventive health measures, installation of public water points, sanitation, etc.; (*b*) user charges should be introduced selectively (according to an income criterion with low-income people either exempted from payment or charged only nominal fees) for the group of intermediate services, comprising, for instance, secondary education, several curative and health services, and piped water; and (*c*) finally, for high-income services, a large portion of the full economic cost should be recovered from all income groups.

3 Community financing

Community financing presents an alternative to user charges or national taxation as a method of financing local services. Community financing has been used for the construction of schools, clinics, and sanitation projects, and to meet recurrent costs.

A survey of over 100 self-financing health sector schemes (Stinson 1982) found nine principal methods of financing, including fees for services and drug sales, financing by contributions from production co-operatives, the use of voluntary labour, exchange of services, special income-generating activities, and *ad hoc* fund raising. The most common objective of the projects was to meet drug costs, followed closely by compensation for health workers. The schemes rarely met hospital costs, nor did they usually defray costs of management or evaluation.

The effects of community-financed schemes on vulnerable groups varies according to whether the schemes are a substitute or addition to nationally financed health services, the wealth of the community, and precisely how the schemes are organized.

Community-financed schemes have mainly developed in rural areas, which are typically poorer than urban areas. 'Community financing ... places a significant burden on persons who have little ability to pay ... It does nothing to reduce disparities between town and country or among geographic regions;

and as health services develop it may accentuate disparities' (Stinson 1982, p. 15). In very poor communities, the vulnerable groups themselves bear the main cost of the schemes. However, in so far as the schemes supply *additional* services to those provided nationally (or prevent cuts that would otherwise occur), they may protect the most vulnerable during the adjustment process.

The diverse methods of community finance have different implications for protection of the most vulnerable, i.e.:

1. *Schemes relying on sales of drugs or payments for services* are a form of 'decentralized' user charges and suffer from the shortcomings discussed above, i.e. they are regressive and discourage utilization of services, particularly preventive services. However, a number of such schemes provide sliding scales or exemptions. For example, village health committees in Lamphun, Thailand, issue fee exemption cards for the indigent. In some cases, it has been found desirable to let a committee determine exemptions, because health workers were pressured by relatives, etc. Sliding scales and exemptions have been rare for drug sales.

2. *Community labour*, provided during the slack agricultural season, has been widely used in construction and maintenance. In this way even poor regions and communities may generate resources to meet their needs. For example, communities in one part of Ethiopia fenced and cleared 3,000 springs, built nearly 38,000 latrines, and dug over 3,000 refuse pits. In most parts of West Africa, while governments finance teachers' salaries, rural communities take care of the construction of primary schools. Community labour has also been used for productive enterprises which generate cash which is used in part to support social services. For example, the Eastern Clinic in Sierra Leone developed an oil palm plantation with a press and soap factory as a way of making money.

3. *Fund-raising activities*, such as raffles, lotteries, etc., are another way that funds have been generated: in Carrizal (Costa Rica), a health committee raised $11,000 to buy land and materials for a health post.

In conclusion, community-financed projects can provide a valuable mechanism for helping provide basic services provided that (*a*) the projects are additional to national supplies, not substitutes; (*b*) the method of financing adopted allows the most vulnerable to benefit from the services with low or zero charges; (*c*) the schemes have adequate leadership, design, and management: (*d*) the finance generated by the local community is matched by outside support to provide essential inputs which are not available from local sources.

It is worth emphasizing the desirability of providing external support for local community projects. In the first place, without some outside resources the projects may not be viable at all, especially in very poor communities which can contribute labour, food, and local materials but not enough finance to purchase inputs from outside the area. Secondly, external agencies (the central government, regional government, NGOs, or official aid donors) may be able to help in design and management, which tends to be weak at a community level. In the third place, the known availability of some external finance to support local efforts may provide a powerful incentive to local initiatives. In an unusual experience in South Korea, 35,000 villages were supplied with cement and steel reinforcing rods to support village improvement projects in roads, bridges, wells, and sanitation facilities. Each village was rated according to its accomplishments; those doing well received further, though modest, support while those doing poorly received nothing. The Saemaul movement has transformed the appearance of South Korean villages, fostered the completion of a large variety of co-operative self-help projects, and promoted more effective working relationships, both among farmers and between farmers and local officials.

4 *Mobilizing international resources: temporarily relaxing regulations on recurrent cost*

Besides its overall level, the effectiveness of external assistance is influenced by specific policies regulating its use. One such policy is that on counterpart funds and recurrent costs. A temporary relaxation in the rules regulating external assistance could result in increased and more relevant financing for the social sector. (A more general discussion of external assistance is presented in Ch. 15.)

At present most externally financed projects require the recipient country to finance recurrent costs, while external assistance provides the capital costs of the project—in some cases, only the foreign exchange component of capital costs. In periods of recession and adjustment government budgetary resources are generally squeezed, and it is not uncommon that local counterpart funds, usually intended to finance recurrent costs, are sharply curtailed. This leads to decline in the utilization of projects already initiated, and newly allocated aid money frequently cannot be disbursed for lack of counterpart funds. Ironically, in this way the negative effects of economic decline are compounded by the norms regulating aid. As a result clinics, schools and water systems (often built with external assistance) fall into disrepair, with almost no drugs, books, or spare parts, while absenteeism often becomes a problem among staff who have been without salary for several months.

The refusal to meet local and recurrent costs therefore has not only biased decisions towards capital-intensive and import-intensive projects, but also reduced the rate of utilization of existing projects and total disbursement of foreign assistance. This vicious circle becomes particularly evident during adjustment periods when both budgetary resources and foreign exchange decline.

This situation is now widely recognized, and it is increasingly accepted that new projects should not be launched until existing ones have been restored to fuller use. This implies the willingness, one way or another, to finance recurrent costs. *The question at issue, therefore, is not whether or not to finance recurrent costs, but how and when.*

A policy on local and recurrent costs could be articulated as follows:

1. *Real local commitment.* To start with, it is necessary to verify that there is a real local commitment to the project under consideration, and that after a few years the project can become self-sustaining. This means that *under normal conditions* local counterpart funds should cover at least, say, 30–40 per cent of the total costs of the project, and that local funds should be able to finance total recurrent costs after a few years. However, in order to avoid the capital and import-intensive bias mentioned above, the choice of what costs (capital or recurrent) to finance in the short run with foreign assistance should be left to the recipient countries. Often, for instance, what is needed is not new projects but revitalization of old ones. This requires funds for repair and maintenance and recurrent costs, rather than new capital investment—which may conflict with donor aid-tying practices.

2. *The exceptional situation of countries either in deep recession or undergoing severe adjustment must be recognized.* Their budgetary and foreign exchange situation must be thoroughly assessed before applying the above criteria. A degree of country differentiation appears necessary at this point. While middle–high-income developing countries—with relatively well developed health, sanitation, and school systems—may not require any change in cost policies, the low-income developing countries of Africa and Asia ought to be treated differently. First, labour and other contributions in kind (construction material, current inputs, food, etc.) should be counted both as counterpart funds and recurrent inputs. Secondly, for a limited amount of time, recurrent costs both for ongoing projects and new projects could exceptionally be met by donors. For instance, recurrent costs might be met for, say, three years, or on a sliding scale for, say, five years. The figures are of course only indicative and should be adapted on a case-by-case basis. Barring exceptional circumstances, after this 'grace period' the project should become self-sustaining without continued external assistance.

These changes should increase resources for adjustment in the social sector in low-income developing countries, as foreign assistance previously blocked by the lack of counterpart funds is released for funding both recurrent and capital costs of ongoing and new projects. Such changes would also result in an increase in the rate of utilization of existing projects and in greater output of the social sector than when external assistance was used exclusively for new capital investment.

III Improving efficiency and equity in the use of social sector resources

The measures described in this section aim at increasing the level of output and at improving its distribution for any given level of resources available to the social sector. The measures proposed broadly aim at maximizing collective welfare by increases in efficiency and equity and changes in the organizational make-up of the social sector. Measures include the following.

1 Promotion and support of the diffusion of self-help practices at the household level

It has been estimated that at least 75 per cent of all health care takes place at the family or individual level, with women having the greatest responsibility for promoting family health and nutrition (Levin *et al.* 1979, cited in Coeytax 1984). The degree of self-provisioning is lower in other social sectors, education for instance. In many societies, however, there is scope for decentralizing many activities in health, nutrition, child care, sanitation, etc. to the family (or community) level. This decentralization is not costless. Important efforts have to be made to mobilize public opinion and create awareness about the need for the adoption of certain health, nutrition, and child rearing practices. Governments, community leaders, and foreign donors must often join forces to organize and sustain massive campaigns of public education. Social communication aimed at the mother is the key element of this strategy. The current UNICEF approach to the treatment of diarrhoea (the number-one infant killer in the world) through home-based oral rehydration is an appropriate example. While until recently diarrhoea was treated at considerable cost in health posts or hospital by means of intravenous rehydration, the new strategy emphasizes home-based treatment consisting of an appropriate mix of sugar and common salt in a litre of boiled water. All the ingredients of the oral solutions are generally available even in very poor families, while pre-packaged mixtures of salt and sugar are produced industrially and sold commercially in many developing countries at extremely low costs (6–10 cents per packet). While such an approach may increase time costs for women (Leslie *et al.* 1986), it will place extremely modest monetary costs on the households; and will lead to substantial savings in the public sector, where a considerable proportion of hospital beds, staff time, and current inputs is absorbed by the care of diarrhoeal disease. Other areas where a similar approach using public education as the main thrust can be applied include breast-feeding, weaning, and growth monitoring.

2 Improving the efficiency of government social expenditure

Despite the conspicuous and growing shortage of budgetary and human resources, the social sector is far from using them in an efficient way. Indeed, in many developing countries, the provision of social services is affected by a long series of biases in favour of expensive, urban-based, capital- and skill-intensive activities, often modelled on those of the industrialized countries. As seen earlier, the capital intensiveness of such services is often influenced by donors' preference for financing capital costs and by the practice of tied aid.

For these and other reasons, some social services often cater to a relatively small, mostly urban, upper and middle class, bearing little relevance to the satisfaction of the most elementary health, nutritional, and educational needs of the population.

In many countries substantial scope exists therefore for improvement in the efficiency of government recurrent and capital expenditure. For ease of exposition, such improvements are grouped into five categories:

1. *Selective rehabilitation.* As far as capital expenditure is concerned, there is the need for selective rehabilitation of the social service infrastructure. Output increases obtained by rehabilitating existing infrastructure are generally substantially cheaper than those obtained through new investment. It is important to underline, however, that this rehabilitation should be selective in nature, i.e. starting from those facilities with the highest potential coverage to meet high priority unfulfilled needs. Selective rehabilitation should also represent an occasion for restructuring social services away from expensive, high-tech solutions and towards low-cost and high-efficiency measures. The study of Ghana, for instance, suggests that in view of the expensive nature of hospital-based care, the government should consider putting a stop to new hospital construction and to major extensions of existing capital. The resources so freed should be used for the rehabilitation of health posts and health centres.

2. *Restructuring of social expenditure.* Within each sector there is a need to restructure social expenditure towards the satisfaction of the needs of the poor majority. The problem of an excessive allocation of health resources to the hospital sector is to be found in many other countries. In Malawi, in 1983, hospitals received over 60 per cent of government health funds (Ministry of Health 1984), while in the Senegal (1981/82) and Tanzania (1980) hospitals absorbed respectively 51 and 58 per cent of government health budgets (UNICEF 1983). Intrasectoral misallocation of resources is not only typical of the health sector. In Burkina Faso, for instance, between 1980 an 1984 secondary and university education received on average a share of the education budget twice as large as primary education, although the latter covered a school population 10 times larger (UNICEF-Burkina Faso 1986), while according to a World Bank study '... in Francophone Africa two per cent of each cohort in the population attain higher education and receive 40 per cent of the public resources devoted to education' (World Bank 1984, p. 42).

Correcting such glaring misallocations is not simple. For technical and social reasons, capital and labour resources are only partially mobile. A large hospital cannot be divided into 50 primary health care posts. Nor is it easy to provide sufficient incentives to secondary school teachers from urban areas to take up service in a primary school of a remote rural area. There are also clear political interests in the misallocation, which typically favours powerful élites. Reallocation is easier at the margin during periods of overall growth of resources. Despite these difficulties, redirection of government social expenditure in favour of basic services is possible. Such restructuring has happened in a number of countries. In Zimbabwe, for instance, the share of preventive health services doubled between 1979/80 and 1985/86, with a similar shift in favour of primary education (vol. II, ch. 10). In a study on the provision of education in Commonwealth countries, Jolly (1977) shows that attainment of the universal primary education target could be substantially accelerated by reducing unit costs in secondary and higher education and by shifting the resources thus saved to primary education.

3. *The adoption of low-cost high-efficiency measures* for the satisfaction of the basic needs of the poor will substantially contribute to more efficient use of social sector resources. In the past, expensive techniques were used to deal with common problems. Several low-cost, high-efficiency interventions have been developed recently. Water pumps have become sturdier, cheaper, and simpler to operate and maintain; vaccines more resistant to heat (thus facilitating their transport) and more potent have been developed at lower costs; and supplements to prevent vitamin A, iodine, and iron deficiency can now be made available at negligible costs. For instance, Cornia (1984*b*), shows that in Indonesia an integrated child-survival package covering 8.9 million children in 1982 and comprising growth monitoring, oral rehydration, breast-feeding, immunization, distribution of vitamin A capsules and nutrition education had an average yearly out-of-pocket cost of $6–7 per under-5 or about $1 per head of population. There is also ample evidence (Grosse and Plessas 1984, Robertson 1984) that *ceteris paribus* the cost of programmes tends to decline with the scale of the service delivered. In this way, a 'virtuous circle' is created between the low cost of an intervention (which allows for increased coverage at any given level of resources) and economies of scale, which by gradually reducing unit costs per capita further stimulate the expansion of coverage.

4. *The adoption of less skill-intensive and more community-based approach to the delivery of social services.* Although highly qualified staff (trained teachers, water engineers, doctors, certified nurses, nutritionists, etc.) are scarce in most developing countries, it is not uncommon that their precious time is absorbed by relatively simple problems, which could easily be delegated to lower-level staff and to community workers. For the health sector, for instance, the Alma Ata Declaration (WHO 1978) explicitly recommends the institution of a three-tier primary health care system in which the first and second tiers are manned by Village Health Volunteers and para-professionals with the ability to treat common ailments, while more complicated cases are referred to the higher tiers. In this way substantial savings on personnel costs and a more rational allocation of highly qualified staff become possible. The introduction of Village Health Volunteers, although not without problems, has further strengthened this approach to cost saving and rapid increase in service coverage. In Indonesia, for instance, the monetary cost per under-5 of the infant and child health programme could be reduced by around 30 per cent by the unremunerated

work of Village Health Volunteers (Cornia 1984*b*). While the use of volunteers requires considerable training, the results they produce are often impressive.

5. *Increasing the overall efficiency of the social sector.* This includes a series of heterogeneous measures which can contribute to cost saving and increased efficiency. Among them, *appropriate procurement policies* play a particularly important role. For instance, in many countries, governments should consider establishing a basic drug list as advised by WHO. Importing these under the WHO/UNICEF Drugs Procurement Facility allows cost savings of up to 40 to 50 per cent. Besides keeping costs down through centralized bulk procurement, the establishment of an essential drugs list could generate substantial financial and foreign exchange savings by explicitly *banning drugs* which have been proven to have no or negative effects. This is particularly the case for some drugs supplied to treat diarrhoea which, although widely used, have no therapeutic value.

Overall efficiency can also be improved by attempts to *reduce wastage*. In an evaluation of a measles immunization campaign in Cameroon, Walsh (1985) reports that out of 100 doses of vaccine, 83 were wasted as they had lost potency or were given to children who were either too young, too old, or already immune. While insufficient or inappropriate investment is at times responsible for these high levels of wastage, increased expenditure on supervision can substantially increase the efficiency of the overall delivery system.

3 Targeting

Targeting is a further powerful way of reducing programme costs and increasing the efficiency of social expenditure. In principle, achieving effective targeting should form an important aspect of sectoral policies to protect the vulnerable during adjustment. But to achieve this requires very careful design of targeting. The discussion here uses food interventions to illustrate the general issues.

1. *Defining the target population* is an essential prerequisite for targeting. Such definition is not easy, since it requires *facts*, which are typically scanty or nonexistent (see Ch. 14), and *norms*, which have to be chosen, the target group being those who fall below the selected minimum standards.

There are further problems in the selection of standards. First, the choice of the *reference dimension*, i.e. the dimension against which the target group is to be defined. For example, in nutrition the target group could be defined with reference to anthropometric data, calorie intake, or household income levels. Choice of reference dimension is partly dictated by availability of data. It also depends on the administrative mechanism and target group being considered: if children are the main target and health clinics the administrative mechanism, then some anthropometric dimension is appropriate. An income reference dimension is more suitable for income-support schemes. Secondly, how is the *cut-off point* to be selected? In general for most needs, including nutrition, there is no scientific justification for any particular cut-off point, so some arbitrariness enters the determination of norms. But the fact that no precise cut-off point is scientifically based, does not mean that no cut-off point is necessary—i.e. malnutrition exists, even though nutrition experts disagree on precisely when this occurs. Thirdly, the target group should be *differentiated with respect to extent of inadequacy*—e.g., distinguishing severely malnourished from mildly malnourished. This is important because failure to meet the needs of the most severely deprived (the ultra-deficient) is more serious than failing to reach the rest of the target population.

2. *Two types of mistakes can occur when targeting.* Assume the target population (T) has been identified and that it is divided into the deficient (DT) and the ultra-deficient (UT). Designing targeting interventions then aims to ensure that all T is covered by the intervention, but no one outside the target group. It follows that the targeting may be subject to two types of mistake:

(a) *Mistake E.* Excessive coverage, i.e. some interventions go to those outside the target group. This may be represented by E. The greater E, the higher the cost of any scheme; or put in another way, the size of the support to each member of the target group could be increased if E-type mistakes were all eliminated.

The major criticism of untargeted interventions (e.g. across-the-board subsidies) is that E-type mistakes are very large, so that total costs are high. For example, in Morocco, it was estimated that 80 per cent of the budgetary costs in the rural areas and 70 per cent in the urban areas 'increased the consumption of the already well-nourished' (Mateus 1983). This means that E was approximately 3, or the costs could have been reduced to one-third by eliminating E mistakes. It should be noted that E mistakes raise incomes of the non-target group. In principle, these could be recouped by taxes (e.g., income tax or indirect taxes).

(b) *F mistakes.* The second type of mistake is failure to cover all the target group. Suppose F represents the proportion of the target group that is not covered, then FT people's needs are not met. From the perspective of protecting vulnerable groups, F-type mistakes represent a serious failure and cannot be compensated for in the way E-type mistakes can. F mistakes are particularly serious if they consist in failures to reach the ultra-deficient group.

Even apparently 'universal' subsidies can involve some F mistakes—e.g. where the subsidies do not cover inferior goods, or subsistence farmers. Increased F mistakes are a normal consequence of moving from a universal to a targeted approach, which may be offset by good design of targeting.

In designing schemes, there tends to be a trade-off between E and F mistakes. The more narrowly focused on target groups the less the E mistakes, and the greater the F mistakes. While the aim should be to reduce both types of mistake, in so far as there is a trade-off, the emphasis—from the perspective of protecting the vulnerable during adjustment—must be placed on reaching *all the target group*, and especially the ultra-deficient.

3. *Types of targeting*. Schemes may be targeted by *income*, e.g. ration shops or coupons provided to those falling below a certain income (the recent Sri Lankan food stamp scheme provides an example); by *needs*, as identified by health workers, with coupons or free or subsidized foods provided to the needy (the Botswana scheme and the Indonesian scheme deliver food to children who are identified as most deficient, using anthropometric measures); by *commodity* subsidizing only basic or 'inferior' foods; by *geography*, locating subsidized ration schemes in areas where a high proportion of the target population live; by *age*, providing subsidies for all those below (or above) a certain age (this can be extended to pregnant or lactating women); through *employment* in food-for-work schemes; and by *season*, providing free or subsidized foods at certain times of the year. Particular schemes may combine elements—e.g. providing food to children of low-income households at certain times of the year.

The first two approaches differ from the remainder in being somewhat *discretionary*, in that the administrators of the scheme decide in any particular case whether the person qualifies. This discretionary aspect can lead to abuse (e.g. through corruption); and people who are needy may be left out because they do not come forward. This seems to occur particularly among the ultra-deficient, who generally have other characteristics (e.g. low levels of education, remote location) which make it less likely that they will come forward. The remaining schemes are *non-discretionary* (and therefore sometimes described as 'self-targeting'), being universally available within a restricted category. How far they generate the two mistakes will depend on the nature of the target group in comparison with the non-target population. For example, if *all* and *only* the target group lives in one remote region, then providing subsidies for everyone in this region would achieve perfect targeting, avoiding both mistakes.

In order to assess how far particular schemes are likely to generate E and F mistakes in any context, it is helpful to draw up a matrix describing the characteristics of the target population (divided into deficient and ultra-deficient) and comparing these with the non-target population.

Where there is a high proportion of the target group included in any category (high percentage in cols. 1 and 2 of Fig. 8.1), then a subsidy based on that characteristic will achieve high coverage of the target group (low F mistakes). If there is a low proportion of the non-target population with the same characteristic (low percentage in col. 3) then there will be low E mistakes

Schemes which combine characteristics may achieve improved targeting: for example in Brazil, common foods are subsidized in shops in certain poor areas (combining commodity and location).

Characteristics	1. Target: deficient		2 Target: ultra-deficient		3. Non-target	
	No.	% of group	No.	% of group	No.	% of group
Age and sex						
Under 5 F, M.						
5–15, F, M.						
15–60, F, M.						
60+						
Pregnant and lactating						
Location						
Urban						
Rural						
Region						
'North'						
'South'						
Consumption						
Of staple 1 as % income						
Of staple 2 as % income						
Occupation						
Formal sector, wage						
Informal sector						
Landless agricultural worker						
Subsistence farmer						
Small cash farmer						
Season						
Jan.–Mar.						
Apr.–June						
July–Sept.						
Oct.–Dec.						
Other relevant						

Fig. 8.1 Matrix of characteristics of the target population

4. *Other considerations in designing targeting schemes.* (*a*) Administrative cost—which depends in part on the existing situation; e.g. in India and Pakistan ration shops have been established, but elsewhere they would need to be set up. Administrative costs tend to be higher for special schemes (e.g., food-for-work and feeding schemes). Discretionary schemes have high administrative costs because they require identification of the target population on an individual basis. (*b*) Potential for corruption and perversion, and liability to pressure from private interest groups 'that want to divert programme funds from the target groups' (World Bank 1986, p. 47). (*c*) Effects on work incentives. (*d*) Effects on local food production incentives—food-for-work schemes supported by food aid can have negative effects on local production incentives. Price controls on foods may also, but need not if accompanied by producer

subsidies (as in Sri Lanka in the 1960s and 1970s). Feeding programmes using locally purchased foods have positive effects on producer incentives. (*e*) Effects on consumption patterns and tastes: subsidies on foods which are not produced locally or are produced locally at high costs may have undesirable effects on tastes. Subsidies on weaning foods or nutritionally superior foods can have positive effects.

In conclusion, targeting can help sustain minimum levels of nutrition and health in the whole population during periods of declining resources by concentrating the provision of benefits on the group facing the most severe deprivation. In several countries there is scope, for instance, for redirecting subsidies from generalized to targeted schemes. This would allow either substantial savings of budgetary resources or a higher benefit for the population in need. The problems encountered in the design of targeting indicate that there is frequently a trade-off between *E* and *F* mistakes. Whenever the aim of reducing both mistakes cannot reasonably be attained, priority should be attached to reaching all of the target group, even if this entails the cost of including some outside the target group.

IV Conclusions

Substantial scope exists for protecting the poor and the vulnerable during economic difficulties through policies in the social sectors. To achieve this objective, the role and scope of social sector policies must be substantially enlarged as economic trends and adjustment policies, however efficient, tend to put enormous burdens—at least for a few years—on the fragile shoulders of low-income households. During such periods, their autonomous capacity to satisfy the most elementary shelter, nutrition, education, health, and sanitation needs declines dangerously. Evidence shows that although the middle and upper class have also been severely affected by declines in standards of living, this has generally not been reflected in serious nutritional and health hazards. The purpose of social policies during adjustment therefore should be to expand the supply of basic goods and services, particularly to the poorest segments of society.

In the course of the discussion three main avenues were identified for achieving this objective: the *mobilization of additional resources* for the social sector; the *improvement in the efficiency* in the use of such resources; and an *increasing emphasis on equity* in the distribution of these benefits. While the potential of the first option might be limited in some countries, greater equity and efficiency are viable propositions for all countries facing severe economic decline.

Better targeting and restructuring of social expenditure, in particular, can substantially contribute to sustaining minimum standards of living of the poor during periods of economic hardship. In most sectors new technological breakthroughs and increased self-help and community participation now make possible the adoption of low-cost, high-efficiency approaches substantially benefiting the poor and their children. Their low-cost and high-efficiency also make them attractive from a political point of view.

9

Policy Approaches Towards Small Farmers

Richard Longhurst

I Introduction

This chapter considers how policies to promote the incomes and productivity of small farmers may contribute to protecting the vulnerable during adjustment.

In many developing countries, the rural sector accounts for the majority of the population, and an even greater proportion of those falling below a poverty line and having grossly inadequate access to basic services—water and sanitation, health and education services. Within the rural sector small farmers are typically the majority of the working population.

In some respects the direct poverty-inducing effects of recession and adjustment policies fall more on the urban population. The urban population suffers most from the decline in formal sector employment and real wages, and cuts in food subsidies. In particular cases, the rural population has been badly affected—where a collapse in primary product prices has occurred (sugar in the Philippines and tea in Sri Lanka), or where severe drought has been a major factor (as in much of Sub-Saharan Africa), and the rural population has generally suffered from the cuts in government expenditure on basic services that have usually accompanied adjustment. However, the rural population has, typically, more natural insulation from external economic shocks, being less part of the monetary economy, and often able to retreat into a greater degree of subsistence. Moreover, the adjustment policies frequently aim to change the internal terms of trade in favour of the rural sector, through exchange rate changes and changes in producer prices, but these policies may also increase rural differentiation, and may not therefore by themselves be effective in protecting the vulnerable in the rural areas.

Precisely how these developments have affected rural poverty varies according to country circumstances and policy package, as the country studies illustrate. For example, in Ghana the rural population have been badly affected by the long recession, and by adverse weather, but have on balance gained by the adjustment policies. In Sri Lanka there was a definite gain for rice producers, following the improved prices, but the tea estate workers have suffered. In the Latin American cases, it appears that the urban population has been worst hit (see vol. ii).

Irrespective of the distribution of net gains and losses, policies to improve the conditions of small farmers can play a vital role in helping the vulnerable during adjustment and in promoting growth. The role of these policies is most significant in those situations where rural poverty is greatest and has increased most, and where most of the rural poor are small farmers, but elsewhere too improving small-farm incomes will help alleviate poverty and increase growth. Raising incomes of small farmers has direct effects in reducing poverty among this group, which accounts for very large number of deprived households in almost every country, but is especially important in Africa and much of Asia. But the effects are not confined to small farmers. Where, as in many places, the urban poor still have ties with the rural areas, and may return if opportunities improve, raising rural incomes may also indirectly improve urban conditions. Some reverse migration has been noted in a few African countries. More often, improved rural conditions will slow down the flow of rural–urban migration, reducing the extent of urban poverty. In addition, the success of small farmers has important linkage effects on the rest of the rural economy. These linkages arise from expenditures by farming families on local goods and services and agricultural inputs, and from local processing of farm produce. In the Philippines, for example, it has been noted that a 1 per cent increase in agricultural output is associated with a 1 per cent increase in non-agricultural rural employment, with this ratio increasing the greater the concentration of the output increase on small farmers (Ranis and Stewart 1987). As non-agricultural employment increases, the position of the worst-off rural families —those with no or little land—improves. Lastly, but by no means least, numerous studies have shown that small farms are more efficient than large, while the agricultural sector as a whole often has a comparative advantage which has been neglected by government policy. Therefore, focusing on the small farmer will promote growth and efficiency, as well as equity.

In the light of these general considerations, this chapter analyses policies to promote small-farm productivity and incomes during adjustment. The second section discusses how typical adjustment packages affect small farmers. The third section reviews the evidence on the social and economic efficiency of the small farmer. The fourth section examines programmes and policies to help the small farmer during adjustment.

II   The economic efficiency of small farmers

A great deal of evidence has accumulated which strongly indicates that small farmers are more productive per unit of land than large farmers. This is the well-known 'inverse relationship' between land area operated and annual net value added per acre which was first identified in the Indian Farm Management Studies 30 years ago with respect to unimproved rainfed farming (Rudra and Sen 1980), and which is found in most parts of Africa today. This relationship, which varies between land types and in different areas of commercialized agriculture, is not entirely uncontroversial. It generally exists because of greater application of family labour. Smallholders find it more advantageous to apply labour to grow high value crops, double crop, or improve land in the slack season, reduce fallows in area and duration, and enhance yields by better cultural practices (Lipton 1985, p. 15). Lower management and supervision costs, and greater need for food compared with leisure, are also among the explanations. The inverse relationship may be weaker in areas where off-farm income is important, such as in northern Nigeria (Hill 1972, Longhurst 1986a). Generally, however, small farmers have a high level of labour use in comparison with large farms, which often have a high proportion of unused land, poor cultivation practices, and high levels of mechanization, dependent on imported fuel and spare parts.

The various caveats apart, the relationship points to the greater economic efficiency of the small farmer. Cornia (1985) has analysed FAO farm management data for 15 countries, looking at the relationship between factor inputs, land yields, and labour productivity. For all but three countries a strong negative correlation was found between farm size on the one hand and factor inputs and yields per hectare on the other.

However, whereas small farmers face low opportunity costs of employing family members, they face high costs of and difficult access to credit, and a higher effective price of land because of high borrowing costs (Cornia 1985). (In addition, small farmers often get lower prices for their produce than large farmers even when holding timing of sale constant, e g. in Thanjavur, India (Swenson 1973).) Large farmers use more capital, with mechanization primarily as a labour-displacing strategy, and also use more off-farm labour, indicating a more capitalistic mode of production based on wage labour. In Cornia's analysis, African countries used more family labour than others.

If a technology is appropriate to their resource base and constraints, small farmers adopt it almost as rapidly as large farmers. The research emanating from the spring of high-yielding rice and wheat varieties in Asia shows that small farmers quickly caught up after large farmers adopted new varieties (Barker and Herdt 1984). In areas where varieties are well suited to small holders, e.g. varieties that out-yield local varieties even with low inputs, disease risk, and some moisture stress, adoption is especially rapid (Lipton with Longhurst 1985).

Small farmers are active entrepreneurs, surviving on a limited resource base and working long hours for low returns. In many parts of the world, Africa in particular, the small farmer is a woman, having to combine household duties and child care with farm production. In addition to economic benefits, the small-farm families provide essential social benefits. They act as a sponge letting out migrants to the towns and absorbing them again if unsuccessful. Food and income are remitted to urban migrants seeking work. Small-farm labour-intensive cultural practices maintain land quality and fertility, minimizing soil degradation; production of by-products generates off-farm income activities. The farm family, through extended community networks, provides support to indigent families in times of stress. They thereby provide a very effective low-cost social security system.

Consquently, small farmers are economically efficient and provide important ecological and social benefits. This suggests that they should play a more central role in an adjustment strategy not only because potential benefits should be spread to the majority of the population, and its poorest sections, but because of the contribution that can be made to food security, reducing food imports, reducing migration, and creating more markets for non-agricultural goods and services in the rural areas (Daniel *et al.* 1984).

The generation of production by small farmers requires support from extension services but need not require large armies of extension agents. Richards (1985) has described for Sierra Leone how small farmers are constant researchers, testing varieties (of upland rice) and new cultural practices. They can quickly assess whether new technologies are suitable or not. This suggests that the per capita support costs of assisting small farmers need not be high. In many countries, for women farmers there already exist indigenous organizations, such as revolving credit societies, which could be used to channel the supply of inputs.

III   Structural adjustment policies and the small farmer

Structural adjustment policies aim *inter alia* to improve the balance of payments. In addition there has been an underlying philosophy of 'market efficiency'. Increased commercialization of this nature is likely to bypass the small producers as much of their effort is devoted to self-provisioning, and they can only be pulled in if production and marketing systems are strengthened. A major means of improving the balance of payments in many countries would be by a reduction in food imports through increased domestic production, which in general can only come through an increased flow of resources to the small farmer.

The impact of structural adjustment policies varies according to the situation of small farmers. In macro-economic adjustment, the prices of goods and services that are traded are increased relative to non-tradeables. Therefore, the small farmer growing primarily for self-provisioning will be worse off than small farmers who produce for export, who will benefit from export-promoting policies. With the exception of those smallholders who are able to produce for export (e.g. growers of cotton, groundnuts, tea, cocoa, and coffee), small farmers are mainly found in the sector producing neither tradeable output nor inputs for tradeables. In Ghana, for instance, adjustment policies have largely ignored the small farm sector while rehabilitating the estate sector. However, the household food supply of subsistence farmers may be protected as it is mainly in-kind income (Pinstrup-Andersen 1986*a*). This could be the basis for the often quoted but poorly documented 'retreat into subsistence'.

Increased commercialization promoted by structural adjustment can have risks for household food consumption and nutritionally vulnerable groups if farmers are encouraged to move into export crops. These risks and the ways in which they can be minimized will be discussed in Section IV. In many cases of extreme foreign exchange constraints, the agricultural sector suffers in general, and small farmers especially, from an acute shortage of all types of inputs (fertilizers, hoes, seeds), and from deficient transport systems. Increased supplies of inputs in these areas are essential for increasing production. Adjustment policies sometimes aim to increase inputs to the agricultural sector, but they rarely if ever make any specific attempt to steer resources to the small scale farmer. An alternative strategy could be devised which would meet both adjustment and equity considerations.

IV Strategies to increase the productive capacity of small farmers

This section proposes strategies which can meet equity and efficiency objectives by increasing the productive capacity of the rural poor. They are not comprehensive in coverage but have a common element: that there should be grater understanding of the pattern of activities of the poor, the constraints faced, and risks taken, and the methods and technology employed to ensure food security at the household level, particularly in times of stress. This is not to suggest that subsistence production can itself be expanded to the level required, but that innovations should be grafted onto mechanisms already employed by the poor.

1 Support for women

Despite the acknowledged predominance of women in agriculture in many parts of the world, women continue to be left out of agricultural strategies. In Africa, 85 per cent of rural women are involved in agriculture, where they produce and process as much as 80 per cent of family food consumption. Reduction in male wage employment and increasing landlessness have led to increased dependence on women's earnings in poor rural households. Where successful structural adjustment requires improving the balance of payments with regard to agricultural exports and food imports, then women must be part of that strategy.

An important corollary to the provision of assistance to women that raises their income or reduces their workload is the impact it will have on child nutrition. Recent research has highlighted the influence of women's time allocation on children (Schofield 1974, Tripp 1981, Popkin 1980). This can have two opposing effects. If women work on cash-rewarded employment outside the home, the income they earn can be used for extra food to the benefit of children; on the other hand, reduced inputs of child care can be harmful to children. Special attention has to be given to agricultural innovations that might alter the seasonal distribution of workloads for women, as it is at the period immediately before harvest that child care suffers and malnutrition reaches its peak (Chambers *et al.* 1981). There are clear linkages between structural adjustment objectives to increase food supply, the economic and technical roles of rural women, and the welfare of children.

Many households in both Asia and Africa are headed by women, representing some of the poorest households. In Africa there are a growing number of households where the male is absent through out-migration (Allison 1985). In Lesotho and Botswana men seek employment in South Africa. Less favoured peripheral areas of Zambia in Western, Northwestern, Luapula, and Northern provinces also have high rates of male out-migration. In Luapula, female-headed units constitute a third of all households. Such areas have about half the average farm size compared to the more favoured central and southern provinces (Chambers and Singer 1981).

Many agricultural strategies have ignored the fact that rural households are not homogeneous production units. In much of Sub-Saharan Africa, households contain several separate granaries and 'purses' (Dey 1984). Most projects and settlement schemes have denied women title to land. In the few cases where the sexual division of labour and differences in crop responsibility and control over product have been recognized, projects have proved successful. However, women generally lack power, assets, and participation in formal institutions to make their views known and take their share of available resources. When given the opportunity, they are vigorous entrepreneurial agents but often require a strengthening of their own organizations such as savings groups, trade associations, and credit networks.

Resources have been directed towards men even in situations where women are the technical experts in crop production, as shown by research on irrigated and swamp rice in The Gambia (Dey 1982). Subsequent investigations have confirmed this in other rice-growing African countries (Dey 1984). Swamp rice cultivation in The Gambia is traditionally carried out by women, but when new projects were designed, the project management discussed proposals with men, not women. Men were invited to take part in the construction work under food-for-work programmes so that the immediate benefits accrued to them. Because of the nature of separate 'purses' no benefits were received by women. As a result they had no interest in cultivating the new swamps because they had lost their traditional control over the crop, and because the siting and construction of the swamps, lacking their expertise, made their labour input especially high. Similar experiences are recounted for Madagascar (Conti 1983), Senegal, and Ivory Coast. When the project management involved women by asking their advice, they were impressed by women's all-round technical knowledge of rice cultivation and water control (Dey 1984, p. 73). As a result, some modifications have been possible in swamp construction and provision of credit to women to enable them to purchase inputs.

Following these experiences, the Jahaly Pacharr Smallholder (irrigated rice swamp) project, initiated in 1981, attempted to tackle the problems faced by women rice farmers (IFAD 1985). This meant, first, the provision of day care centres for children of women whose workload increased due to the introduction of double cropping; and secondly, the upholding of their traditional cultivation rights. Previous approaches with the use of improved technological packages had led to women losing their traditional tilling rights. As a result, the project arranged with the village communities that the swamps would be leased to the project authority, which would then distribute it to the original tillers after development. This redistribution was to be done by two communities, which would have both men and women represented. Initially women were underrepresented and land allocation was heavily biased in favour of men. After intervention by project authorities, the number of women on the committee was increased to more than half. Under these new arrangements 95 per cent of over 3,000 beneficiaries are women with credit and inputs provided directly to them, and extension workers are using womens' groups. Over the period 1982–84, rice yields averaging six tonnes per hectare have been achieved by women cultivators, compared to $2\frac{1}{4}$ tonnes before the project (Dey 1982).

In Zanzibar a large-scale scheme to develop nearly 3,000 hectares of double-cropped irrigated rice land and 800 hectares of rainfed rice land also recognizes women's dominant role in the production of rice and other subsistence food crops. Both men and women are able to register as tenants, each being allocated one-tenth of a hectare of irrigated land or one-quarter of a hectare of rainfed rice land (Conti 1983). The whole area was developed by the end of the second season in 1984, with women accounting for just over half of the registered tenants and playing an active role in the scheme's tenants' association. The project provides labour-saving equipment such as tractor ploughs, rotary hoes, and threshers for hire, although the plots are sufficiently small to permit manual cultivation if this equipment is not available when needed. The scheme is popular with women, since irrigation makes a new dry season crop possible and ensures reliable water supplies so the grain available to the family and returns to labour have been increased. The tenants' association is also proving a means of increasing women's participation in village-level decision-making.

Sufficient evidence exists to show that the twin objectives of increasing national food supply and increasing the allocation of resources to women small farmers can be achieved with appropriate project and policy design. Agricultural policies have to avoid the misconception that women will automatically benefit if resources are targeted exclusively to the male head of household.

2   Provision of inputs to small farmers

Incorporating the responsibilities and activities of women into agricultural project design is an important element in the overall means of providing inputs—fertilizer, seeds, credit, water—to small farmers. This is a most complex problem involving difficult technical, economic, and political issues. But the evidence supports the view that small farmers can out-produce large farmers.

In project design there has often been a hasty top-down approach encouraging farmers to adopt strategies which fail to recognize small farmer priorities. In formal agricultural research the same is also true (Richards 1985). Northern Nigeria has been the location for a lot of World Bank-supported investment in rural development. Such small farmer priorities and constraints as mixed cropping as a strategy of maximizing profit and minimizing risk, the labour peak around the time of first weeding, and the allocation of farm labour preferentially to food crops were ignored in the formulation of the Funtua Project (Longhurst 1981). The project emphasized technologies based on sole cropping, improved varieties less resistant to local weeds (so increasing weeding labour needs), and encouraged cotton as a cash crop. Such an approach was of great benefit to the large farmers who, with oxen technology, found it more advantageous to sole-crop. The project management chose to work through existing patronage relations, assuming that this was necessary to get local co-operation, and focused its attention on 'progressive' farmers who were wealthy and combined farming with trading. As a result a small class of 'overnight' farmers, recruited from a wealthy urban élite, was created by the liberal provision of subsidized bank loans to buy tractors and pay for labour and fertilizer (Collier 1983). An evaluation of the project in one of its villages showed that the great majority of fertilizer went to the richer farmers (Longhurst 1986a). Equally worrying was the finding that the subsidized fertilizer encouraged all farmers who used it to abandon their traditional manuring practices. Finally, in the village surveyed, none of this lead to production increases: the per hectare yield of the staple crop of sorghum when sole-cropped was the same for project participants as for non-participants (p. 80).

Alternative strategies in relation to the small farmer might have led to increased production. A pilot project based at Ahmadu Bello University in Zaria (the Guided Change Project) distributed small amounts of fertilizer directly to its participating farmers rather than through local power authorities (Collier 1983, p. 211). This also avoided excessive amounts of fertilizer being appropriated by large farmers and wasted. Credit institutions could be established without involving the local élites.

In Zimbabwe the political commitment of a socialist government combined with the existence of a strong agricultural research programme and suitable technology is now extending benefits to Communal Areas from the Commercial Areas: over 50 per cent of the total population and 70 per cent of the rural population lives in the Communal Areas, which until Independence were neglected in favour of the approximately 6,000 large-scale farmers who farmed a similar area in the Commercial Areas. In 1980, after drought and war, the produce price for maize was doubled, and maintained ahead of inflation. The government also distributed packs of hybrid maize seed and chemical fertilizer;

the farmers organized themselves into a wide variety of effective organizations (for mutual work exchange, bulk purchases of inputs). As a result of these and other factors the share of national maize sales originating from the peasant sector increased from 8 to 45 per cent (Bratton 1986).

Political will is required to reach small farmers so that benefits are not appropriated by the few large farmers. However, in periods of scarce development funds, emphasis on the small farmer appears to be a more cost-effective approach.

3 Agricultural research

Agricultural research has a long time-horizon so some research strategies initiated today will not provide benefits for the small farmer for about 10–15 years. However, new varieties of seeds developed over the last 20 years have led to benefits for the poor; the evidence suggests that where improved rice, wheat, maize, and sorghum varieties have been introduced, the poor are better off with than without them (Barker and Herdt 1984, Lipton with Longhurst 1985).

In Asia the modern varieties have produced more food and the consequent reduction in scarcity has moderated price fluctuations. Since this has also raised the demand for labour there has been more employment, and hence income for landless labourers. Seasonal shortages have also been reduced. But it does not appear that these increases in aggregate production and reduction in food imports, especially in India, have led to significant reductions in malnutrition among vulnerable groups. Supplementary policies are needed to improve income and food distribution.

However, the impact of the new wheat and rice varieties has been almost entirely confined to Asia and Central and Southern America. Sub-Saharan Africa has benefited very little from improved varieties to date, with the exception of hybrid maize varieties in Kenya, Zimbabwe, and Zambia and, to a much lesser extent, cassava in West Africa. Little progress has been made on the crops African farmers grow or on the ecological and farming systems in which they cultivate. In particular, no new high-yielding varieties of sorghum and millet suitable for African countries are apparent, and many new maize varieties have proved susceptible to drought.

Agricultural research for African smallholders needs to be increased, especially on food crops: coarse grains, roots, and tubers, i.e. millet, sorghum, yams, cassava, and sweet potatoes. Shorter-duration varieties will fill seasonal shortages, although there is a trade-off between total crop yield and its distribution through the year, as early maturing varieties are expected to be inherently lower in yields than the longer-duration varieties. With so many poor people now being pushed onto semi-arid lands because of population pressure and drought, improvement of the crops that grow in such areas is an urgent priority.

A further priority with regard to the small farmer is secondary food crops and the conservation of gathered foods. There is an enormous range of vegetables, secondary grains, tubers, legumes, and fruits which supplement the diet in important respects: by providing a large proportion of food intake at certain times of the year or key nutrients year-round. They are of special importance in the nutrition of vulnerable groups; women are not only the cultivators and gatherers of these crops, but also the preservers and promoters (Longhurst 1986*b*). For example, in The Gambia a grass-like millet called *findi* that matures in about 60 days is very low-yielding (about 100 kilograms per hectare) but provides vital food supplies in the hungry season before the main cereal harvest. Findi is drought-resistant, tolerates poor soils, and has low labour requirements. The human energy expended on growing findi in relation to the energy produced is low, compared to late millet (Haswell 1981); findi covered 11 per cent of the cultivated area in one village but 'cost' only 1.3 per cent of the total human energy input into subsistence agriculture, with a ratio of energy gained to that expended of 16:8. Late millet covered a similar area but the percentage of human energy input was greater, with a ratio gain of 8:1. Of course, findi yields per hectare are much lower but this illustrates an essential element of small farmers' efforts: where labour is the constraint rather than land, their priority is to maximize food per unit of time rather than of land.

A research strategy needs to be developed for subsistence and secondary crops. Many crops have been neglected by research workers, partly because the costs of improving yields, adaptability, or processing may not be justified given the small coverage and diminished consumption as incomes rise. Research in new crops also has high start-up costs. However, income setbacks and the spread of poor people onto marginal land means that these crops are becoming more, rather than less, important (Longhurst and Lipton 1985). Also, their income-generating potential, especially for women, is often under-rated. Many secondary crops are processed within the household to provide foods or oils; a study from Tanzania has shown that gathered foods also generate cash incomes, being bought and sold in markets in considerable amounts (Fleuret 1979).

4   Export crops

There has been excessive concentration on large farmers in the production of export crops, although export crops can also play an important role in improving the incomes of small farmers. Income growth among small farmers can only be achieved through increasing commercialization, although this has to be in a manner compatible with attaining household food security. The concept of comparative advantage should apply to crop production, taking into account dynamic trends and risk distribution as well as static returns, and ensuring that appropriate institutions and efficient marketing structures are in place to bring smallholders those essential products which they are not producing for themselves. Blanket condemnation of the role of export crops, especially for their impact on human nutrition, is not appropriate; rather, there should be a careful examination of the economic and policy circumstances in which they are introduced (Pinstrup-Andersen 1983). The issues involved touch on some already discussed in this chapter, including those of the scale of production, the relative roles of men and women, and price policy for crop output and inputs (Johnston and Clark 1982).

The economic and social viability of the export crop must be considered together with the potential loss of alternative production (Daniel *et al.* 1984). The poorest can become involved in three ways: (*a*) where food crop and export crop expansion can be sustained by the same infrastructure and technical support services, so reinforcing each other (e.g. cotton as export crop and millet and sorghum as food crops in Mali and Burkina Faso); (*b*) where the provision of additional cash income will increase food security and reduce nutritional risk; and (*c*) where food requirements and cash supplements can be met from the same source, e.g. in maize production, livestock-based system, or the development of smallstock (Daniel *et al.* p. 13).

In terms of their impact on food security the enormous range in export crop type has to be considered. At one extreme there are those non-food crops, where total control is vested in the male head of household, where all national extension advice and research is concentrated on the crop, and where a marketing board is the sole outlet depositing one cash sum for the year's crop in the hands of the head of household. Such crops have the potential for doing most nutritional harm, decreasing food availability at both the household and community level. Other export crops are also food crops (e.g. groundnuts); some have an alternative outlet at local level (e.g. also groundnuts, for oil) and can provide payments spread throughout the year (e.g. tea). Cocoa, cotton, coffee, tea, and groundnuts can all be grown by smallholders; in some countries women have access to export crops, grow them and benefit from the proceeds (e.g. cotton grown by secluded women in northern Nigeria (Longhurst 1981)).

In the 1950s cocoa was a smallholder crop associated with declining nutritional status among growers' families (Collis 1962); it represented most of the undesirable aspects discussed above. Other studies have shown that the allocation of land and labour time towards cash crops has diminished local food availability, thereby increasing food prices (Fleuret and Fleuret 1980; FAO 1984). In the case of groundnuts in Senegal and The Gambia, however, the impact of the crop on nutrition has been beneficial (IAI 1982). The nature of world prices over the period 1970–80 made it good sense for these countries to encourage groundnuts as a cash crop and import rice. Good transportation and marketing contributed to this, but it is an example of how foreign exchange and farm-level objectives can coincide.

Export crops can be an important element in smallholder development as a means of diversifying sources of income and to provide cash for buying food during seasonal shortages. In some drought-prone areas, small peasants should grow both cotton and food crops, with the former an anti-famine safeguard as low rainfall affects cotton much less (Green 1986). Excessive concentration on income-inelastic food crops can lead to surpluses which cannot be sold. However, food availability must not be undermined, especially to provide for the landless and to minimize import requirements. The essential need is productivity increases in both sectors, coupled with improvements in marketing systems so that the shift from semi-subsistence agriculture into more commercialized farming is achieved without dislocation.

5 *Seasonal aspects of household food security*

Poor rural households in many developing countries suffer a coincidence of peaks in work requirements, levels of infection, food prices, and informal-loan interest rates, and troughs in food stocks, food intake, and body weights. This occurs during the 'hungry season' which is in the middle of the rainy season in most unimodal and, to a lesser extent bimodal, seasonal societies. This includes most of Africa and large parts of Asia (Chambers *et al.* 1981). As a result, child malnutrition and adult health are at their worst at this time.

Such a regular phenomenon which is not only climatic but also economic in nature, in so far as the poor suffer from deleterious terms of trade while the rich are able to exploit these fluctuations to their advantage, is a constraint on smallholder development. Negotiating this period and its damaging effects on household food security inhibits farmers in their ability to adopt riskier innovations. Therefore the introduction of a seasonal perspective into agricultural planning to provide resources in the lean season may be more cost effective and more immediately feasible in terms of improving rural welfare than providing resources year-round.

Encouragement should be given to farmers' efforts to produce food and income at critical periods. Appropriate policies include the use of irrigation to extend the growing season, improved dryland farming methods, technology to reduce labour peaks in the household for women without reducing income from such work, intercropping, crop varieties with short maturation periods, and crop breeding for drought resistance. Some of these have been discussed earlier in this chapter. Government food policy to offset problems of seasonality would involve maintenance of buffer food stocks and their decentralization; food price regulation; and market improvement. Community grain banks can prove effective, whereby grain is sold to a community store at a stated price and the seller has the option of buying back at another known price or obtaining the grain on credit. In Indonesia such banks are also being used by the government to inject grain into food-deficit areas (Levinson 1982).

Farmers employ a number of means to navigate seasonal periods of shortage, such as crop diversification, mixed cropping, choice of crop variety, off-farm income sources, and food gathering if shortages become severe. Agricultural strategies should build on these rather than disrupt them.

V Conclusions

The macro policy adjustment package frequently includes a change in the internal terms of trade in favour of the agricultural sector, correcting the bias against this sector often exhibited in the past. While this correction can be an important element in improving resource allocation, by itself it may not do much for the vulnerable in the rural areas. To date, the system of development in most countries, taken as a whole, has been biased towards large farmers. They have been the chief beneficiaries of technology, research, extension, credit availability, and marketing services. Yet this bias has not led to the levels of agricultural productivity required in most African countries. A structural adjustment policy has both the potential to exacerbate this bias and the opportunity to restructure resources towards small farmers. A focus on the small-scale farmer is also essential to realize the increase in agricultural productivity, and especially food production, necessary for countries in which there is a chronic food shortage.

A coherent approach to increasing productivity among small farmers combines both short- and long-term strategies. Small farmers require immediate help in the form of essential inputs, marketing infrastructure, and short-term credit. Price policies can also be introduced with some immediate impact, although they can be a double-edged sword if the poor are both producers and consumers. Other policies—e.g. those involving investment in infrastructure, land and tenancy reform, land improvement—will take longer, while policies towards research and development typically have the longest gestation period. However, all should form part of the adjustment strategy because adjustment problems are likely to persist in many countries for some years at least, and it is therefore essential to incorporate policies today that will permit more growth and higher incomes for the vulnerable over the next five years and beyond. The main argument in this chapter has been that the increased productivity required in countries undergoing chronic food shortages and structural adjustment can be achieved by policy measures that focus to a greater extent on small farmers. In this way overall poverty can also be reduced. The political and social problems cannot be minimized but it is apparent that development cannot be achieved by an excessively bimodal distribution of income and resources. Comprehensive asset redistribution, involving land reform is often regarded as a prerequisite for such a strategy and the need for this should not be de-emphasized. However, it has been seen that much can be done by providing appropriate technology and incentives to enhance the latent entrepreneurial talent existing among poor groups.

Small-farmer projects, especially those aimed at women farmers, have shown that much can be achieved by redesigning programmes and projects so that they are based on a more accurate conception of the needs of rural people.

10

Supporting Productive Employment Among Vulnerable Groups

Frances Stewart

I Introduction: incomes of the poor, employment, and productivity

Low and falling household incomes are a major cause of malnutrition among vulnerable groups, as deficient food entitlements make it impossible for households to meet their minimum food needs. While this is a chronic problem of poor people in poor societies, it is often accentuated following recession and adjustment as employment and wages fall and food prices rise. Consequently, one important aspect of adjustment policies to protect the vulnerable are policies to support the incomes of the low-income during the adjustment process, before economic growth is resumed and the trends in real incomes are reversed.

The appropriate mechanism varies according to the *source* of the problems. Where—as is typical in the urban areas—the collapse of formal sector employment is the major cause, together with knock-on effects on opportunities in the informal sector depressing incomes and opportunities there, an urban labour surplus emerges and job creation can play a valuable role in relieving the crisis. Similarly, labour surplus may also emerge in the rural areas, seasonally, or even throughout the year with growing population. But in both rural and urban areas, many people are fully employed, in hours, but are receiving very low incomes because of the low productivity of their activities. For this class of people, the appropriate solution is not to create alternative temporary employment—which could disrupt production while adding only a little to incomes—but to assist in improving long-term productivity.

Consequently, the adjustment crisis calls for two different approaches: temporary employment creation, and improvement of productivity of low-income activities.

Public works schemes offer very substantial potential under the first approach. As discussed in detail below, these can provide considerable employment at relatively low cost. Moreover, properly designed, they also improve long-term productivity by helping maintain or create economic and social infrastructure. Since they can be introduced on a short-term and temporary basis, they are particularly suitable for the type of income support needed during adjustment. For the longer term, policies are needed to help raise productivity of small-scale activities; these include policies towards credit for the small-scale and low-income, support for appropriate technology, and community development in support of income-creating projects in low-income areas.

This chapter reviews experience in these categories. While the employment-creating schemes may have immediate effect, the productivity-raising schemes are likely to take longer to have a substantial impact on incomes. Consequently, in the short term, direct support (e.g. in the form of direct feeding schemes) may be an essential but temporary measure, to help the vulnerable until the productivity-raising schemes take effect.

II Public works

Labour-intensive public works are designed to use surplus labour in order to create economic and social infrastructure and thereby to raise long-run productivity. Such public works schemes were recognized as a potentially important aspect of development strategy in the 1950s; and some major schemes were adopted in the 1960s (notably the Moroccan Promotion Nationale and the schemes in East and West Pakistan).

Keynes (1936) and Nurkse (1953) provided the intellectual origins and justifications: Keynes focused on multiplier aspects, and from this perspective digging holes and filling them up would permit the public works to fulfill their essential function. However, for a variety of reasons, multiplier consequences are of lesser relevance in developing countries, where production aspects are of more relevance, as Nurkse pointed out: public works could call on a country's surplus resource (labour) and use it to create capital. In the 1970s, with the emphasis on poverty alleviation and basic needs, the distributive implications of public works gained importance. However, the critique of Nurkse's concept of surplus labour—theoretically and empirically—weakened the case for public works, since if marginal product per worker was positive in agriculture, moving people into public works would reduce agricultural production. Labour-intensive public works then could only be justified either where there evidently was surplus labour, or if the productivity of the works were so great that it justified reallocating labour from agriculture.

Labour-intensive public works acquire renewed justification as an emergency mechanism for redistributing income during periods of recession and adjustment for three reasons. First, because of the critical need to maintain incomes of vulnerable groups at a time when GNP per capita is falling and this decline is shared (sometimes disproportionately) by low-income groups. Hence the income distribution function becomes especially important. Secondly, the cuts in public investment that typically accompany macroeconomic adjustments eat into social and economic infrastructure, thus reducing future economic and social capacity. Hence the production aspect of public works gains especial importance. Thirdly, in the urban areas, the size of the pool of surplus labour usually increases following adjustment policies. Consequently, in the urban areas, the surplus labour aspect of public works becomes especially important. This is not necessarily true in the rural areas: there, while the income and capital creation reasons for the public works are at least as powerful as in the urban areas, care is needed to identify the existence, extent, and seasonality of surplus labour and to design public works to fit in with these facts.

Public works are also especially suited to fulfilling an adjustment role because in principle they are fairly short-term interventions (typically three years) which can be added to (or subtracted from) other investment plans without causing major disruption.

In fact, there is a long tradition of using public works as a relief measure in drought-prone states in India and also in North-East Brazil, and more recently in Botswana, where works are activated in response to drought and terminated with recovery. Sometimes these projects are very large: in 1972–73, during a severe drought in Ahmednagar, relief expenditure was $11.6 million and covered 350,000 workers (Guha 1975a, Costa 1974). Using such works as a component of adjustment policies would represent a logical extension to crises caused by economic as well as climatic forces.

Clearly, however, if they are to be an effective component of adjustment policies their characteristics must be such that they do fulfill the required functions. This means that:

1. They must be effective in generating additional incomes for target groups—therefore, the employment created must be secured by members of low-income households.

2. They should be on a sufficient scale to make a significant contribution to short-run income maintenance.

3. They should contribute to the medium-term capacity of vulnerable groups to meet their basic needs—by increasing their employment oppor-tunities and/or productivity, or by increasing relevant social capital.

4. Cost per work-place should be reasonable, with a high proportion of total costs going to wages.

5. The works should be worthwhile investments, in the sense of raising long-run productive potential (or capacity to meet social needs) of the economy. It is desirable that such investments should generate a rate of return that is as good as alternative projects. If the economic rate of return is significantly below some minimum, careful consideration is needed as to whether the distributional objective is sufficiently important to justify the project, or could be achieved more effectively in some other way. (Unavoidably, all minima of this sort are somewhat arbitrary; an internal rate of return of 10 per cent or more is typically what is required of conventional projects, so should be sufficient for these; below 5 per cent is typically regarded as unacceptably low.)

6. There must be viable mechanisms for financing and administering the schemes, and for their subsequent maintenance, in the context of economies with acute financial and management problems.

During the past 20 years, considerable experience has accumulated on the operation of public works schemes. The ILO and UNDP launched Special Public Works Programmes (SPWPs) in 1979. By March 1986, 28 countries had participated in these projects. As the following review (based heavily on previous ILO assessments—see Gaude *et al*. 1984 and Guha 1981) shows, labour-intensive public works can and often do fulfill the functions required to make them a highly effective component of adjustment policies.

1   Direct employment and incomes

Public works schemes have provided a very large amount of employment. In general, this employment has been secured by low-income workers (the target population), who have been able to make substantial additions to their incomes as a result of the schemes. For example:

1. Indonesia's Kabupaten Programme (1970–73) provided nearly a million workers with employment. Studies of three projects showed that between 54 and 90 per cent of the labour were casual landless labourers.

2. The Employment Guarantee Scheme of Maharashtra employed 800,000 workers in 1978/79, most of them landless workers and marginal farmers. Earnings from the scheme were 69 per cent of total earnings of the landless labourers and 30 per cent of those of small landowners (Costa 1978).

3. In Tanzania, an SPWP-generated 864 million man-days' employment (1980–82), and a further 54 million through self-help, among small farmers.

2   Medium-term effects on incomes of vulnerable groups

Public works have been criticized for enhancing long-term inequalities, and doing little to improve the position of vulnerable groups in the medium to long term. It has been argued that the assets created 'tend to benefit the better-off both because infrastructure adds value at least proportionately to existing assets and hence increases the income and wealth of the better off and because the better off tend to influence assets creation in such a way that they gain more than proportionately' (Harvey *et al*. 1979).

A World Bank study of one of the Bangladesh schemes found that the ratio of returns to landowners to those of labourers was 5 : 1 (Burki *et al*. 1976). An FAO expert engaged on a Tunisian forestry project said it was 'a good example of the way in which aid, in principle intended to satisfy the basic needs of poor rural people, in fact ends up by increasing the power and control of land by the large growers' (Bertholot 1979).

In view of this it has been contended that public works schemes cannot improve the long-term welfare of the poor unless they form part of a comprehensive plan of redistribution of assets (Griffin and Ghose 1978). However, this is an over-simple view.

Long-term effects on vulnerable groups depend on precisely which assets are created or improved, and also on the long-term employment effects of the schemes. Even where long-term benefits go disproportionately to non-target groups, target groups may still benefit substantially. There are enough examples of schemes which have significantly improved the long-term prospects of the low-income to show that this is possible if the schemes are properly designed and controlled:

1. In a Pilot Intensive Rural Employment Project in Kerala State, of 328 farmers who benefited from the irrigation, 257 were marginal farmers, while the rest were small and medium farmers; on average, incomes for beneficiary farmers rose by over 20 per cent. In addition the scheme created long-term extra employment of 436,000 man-days in maintenance on the irrigation and road works, and 136 days in agriculture per additional hectare of paddy. The scheme also improved the housing of Harijans (Guha 1979).

2. Indirect income and employment effects of the Tanzanian SPWP are expected to exceed the direct effects. Since land distribution in Tanzania is distributed fairly equally (and some land is farmed communally), the indirect employment and income creation will mainly assist low-income farmers.

3. A number of schemes include creation of social capital in low-income areas, which will benefit the low-income in the long run—e.g. a scheme in Tamil Nadu included construction of 19 community wells, 26 school buildings, and 4 playground wells; a Sierra Leone SPWP included construction of primary schools and health centres.

It is evident that even in a context of unequal asset distribution, public works schemes can support low-income households in the long-term. This will certainly be the case, to some extent, if the schemes are employment-creating, as with most agricultural improvement schemes. Explicit effort is needed to prevent disproportionate long-term benefits going to the richer farmers. Such efforts are strengthened if target groups participate in design, execution, and maintenance.

The distributional impact of the project may also be altered by its method of finance and cost recovery. On the one hand, the schemes may be financed by progressive taxation; on the other, cost recovery may be imposed on richer farmers. The Indian Rural Works Programmes of the 1960s required that certain schemes benefiting landowners should be regarded as loans, requiring repayment by beneficiaries. In the Maharashtra Employment Scheme, cost recovery is applied where the beneficiaries are easily identifiable— viz. in land improvement, soil conservation, and irrigation, with both direct cost and indirect recovery in the form of a progressive betterment levy (Guha 1979).

3. *Costs per job created*

Typically, public works schemes have relatively low costs in relation to jobs created because (*a*) they use labour-intensive technologies, (*b*) wages form a large proportion of total costs, and (*c*) because low wages are offered (normally in line with minimum wages in the area).

TABLE 10.1   *Public works: costs of some recent schemes*

	Duration of works considered	Cost per work-day[a] ($)	Wage per work-day ($)	Wage as % total costs (%)	Costs per worker as % GNP per capita, 1984 (%)
Tamil Nadu	'73–'76	0.2	n.a.	66.6	0.1
Maharashtra	'74–'79	0.3	0.25	76.5	0.1
West Bengal	'80–'82	1.3	1.11	86.0	0.5
Rwanda	'80–'83	2.2	1.1	60.8	0.8
Burundi	'79–'82	2.5	0.89	40.9	1.1
Nepal	'80–'83	3.1	n.a.	56	1.9
Tanzania	'80–'82	3.8	1.9	46.5	1.8
Jamaica	'74–'76	4.8–13.8	4.4–6.0	40–59	0.8
Dominica	'81–'82	11.2	5.0	62.3	1.2

Sources: Gaude *et al.* (1984), UNDP/ILO (1986), Costa (1978), Phan-Thuy (1978), Girling and Keith (1977).
[a] Work-day is the work of one person for one day.

As Table 10.1 indicates, costs per work-day of employment vary greatly, from as little as 20 cents to as much as $13.80. The variation is due in part to variations in the daily wage-rate, from (an estimated) $0.25 in Maharashtra to $6.0 in Jamaica. In addition, the proportion of wages in total costs showed substantial variation—with a low average of 41 per cent (Burundi) to a high of 86 per cent (West Bengal).

Experience suggests that it is not difficult to achieve labour costs of at least 60 per cent, and this ought to be taken as a cut-off point for such schemes, where short-run income maintenance is a prime objective.

4   *Rate of return and effects on productivity*

Many public works schemes have had very substantial positive effects on productivity. This is particularly evident in agricultural improvement schemes, especially irrigation. Two examples illustrate:

1. In Bhorktar, Nepal, irrigation projects allowed farmers to grow one or even two extra crops a year. In addition, they have permitted a switch towards

high-yielding varieties. Annual cropping density rose from 128 per cent to 212 per cent, and is expected to increase further. Production per hectare rose by a factor of 2.4 and is expected to increase to 3.7 times the initial level. The agricultural surplus rose by 350 per cent in 1985, and farmers' cash incomes rose by 250 per cent. Considerable indirect effects also occurred—including expansion in agro-processing.

2. A school-building project in Sierra Leone increased school enrolment by 30 per cent. Construction of village wells has freed women's time (by 1–2 hours per day), noticeably reduced water-borne diseases, and is expected to increase palm-oil production.

Calculations show that most projects have generated satisfactory rates of return, even without taking into account the social return arising from their distributional aspects. Some evidence is summarized in Table 10.2. Although benefit–cost ratios are not very meaningful without a full account of assump-

TABLE 10.2   *Benefit–cost ratio of selected public works projects*

Project location	Project type	Benefit–cost ratio	Assumed discount rate (%)
Tamil Nadu	Total	3.9	
	Roads, gravel	1.8	
	Roads, metal	0.9	
	Minor irrigation	7.4 [a]	10
	Afforestation	5.1	
	Wells	2.0	
	Schools	0.2	
	Playgrounds	0.8	
Indonesia	Roads	3.6	n.a.
Bangladesh	Roads, drainage, flood control	3.4	12
Ethiopia	Irrigation	2.0	n.a.
West Bengal	Irrigation 1	1.7	n.a.
	Irrigation 2	0.7	n.a.
Dominica	Feeder road	1.8	n.a.
Nepal	Irrigation	1.5	10
Morocco	All projects	1.4	10
	Small-scale irrigation	2.3	10
	Medium-scale irrigation	1.3	10
	Restoration of soil	0.6	10
Tanzania	Irrigation	1.4	n.a.

Sources: Gaude *et al.* (1984), UNDP/ILO (1986), Andriam-Ananjaro (quoted in Arles 1974), Thomas (quoted in Arles 1974), Thomas and Hook (1977), Phan-Thuy (1978).
[a] Calculations assume a shadow wage two-thirds of the actual wage; benefits assessed include redistribution to target groups.

tions made, the ratios are generally above one at what appears to be a reasonable discount rate, and (except in one case), without allowing for distributional benefits. This suggests that *public works could generally be justified on the basis of their economic effects alone.* The ranking of the returns (highest for irrigation and lowest for social investments) largely reflects the method of calculation, which generally does not incorporate indirect or intangible benefits so readily as direct measured benefits, for example of increased crop output associated with irrigation.

5   Financing public works schemes

Public works schemes—like other infrastructural projects—may be financed in a variety of ways. Some have involved a heavy aid component and many have made use of food aid; others have been financed largely or wholly domestically (by central or local government), sometimes with the support of special taxes. The Maharashtra Employment Guarantee Scheme imposed taxes on irrigated farms, gainful professions, and organized industry to finance half the costs. Some schemes have been partially financed by volunteer labour (e.g. the Sharmadana System in Sri Lanka, and the SWSPs in Tanzania and Sierra Leone). However, self-help projects relying on volunteer labour do not assist in short-run income maintenance, which is a prime objective in the use of such projects during adjustment. Consequently, in their adjustment role, they should normally be accompanied by payments in cash or food, which also help to improve incentives and productivity, as indicated by experience in Sri Lanka and Sierra Leone.

Financing has varied from 100 per cent domestic financing (e.g. the Maharashtra Employment Guarantee Scheme and the Indonesian Kabupaten Programme) to complete dependence on external funds (such as some of the SWSPs). External finance typically consists of a mixture of technical assistance, food aid, and finance. Food aid is sometimes used as direct payment to workers (as in the Sharmadena Project in Sri Lanka), and sometimes indirectly, through finance raised by the sale of food aid. PL-480 played an important indirect financing role in the 1960s Bangladesh Programme.

The appropriate financing mechanisms depend on a number of factors: (*a*) the extent to which the government has sufficient resources to finance the schemes; (*b*) the availability of external resources, of finance and of food aid; and (*c*) the effects on distributional equity, and on costs and incentives of alternative methods of financing.

Greater local financing helps generate local commitment to the success of the schemes, both in construction and in operation. However, this consideration may often conflict with considerations of financial capacity and equity. The aim, none the less, should be to require some degrees of local financing.

Food aid tends to involve higher administrative costs than financial aid (Thomas *et al.* (1975) suggested 25–50 per cent higher administrative costs). In regions where there is an agricultural surplus, it is inappropriate as worker payment since it has a depressing effect on local prices and incomes and involves unnecessary transport costs. Food aid may therefore be used directly in urban schemes, but normally only indirectly (through the use of counterpart funds) in rural schemes, except where there has been a collapse of local supplies. Food aid is particularly appropriate where drought and food supply problems are the basic cause of income decline, but not where food supplies are unchanged and the problems arise from other economic developments.

6 Drought-relief schemes

As noted above labour-intensive works have been used as special and temporary alleviation during times of drought, a role which is closely parallel to the adjustment role. The study of Botswana shows the important role employment schemes have played in drought relief. Both India and Brazil have major schemes directed at drought relief.

In India, the Drought-prone Areas Programme has a dual objective: to provide income maintenance as and when necessary, and to improve infrastructure and farms so as to raise long-run productivity and reduce vulnerability to drought. The two functions are fulfilled by a large ongoing programme of irrigation and farm improvement; and a shelf of labour-intensive projects to be activated during emergency.

The Frentes de Trabalho, North-East Brazil, started as early as 1909, to provide work for those unemployed as a result of drought. Weaknesses in the programme revealed by a very severe drought of 1958 led to more emphasis on development programmes. Comprehensive annual emergency schemes are prepared in advance for emergencies, while there is a long-term integrated programme of preventive works in semi-arid areas. Emergency funds are available for immediate use.

7 The use of labour-intensive schemes during adjustment

This survey of experience with labour-intensive employment schemes has shown that they can play an important role in maintaining incomes and improving economic and social capital during the adjustment process. They can be low cost and offer high returns. They invariably provide employment and incomes for low-income households during the construction phase; most schemes also lead to improvement in incomes and employment of target groups in the longer run, sometimes of such substantial magnitude that they exceed the short-run effects. Public works schemes are self-targeted to the needy, since joining is voluntary and only the unemployed, or those on very low incomes, would seek such employment. They can contribute to rehabilitation of social and economic infrastructure, which is often an urgent priority in the adjust-ment period. The schemes have short-run multiplier effects by increasing local purchasing power, as well as positive long-run development effects. However, special care is needed to ensure that the long-run effects do not go dis-proportionately to middle- and upper-income groups. Participation of target groups in design and control of projects is an important element in securing worker commitment to the project, and responsiveness of the project to the long-run needs of target groups. Weak participation of target groups has tended to be a feature of schemes which have suffered especially from low efficiency and worker productivity and maldistribution of long-run benefits. In contrast, highly successful schemes (from the point of view of efficiency and equity), such as the Maharashtra Employment Guarantee Scheme and the Kottar Scheme in South India, have included a strong element of par-ticipation.

The role of such schemes during adjustment is akin to their long-established role as a drought-relief mechanism. Here certain aspects of the considerable accumulated experience are relevant to the design of adjustment programmes. First, it is desirable to establish a stock of potential projects, ready for use in a crisis, to avoid delays or poor design. Secondly, the projects need to be integrated into long-run development programmes for the region, which should aim to reduce vulnerability of target groups to economic and climatic crises.

Labour-intensive schemes are appropriate where there is surplus labour, and are therefore especially suitable for us in the urban areas. In some parts of the world, rural surplus labour is a seasonal phenomenon, although Lipton has shown that the very poor among rural households tend to be more unemployed (have more surplus labour) than other groups (Lipton 1983*b*). In rural areas where surplus labour is mainly seasonal—as in much of Africa—care must be taken to incorporate a seasonal dimension into the design of the projects. Problems have emerged in the past in Tunisia, Morocco, and Tan-zania due to insufficient attention to this factor.

A brief review of the finance of programmes has shown considerable vari-ations in financial arrangements: a pragmatic approach seems appropriate, selecting financing according to the possibilities open to a particular country. While food aid represents an important potential source of finance, care must be taken not to use food aid where it would depress local agriculture. (See Costa *et al.* 1977 for very useful guidelines for the design and organization of labour-intensive projects.)

III Labour-intensive and small-scale activities

Support for labour-intensive—and especially small-scale—activities provides a vital element in a strategy to protect the incomes of vulnerable groups by supporting productive employment.

Labour-intensive technologies generate very substantially more employment than capital-intensive alternatives in many industries (Table 10.3). For example, in Botswana it has been estimated that home brewing would provide 6,500 full-time equivalent jobs, compared with 1,100 in factory brewing (Haggblade 1985).

TABLE 10.3 *Employment and capital–labour ratios*

	Employment[a]		Fixed capital per worker		Ratio of (3) to (4)
	Appropriate[b]	Capital-intensive	Appropriate ($000)	Capital-intensive ($000)	
	(1)	(2)	(3)	(4)	(5)
Beer brewing	7,460	4,316	12.1	18.3	1.5
Brick making	29,909	2,182	3.3	45.8	13.9
Cotton spinning	10,747	4,528	2.0	14.7	7.4
Cotton weaving	10,488	2,538	8.7	37.6	4.3
Fertilizer	772	691	122.3	137.6	1.1
Leather processing	4,502	2,108	15.5	36.2	2.3
Maize milling	19,231	7,574	2.9	9.7	3.3
Shoes	31,589	18,158	0.8	2.2	2.8
Sugar processing	123,980	15,925	0.8	6.2	7.8
TOTAL	238,678	58,017	5.8[c]	21.3[c]	3.7[c]

Source: Pack (1982).
[a] For an equivalent level of output.
[b] 'Appropriate' is here defined as the technique which was most profitable using prices typical of a low-income developing country. In fact more labour-intensive technologies were also available, but these would only have been profitable at shadow prices.
[c] Excluding fertilizer (averages).

TABLE 10.4 *Capital–labour ratios in manufacturing in the Philippines, 1974*

Number of employees	Fixed assets per worker (P 000)
Household	1.4
5–19	4.7
20–49	8.7
50–99	15.2
100–199	19.7
200 or more	25.8

Source: Anderson and Khambata (1981).

The small-scale sector almost invariably adopts more labour-intensive technologies than the large-scale sector, as illustrated for the Philippines in Table 10.4. This finding is supported by numerous studies (see Berry 1972, Berry, and Pinell-Siles 1979, Byerlee *et al.* 1979, Child 1977, Joshi *et al.* 1976, Liedholm 1973, Liedholm and Mead 1985, Morawetz 1974, Nihan *et al.* 1979, Roy 1986, Shetty 1963, Steel 1977, Todd 1971).

In some industries (e.g. steel production or car assembly), economies of scale rule out small-scale production, but in many industries where both large and small firms coexist, most empirical studies have shown that small firms use capital more productively than large firms (i.e. have higher output per unit of capital). (See e.g. Liedholm and Mead (1975).) It follows that focusing on small-scale firms in those industries will maximize short-run output as well as employment. Studies from countries in Africa and Latin America summarized in Table 10.5 show that in a variety of industries capital productivity and economic profit of the small-scale sector is substantially greater than that of the large scale.

The small-scale sector is especially important as a source of employment and incomes for low-income groups. This was also illustrated in the case of brewing in Botswana. Over half of the earnings of the home-brewing alternative were estimated to go to those with incomes in the bottom 65 per cent of households, and 13 per cent to the richest 5 per cent, while for the factory alternative 29 per cent went to the bottom income category and 47 per cent to the richest 5 per cent. In addition, the small-sector is much more accessible to women. A survey in Zambia showed that in small-scale enterprises, women accounted for 65 per cent of ownership and 55 per cent of employment. Altogether the small sector in Zambia employs six to eight times more full-time-equivalent female workers than the formal sector, where women account for only 8 per cent of the employment (Fisseha and Milimo 1985). The small-scale sector also often produces more appropriate products than the large-scale, catering to the needs of low-income consumers by providing simple products in small quantities. All these features are especially true of the informal sector, which provides essential support for very low-income households by generating incomes and supplying low-quality and low-price goods and services (see Ch. 4). It is especially important for women providing the sole source of income for many female-headed households; women play an entrepreneurial role there that they generally do not in the modern sector.

While the informal sector benefits when the modern sector is growing, its most critical role is during recession and adjustment, since it provides the only source of livelihood for many of those who become unemployed (see Ch. 4). But conditions in the sector tend to deteriorate at these times because markets are declining while the numbers dependent on the sector increase. It follows that *providing additional support for small-scale activities, especially in the informal sector, is a vital element of any strategy to protect the incomes of the vulnerable during the adjustment process.*

The activities of the small-scale sector are very often associated with very low labour productivity, and consequently with low incomes. In order to raise incomes of low-income households, it is essential to raise productivity as well

TABLE 10.5   *Capital productivity and economic profits: large and small-scale enterprises in selected countries*

	Ratio of value added to capital services		Economic profit as % of capital stock[a]	
	Large-scale	Small-scale	Large-scale	Small-scale
Botswana (1982)				
Sorghum beer	6.2	19.6	+130	+190
Egypt (1982)				
Clothing	2.6	8.5	+17	+42
Metal products	1.5	18.5	−3	+103
Honduras (1980)				
Clothing	2.5	6.9	−21	+45
Furniture	1.9	13.9	−26	+58
Shoes	0.9	12.5	−22	+102
Leather products	1.5	10.6	−21	+79
Metal products	1.4	12.1	−24	+23
Jamaica (1979)				
Clothing	1.6	10.5	−11	+86
Furniture	2.3	13.1	−0.4	+173
Shoes	2.3	17.8	−6	+247
Metal products	2.8	6.6	16.9	+56
Sierra Leone (1974)				
Clothing	1.7	8.3	−27	+59
Bread	1.7	12.4	−11	+12
Rice milling	1.4	57.1	−30	+80

Source: Liedholm and Mead (1985).
Note: Large-scale firms are those employing 50 or more workers. Small-scale firms are those employing less than 50 workers.
[a] 'Economic profit' is defined as value added less capital services (valued at shadow interest rate) and labour costs (including family labour, valued at the competitive wage rate in the industry).

In estimating economic profit the following have been subtracted from value added: (*a*) capital services valued at shadow interest rate; (*b*) labour costs, including inputs of family workers and proprietors valued at the competitive wage in that industry. A marginal firm or industry would generate economic profits of zero.

as expand the opportunities of this sector. This involves increasing access to capital, improving the technology available, and helping to improve management. Policies to achieve these objectives are broadly of two sorts: on the one hand, *macro policies* which determine the general incentives, opportunities, and constraints facing the small-scale sector; on the other hand, special *micro interventions* to support small-scale activities. Macro policy change is likely to have more extended effects than micro interventions, which by their nature are limited in time and place and may be unsuccessful in a hostile macro environment. The best results for the small-scale sector have been achieved in economies which have achieved both a good macro environment and special schemes (of credit, technology) to support the small-scale sector. This occurred in Taiwan, for example, during the 1960s. Between 1956 and 1966, non-agricultural employment in the rural areas grew by 7.5 per cent a year. Rural industry in Taiwan was small-scale and comparatively labour-intensive. Non-agricultural activities accounted for over half the income of rural families in 1974 and had a definitely equalizing effect on the income distribution (Ho 1976, Fei *et al.* 1979).

1   Macro policies

In many countries, the macro environment is actively hostile to labour-intensive, small-scale, and especially informal sector activities. Simply neutralizing this hostility is sufficient to provide a major boost to the small-scale. The main areas involved are *resources, infrastructure, markets,* and *technology.*

1. *Resources.* The resources available to each decision-maker, in price, quality, and quantity, determine the quantity of investment each could make, and also influence the nature of investment decisions. Policies towards resources include those influencing the prices of different resources (e.g. subsidies and taxes, investment allowances, and minimum wage laws); policies towards imports (tariffs, quotas, exchange rates), which determine the price and availability of imported resources; and policies towards credit, which determine access to finance for investment by different decision makers.

The most important source of discrimination against the small-scale sector lies in the distribution and price of credit. Frequently, borrowing finance for capital is very expensive, and may not be available at all for the small-scale sector, while it is artificially subsidized for large-scale enterprises.

Investigation into sources of finance in small enterprises in four African countries showed that the predominant source was own savings, while both banks and government supplied 1 per cent or less of finance used (Liedholm and Mead 1985).

The very substantial difference in interest rates between the sectors in many countries is shown in Table 10.6. This difference is often compounded by investment subsidies, reduced tariffs, and overvalued exchange rates which reduce the relative price of capital to the large-scale sector. (See Haggblade *et al.* (1986) who found capital costs in the large-scale sector were 60 per cent below those of the small-scale in Pakistan (1961–64) and 65 per cent in Sierra Leone (1976), with the interest costs and the trade regime roughly equally responsible.)

The high cost of capital and the low incomes in the informal sector have led to very low rates of capital accumulation, which is largely responsible for the low levels of productivity. For example, a survey of tinsmiths, carpenters, cobblers, mattress makers, and tailors in Nairobi in the 1970s showed an average investment of $15 (Chana and Morrison 1975).

The bias against the small-scale sector in interest and capital access arises partly from a policy decision to maintain interest rates below a market clearing

TABLE 10.6   *Interest rates in selected economies (percentages)*

	Informal rate		Formal rate		Ratio of informal real to formal real
	Nominal	Real	Nominal	Real	
Africa					
Ethiopia	70	66	12	8	8.25
Ghana	70	64	6	0	*
Ivory Coast	150	145	10	6	24.2
Nigeria	200	192	6	−2	*
Sierra Leone	75	60	12	−3	*
Sudan	120	120	7	7	17.1
Asia					
Afghanistan	33	n.a.	9	n.a.	n.a.
India	25	15	9	−1	*
Indonesia	40	29	14	3	9.7
Jordan	20	15	7	2	7.5
Korea, Republic of	60	49	6	5	9.8
Malaysia	60	58	18	16	3.6
Pakistan	30	27	7	4	6.8
Philippines	30	24	12	6	4.0
Sri Lanka	26	20	5	−1	*
Thailand	29	27	9	7	3.9
Vietnam	48	20	30	2	10.0
Latin America					
Bolivia	100	96	9	5	19.2
Brazil	60	38	15	−7	*
Chile	82	52	14	−16	*
Colombia	48	40	24	16	2.5
Costa Rica	24	20	8	4	5.0
El Salvador	25	23	10	8	2.9
Haiti	140	122	15	−3	*
Honduras	40	37	9	6	6.2
Mexico	60	57	10	7	8.1

Source: Haggblade *et al.* (1986).
* Ratio not calculable where formal sector real interest rate ≦0.

rate in modern sector institutions, in order to encourage investment. This may be corrected by interest rate reform. But there is a more fundamental problem at work, which arises from two sources. First, small and informal sector enterprises lack the kind of financial collateral that formal credit institutions require. Secondly, there is a high risk of lending to the sector with 'normal' modern sector procedures. These facts mean that lending to the small-scale sector and especially enterprises in the informal sector is unprofitable except at very high interest rates. If a bank borrows at 8 per cent a year and wishes to earn a return of 10 per cent on its lending, with a 50 per cent default rate it would have to charge 30 per cent a year on all loans to recoup losses over a five-year period and earn 10 per cent on the total capital. Even promising projects offering a return of as much as 20 per cent a year, would not qualify.[1] Consequently, institutional innovation—to change the type of collateral acceptable and to reduce the risk of default—is essential. Most of the micro interventions described below are designed to achieve these changes.

While the cost of capital in most countries is the major source of discrimination against the sector, there are also other important biases which raise costs and reduce opportunities. For example, most inputs (e.g. raw materials) are more expensive in small quantities. Import duties are often levied on the capital equipment of the small-scale sector since it is classified as 'consumer goods'—e.g. Burkina Faso levied import duties of 72 per cent on hand tools, and 41 per cent on sewing machines (Haggblade 1984). In addition, many administrative interventions (e.g. import licences and export subsidies) have been shown to favour large-scale enterprises (Haggblade *et al.* 1986).

2. *Infrastructure.* The extent and distribution of infrastructure is often biased against the development of the informal sector, and especially of small firms in the rural areas. Table 10.7 contrasts the availability of infrastructure in Taiwan—which experienced decentralized industrialization with a rapid growth of small firms— with the Philippines, where industrialization has been much more centralized and large-scale.

3. *Markets.* The small-scale sector tends to serve low-income domestic markets, providing some goods and services for the large-scale local modern sector. In the rural areas, the size of markets for the informal sector is strongly influenced by developments in agriculture. High growth in agriculture— especially if the increase in agricultural incomes is not too unequally distributed—generates demand for the local informal sector to provide consumer goods and inputs for the agricultural sector and to process agricultural produce.

Government policies to extend the markets for the informal sector include policies to support incomes of the poor, which will generate demand for the products of the small-scale sector; policies promoting agricultural output, especially where it involves small farmers and increases employment in agriculture; and policies towards appropriate *product standards*: many governments introduce Western-type produce requirements, which the informal sector cannot meet (e.g. in their own contract purchases, in standards specified for food and drink, and in building regulations).

4. *Technology.* The informal sector generally has limited access to knowledge about improved technologies. Moreover, research and development is concentrated in advanced countries and focuses mainly on developing large-scale techniques for the modern sector. Even R and D which takes place in the developing countries mainly relates to the modern urban sector. Technology policy therefore requires a redirection of R and D towards small-scale activities;

[1] The formula used to determine lending by financial institutions is $(1-p)(1+r) > (1+i)+a$, where p is fraction of loans and interest expected to be unpaid, r the interest rate charged borrowers, i the interest financial institutions pay raising finance and a the administrative cost of handling loans as a per cent of principal. Consequently a high r arises where p is believed high (see Anderson 1982).

TABLE 10.7   *Infrastructure in the Philippines and Taiwan*

	Philippines	Taiwan	Ratio Taiwan:Philippines
Utilities			
Installed electricity capacity, kw per 1,000 people	95.8[a]	719.3[a]	7.5
Households with telephone, %	1.1[b]	71.3[c]	64.8
Households with piped water, %	23.8[b]	63.8[c]	2.7
Transport			
Highways, metres per square kilometre	179[d]	458[e]	2.6
Paved roads as percentage of total	26.3[d]	51.7[e]	2.0
Railways, metres per square kilometre	7[d]	153[e]	21.9

Source: Ranis and Stewart (1987).
[a] 1970.   [d] 1983.
[b] 1975.   [e] 1974.
[c] 1979.

and development of an information network to improve access of the informal sector to new technologies.

2   *Micro interventions*

Well designed micro interventions are an essential complement to appropriate macro policies, and can play a critical role in supporting the income-earning capacity of the most vulnerable groups during economic crises. Not only do they give members of poor households immediate access to income, but when successful, they also provide the basis for long-run growth in productive employment.

Over the past decade considerable experience has accumulated in projects directed towards production by very small enterprises. This shows that, while there have been plenty of failed projects, projects *can* succeed in raising incomes and productivity, offering a return on the capital (or aid) involved in the projects which can be very high, often higher than that associated with large-scale conventional projects.

Micro interventions to support small-scale and informal sector activities normally offer credit at rates below the exorbitant informal sector levels, often advice on management, and sometimes also on technology. Provision of credit is especially important, because of the failure of conventional credit institutions to reach the informal sector and the extremely high cost of borrowing from informal sources, as shown above.

The most appropriate interventions depend on the particular context. This section indicates major elements of such interventions by providing a brief description of three successful projects. 'Success' has to be judged by two criteria: (*a*) success in reaching target groups; and (*b*) commercial efficiency in a conventional sense, which will ensure the longer-term positive effects on the incomes of the people involved, and is also a necessary condition for widespread replication.

(a) Grameen Bank, Bangladesh The Grameen Bank, founded by Professor Muhammed Yunus in 1978, is designed to meet the credit needs of the landless in rural Bangladesh. The Bank was intended to help loosen the grip of the moneylenders, and assist the unemployed and underemployed to find gainful employment for themselves by undertaking income-generating activities, with a special focus on women (see Yunus 1982, 1984).

The bank soon gained the support of the Bangladesh Bank and the nationalized commercial banks, and a loan of $3.4 million from the International Fund for Agricultural Development. The Bank now has 25 per cent equity capital coming from government sources, and 75 per cent from the landless borrowers. There has been rapid expansion. According to the June 1986 report, the bank operates 241 branches and encompasses about 171,000 members in 3,600 villages. Seventy per cent of the members are women. The bank's activities are reviewed below.

1. *Operational procedures.* Each branch is headed by a manager with a field staff of three men and three women, all of whom are required to live in the villages in which they work. Anybody who owns less than 0.5 acres of land or whose family assets do not exceed the value of one acre of cultivable land is eligible for a loan for income-generating activities. Women are especially encouraged to improve their household skills in order to produce goods and services in demand.

Villages wanting a loan form groups of five. All loan proposals are discussed publicly in the village in order to minimize exaggeration and misinformation. Initially, two members from each group are given loans, for repayment in weekly instalments at the rate of 2 per cent of the total loan for a period of 50 weeks. The interest charged was 13 per cent a year up to the end of 1983 and 16 per cent a year since then (Mridha 1984). All loans extend for one year. The first two loanees in the group are observed for their utilization and repayment, and loans to the remaining members depend on this behaviour. The members therefore put peer pressure on the loanees to insure proper use and repayment. The male groups in a village together constitute the Village Landless Association, and the female groups the Village Women Association.

Every member deposits one taka (around 3 cents) every week as personal savings to form the Group Fund. Total savings in the Group Fund stood at nearly $3 million by the end of June 1986. An Emergency Fund has also been established as a form of insurance against accidents, loss of crops, etc.

2. *Impact of credit availability.* Loans have been used for a huge variety of

activities in agriculture and forestry, livestock and fisheries, processing and manufacturing, trading and shopkeeping, and transport services. The bank has been particularly successful in creating new employment opportunities for women, who received 56 per cent of the disbursements.

3. *Rate of return.* The rate of return on male loans is high—57 per cent, using the agricultural wage as the opportunity cost of labour. Around 40 per cent of the women's activities give labour productivity below the market wage (Hossain 1984). On average, the rate of return on the capital would be negative if the opportunity cost of female labour is valued at the agricultural wage. But women in rural Bangladesh generally do not work for outside employment, so that the opportunity cost of female labour is below the agricultural average. Assessing family labour at 80 per cent of the prevailing agricultural wage, the return on women's loans becomes positive—29 per cent.

Women loanees have been shown to spend substantially more on medical expenses and to consume significantly more meals than non-loanees. The differences are much smaller for male loanees (Rahman 1986).

4. *Repayment performance.* One of the most successful aspects of the Grameen Bank, from a banker's point of view, is the very high pay-back—99 per cent on average, while the women have a 100 per cent repayment rate (Hossain 1984, Rahman 1986).

In summary, the Grameen Bank has succeeded in extending loans for income-creating activities to the very poor and landless; the default rate has been almost negligible; the rate of return has been positive; the Bank has reached women in a society where they are traditionally excluded from outside activities; group solidarity has been increased; and substantial savings have been generated among very poor households.

(b) The Self-employed Women's Association, India The Self-employed Women's Association (SEWA) was established in 1972 when a group of women headloaders, used-garment dealers, junksmiths, and vegetable vendors came together in Ahmedabad, India to form a workers' association. By 1982, the SEWA trade union consisted of over 5,000 poor women workers. The Union was established to struggle for higher wages, and improved working conditions, and to defend members against harrassment by police and exploitation by middlemen. It provides further support through a women's bank, skills training programmes, social security systems, production and marketing co-operatives, and other programmes for developing trades (Sebstad 1982).

The SEWA Bank developed following a decision by the Indian government in the early 1970s to take action on behalf of informal sector workers and small businesses that were normally denied credit in traditional banking. All banks were required to lend 1 per cent of their portfolios to the so-called 'weaker sector'. As a result, SEWA received loans from the Bank of India and other banks, to be administered through them to poor women.

Early trials and errors showed that credit alone was not enough. Despite the availability of capital, poor women faced other problems. Consequently,

SEWA provides borrowers with complementary services such as assistance in marketing, supply of raw materials, and training.

The majority of loans advanced have been 500 rupees or less, with an average loan amount of 575 rupees. Home-based products received the largest share of the loans (46 per cent), followed by small-scale vendors (33 per cent), agricultural workers (10 per cent), and service workers. The repayment rate has for the most part been good, with an almost negligible default rate but some late payment.

The SEWA Bank has shown that banking with poor women can be very successful. The Bank is one part of a much larger movement towards liberating the lives of poor working women from the often oppressive structures of traditional Indian society. As the success of the bank has gradually increased, so have SEWA's other activities.

(c) **Banco Popular, Costa Rica** A project for support of micro enterprises was initiated in San José, Costa Rica, by the Banco Popular (see Ashe 1985). The project relies on the solidarity group system, each group being made up of five to eight micro businesses which join together to qualify for a loan. The project has extended loans to 447 clients (of whom 40 per cent were extremely poor with income inadequate to buy a basic basket of food). Over half the loans were for small stores or street vendors, and one-third for micro industries and services. Each received a loan of $247 for one year. Assistance is given with book-keeping, and follow-up visits are made.

After one year of operation, the project appeared outstandingly successful:

(*a*) Median income was 145 per cent higher and average income 240 per cent higher.
(*b*) 119 new full-time and 48 part-time jobs were created.
(*c*) 60 per cent of the clients had increased their savings.
(*d*) Record-keeping improved.
(*e*) Dependence on informal sector moneylenders was reduced.
(*f*) Solidarity increased within the groups (79 per cent provide business advice to other group members, 74 per cent help in payments where necessary, 16 per cent have created an emergency fund).
(*g*) The pay-back record is good, with only 12 per cent late payments (after six months).

3 *Appropriate technology*

Many micro interventions focus on providing credit, mostly combined with some technical assistance for management, but do not include advice on appropriate technology. Consequently, some are associated with activities involving very low labour productivity and therefore low incomes for participants. Ideally, these financing schemes should be combined with advice on how to upgrade the technical efficiency of the activities being financed and/or adopt new activities and technologies. Despite relative neglect in aggregate

R and D efforts, numerous technological innovations have occurred improving the productivity of small-scale traditional technologies.
Some examples illustrate the possibilities:

1. Improvements to small-scale sugar processing (open pan sulphitation) have made it competitive with the large-scale (vacuum pan) technique, with a capital cost per work place of 1/4 to 1/20 of that in large-scale plants. In India, 30 per cent of output is processed with the small-scale technique, but elsewhere the proportion is much lower (e.g. only 1.7 per cent in Kenya) (Kaplinsky 1983).

2. In Ghana, a redesigned stove for smoking fish raised household incomes fivefold (UNICEF–Ghana 1984).

3. In the Philippines, modifications to small-scale rice-milling methods have raised the quality of the product so that it is equal to that of large-scale mills, while costs per bag processed are lower and capital costs per worker are less than half. Moreover, the small mills are located in villages and owned by local people (IRRI 1978).

4. In Bangladesh, hand- and foot-operated pumps enable farmers with very small holdings to irrigate their land. It is estimated that around 0.5 million pumps have been distributed, over half being used to supply drinking water; each pump irrigates a half-acre of land, together increasing incomes and nutrition for over a million people. The pumps have much lower investment costs than conventional techniques, lower maintenance costs, no fuel costs, greater reliability, and offer high financial returns to users (Darrow 1985).

5. In Papua New Guinea, the Appropriate Technology Development Institute has applied small-scale processing to sago to develop new products including biscuits, cereals, and snacks, which has introduced new income opportunities for local women and improved the local diet (New 1985).

6. In Sri Lanka, the Eastern Technical Institute has developed a highly labour-intensive way of processing cassava to make starch for use in the manufacture of textiles and paper. The enterprise has increased rural employment and incomes from the production as well as the processing of cassava (J. Kennedy 1979).

These are just a few of many examples of improved traditional technologies or new small-scale technologies which increase labour productivity and enlarge income-creating opportunities for low-income households. Institutional support is needed to disseminate knowledge about such improved small-scale technologies. One possiblity is for credit institutions to include technology advisory services. In addition, appropriate technology centres can collect and provide information suitable for local activities.

Micro interventions which combine credit, management training, and information on improved technologies are likely to be most effective in raising the incomes of low-income households and supporting the incomes of vulnerable groups during adjustment.

Health Policy and Programme Options: Compensating for the Negative Effects of Economic Adjustment

W. Henry Mosley and Richard Jolly

I Introduction

As the global recession spreads in the developing world, governments have found it necessary to reduce overall levels of expenditure. In this process, social services, including health services, which are too often looked upon as consumption items, have experienced reductions in expenditure. When this has been coupled with other policies, such as a freeze or reduction in real wages and an increase in the prices of food, clothing, and other necessities, the adverse health consequences for impoverished families, particularly mothers and children, have been severe. As illustrated by some of the country studies in Volume II, however, deterioration in the health conditions of populations does not need to accompany economic recession and economic adjustment. Governments can take selective measures which are economically feasible to protect and even improve the health of the most disadvantaged groups during periods of financial stringency.

This chapter will examine the strategic options that may be available to ministries of health to protect vulnerable groups during periods of economic recession and adjustment. It begins with a set of principles that can provide guidelines for policies and programmes, and then illustrates these with the experiences of health programmes in the developing world. The chapter concludes with a list of concrete actions that could be undertaken in a number of developing countries to protect adults and children from the adversities of recession and adjustment.

II The cost of good health

Before beginning a detailed analysis, it is useful to look at the current global picture to assess what level of health might be achievable within the economic constraints faced by poor countries. The 1986 UNICEF report on the state of the world's children identifies 36 countries with a per capita GNP below $400. The median infant mortality rate for this group of countries is 130; however, the variation is enormous, ranging from a high of 195 to a low of 39. At one extreme, exemplified by Afghanistan, one child in three may be expected to die before reaching the age of five, while at the other extreme, represented by China and Sri Lanka, the risk of death in the first five years of life approximates 1 in 20. The high level of achievement in China and Sri Lanka did not require heavy investments in the health sector (Halstead *et al.* 1985). The public expenditures for health services in these two countries in 1982 were approximately $4 and $10 per capita, respectively. The state of Kerala in India, under similar economic conditions, has achieved an even higher rate of child survival with a public expenditure of only $4 per capita. These three cases do represent the extreme examples; however, there are a sufficient number of other countries, notably Burma, Kenya, Costa Rica, and Cuba, where the level of child survival is far higher than one would predict on the basis of national income, to give confidence in the assertion that the health status in a country is constrained far more by the nature and structure of social institutions, including health services, than by lack of financial resources (Preston 1978).

III The achievement of health

Chapter 1 provides a comprehensive analytical framework identifying the determinants of child health and survival (see Fig. 1.3). Within that conceptual framework the primary producer of health is the family, particularly the mother. Critical to the mother's ability to produce healthy, surviving children is her own physical condition as well as her knowledge, skills, time, and autonomy. Her capacity to produce healthy children will be constrained by the resources available at the household level. Governments can help (or hinder) her performance by a variety of policies and programmes affecting the resources available to the household, such as those affecting wages and prices. Additionally, governments can intervene directly in the health production process by controlling the flow of information and technologies to the mother, by mobilizing social support, as well as by implementing environmental control measures.

This conceptualization has close parallels with other views which put the mother or the household at the centre of health care. In this framework, such items as physicians, services, and drugs are treated as inputs to a production process which is carried on by producers at the household level to generate health as an output (Cumper 1983). Social mobilization, including government effort to make health knowledge available to the family through the media or the school system, can be seen as another input. This framework more accurately depicts reality than the traditional view of health care as a consumption good. More importantly, from the standpoint of strategic planning, it clearly shows that the role of the health sector should be to organize service inputs and other measures in ways that will enhance a mother's ability to effectively and efficiently assure her child's survival. Finally, it helps to clarify how resources directed toward health care can represent a productive investment that contributes to national development.

IV Basic principles

Although the cost of technically qualified manpower forms an important share of health expenditure, most developing countries rely upon a variety of health workers with more limited skills for part or all of the front-line service. The philosophy of primary health care has set out a strategy for ensuring 'health for all', which is increasingly influencing the approach in many countries. The challenge to adjustment policy presented by the health sector is how to turn the constraints of adjustment into an opportunity for restructuring the health sector to make more rapid progress toward these basic health goals.

While universal access to basic health services is one important goal of this set, the choices presented and specific issues for strategy are in fact more complex than, for example, for universal primary education, where for reasons of equity and because of contemporary thinking about the need to introduce a common core of basic knowledge, the dominant emphasis is on universal access to a basic form of primary education, country by country. In contrast, for primary health care, a clear focus on the basic health needs of the majority must be coupled with some selectivity in the services provided.

There are at least three basic points to be made regarding health priorities for adjustment policy:

1. *Priorities for health activities need to be judged in relation to the health needs, health infrastructure, and basic economic and social characteristics of each situation.* Health needs should be assessed not only from the basic epidemiology of the area but also by anticipating ways in which risks of illness and stress are likely to change because of current economic strains. Programme choices can only be made rationally on the basis of data which accurately measure the magnitude of health problems in the population and identify the relevant factors causing these problems. The social monitoring system set out in Chapter 14 would contribute directly to this.

Although it is often necessary initially to allocate priorities on the basis of incomplete data, it is important to begin to collect input–output and impact data as soon as the programme is initiated so that better analyses can be undertaken. Frequently this may result in substantial revisions of strategy or even a reallocation of priorities.

For example, in the case of Botswana, reported in Volume II, Chapter 1, two feeding programmes have been implemented: a supplementary feeding programme for vulnerable groups, and a direct feeding programme for rehabilitation of severely malnourished children. Follow-up analysis of the supplementary feeding programme revealed as an unplanned benefit a quadrupling of the attendance of under-5s at health facilities. This increase in attendance helped to improve the immunization coverage and nutritional assessment of children as well as bringing in more mothers for health education activities. From this perspective, the benefit-to-cost ratio of this programme would be very high.

On the other hand, the direct feeding programme in Botswana encountered a number of problems. Because of poor screening, many healthy children were being enrolled. At the same time, many of the most vulnerable children were not being adequately fed, often because poor mothers whose husbands were absent could not bring their children in daily or remain the entire day for the children to receive a full day's ration. In addition, the most vulnerable, who lived in remote areas, were not being reached at all. This analysis suggests the benefit-to-cost ratio of this programme is substantially lower than originally conceived, and consideration might be given to reallocation of these resources to an alternative programme.

2. *A broad-based, long-term view of health strategies and infrastructures is needed* both to take account of recent innovations in public health practices and to gain a sustained multiplier effect from health programmes. Maintaining and extending safe water supplies and sanitation is a basic part of primary health care, yet often outside the responsibility of the Ministry of Health. Similarly, health education and social mobilization through the school system or through women's organizations or in factories is a vital part of the health care system, and one to which bureaucratic economies, in the name of adjustment, can do serious damage. Adjustment with growth and human development may well require an expansion of such health-related interventions outside the Ministry of Health, since these often provide the essential institutional and social supports for home-centred health activities which can produce sustained reductions in risks of many diseases by improving mothers' skills and assisting them to use their time and resources more effectively and efficiently.

The importance of the multiplier effect on child health and survival that can be produced by broad-based interventions that change individual and community health behaviour, such as provision of water and promotion of hygiene, or nutrition programmes to support proper diets during pregnancy as well as breast-feeding and proper weaning and child nutrition, cannot be overemphasized.

In high mortality situations, mothers and their children are constantly exposed to multiple recurrent infections and nutritional deficiencies which cumulatively produce increasing frailty, growth faltering, and ultimately death. In these circumstances, therapeutic interventions, even those which are lifesaving for a given episode of illness, like oral rehabilitation therapy (ORT) may have achieved only a fraction of their potential impact on survival because the child will be returned to its home environment only to suffer other illness that may lead to death. Preventive measures that reduce the risk of death either by increasing individual resistance, such as with immunizations and nutrition programmes, or by reducing the child's exposure to multiple infections through improved hygiene can potentially have a far greater survival impact. The self-reliance generated by such broad-based strategies assures their viability in the long run. Moreover, by virtue of the fact that improved health practices are preventing a multiplicity of diseases, a substantial improvement in productivity and cost savings to families and to the health system can be anticipated over time.

Family planning is a broad-based health intervention which can have multiple long-term cumulative benefits both for mothers and children. The study from Chile is instructive in this regard. In the space of only six years from 1972 to 1978, the infant mortality rate dropped dramatically by 45 per cent, from 72.7 to 40.1 per cent (Foxley and Raczynski 1984). This was associated with a fertility decline of 23 per cent coupled with a reduction in births to older high parity women and to less-educated women. Taucher (1983), in analysing the relationships of child-bearing patterns to infant mortality, estimated that the structural changes in child-bearing by age and parity accounted for one-fifth of the reduction in infant mortality in the period. More significantly, she noted that the reduction in the number of births, by increasing the ratio between health resources and children to be served, greatly facilitated Chile's efforts to improve the quality of health care to mothers and children in the mid-1970s.

3. *Political leadership and commitment are required* to mobilize public interest and action and to galvanize government administration and health services into active support if adjustment with a human face is to be made a reality. In the last few years many remarkable examples of such social mobilization have emerged in Africa, Asia, Latin America, and the Middle East. With political leadership and 'people support' from a wide variety of both government and non-government organizations, major advances have taken place in a number of priority areas of child health and survival: immunization against six basic communicable diseases (diphtheria, tuberculosis, whooping cough, measles, polio, and meningitis) and also tetanus, which together still account for an estimated 3.5 million deaths of under-5s each year; oral rehydration therapy against dehydration from diarrhoea, which accounts for an estimated 4–5 million deaths of under-5s each year; and a variety of other low-cost, high-effectiveness actions against health problems affecting millions of children, and in many cases adults as well. The significance of these advances is that they provide practical examples of what can be achieved with limited financial resources when other resources—of manpower, the media, and individual households' awareness and energy—are directed to basic health objectives.

V   Strategic choices

Which choices are to be made? Here four basic points must be noted, each of enormous importance in deciding how to provide a minimum level of health care and to make progress toward reducing mortality and increasing child health as part of an adjustment programme.

1. *Basic health care can be relatively low-cost.* In the first place, many basic health actions can be undertaken at relatively low cost, at much lower cost than other forms of treatment and service and, it seems, at a much lower cost

than is often perceived by general economic planners or political leaders. The Minister of Finance in Pakistan has already been quoted as stating that it proved possible to finance the total cost of a nation-wide immunization effort with what was saved by postponing one expensive urban hospital. The example of Tanzania, to be given later, shows that a regular supply of essential drugs for virtually the whole of the 20 million rural population has been provided for barely 30 cents per person. In a number of countries where the data have been analysed, the total cost of providing sufficient packets of oral rehydration salts for nationwide action against dehydration through diarrhoea would be less than current expenditures on inappropriate, ineffective, and sometimes dangerous remedies for diarrhoea. In the area of manpower, which often consumes 40 per cent or more of the health budget, it has become increasingly clear that many functions performed by physicians in primary care pro- grammes can be carried out at far less cost yet just as effectively by properly trained and supervised lower-level workers (Waife and Burkhart 1981). The use of indigenous medications and therapies in place of imported drugs and expensive technology can also dramatically reduce costs. China has pioneered this approach with the strategy of integrating traditional and modern medicine. Other nations are beginning to consider this more seriously as a means of improving operational efficiency in the face of declining health resources. The Philippines study in Volume II, Chapter 7, notes that indigenous health care technology is being increasingly stressed, with the development and use of herbal medicines and acupuncture in public hospitals as substitutes for expen- sive technology and services.

Conscious attention to greater cost-effectiveness within the budgets of large hospitals can be a major source of savings, with no loss of health effectiveness. It is quite common for hospitals to account for two-thirds of total government expenditure on health, and for one-half of this to be the cost of one or two major national hospitals. If the serious application of cost-effectiveness principles reduces costs in a country's hospitals by 30 or 40 per cent (which experience shows as sometimes possible), some 10 per cent of total health resources can be freed for the support of more basic health services, reaching many times more patients with preventive as well as curative care.

In short, a serious restructuring of existing expenditures on medical services would in many countries, perhaps in most countries, provide all the resources needed for achieving a basic level of effective health care for all the population.

2. *The basic components of a child survival and development strategy, while low cost and simple, often can raise the quality of health programmes.* For example, as oral rehydration therapy has been introduced into hospital and clinical settings, it was revealed that many institutions had inordinately high diarrhoea fatality rates (5–30 per cent) because of the ineffective use of intravenous rehydration and the inappropriate use of expensive and sophisticated drugs. The intro- duction of ORT not only resulted in a cost savings but also in dramatic improvements in the effectiveness of treatment, typically reducing fatality rates

below 1 per cent (PAHO/WHO 1983). Similarly, as programmes to promote breast-feeding expanded, it was often found that medical professionals, in conjunction with commercial industry, had been encouraging mothers to switch to bottle-feeding. The Western medical tradition of separating mothers from their newborn infants at the time of childbirth supported this practice. The introduction of rooming-in not only encouraged new mothers to adopt the least costly and most healthy feeding practices, but also revealed that in some instances the newborn nursery was, in fact, a major focus of disease transmission which dramatically increased neonatal morbidity and mortality rates (Clavano 1981). Recent efforts to introduce essential drug lists have uncovered the common practice of 'polypharmacy', with many health practitioners prescribing a multiplicity of expensive drugs directed to every symptom the patient described, usually with little therapeutic benefit. More fundamentally, with the growing emphasis on increasing mothers' self-reliance, the inadequacies of the usual clinic-based strategies in effectively communicating health information and motivating the population toward effective health practices are coming to light.

3. *Greater cost-effectiveness can be achieved by selective targeting* in both the design and strategy of health programmes. Fig. 11.1 illustrates the issue with respect to reductions in under-5 mortality by measures requiring mass application such as immunizations or public health education campaigns. The vertical axis shows the rate of under-5 mortality and the horizontal axis is the percentage coverage of the relevant part of the population.

The point of the figure is made clear by referring to the straight-line relationship ABE which is often presumed to hold between extension of coverage and reduction in mortality. In fact, other relationships are not only possible but typical. For measles, infant and young child deaths tend to be concentrated among poorly nourished children, usually from poorer households. If they are reached last in an immunization effort, the actual curve is more likely to appear as ACE. But in contrast, with careful planning and targeting to give priority to reaching the most vulnerable, the relationship could be made into ADE. In the case of smallpox, complete eradication was achieved by selective targeting on, at most, a small percentage of the population, the AFG shown in Fig. 11.1.

There are two recent examples illustrating highly effective targeting to selected disadvantaged socio-economic subgroups. In the 1970s, during a period of rapid economic expansion, Costa Rica introduced major changes in health strategies that were designed to achieve complete coverage of the entire population with basic health services (Halstead *et al.* 1985). Elements of this programme involved extending social security coverage from 39 per cent to 78 per cent of the population and decreasing the number of hospitals from 51 to 37, while increasing out-patient installations from 348 to 1,150, with the establishment of a programme of home-visiting by health workers in remote areas documented as having poor health conditions. Coupled with this was a

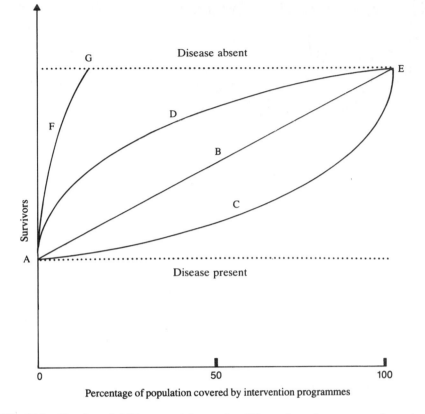

Fig. 11.1 Number of children surviving under different hypotheses concerning extension of health interventions

major programme to improve rural water supply and sanitation. As illustrated in Fig. 11.2, the impact of this new programme on neonatal and particularly post-neonatal mortality was dramatic. Overall, infant mortality declined by over 60 per cent in the eight years from 1972 to 1980. Major reductions were seen in deaths due to diarrhoeal, respiratory, and vaccine-preventable diseases, as well as in deaths attributed to immaturity (low birth weight). This programme, however, was relatively expensive, costing $155 per capita in 1980, or about 7.6 per cent of the GDP (30 per cent of government expenditure).

Chile also implemented a programme of selective social targeting in the mid-1970s; however, this was under circumstances of a substantial reduction in public expenditures for health. As noted in Volume II, Chapter 3, this targeted health programme concentrated almost exclusively on maternal and child care. Further focus was achieved by a screening programme in conjunction with well-baby clinic check-ups (which were already reaching almost all infants) that detected children suffering from malnutrition, who were then

Source: Rosero-Bixby (1985).

Fig. 11.2   Costa Rica: Infant, post-neonatal, and neonatal mortality rates, 1955–1982

given specialized psychological, medical, and nutritional care. Finally, if there were children under two years who were still malnourished, they were admitted to a network of recovery centres. As illustrated in Table 11.1, between 1975 and 1980, during a period of economic instability, this programme proved highly effective in protecting the vulnerable groups (Foxley and Raczynski 1984). Infant mortality declined by almost 40 per cent. There were equivalent declines in deaths due to pneumonia, diarrhoea, and infectious diseases, while malnutrition deaths declined by 65 per cent. While this experience illustrates what can be achieved by selective targeting in the face of contracting resources, it must be recognized that such gains cannot be sustained indefinitely in the presence of continuing economic decline. In fact, as Chapter 3 in Volume II indicates, health conditions in Chile had begun to show serious signs of deterioration by 1983.

     4. *Non-government organizations and political leadership* have a vital role to play through the mass media in mobilizing the population fully to participate in

health programmes. One problem common to the usual clinic-based programmes has been that simply making the services available did not guarantee
that they would be accepted or effectively used, particularly by the most
disadvantaged subgroups of the population who may have the highest health
risks. This problem has been variously defined as 'poor patient compliance' in
programmes of long-term therapy for conditions such as tuberculosis and
leprosy, 'low continuation rates' among contraceptive acceptors, and 'high
drop-out rates' among children in immunization programmes. Over a decade
ago, the Narangwal Project in India provided a well-documented illustration
of how an intensive personal motivation programme could affect the demand

TABLE 11.1   *Infant mortality rates by cause, Chile, 1972–1980*

Year	IMR	Cause-specific infant mortality rates						
		Pneu-monia	Diar-rhoea	Infectious diseases	Mal-nutrition	Birth lesion and other peri-natal	Con-genital anomalies	Other
1972/73	69.3	17.8	9.5	5.0	2.8	14.3	3.1	16.7
1975/76	57.1	11.7	6.2	5.5	2.6	9.5	3.5	18.0
1977/78	45.1	7.6	4.8	3.7	1.8	5.0	3.4	18.8
1979/80	35.4	5.8	2.4	2.6	0.9	3.7	4.0	16.1

Source: Derived from data in Foxley and Raczynski (1984), Table V.6 (p. 230) and Table V.7 (p. 231).

for and use of health interventions (Kielmann *et al.* 1983). Two groups of
villages were offered a comprehensive package of primary health care services,
including a twice-daily feeding programme for malnourished children and a
weekly clinic for health care. In one group this programme was augmented
by a motivational home visit to every family once a week, while in the other
group families were visited only every two months. After three years, substantial
differences in the programme impact between the two groups of villages were
observed. In the motivated group essentially all social classes utilized the
services, resulting in a significant mortality decline, while in the other group
the clinical services were used primarily by upper-class families, resulting in a
widening of health differentials in the community but having little overall
impact.

In the last few years, many examples have appeared of motivational programmes and social mobilization on a national scale, often but not always
focused on immunization programmes.

Three elements in the chemistry of social mobilization have usually been
combined to produce these dramatic results: political leadership, non-government voluntary organizations, and mass communications. Political leadership

is needed to give a lead from the top, to accord national priority to these basic health actions, and to involve education, local government, and the mass media, beyond the Ministry of Health. Non-government organizations are also vital if the movement is to involve people and be more than a government effort. NGOs are often also the critical means for reaching and mobilizing women, young persons, and community-level organizations in general. The churches and religious groups, with their wide links and community organization, have also demonstrated their power to motivate and mobilize in all parts of the world. The media provide the third ingredient—television, radio, and printing—in a mix which matches the situation and structure of the country. The media have the power to persuade as well as to inform and to motivate and mobilize.

In the context of recession and adjustment, these elements of social mobilization are of added importance because they often have underused or misdirected potential, which at little cost can be turned to social use for health. In many countries, advertising time and skills have been provided without charge to publicize national health efforts; newspapers have carried for weeks the build-up to an immunization campaign; the churches, the Boy Scouts, the Red Cross, and national women's organizations have mobilized their memberships in support of health actions. No doubt there has been some 'opportunity cost' in all these efforts, but in general the phrase 'social mobilization' seems an apt description of the process. It is mobilizing for social purposes vast individual and community resources, many of which seem unlikely to have been fully used without some social purpose of this sort.

VI Essential drugs

The availability of a regular supply of basic medicines is a vital part of ensuring basic health services, preventive and curative (see WHO 1985). It is one of the major components of primary care. Yet in country after country in Africa over the 1980s, health centres and dispensaries, rural and urban, lack basic supplies of medicines, often going for many months with only two or three items, if any at all. Medicines available on the private market are very expensive, far beyond the reach of most of the poorer sections of the population. Shortages and high prices in a less extreme form are often the situation in Latin America and certain countries in Asia, especially in the rural areas.

Before turning to what can be done, it is worth underlining the triple and synergistic inefficiency of this situation: health workers are deprived of a critical element for much of their work, reducing their efficiency and destroying their morale; the health of the population suffers; deprived of support for self-cure and prevention, there is a prolonging of illness among the sick, increasing the probability of cross-infection, especially for the young and vulnerable; work efficiency in the home, on the farm, and at other work-places suffers, reducing output and real incomes, welfare, and happiness to the detriment of family members, young and old, in countless households and communities.

It is obviously possible to exaggerate this downward cycle of deprivation and to ignore the remarkable capacity of people (and the human body, even when short of food, to throw off illness) to carry on with work and household activities with considerable efficiency. One can see many such examples in villages and slums. But equally, it is possible to underestimate the widespread and deleterious effects of a growing incidence of illness and weakening health services spread in varying degrees over whole communities. The net effect is likely to be a general and significant lowering of health, efficiency, and welfare across the community, but because data and hard evidence are limited the whole effect may be largely missed.

Much of this is unnecessary. The provision of essential drugs need not be expensive; if effectively handled as part of national policy, an adequate supply can be provided for all at a cost which can almost certainly be afforded.

The essential drugs programme of Tanzania provides an example. This programme, started in 1983 with the support of the Danish International Development Agency and in collaboration with WHO and UNICEF, had the purpose of providing a regular supply of 32 to 36 essential drugs to all 3,000 clinics and dispensaries in the rural areas of Tanzania, covering in theory roughly 20 million rural Tanzanians and in practice reaching an estimated 75 per cent of them. Under this scheme, the drugs are supplied each month in a pre-packed box, with standardized contents matched to the broad health needs of the region of the country. The boxes are taken to subregional centres by the Ministry of Health, but from there to the village the local community is responsible for collection and transportation on the final stages of the journey. This reduces costs to the central government and also introduces an element of community involvement and monitoring; members of the community know of the box's arrival and thus that supplies should be available for the next month.

In support of the scheme, a crash training course was held during the first year to provide some 5,000 basic health workers with refresher courses designed to improve the diagnosis, prescription, and use of essential drugs in relation to the most common illnesses and needs. This helped improve efficiency in the use of drugs, though subsequent evaluation still showed that only 65 per cent of patients were correctly diagnosed and prescribed drugs in the appropriate quantities. Further training is therefore planned.

From the viewpoint of adjustment policy, four points are of major importance:

1. For barely 30 cents per person a year, it has proved possible to provide essential drugs through basic rural health services covering 20 million people. This cost includes the essential drugs themselves (about $5 million), and related transport and training. This is only a fraction of what many countries at

present pay for essential drugs—even countries short of foreign exchange and with many clinics desperately short of essential drugs.

2. There are three major reasons why the nation-wide provision of essential drugs can be achieved at very low cost:

(*a*) The concentration is on 32–36 essential and generic drugs.

(*b*) International competitive procurement has helped to reduce essential drugs prices (in dollar terms) by some 50 per cent over the last four years. The total cost in Tanzania is some 60 per cent of that originally estimated.

(*c*) A separate distribution system with its own source of supply has been established which concentrates solely on regular provision to each and every basic level clinic or health post in the rural areas. At the same time, the insistent claims of hospitals or urban centres are controlled by specifically prohibiting their access to the rural essential drugs scheme.

3. In many countries much higher prices have been and still are being paid through using privately negotiated contracts and special arrangements rather than competitive procurement. The situation is especially bad in those countries with severe balance of payments problems, since uncertainty over debt payments and exchange rates enables the drug-supplying companies to ask for, and often get, high prices as part of a package deal of drugs, credit, and transport.

To gain full benefit, there is a need to carry success in one area into nation-wide application. In the case in question, essential drugs for the rural clinics still form only a fraction of the total annual use of drugs in Tanzania—an estimated $5 million out of a total of $28 million. Much of the remainder is apparently bought at higher prices and is less focused on priority needs. On the face of it, there is ample scope for making further savings while increasing the curative and preventive efficiency of the whole health system.

4. It is too early to assess the benefits of the Tanzania essential drug programme in terms of health impact, but the benefits in terms of political popularity, health worker morale, and apparent health effectiveness are already considerable. One interesting by-product is the easing of the load on district hospitals which has followed as patients find clinic visits more satisfactory and are therefore less inclined to go to a hospital for minor problems.

VII   Conclusions

The recent global economic recession, while having serious short-run adverse consequences, can possibly have benefit in the long run by forcing nations to look critically at their resource allocation priorities and operational efficiencies. As this chapter has shown, such a critical examination is essential in the health sector. Up to the present, health services have usually been programmed and delivered as consumption goods, with little or no consideration given to their impact in promoting the production of health and overall growth. A reformulation of health strategies should also place health expenditures as productive investment in building up the quality of human capital. Assisting mothers in reducing morbidity and mortality in their children and in controlling their own fertility would clearly increase the 'efficiency in production' of healthy offspring. Simultaneously this strategy would drastically reduce the numbers of disabilities among the survivors, which would assure a higher quality of productive citizens for the next generation.

A primary health care strategy incorporating such basic elements as immunizations, oral rehydration therapy, and essential drugs covering the entire population will not only lead to substantial improvement in health but can be implemented at less expense than the cost of constructing and operating a single major urban hospital in most developing countries. Furthermore, when effectively carried out, a well-formulated child survival and development programme can substantially improve the overall quality of medical care available to the people.

Essential elements in primary health care strategies are the effective use of the media coupled with mass social mobilization. This approach not only permits Ministries of Health to draw upon far more resources than are ordinarily available in their own budgets, but it also increases the efficiency of programmes by generating popular demand for, and effective use of, the technologies and interventions being made available.

There is now abundant international experience attesting both to the popularity and effectiveness of the child survival and development programme strategies. In the final analysis, political will and commitment are the underpinnings of any programme to achieve adjustment with a human face.

12

Education

Richard Jolly

I Introduction

Earlier chapters have indicated some of the major problems of education that arise from the impact of recession and often also from the misplaced emphasis in adjustment policies. The challenge of giving a human face to education policy should give highest priority to primary education and, to the extent this is secure in access and quality for *all* children of primary school age, to the other levels of education, including adult education and pre-school. But there are often other long-standing problems of education which need to be tackled yet which frequently get shelved given the pressures of adjustment. The very challenge of bringing human concerns into adjustment policy should be made into an opportunity for also tackling these problems of education:

1. Making the curriculum itself more *relevant for social progress* and strengthening linkages between the education system with the world of work.

2. Modifying what is often an *inequitable structure of fees and subsidies*, replacing it with a structure which helps the educational system provide equal opportunities, with special financial support for those who need it. As many analysts have pointed out, education has the *potential* for being a major force for greater equality, but too often this potential is obstructed by perverse effects of structure and fees.

3. In many poorer countries, there is also need for action *to encourage female participation* on a more equitable basis in the school system—in terms of initial enrolments, avoiding drop-outs, and ensuring balanced progress up the system, including into the various professional streams.

4. Strengthening the *wider social and development role of the school system* by making it a centre of community action in both rural and (poorer) urban areas. Schools can become centres for adult education for mobilizing public health action, and catalysts for action on a wider variety of topics. Similarly, teachers can often be natural community leaders for development, providing the extra burdens this places on them is adequately recognized and they receive training and support.

These needs and possibilities are set out in other documents more fully than is possible or appropriate here. For present purposes only two points need be stressed. First, that the very constraints of adjustment policy often set back progress towards these broader education goals and roles, thereby making less effective use of even those resources which remain committed to education. Secondly, following directly from this, that specific concern with the above issues should be made part of the restructuring process in adjustment policy, and neither postponed nor abandoned. The question should be how, not if or when.

II Current situation and trends

The potential for restoring momentum to expansion in spite of constrained resources is shown by the large differences in the unit costs of education in different countries. The unit costs of primary education, for example, differ by a factor of one to three. Generally the poorer countries spend a much higher share of their national resources on education than the richer countries, in part because the higher rates of population growth in developing countries mean that they have higher proportions of school-age children relative to their working population; but in part also because their unit costs of basic education in relation to per capita income tend to be higher than in better-off countries. A move to expansion in spite of constraints lies in changing these structural factors to facilitate expansion at lower cost.

The reason for the relatively high unit costs can be made clear by identifying the factors which explain the dominant level of unit costs for any country.

1 Recurrent costs

Recurrent costs are affected by the following factors:

1. *The level and structure of teachers' salaries*—which in turn reflect (*a*) qualifications and grading of teachers at each level of education, (*b*) the relationship between teachers' salaries and that of others in the educated professional groups, and (*c*) the level of salaries of the educated professional group as a whole.

2. *The average pupil–teacher ratios at each level of education*—which in turn reflect (*a*) class size, (*b*) staffing, and (*c*) school organization, especially length of the school cycle and drop-out rates.

3. *The non-salary costs of education*—which at primary and secondary levels in all countries are almost always a minor part of total recurrent costs, frequently less than 20 per cent. At tertiary level, these may become more important— and occasionally a cause of unnecessary waste.

2 Capital costs

The capital costs per place usually reflect (*a*) the standards and general quality chosen for school and university accommodation as much as (*b*) actual space provision and (*c*) general building costs. Critical also is (*d*) the efficiency of school organization—notably whether shift use is common or exceptional, whether school and university facilities are left vacant during vacations, and whether subject options and timetabling make intensive use of specialist facilities like laboratories and assembly halls instead of requiring extra provision.

These are the main factors which explain why countries spending roughly the same proportion of national incomes on education differ by factors of two, three, or more in the proportion of their school-aged children attending school and reaching each level.

This leads to the critical question of resource allocation and the options open midst the constraints of adjustment. If this central issue is to be adequately analysed, the following points must be kept in mind.

1. In most countries, in spite of primary schools accounting for 80 or 90 per cent of total school enrolments, primary education generally accounts for half or less of total educational expenditure, the rest being the share of secondary, higher, and any other vocational education the country may be supporting. Tertiary education, typically extending to a small minority, often one per cent, if that, of the population, often takes a large share of total revenues—one-quarter or more.

2. Teachers' salaries form the bulk of educational expenditure at all levels, but overwhelmingly at primary levels in developing countries where they usually comprise 80–95 per cent of recurrent expenditures. Even at secondary level, teachers' salaries may well comprise 65 to 85 per cent of recurrent expenditures.

3. Teachers usually also form an important fraction of the educated manpower of a country, especially of those employed in the public sector. This has two consequences. In the first place, it means that the level and structure of teachers' salaries are really part of a wider whole: the level and structure of salaries of all the labour force with formal levels of education. These often form an identifiable group, since salaries in the public sector are frequently fixed directly by reference to educational qualifications. The second consequence is that attempts to alter teachers' salaries will usually need to be made as part of a wider set of changes in the salaries of all those with salaries set by reference to educational qualifications.

4. Moving to universal primary education at a time of severe budgetary constraints may seem brave, if not foolhardy. Many a low-income developing country has embarked on educational expansion only to see education costs soar much more rapidly than enrolment. Indeed, experience over the last two decades shows that:

(*a*) Enrolments have risen rapidly in most developing countries, but almost always more rapidly at higher levels than at secondary and very much faster at secondary than at primary level.

(*b*) Enrolment ratios, however, have risen more slowly, and still spread over a wide range. About one-third of primary school enrolment ratios in 32 low-income countries in 1982 were under 50 per cent, another third between 51 and 80 per cent, and a final third were over 80 per cent.

(*c*) Public expenditure on education has risen rapidly in virtually all countries, often faster than total enrolment, and in almost all cases in the 1960s and early 1970s considerably faster than either government revenue or GNP.

III Priorities for maintaining and restoring the effectiveness of basic education

The pressures to maintain salaries and avoid any reductions are such that the typical pattern is for expenditure on maintenance of building and equipment, books, and teaching supplies to be cut to the bone. This in many countries has produced grotesque educational inefficiency. One can readily find secondary schools attempting to carry on with literally half a small cupboardful of books, and even at university level, students in some countries are having to rub out their notes in exercise books in order to reuse them. At primary level, one can still find children sitting on the floor, without desks, reading from a crude blackboard with no books or exercise books for themselves, possibly a slate or two and a piece of chalk picked from the nearby pit as writing material.

Yet these inefficiencies need not exist if, in one form or another, an attempt is made to give priority to the basic minimum requirements for an efficient education system. Some ideas are given below.

1 Books and teaching materials

One must repeat that the main issue is priority not resource availability, since the quantity of resources required will be small in relation to all other resources required. Even so, priority is probably best assigned in the order of:

1. Minimum teaching books and aids for the teachers.
2. Exercise-books and writing materials for the students.
3. A minimum supply of basic books for the students.

A critical issue is the reuse of books from year to year. Important as this is, often the quality of the books provided and the incentives and discipline to ensure their careful use and thus protection for use in subsequent years is less than desirable and possible. A lot might be achieved by ensuring that new books, when provided, are designed and protected for longer-term use. Incentives to students and parents to pay for and protect materials is also important. Countries often charge parents for the materials and books, which on the one hand increases the care usually given them, but on the other hand often prevents some students obtaining even basic materials. A compromise often used is to make new books on sale available to the parents but to ensure a secondary market in used books, to make earlier copies available at lower prices.

There are also opportunities to use publications and printing presses at present used mainly for news and leisure publications for education purposes as well. At least one country has used its glossy magazine presses to roll off a series of impressive 'school books' with more lively illustrations than the typical textbook. Newspapers in many countries have been used to carry a special centre spread for new literates.

Donors might be prepared to make available paper and possibly text-books in support of maintaining basic education materials. Such support can be given in cash or even in kind, making use of the underutilized capacity of paper mills and printing facilities in some industrialized countries.

2   Building maintenance

Often, unnecessary deterioration has been allowed to occur. Repair and maintenance of buildings, particularly of primary schools, can draw on community effort, whether for a basic mud hut and grass-roots school or for more solid buildings. What may be needed is minimum support for critical building supplies, such as paint or nails, although even here community action to raise the limited resources can often be generated with effort and community leadership.

The critical need is for better community understanding of the challenge of adjustment policy and a sense of hope that people, their children, and community welfare need not suffer if community effort can be mobilized. This is an important area for strengthening understanding of the adjustment process, especially of the tough choices it poses for all levels of the country and its government. Clearly also the response generated is likely to depend on the sense of fairness and equity with which the burdens of adjustment are shared. If community action is simply a way of relieving the costs of services for the masses while those better off and services in the capital city continue much as before, the chance of effective community response is likely to be severely limited.

3   Teachers' salaries

Because these form by far the largest part of educational expenditure, the need to review their cost in real terms is an important issue for policy. In many countries, significant reductions in real salaries are likely to have taken place through rapid inflation. If this is part of a general reduction in salaries of this level of worker through inflation, a rough equity may well have been maintained, though even so a major programme of public information and explanation may be needed. In some cases, teachers' salaries may still be high relative to the earnings of other workers.

Two considerations are necessary in consciously deciding how much change in salary is possible and desirable:

(*a*) The need to maintain basic salaries of teachers, as other groups in communities, at a level sufficient to ensure, in cash or kind, the provision of basic needs to the households of the teachers concerned.

(*b*) The need to maintain or provide some incentives, in finance or otherwise, to help sustain motivation and commitment of the teaching force.

Neither of these considerations is easy, but experience in different countries shows many possible approaches. These have often proved successful when used, but have also been used too little.

For instance, with respect to basic needs priorities, Ethiopia at one time ensured that a community was committed to provide the teacher the equivalent of food from an acre of land, farmed by the community but made available for the teacher as part-payment in kind. Similar action has been undertaken in other countries to make up for a limited salary. Other countries have chosen consciously to maintain teachers' monetary salaries at an adequate level.

As regards incentives, this is a critical but even more neglected issue. In the first place, some element of financial incentive can often be introduced into the salary structure of the teaching force, to reward those who have made special efforts or attained special achievements. Here the issue is fairness and objective criteria in awarding the extra payments, and keeping them in proportion in relation to basic salaries. Again, such incentives need not only be provided in financial terms. Often recognition or rewards in kind can be important incentives.

Provision for training and self-improvement and self-education is often also an important form of incentive for primary teachers, many of whom hope to advance themselves and often are prepared to work hard for this, particularly in their earlier years. It is important to ensure adequate facilities for training and self-improvement, which often requires special efforts for rural teachers in remote areas. But these efforts, while small in relation to the costs of primary education, can make a major difference in maintaining the efficiency and even enthusiasm of the primary school teaching force.

IV The choices ahead: difficult options but real opportunities

Most people are so accustomed to treating the financial constraints of education and its cost-determining structure as given that they often fail to sense the magnitude of what is sacrificed through not exploring options with sufficient imagination. In order to make this clear, one can calculate the extent to which it would be possible to move rapidly to universal primary education without any increase in total educational expenditure. This goal is of course only one of several basic goals which could be identified. It is chosen partly because it is one of the fundamental goals and partly because it illuminates more general issues. It is also in an area which in many countries is already accepted as one of high political priority. Many politicians might reassess the difficulties of adopting certain cost-saving measures if they realized the extent to which such savings would make possible a rapid move to universal primary education.

Can nothing be done? In principle, there are two ways around these constraints. One can 'wait for growth'—for additional production to become available which will provide the foreign exchange and local resources needed for additional teachers' salaries and their additional consumption. Quite apart from the delays, however, this strategy may never succeed. Salaries and consumption levels have frequently shown a tendency to rise along with overall growth of national income, thus absorbing the gains in paying teachers more rather than in providing for more teachers.

What is the alternative to 'waiting for growth'? Essentially it is to provide for educational expansion (and to tackle other educational problems) within the resources already available, especially within available human resources. This means working out how educational goals can be achieved by adapting institutions and incomes structure to achieve them rather than by taking these elements as given and adapting the goals.

Given the determinants of educational costs identified earlier, there are five major ways in which this can be done: (*a*) the share of primary education in total education must be increased; (*b*) a revision in the effective salary structure of teachers and other employees with comparable education; (*c*) changes in pupil–teacher ratios; (*d*) changes in the length of the cycle, reduction in dropout rates and other structural factors determining the major part of educational costs; and (e) much greater provision of support and resources from their communities and abroad.

A revision in the effective salary structure of teachers and other educated persons would make it possible to employ more teachers within a given budget. In those countries still with high salary scales for teachers, it would also make possible a general narrowing of excessive differentials and incentives, one of the critical requirements for the eradication of educated unemployment and the establishment of an incentive structure related to the priorities of rural development and basic needs.

A wholesale restructuring over time of wages and incomes implies a major and sustained incomes and wages policy applying to all educated persons and not just teachers. One must frankly admit that in spite of the obvious difficulties in many countries, this seems to be an inescapable need if educated unemployment is to be eliminated and basic needs met.

In addition, important though less wholesale alternatives are available, both as positive measures in themselves, and as steps towards more fundamental reforms. Such measures include the adoption of national-service wage scales for teachers and others in the first two or three years after training, the use of volunteer teachers or pupil-monitors, and a revision of the automatic link between teachers' qualifications and individual salary grading. Some reduction of excessive salary differentials in general has often been achieved as a by-product of inflation, by providing only partial compensation for cost of living increases among the higher-income groups but full compensation for those at the minimum wage level. All these approaches are or have been in operation, though often their broader significance as steps towards more general changes in salary and incentive structures has not been emphasized.

A quite different approach is for government to provide its financial support for education to the local community—and to leave it to the community to supplement in cash or kind the teacher's remuneration, in the form of free housing, free food, or assistance with work on the teacher's farm, etc. Such an approach, in principle, offers a major way to bridge the gap between limited government financial resources and the additional consumption which employing more teachers would generate. It does this by building on the productive resources of the rural area and not just by finance from central government (though it implies the need to diminish urban bias elsewhere in the community).

Each of these measures can be used, alone or in concert, to make possible changes in education expansion and improvements in the short run and at the same time to move towards broader changes in salary structure. The extent of the salary changes required will naturally vary with the particular circumstances of each country. If at all possible, the measures should be applied to all salaried workers with educational qualifications, not just to teachers.

In addition to direct changes of the wage and salary structure, changes of the pupil–teacher ratio and of the share of primary education in the total education budget also incorporate promise for reform. An earlier study (Jolly 1977) has shown that a large proportion of the countries not yet having achieved universal primary education could achieve this goal by changes in these two factors with no change in educational expenditure in total.

Two facts point to the conclusion that achievement of universal primary education *is* possible, even at times of severe resource constraint. First, is the fact that some very low-income countries have achieved 100 per cent primary enrolment—for example, Togo, Sri Lanka and China. Secondly, the costs per student-year of primary school are a fraction—one-eighth to one-tenth—of the cost per student-year of tertiary education. Consequently—even without cost savings at the primary level—a small switch in resources from tertiary level to primary could achieve universal primary schooling. If government finance of tertiary education were replaced in part by fees and loans, this could be achieved without reducing the quantity of tertiary education. The education sector, and especially primary education, makes use of resources which are generally abundant in most developing countries, even during recession and adjustment—labour and locally available materials. The sector also contributes to the long-run productive potential of the economy. Consequently, there is no case in economic logic for cutting back on this sector. What is needed is the political commitment and administrative creativity to sustain and expand the sector despite financial limitations.

13

Nutrition Interventions

Per Pinstrup-Andersen

1 Introduction

Governments faced with proposed adjustment programmes that are likely to have negative effects for the poor may either modify the programmes or introduce compensatory programmes and policies alongside the adjustment programmes. While both may be important, this chapter focuses on compensatory means to counter negative impacts on the absolute poor in general and their nutritional status in particular, through food-related programmes.

Such interventions are necessary because according to a recent World Bank report (1986*b*) 'economies cannot be expected to grow quickly enough to eliminate the chronic food insecurity of some groups in the near future even under the best of circumstances'.

II Ways of providing compensation

There are essentially four ways in which compensatory measures to avoid negative nutrition effects among the poor may work. First, expected real income losses of poor households may be offset by equal size transfer of income-generating programmes, thus leaving real household incomes unchanged. Secondly, programmes and policies may be introduced to maintain household food consumption constant during a period of decreasing real incomes. This may be attempted by inducing households (*a*) to spend a larger share of their incomes on food, or (*b*) to substitute toward a lower-cost diet. Reducing food prices, both absolutely and relative to non-food prices, and changing relative prices among food commodities may contribute to achieving these aims. Improved nutrition information, changes in budget control among household members, and increased availability of food from own production may also be effective. The major drawback in efforts to increase the share of the budget being spent on food is that less will be available for other goods and services that may be as important as good nutrition—e.g. housing and health care.

If neither of these approaches, i.e. compensating for potential decrease in household income or food consumption, are likely to be sufficient, two additional ways may be considered. First, expected decreases in the food consumption of individual household members most at risk of malnutrition, e.g. pre-schoolers and pregnant and lactating women, may be avoided by increasing the share of total household food consumption allocated to them. Nutrition information and education as well as food supplementation schemes effectively targeted to those individuals are the most common measures to reach this goal. The principal drawbacks of such measures are that other household members who may also be at risk of malnutrition may experience a reduction in their share of the total household food basket. Furthermore, it is usually difficult effectively to target food supplementation schemes to specific household members if such targeting conflicts with the desires of the head of the household. Measures to reduce the occurrence and severity of anorexia (i.e. loss of appetite) may also be effective in increasing the share of total household food going to high-risk individuals.

Finally, potential negative effects may be avoided by introducing measures that increase the physiological utilization of the food consumed by the individuals most at risk of malnutrition. Such measures include primary health care, improved sanitation, and child care and nutrition education.

In summary, government efforts to compensate for expected negative nutrition effects may be aimed at avoiding declines in (*a*) household real incomes, (*b*) household food consumption at a lower income, (*c*) food consumption of high-risk individuals at lower household food consumption, or (*d*) the amount of utilized calories and nutrients in high-risk individuals at lower total intakes by those individuals. A schematic overview of the aims of compensatory programmes and policies as discussed above is presented in Fig. 13.1.

The question as to which of these four ways of avoiding negative nutrition effects should be the focus of government intervention depends on the nature of the existing nutrition problem, household food acquisition and allocation behaviour, and the capacity of the government to implement various types of programmes.

In cases where a low level of physiological utilization is prevalent due to, say, frequent and severe diarrhoea in children, the potential negative effect of reduced food consumption may be offset by improved sanitation and health care. Similar efforts may lead to reduced occurrence and frequency of anorexia, thus increasing the share of household food consumption obtained by high-risk individuals. Where serious food deficiencies in some household members are found alongside excess consumption by others, efforts to change household food allocation behaviour may prove useful.

Households spending a relatively large share of their incomes on non-essential goods and services, and households that consume a relatively expensive diet, are more capable of making—and usually do make—adjustments in food acquisition to cope with decreasing real incomes and mitigate the negative nutrition effects. On the other hand, many low-income households spend a very large proportion of their real incomes on food and other essentials without being able to meet nutritional requirements of most or all household members.

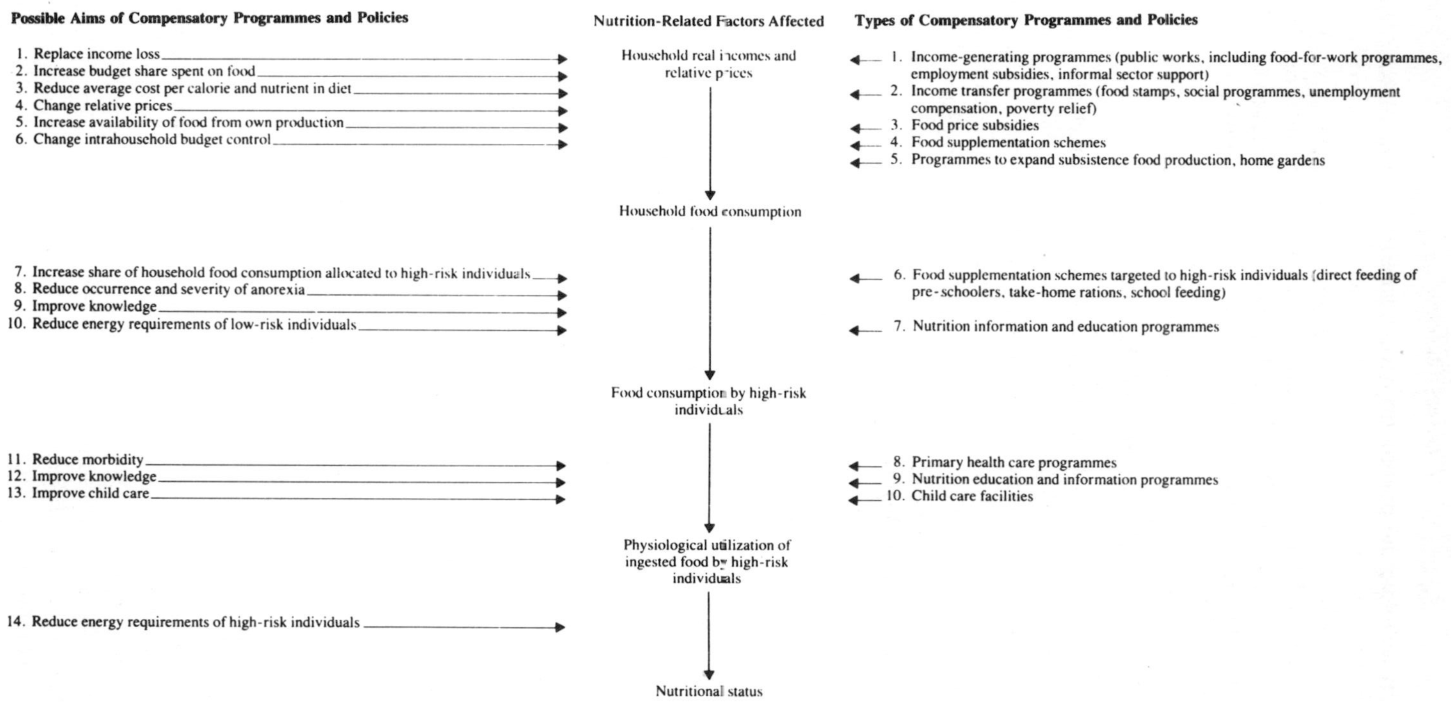

Possible Aims of Compensatory Programmes and Policies

Types of Compensatory Programmes and Policies

1. Income-generating programmes (public works, including food-for-work programmes, employment subsidies, informal sector support)
2. Income transfer programmes (food stamps, social programmes, unemployment compensation, poverty relief)
3. Food price subsidies
4. Food supplementation schemes
5. Programmes to expand subsistence food production, home gardens

6. Food supplementation schemes targeted to high-risk individuals (direct feeding of pre-schoolers, take-home rations, school feeding)
7. Nutrition information and education programmes

8. Primary health care programmes
9. Nutrition education and information programmes
10. Child care facilities

Nutrition-Related Factors Affected

Household real incomes and relative prices

Household food consumption

Food consumption by high-risk individuals

Physiological utilization of ingested food by high-risk individuals

Nutritional status

Possible Aims of Compensatory Programmes and Policies

1. Replace income loss
2. Increase budget share spent on food
3. Reduce average cost per calorie and nutrient in diet
4. Change relative prices
5. Increase availability of food from own production
6. Change intrahousehold budget control

7. Increase share of household food consumption allocated to high-risk individuals
8. Reduce occurrence and severity of anorexia
9. Improve knowledge
10. Reduce energy requirements of low-risk individuals

11. Reduce morbidity
12. Improve knowledge
13. Improve child care

14. Reduce energy requirements of high-risk individuals

Fig. 13.1 Schematic overview of aims and types of compensatory programmes and policies.

For these households, the possible nutritional gains from increasing budget shares of food, reducing the cost of attaining calories and nutrients, and improving allocation of food among household members, may already have been exhausted and reductions in real incomes may be fully reflected in worsening nutritional status. The only viable policy options for such households are to avoid or replace income losses and to improve the physiological utilization of food.

III   Programme and policy options

Governments wishing to avoid the potential negative nutrition effects of macro-economic adjustment programmes may choose from an array of compensatory programmes and policies. If the aim is to compensate for losses in household incomes, then income generation, income transfer, and price subsidy programmes are the most obvious choice (Fig. 13.1). Income-generating programmes are discussed in Chapters 9 and 10. Income transfer and subsidy programmes are discussed below.

Food price subsidies may also be used to make food or certain food commodities cheaper relative to other goods. This may induce the household to make adjustments in the budget allocation in favour of the cheaper commodity. Food supplementation schemes may be viewed as income transfer programmes because they add resources to the household. Depending on their design, they may also induce households to expand the share of total real income spent on food and/or change the food allocation within the household in favour of the most malnourished. Nutrition education programmes may assist in mitigating the negative nutrition effects of income losses by influencing household food acquisition and allocation behaviour. Finally, primary health care programmes may play a major role by increasing the physiological utilization of ingested food and by reducing the occurrence and frequency of anorexia.

In summary, the following programme types are available for the policy-maker who wishes to avoid or compensate for negative nutrition effects of macro-economic adjustment programmes:

1. *Income-generating programmes*
    (a) Public works, including food-for-work.
    (b) Employment generation with or without subsidies.
    (c) Informal sector support.
    (d) Programmes to expand subsistence food production, including home gardens.
    (e) Programmes to increase agricultural production and incomes on small farms.
2. *Income transfer programmes*
    (a) Food stamp programmes.
    (b) Social programmes, poverty relief.
    (c) Unemployment compensation.

3. *Food price subsidies*
4. *Food supplementation schemes*
   (*a*) On-site feeding schemes.
   (*b*) Take-home schemes.
   (*c*) Nutrition rehabilitation centres.
5. *Nutrition education programmes*
6. *Primary health care*

Income transfer schemes, food price subsidies, food supplementation schemes, and nutrition education are discussed below. Primary health care is considered briefly in this chapter and in more depth in Chapter 11.

IV Income transfer programmes

Income transfer programmes may be preferred over income-generating programmes because they are easier and faster to implement. They may be effective to compensate for short-term transitory declines in incomes of certain groups of low-income people. However, if the income declines are expected to be of a longer-term nature, it is important that transfer programmes be accompanied with measures that will assure a self-sustaining enhanced capacity of the poor to generate more income.

Income transfer programmes may be designed and implemented in a variety of ways. The transfer may be provided in cash as poverty relief, unemployment compensation, etc., or it may be linked to foods, housing, or some other essential commodities.

Food-linked income transfer programmes take many forms, of which food stamps and food supplementation programmes are the most common. Both types of programmes are attempts to transfer incomes to families or individuals in target groups in the form of food or food-purchasing power, in order to assure that dietary intakes increase. The most common arguments for transferring food or food-linked incomes rather than cash are that (*a*) a larger proportion of the additional incomes is spent on food (a higher marginal propensity to consume food) when food and food-linked incomes are transferred than when the transfer is cash income, and that (*b*) food is available to the government at a cost below market prices, that is, as foreign food aid or surplus production.

In many cases transfers are limited to specified rations smaller in quantity than those that would be acquired without subsidy—that is, the quantity is intramarginal. This implies that the nutritional effect would be expected to be no different from that of a transfer of cash income equal to the real income embodied in the transfer.

But food-linked income transfers need not be intramarginal. One way to design transfer programmes that will have an effect on the acquisition of food beyond the income effect is to require the household to pay an amount close to that which it now spends on food in order to obtain food stamps that will cover a larger quantity. Such a 'purchase requirement' was included in the US food stamp programme until 1979. Programmes designed in this fashion are likely to have a greater effect on the acquisition of food by a household because in addition to the income effect, they make food cheaper at the margin.

Purchase requirements are difficult to implement in a socially just manner. If the amount to be paid for the food stamps is based on the average expenditures for food by the target group, the programme will tend to be regressive among target households and may exclude the neediest from participating because the amount may exceed what they are able to pay. On the other hand, in most societies it is impossible to extract a different amount from each household on the basis of the ability to pay.

But even if food-linked income transfers do not influence nutrition any differently than cash transfers of the same magnitude, the former may be politically feasible when the latter are not. Better-off population groups are generally more willing to support income transfers aimed at the alleviation of overt human misery, such as extreme and highly visible malnutrition, than general income transfers for which the spending decisions related to the transfers are left in the hands of the recipient households. For this reason, income transfers to the poor may be politically desirable or feasible only if earmarked for alleviation of.extreme human misery, even though the final result is not different from that obtained from transfers that are not earmarked.

Three developing countries—Sri Lanka, Colombia, and Jamaica—have experience with food stamp programmes. In the absence of a purchase requirement and with the value of stamps appreciably less than pre-stamp food expenditures, the Sri Lankan programme has served primarily as an income transfer (Edirisinghe 1986). The Colombian food stamp programme, which was discontinued in 1982, was part of a larger food and nutrition plan, including nutrition education and growth-monitoring of children. The programme was targeted to low-income regions, and within those regions to households with pre-schoolers and pregnant and lactating women. The value of the food stamps was low—less than 2 per cent of average incomes of participating households—and it was not possible to detect any impact on the nutritional status of the target individuals (Pinstrup-Andersen 1984). The impact on household food consumption was not significantly different from the impact of wage incomes of the same magnitude. Thus, like the Sri Lanka food stamp programme, no difference was detected in the marginal propensity to consume food from food stamp and other income.

There is evidence from other studies, however, that the marginal propensity to consume food varies with income source. Thus, results from a Philippine study indicate that the income transfer embodied in food subsidies for intra-marginal rations have a larger impact on household calorie consumption than an equal amount of wage income (Garcia and Pinstrup-Andersen 1986). Similarly, Kumar (1979) found that in Kerala, India, the marginal propensity to consume food varied among women's incomes, men's incomes, and incomes in-kind from home gardens. One possible explanation for different marginal propensities among income sources is that intrahousehold budget control is a function of the source of income, and that the marginal propensity to consume food varies among members of a household.

V   Food price subsidies

Food price subsidies have made significant contributions to improved nutrition in a number of countries, as further discussed in Pinstrup-Andersen (1986*b*). Food price subsidies may influence the nutritional status in three ways. First, subsidies increase the purchasing power of recipient households because they can purchase a larger amount of food at the same cost. Secondly, they may reduce the prices of food relative to the prices of other goods, thereby encouraging households to buy more food. Thirdly, they may make certain foods cheaper relative to other foods, and in this way change the diet composition.

Food subsidies have significantly increased real incomes of the poor in a number of countries. In several programmes analysed by the International Food Policy Research Institute (IFPRI) (Pinstrup-Andersen 1987), the value of the food subsidies received by low-income households accounted for 15–25 per cent of their total real incomes. As a general rule, better-off households received larger absolute benefits than poorer ones. However, benefits as a percentage of current incomes are larger for the poor. Both the value and the distribution of benefits varied among programme types and countries. This variation offers opportunities for increasing benefits or reducing costs of consumer-oriented food price subsidies through appropriate programme choice and design.

Household food consumption was also positively influenced. Thus, the subsidized ration shop scheme in Sri Lanka increased daily energy consumption by 63 calories per capita on the average, and by 115 calories among the poorest decile (Gavan and Chandrasekera 1979). A pilot food price subsidy scheme in the Philippines increased average daily calorie consumption per adult-equivalent unit by 130 calories (Garcia and Pinstrup-Andersen 1986). Ahmed (1979) estimated that low-income urban consumers in Bangladesh consumed about 250 calories more per person daily due to the rations, and George (1985) estimated that the poorest Indian consumers increased their calorie consumption up to 18 per cent. This is similar in magnitude to the impact of the Sri Lankan food stamp programme, which was estimated to have increased calorie consumption among the poorest population decile by 15 per cent in 1981 (Edirisinghe 1986).

Very little is known about the effect of food subsidies on intrahousehold food distribution and consumption of individuals. Evidence concerning the impact of subsidy programmes on food consumption by pre-school children is available from Mexico (E. Kennedy 1987) and the Philippines (Garcia and Pinstrup-Andersen 1986). In both cases, the impact was positive and significant. In the case of Mexico, the increase in the consumption of milk—the subsidized commodity—by pre-schoolers was partially offset by decreased consumption of other commodities. Furthermore, in both cases, calorie consumption by other household members increased significantly due to the subsidies. In the Philippines a disproportionately large share of the net increase in household food consumption went to adults, although the goal of the programme was to increase food consumption by pre-schoolers. Although this implies large 'leakages' from the point of view of programme goals, the households that received the subsidies were very poor and all household members, including adult males, were calorie deficient.

There is very little direct empirical evidence on the effect of food subsidies on the nutritional status as measured by anthropometrics. Kumar (1979) found that the weight for age of children in Kerala would fall by 8 per cent if the ration scheme was discontinued. Similarly, results from a pilot food price subsidy scheme in the Philippines showed a positive effect on the weight for age of pre-schoolers (Garcia and Pinstrup-Andersen 1986).

The effect of food price subsidies depends on the nature of the subsidy scheme, including the degree of targeting, the choice of commodities to be subsidized, and the design and implementation of the distribution scheme. Targeting is a particularly important consideration because it is a means of reducing fiscal costs of untargeted subsidies without reducing the benefits obtained by the target group. Some of the schemes are targeted to urban households either explicitly through the issue of ration cards or implicitly by limiting the distribution of subsidized commodities to urban areas. However, very few of the existing food price subsidy schemes are targeted to low-income households. Thus, existing subsidy schemes may be modified to provide larger benefits to those groups of low-income people who are likely to lose from adjustment programmes while at the same time reducing overall costs. This is a very important consideration, since reduced government spending is a major goal of most adjustment programmes.

The choice of commodity and commodity quality is important in price subsidies. In a study of Brazil, it was found that a shift of existing explicit subsidies from wheat to cassava would lower incomes of the rich and increase incomes of the poor. Shifting the subsidy to milk, on the other hand, would result in a large decrease in incomes of the poor and a corresponding increase for the rich (Williamson-Gray 1982). Thus, if the goal is to transfer purchasing power to the poor through a fixed government outlay on food price subsidies, the choice of commodity is important. Similarly, the choice of commodity as a carrier of the subsidy is important if nutritional improvements are a goal. Williamson-Gray found that the current wheat bread subsidies in Brazil caused a slightly lower total calorie consumption by the poor because the increased bread consumption was associated with larger decreases in the consumption of rice and other foods. Shifting the current government outlays on wheat subsidies to rice would greatly increase total calorie consumption by the poor.

Findings from Egypt show that subsidies on bread are more beneficial to the urban poor than subsidies on wheat flour, while the opposite is the case for the rural poor (Alderman and von Braun 1986). A study of Bangladesh concluded that distribution of sorghum at the ration shops would provide larger relative gains to the poor than the rice and wheat currently distributed because sorghum is acquired almost exclusively by the poor (Karim *et al.* 1980).

A study of maize subsidies in Mexico provides further insights into the importance of the choice of product to be subsidized (Lustig 1986). In Mexico, maize prices to producers are supported through a policy of government price guarantees, while consumer prices of tortillas—a commonly consumed processed maize product—are subsidized. The price of unprocessed maize for final consumption purposes, however, is not subsidized. Although maize is a basic staple for both urban and rural households, the former usually buy subsidized tortillas while the latter make tortillas at home and thus do not benefit from the subsidy.

Limiting price subsidies to products that are perceived to be inferior or of low quality offers another possibility for altering the transfer patterns in favour of the poor. Distribution of subsidized wheat flour with a high extraction rate (since although nutritionally equivalent such flour has a less attractive appearance) in Pakistan is a case in point (Rogers and Levinson 1976). In a study of wheat flour consumption in Rawalpindi City, Khan (1982) found that although it was available to all consumers, poor households purchased more than 30 kilograms of subsidized wheat flour from ration shops per month compared to about 20 kilograms for the highest income households, while purchases of non-subsidized wheat flour from the open market was about 16 kilograms per month for the poor and 58 kilograms per month for the highest income group. Thus, the perceived low quality of the subsidized commodity resulted in some degree of self-targeting to the poor.

VI Food supplementation schemes

Food supplementation schemes differ from income transfer programmes such as food stamps in five major ways: (*a*) they do not usually rely on the private sector for food distribution; (*b*) they are usually targeted on individual household members rather than merely on households; (*c*) they usually involve relatively small total quantities of food; (*d*) they are often limited to relatively small geographical regions; and (*e*) they usually require more administrative support in implementation.

Food supplementation schemes are usually aimed at household members expected to be malnourished or at risk of becoming malnourished—e.g. children and pregnant and lactating women. Three types of delivery systems are generally used for supplementary feeding. These are on-site feeding, including school feeding, take-home feeding, and nutrition rehabilitation centres.

Studies of infants and children have shown that supplementary feeding programmes are often associated with improved growth, decreased morbidity, or improved cognitive development (Gopaldas *et al.* 1975, Freeman *et al.* 1980, Kennedy and Pinstrup-Andersen 1983). However, the benefits are usually small. Increments in birth weights attributed to the supplementary feeding programmes are typically in the range of 40–60 grams. Similarly, the increases in growth seen in pre-schoolers, although significant, are small.

A number of reasons are given for the comparatively small benefits. First, it appears that only a part of the food given is actually consumed by the target population. Leakages of the supplemented foods occur when the food is shared by non-target family members or when the food is substituted for other food that normally would be consumed. Beaton and Ghassemi (1979) have estimated that leakages can account for 30–80 per cent of the food distributed. Partly because of these leakages, supplementary feeding programmes usually fill only 10–25 per cent of the apparent energy gap in the target population. Given this small net increment in energy, it is not surprising that the observed effect on growth is small.

Most studies have concentrated on growth as the sole measure of the outcome of supplementary feeding. Beaton and Ghassemi (1979) have suggested that physical growth may not be the only benefit nor even the most important benefit of supplemental feeding. In one study, an increase in voluntary activity was found as a result of the additional food; in children this increase in activity may affect cognitive development (Rutishauser and Whitehead 1972).

Beaton and Ghassemi (1979) also make the point that any leakage in the food supplement is seen as inefficiency in the distribution programme. It cannot be assumed, however, that the energy unaccounted for provides no benefit to the family or community. Attention needs to be focused on a better assessment of the potentially wide range of benefits that can be produced by supplementary feeding. Given the magnitude of reported food leakage, the effect on household income may be substantial and the resultant effect on the nutritional status of non-targeted members of the family may also be significant. Few studies have documented the potential income-maintenance effects of supplementary feeding.

In addition to the quantity of food distributed, factors such as the timing of supplementation, duration of participation, and nutritional status of recipients influence the effectiveness of supplemental feeding (Kennedy and Pinstrup-Andersen 1983). Pregnancy and the period from 6 months to 3 years of age are the most nutritionally vulnerable periods. Inadequate nutrition during pregnancy may lead to low birth weights of babies and a resulting higher probability of infant mortality. Children below the age of three years are particularly vulnerable due to inappropriate weaning practices and infections. With respect to the duration of the feeding, on-site and take-home feeding programmes take much longer to produce a significant growth increment than do nutritional rehabilitation centres. The latter may be effective in three months or less, but no general rule for the minimum duration can be given for any of the programme types due to the influence of a number of other factors. Continuous growth-monitoring is necessary to establish the most appropriate time for discontinuing the feeding of a particular child. Furthermore, before discontinuing the participation by a child in a feeding programme, it is important that efforts be made to remove the reasons why the child became malnourished in the first place. Supplementary feeding treats the symptoms, not the causes. Therefore, unless the causes are removed, children who are no longer eligible for supplementary feeding may quickly return to their nutritional status prior to the feeding. In conclusion, it appears that food supplementation schemes may be an effective means of protecting or compensating high-risk members of poor households from potentially negative effects of macro-economic crises and adjustments provided that substitution between the supplement and food from other sources, as well as sharing among household members, are taken into account when designing the schemes and deciding on the size of the supplement. Failure to do so will yield disappointing results and only partial compensation will be provided. In view of the substitution and sharing that is likely to occur within the household, efforts to target on individuals rather than on households cannot always be justified.

VII Nutrition education

While inadequate knowledge undoubtedly has been and still is an important cause of malnutrition, care should be taken to introduce nutrition education programmes only in those cases where insufficient knowledge is the most limiting constraint. The need for nutrition education is most pronounced where large changes have occurred in the environment and constraints within which household decisions are made, such as rural to urban migration, shifts from subsistence to cash cropping, and other changes that significantly alter the magnitude and source of household incomes and availability of food and non-food commodities. However, nutrition education is often promoted in situations where households are unable to respond because of other constraints. Households with severely malnourished members are frequently deprived of other basic necessities as well, and insufficient incomes are the most limiting factor. Nutrition education aimed at reallocating a given amount of real income or food in such households is not likely to be successful. This is illustrated in a recent study in the Philippines where nutrition education was effective only in households that also received a food subsidy (Garcia and Pinstrup-Andersen 1986).

However, nutrition education may be effective in households where a significant budget share is spent on non-essential goods, where the cost of the diet is high due to lack of emphasis on available low-cost foods, and where the allocation of household food is biased against high-risk groups. Nutrition education focused on behavioural changes related to breast-feeding, feeding of weaning-aged children, diarrhoeal diseases, and sanitary practices has also proven to be effective in a large number of cases (Hornik 1985). While, as mentioned above, nutrition education is most likely to be successful when linked with other resource changes (Hornik 1985), a recent project in Indonesia illustrates that it may also be successful by itself (Manoff 1985). This project, which was based on mass media communication, contributed significantly to food intakes and growth of children at a relatively low cost.

High correlation between the needs and constraints of the target households and the design and implementation of the programme is undoubtedly the most critical feature of a successful nutrition education programme. Programmes based on a thorough understanding of the problems and the constraints within which they may be solved are more likely to be successful than those based on preconceived ideas about what households and individuals 'ought' to do.

VIII Primary health care

It is now well established that insufficient intake of nutrients and/or their inadequate utilization leading to child malnutrition can be caused by health problems unrelated to food access. Various forms of pathogenic invasion in the child (and in the adult), such as intestinal affections, worm infestation, respiratory infections, and communicable diseases either depress the appetite— particularly in the under-5s— and therefore reduce food intake or, as in the case of worm infestation and diarrhoea, provoke severe losses of nutrients.

Poor nutrition and pathogenic invasion tend mutually to reinforce each other, particularly in babies and small children. For instance, resistance to disease declines and risk of death increases substantially if a child suffers from malnutrition.

This means that in certain contexts, the best approach to reducing malnutrition, particularly for young children, consists in launching appropriate health programmes, which can have significant positive nutritional effects especially when there is integration between health and nutritional interventions. Evidence (as in the case of programmes in Chile) shows that the fastest reductions in child malnutrition were obtained when health, nutrition supplementation and rehabilitation, as well as nutrition education, were combined in a single programme.

Chapter 11 discusses health sector policies in detail. The most useful health programmes, with wide applicability in many developing countries and with positive effects on nutrition are: diarrhoea control, immunization against the six communicable diseases and control of acute respiratory infections, and supplementation of micro-nutrient deficiencies such as vitamin A, iron, and iodine. As indicated elsewhere in this book, these programmes are particularly needed, and because of their low costs they are especially suitable for introduction or acceleration during adjustment periods.

IX   Designing cost-effective compensation

Compensatory programmes and policies must be tailored to the existing opportunities and constraints in a particular setting. No one programme is likely to be the most cost-effective in all cases. Key considerations for programme design are shown in Fig. 13.1. Others include the administrative capacity, and existing institutions and infrastructure. In order to design and implement the most appropriate compensatory programme, the following six-step approach is suggested:

1. *Identification of the groups of households that* (a) *are poor,* (b) *have members who are either malnourished or at-risk of becoming malnourished, and* (c) *have been or are likely to be adversely affected by macro-economic adjustment programmes.* These groups should be the targets of compensatory programmes. The necessary information for such identification is not readily available; real incomes of individual households or groups of similar households vary over time and are not usually known in most developing countries. Attempts to obtain reliable information on a periodic basis are likely to be expensive. Thus, the challenge is to identify proxies or indicators of poverty, and malnutrition that are sufficiently reliable for targeting purposes and not excessively expensive to monitor, including asset ownership, employment status, geographical location, etc. A number of other indicators are suggested by Rogers (1987). The appropriateness of each depends on a variety of country- and programme-specific factors.

Since groups of poor households may be affected differently by macro-economic adjustment programmes, identification of the poor and potentially malnourished is necessary but not sufficient. Which of these groups is likely to benefit and which is likely to lose from the macro-economic changes must be known. Furthermore, the magnitude of losses should be estimated or predicted. Once the groups have been identified, policies and programmes must be designed in such a way that the benefits are captured by those households while the costs are borne by others. The design and implementation of programmes to reach them and exclude non-target households are difficult. The difficulties are due to political and logistical factors as well as insufficient information. Non-target households will oppose successful targeting, in some cases to the point of threatening political and social stability. Furthermore, the administrative costs of operating subsidy and transfer programmes increase with increasing degree of targeting. This is of particular concern in those developing countries where trained manpower is very scarce.

Thus, for the above reasons, perfect targeting should not be attempted. There is a point beyond which increases in administrative costs, including the cost of identification of target households, exceed the cost savings from further reducing benefit leakages to non-target households. Furthermore, as a programme gets more narrowly targeted, the risk of excluding target households increases due to insufficient information. Finally, a programme narrowly targeted on the poor is likely to have little political support in all but the most enlightened societies and if implemented may have a short life, as exemplified by the Colombian food stamp programme.

Geographical targeting, which was successfully used in the Philippines (Garcia and Pinstrup-Andersen 1986), offers great promise in cases where the poor tend to be concentrated in certain localities. In cases where the nutrition problem is principally found among pre-schoolers, growth-monitoring may be an appropriate targeting mechanism. However, this approach is strictly speaking curative while ideally the programmes would be preventive, i.e. target households should be identified *before* the children become malnourished, not *after*.

A large number of other targeting mechanisms have been tried, some with success, others with failure. These include targeting by the nutritional status of household members, or by employment status; choice of inferior commodities or commodity qualities for subsidization; and targeting on certain periods of the year in cases where seasonal fluctuations in ability to acquire sufficient food are severe. The most appropriate choice among the various targeting approaches depends on the particular circumstances in which subsidies are introduced (Rogers 1987).

2. *Assessing the food acquisition and allocation behaviour of the household target groups*. The purpose of the assessment is to explore to what extent the households can counter the potential negative nutrition effects of reduced real incomes through increases in the budget share spent on food, reduced dietary costs, increased food shares to high-risk individuals, and other measures as listed in Fig. 13.1. Information on these matters is important to assist in proper choice among programme types. In some cases, existing poverty may have forced households to make all feasible adjustments, while in others there may still be room for 'coping' with reduced incomes, particularly if supported by the appropriate programmes. Introducing a nutrition education programme, for example, is likely to be useless for the former but not for the latter, while income support may be essential only for the former.

3. *Identifying the constraints to improved nutrition at the level of the individual with emphasis on assessing the potential contribution of food vs. non-food health factors*. The extent to which increases in calorie consumption by malnourished household members leads to improved nutrition depends on the relative importance of food deficiencies versus health and sanitation factors in the existing nutrition problems. In order to design the most appropriate compensatory programmes, it is essential to have information about the constraints to nutritional improvements. Food-related compensation will have little or no effect if the most limiting constraint is infectious diseases leading to diarrhoea and/or anorexia.

4. *Assessment of household resource availability and constraints*. The purpose of this assessment is to assist in identifying programmes most likely to be compatible with household resource constraints and so enhance the contribution of these resources to improved nutrition. Time demands and constraints, particularly

for women, as well as access to land for subsistence food production, should be assessed along with opportunities for expanded output in self-employment and assistance toward increased employment.

5. *Assessment of institutional and administrative capabilities for programme implementation.* Some programme types require more institutional support than others. For example, food stamp schemes and food price subsidies may be based exclusively on private sector distribution, while food supplementation usually requires separate distribution channels. If a solid primary health care system is in place, compensatory measures may be linked to such a system at relatively low cost, particularly if excess capacity exists.

Integrating food-related programmes with primary health care programmes offers great promise because they address several interacting constraints simultaneously. The drawback is that integrated programmes are very demanding on administrative and institutional capabilities. For this reason, many such programmes which have been successful as small pilot schemes fail when extended nationally. This does not mean that no integration should be attempted but rather that the administrative and institutional capabilities should be assessed prior to programme design and implementation. Distribution of food at health posts has been done successfully in a large number of cases and should be considered as one of several programme options. However, the logistical problems associated with public sector food distribution should not be underestimated. These problems may be avoided by issuing food stamps which may be redeemed at private sector retailers. This was successfully done in Colombia (Ochoa 1987). Multiple use of growth-monitoring of children—e.g. to identify target children, households, or villages; to assess programme impact; and as an educational tool to assist mothers in assessing the nutritional status of children—is another promising but as yet underutilized component of an integrated approach.

6. *Identification of sources of financing.* Deficit government spending is usually an important element of macro-economic crises, and adjustment programmes usually attempt to reduce such deficits. Depressed prices to farmers are also a common component of economic crises, and higher agricultural prices are often pursued as part of adjustments. Therefore fiscal as well as economic costs are important considerations in the choice and design of policies and programmes to protect or compensate the poor.

In general, explicit consumer food subsidies need not have adverse effects on agricultural incentives. On the contrary, such subsidies enhance the purchasing power of consumers, who in turn increase their demand for food and thus provide opportunities for increasing prices to the producers. Implicit consumer food subsidies, on the other hand, are likely to be harmful to producers because they are usually maintained through artificially low producer prices. Countries having explicit subsidies frequently also have implicit ones, and the impact of each of these on agricultural incentives is often confused.

Alternative sources of revenue to cover the cost of subsidy and transfer programmes should be explored. These would include the possibility of using external aid either in the form of food or cash. Food aid has played a major role in financing food subsidies and supplementation schemes in many developing countries, such as Egypt and Bangladesh, although food aid can have negative effects on farmer incentives and incomes. Innovative ways of integrating external aid for alleviating adverse short-term nutrition effects into more traditional macro-economic adjustment programmes may assure the achievement of short-run welfare goals for the poor as well as long-run growth objectives.

14

Monitoring and Statistics for Adjustment with a Human Face

Frances Stewart

I Introduction

Good, appropriate, and timely statistics are essential for identifying what has
been happening and why, formulating policies, and monitoring progress.
Where recession, shocks, and adjustment are concerned, the information is
needed *fast*—so as to permit compensating action before irreversible damage
has been done. These needs are broadly recognized for much economic data:
for example, institutions concerned with adjustment (both national governments and international institutions such as the IMF) require regular and
speedy information on such variables as the money supply, the rate of inflation,
foreign exchange reserves, and exports and imports. There is an equally urgent
need for information on the human dimension: to know, for instance, what is
happening to infant mortality rates, and to nutrition levels so as to see whether
policy interventions are required. There is need also for data on the factors
bringing about such changes so that the appropriate policy interventions may
be devised and then monitored. Yet, while the economic data are generally
available (if not always of the highest accuracy), in many countries there are
extremely few data on the human dimension. What is available is often many
years out of date, while current data consist of an extrapolation from the past
(e.g. this is generally the case for infant mortality rates, which are extrapolated
from census years). This is a singularly inappropriate procedure where big
changes are involved, as is the case with recession and adjustment. Sometimes
more recent data exist, but they are scattered around the country and not
systematically, routinely, regularly, and speedily published. This absence of
adequate data is both a symptom and a cause of the low priority given to (or
complete neglect of) the human dimension in the adjustment process. In
general, where there is commitment to protecting vulnerable groups there are
also good statistics on the human dimension, as is illustrated below in some
country examples.

The aim of this chapter is to identify the improvements urgently needed in
collection and publication of statistics for adjustment with a human face. It is
organized as follows. Section II elaborates on the need for statistics on the

human dimension, showing why economic data are not sufficient. Section III identifies more precisely the type of statistical information needed. Section IV suggests the main steps that should be taken, nationally and internationally, to improve the situation.

II Why data on the human dimension are required during adjustment

The objective of adjustment with a human face is to protect vulnerable groups—and especially women and children—during periods of recession and adjustment. Such protection involves safeguarding children's health and nutritional status in particular and, as part of this, their regular monitoring. Consistent and meaningful monitoring of child welfare must be derived from an understanding of the main causal linkages by which child survival and development are related to social and economic factors.

Annex I to Chapter 1 presents an analytical framework which integrates the two predominant research approaches to child survival and development— i.e. that of medical and of social science. Such an integration is particularly useful during periods of economic instability, when it is important to know not only the extent and immediate causes of deterioration (i.e. information needed for the design of specific programmes of disease control, nutritional rehabilitation, etc.), but also the social and economic origins of the deterioration so as to take remedial action at this (often fundamental) level. The framework identifies six types of deterioration in child welfare, i.e. death, malnutrition, disease, disability, declining school achievement, and abandonment and delinquency. Changes in these indicators (generally known as status or *impact indicators*) can usually be related to some immediate causes, reflecting increasing dietary deficiencies, reduced health care and immunization coverage, declining educational opportunities, etc., which can be measured by means of appropriate indicators (known as *process indicators*), which reflect access to, and availability and use (or intake) of basic goods (as food) and services. The worsening in process indicators is, in turn, due to a number of underlying factors (normally measured through *input indicators*) which can be grouped into three sets of different resources for the production of child welfare. They are: (*a*) *real resources in cash or kind at the household level*, influenced by the level of subsistence production, money incomes, and inflation, particularly for food; (*b*) *government expenditure and policies* on health, education, child care, water and sanitation, and food subsidies; and (*c*) *family and community characteristics*, reflecting not only socio-cultural values but also the time, health, and skills of the parents, and especially of the mother.

Efficient monitoring of changes in child welfare for the purpose of policy-making requires the regular collection of these three sets of data, i.e. status, process and input indicators. The macro-economic indicators normally used for monitoring economic adjustment (such as money supply, trade data, etc.)

are utterly unable to capture—even indirectly, the changes occurring in child welfare. Reliance on macro-economic data not only completely neglects non-economic factors, but is also inadequate—because of the variables selected and the level of aggregation—to capture those economic processes which affect children, especially in poor households. The traditional approach to data collection on children is also deficient for monitoring developments during adjustment, since this approach has been mostly concerned with levels and long-term rather than short-term changes, relying on data collection at relatively long intervals of time (3, 5, or even 10 years) and on projections. For monitoring during economic adjustment, more frequent, disaggregated, and speedily processed data are required in the areas of mortality, nutrition and health, and education.

III Data requirements for adjustment with a human face

1 Features of an ideal child-monitoring system

An 'ideal' child monitoring system would require:
  (*a*) Data to be available regularly and speedily;
  (*b*) Provision of indicators of the *status of the population* at large and *of vulnerable groups*, broken down by major socio-economic category and by region, to record how vulnerable groups are being affected by changing economic circumstances and by policies;
  (*c*) Provision of indicators of the immediate as well as underlying causes of the changing status of the various groups;
  (*d*) A well-functioning system for the timely reporting, aggregation, analysis, and diffusion of the information collected.

These requirements are discussed individually below.

(a) **Speed, regularity, timeliness** A prime requirement—as noted earlier—is that data should be collected regularly and speedily to permit identification of developments during changing economic circumstances. This requires, at minimum, yearly collection of data, with a shorter interval being desirable for much of the data, especially where seasonal variations are important. (For example, an apparently sufficient supply of food taken over the year as a whole can be associated with severe malnutrition at certain times, as data on malnutrition in some African countries show.) The data need to be made available to policy-makers within a very short time after collection—say, a maximum of three months. Longer intervals between observations and data collection and transmission—which are typical in this area—may mean that there can be much human suffering, including unnecessary deaths, before note is taken of the deteriorating situation and appropriate policy interventions are designed. This is now widely acknowledged with respect to food production and the FAO has been developing an early-warning system in this area. Food production is only one element: equal urgency is necessary with respect to other factors relating to the status of vulnerable groups. Regular collection and transmission of data is also necessary to monitor policy interventions and assess how effective they are.

It is difficult to overstate the need for regularity and speed in data collection, or to exaggerate the deficiencies—in these respects—of much of official statistics in this area. Regular monitoring of human status is a general requirement of any human-oriented approach to development. But the critical and *changing* economic situation of the 1980s has added the need for *speed* in collection and transmission because of the rapidly evolving—and often deteriorating— situation.

The study on Ghana (vol. ii, ch. 4) highlights deficiencies in official statistics in these respects. In Ghana, the last comprehensive survey of nutrition took place in 1961. Since then there have been a few village studies but no comprehensive national survey. The most recent official survey of urban incomes was in 1981/82 but these data had not yet been processed at the time of writing 'Infant and childhood mortality rates have been difficult to measure accurately in Ghana' (UNICEF-Ghana 1984). There are no official estimates of infant mortality after the late 1970s, although it was in the 1980s that the most critical situation emerged as a result of prolonged economic stagnation, acute drought and the introduction of major shifts in macro policies. The data that are available do not permit unequivocal conclusions. Official estimates based on fertility surveys put the IMR at around 70 per 1,000 at the end of the 1970s. However, estimates based on life tables suggest considerably higher rates, perhaps 120.

While information on infant mortality, on nutrition, and on incomes of low-income households has to be pieced together painfully and uncertainly, much more official effort is devoted to collection of economic data. The Central Statistical Office was spending time in 1985 processing the 1982 trade statistics despite lack of comprehensive information on the evidently poor situation in health and nutrition.

While official statistics were blatantly inadequate in Ghana, this did not mean that there was no evidence beyond casual observation. For nutrition, there were a series of village studies in the 1970s and more recently the Catholic Relief Services has been collecting nutritional data in the course of its feeding programmes. Data on hospital attendance were collected by the Ministry of Health. Some hospitals and clinics have been recording information on birth weights. There have been a few small surveys of urban incomes. There are enough data to obtain a convincing picture of the deteriorating status of vulnerable groups during the 1980s and to suggest major causes of this development. Consequently, complete agnosticism and inaction pending the collection of better data is *not* justified. More systematic and centralized collection of the data that are available, however, is a high priority, along with longer-term efforts to improve data collection.

Work elsewhere suggests that the Ghana situation is very typical. This was shown in each of the country studies in UNICEF's study of the impact of recession on children. Examination of basic needs in Nigeria and Tanzania also revealed a very similar situation: lack of comprehensive data on health and nutrition status, and also a considerable amount of bitty data which could be patched together to give a more comprehensive picture (see 1LO/JASPA 1981, 1982).

In each case, with a big effort it was possible to arrive at a description and diagnosis of the changing situation of vulnerable groups which is probably pretty reliable. But it is not good enough to wait on special efforts involved in *ad hoc* country studies—which by their nature are intermittent. Data collection on the human situation needs to be an intrinsic and central part of government statistical activities.

A recent survey of the situation in India revealed a similarly unsatisfactory situation in relation to monitoring child health and nutrition. There is a National Census carried out once every 10 years, with a time-lag of 3–7 years between collection and publication. 'The Health information systems suffer from many deficiencies including the poor quality and lack of reliability of data, and also large time lags' (UNICEF-New Delhi 1985). The National Sample Survey Organisation carries out sample household surveys once in five years, with a time lag of five years. There are areas (especially the 10 states covered by annual surveys of the National Nutrition Monitoring Bureau) where information is collected annually and a large number of special studies throughout the country. But despite the considerable statistical capacity in India, information has not been collected systematically and processed quickly, nor has there been a real effort to assemble the information that is available centrally.

(b) Status indicators The prime objective of adjustment with a human face is the protection of vulnerable groups, especially children, during recession and adjustment. The most appropriate indicators of status therefore measure success or failure in meeting this objective. Health, nutritional, and educational status of children are assumed to be the most fundamental aspects of their welfare.

1. *Prime indicators of health and nutritional status are:*
   (*a*) Infant mortality rates.
   (*b*) Child death rates.
   (*c*) Indicators of nutritional status for the under-5s.*
   (*d*) Low birth weights.*
   (*e*) Indicators of morbidity (disease prevalence and incidence).
2. *Indicators of educational status are:*
   (*a*) Literacy levels.
   (*b*) Primary school completion rates.
   (*c*) Drop out rates.*

* The asterisk indicates that the indicators will show deterioration in a short-time frame, and are therefore especially relevant for monitoring adjustment.

(*d*) Repetition rates.
3. *Additional indicators of child welfare are:*
   (*a*) Rates of child labour.
   (*b*) Number of street children.*

Many of these indicators not only represent the status of children directly but are also factors influencing attainment of other status indicators. For example, low birth weights are a major factor influencing infant mortality rates; morbidity and malnutrition also affect infant and child death rates.

To capture changes the data need to be collected regularly over time. Some indicators are more sensitive to changing conditions than others, and therefore should be reported on at short time intervals. Information on nutritional status of infants and children is especially sensitive and requires near-continuous monitoring in difficult times.

Nation-wide averages conceal variations. To devise appropriate policy interventions, it is necessary to disaggregate the date, especially if interventions are targeted to the specially needy. Disaggregation is necessary for targeting interventions (see Ch. 8). Without disaggregation and categorization, policies may be devised which do not at all (or only partially) reach the children most in need, and/or which are extremely expensive, and therefore limited in quantity. For example, an across-the-board food subsidy may not reach the children in need at all (if they are in subsistence households), while it may be extremely expensive compared with a more targeted approach. Disaggregation is also required to reveal causal connections, and consequently to help in improving policy design.

The appropriate disaggregation obviously varies among countries. In general, however, a broad regional breakdown is needed, and also sufficient socio-economic detail to identify the nature of the vulnerable groups—that is whether they are formal sector wage-earners, informal sector, urban, rural—because this information is critical to devising relevant policies. For example, where one region is specially deprived—as for example, Northern Ghana, or Negros in the Philippines—interventions to support incomes, nutrition, and services should be located in this region. More highly focused and more appropriate policy interventions can be devised if the socio-economic group is also identified, e.g. small farmers in Northern Ghana, sugar workers in Negros. While, for example, small farmers would be assisted by policies to improve their incomes through improved credit, better technology, etc., and better prices for their products, such measures would not help for estate workers, and food subsidies and alternative employment opportunities may be needed to raise their nutritional status. Information is not a luxury to be added on as an after-thought to other programmes, but an essential prerequisite for devising good programmes.

(c) Causal indicators: process and input indicators These are indicators of the *causes* of changing health and education of children. While process indicators are the most immediate cause of changing status, the inputs are most directly affected by macro-economic policies. From the perspective of monitoring adjustment policies and devising policy interventions, it is necessary to know how the adjustment policies affect the inputs, and how these in turn affect processes.

There are a great number of factors which affect child status directly or indirectly as is clear from the analytic framework (see Ch. 1, Annex I). From our perspective, indicators should be selected which: (*a*) are of the greatest importance—in magnitude—in determining child status; (*b*) may be amenable to special policies for the protection of vulnerable groups; and (*c*) are affected by changes in the economic environment and macro adjustment policies.

Process indicators include the prevalence of breast-feeding, distribution of oral rehydration immunization level, availability of potable water, health service access rate, and primary school enrolment rate. Regular monitoring of these and other variables is needed to assess the long-term development strategy with a focus on improving the human condition. However, from an adjustment perspective, information is particularly needed on the items which *change* with economic recession, adjustment, and policy interventions.

Input indicators include real incomes of low-income groups; real government expenditures per head on social services; and maternal education, time and health.

In principle, measures of real incomes should capture the effects of changing food availability and changing food prices. In practice, real income data are often deficient, so that it is helpful to have other, more accessible data on basic food prices, levels of money income or expenditure in money terms, and employment and unemployment.

Macro policies impinge most directly on these *input* variables: in particular, on levels of income and employment, levels of government expenditure per capita, basic food prices, and money incomes of those employed in the formal sector (see Ch. and Annex I). Consequently, to monitor the effects of macro developments, the first stage is to see how these input variables are affected, and then in turn how the process variables change.

As with the status indicators, a regional, locational, and socio-economic breakdown of process and input variables is desirable both for identifying appropriate actions and for monitoring their effects over time.

(d) A well-functioning system to analyse and give feedback on the data collected Actual use of the data described above for policy purposes not only requires timely, speedy, and regular collection, but also that the information is brought together at the appropriate geographical level, added up, tabulated and analysed, and reports written summarizing the main evidence clearly and succinctly for policy-makers. At present, the most common weakness in country after country is the failure to co-ordinate, analyse, use, and rapidly publish data already being collected.

The establishment of an effective feedback system to planners and policy-makers is often one of the most difficult tasks. As will appear clearer from the examples given later, the two main constraints are management and resources. The establishment of such a system requires clear identification of the units in charge of data collection—for each indicator—at the primary level, as well as of those in charge of aggregation of data at intermediate (provincial, regional, etc.) and central levels, and the establishment of a national co-ordinating unit centralizing the information coming from the different sources and institutions (Ministry of Agriculture, of Health, the Central Statistical Office, etc.) and in charge of final aggregation, processing, and analysis. This unit would be responsible for feeding regular reports to policy-makers. In view of its crucial role it is important that such a unit is attached to a powerful decision-making body, such as a Presidential Committee, the Cabinet, or the Ministry of Finance.

2   The possible versus the ideal

The requirements described above are ambitious, especially when full disaggregation into regions, location, and socio-economic groups, is included, and particularly as the data are required regularly so as to monitor developments over time. There is a huge gap between these requirements and the actual situation in many countries. But the data requirements are not so ambitious when compared with the sort of information that is routinely demanded and provided in national income accounts. In the longer run it is important to aim at a systematic set of human accounts, on a par with the economic accounts. However, in the short term what is desirable must be tempered by what is possible. In many countries, partial data are all that is available.

Only a subset of each type of indicator may be available, or data which cover only a part of the population. In such cases, process indicators may have to act as proxies for status indicators, or partial evidence be used to suggest the broader picture. Where samples are unrepresentative (e.g. as with low birth weight proportions recorded in hospitals in a country where hospital births account for only a fraction of total births), the absolute data may not be meaningful, but marked changes over time may be indicative of what is happening in the country as a whole; similarly with data on nutritional status derived from pre-selected samples. Consistency of fragmentary evidence may confirm the reliability of what is available, while inconsistency suggests caution is needed. Where the available evidence is incomplete in one major respect, small rapid surveys can be very helpful in filling out the picture.

3   Leading indicators of social stress

A considerable advance on the system prevailing at present in many countries—where relevant information on vulnerable groups is usually published rather randomly, if at all, and often after considerable delay—would consist in the collection, publication, and wide dissemination of a set of *forward* indicators of social stress—which if desired could be aggregated in a single index (as in the case of the US Index of Leading Economic Indicators). This data set should be published every two months, including all recent evidence on the situation of vulnerable groups. It would include the most recent data both on actual developments (e.g. levels of malnutrition) and prognostications (e.g. making use of the FAO system of early warning on food shortfalls).

The precise data to be included in a set of forward indicators will vary according to what is available, as well as to country circumstances. For example, in Indonesia a reliable indicator of the food situation is the proportion of food derived from 'wild foods' in certain villages. This is clearly a country-specific indicator. Availability of data may alter over time within a country as well as between countries, but this should not prevent regular compilation of the data, individually and possibly a composite index, using whatever is available.

Each of the indicators discussed above within the three categories—status, process, and inputs—are suitable for inclusion. In a country like Ghana, where many of these data are not available at all, or only with long intervals and considerable margins of error, there are still enough data to provide a useful index. In such a case, the index could include:

Indicator	*Source*
1. Measures of second- and third-degree malnutrition	Catholic Relief Services
2. Cases of kwashiokor and marasmus	Major hospitals
3. Proportion of low-birth weight	Major hospitals
4. Deaths from measles	Clinics/hospitals
5. Standing crop and/or crop conditions	Farmers' own assessment
6. Food prices in regional markets throughout the country	Ministry of Agriculture
7. Rainfall	Ministry of Agriculture

This represents a rather minimal set of indicators, but none the less of major significance—not in absolute terms, but to indicate changes.

As the statistical base improves, it would be desirable to include rates of infant mortality; changes in sales of assets; changes in indebtedness; changes in migration; FAO early-warning system for food supplies; school drop-out rates; real incomes in the urban informal sector; and the proportion of expenditure devoted to food in low-income sectors.

Developing leading indicators of social stress along these lines would fulfill a number of purposes:

(*a*) Provide early warning and assist in monitoring programmes to protect vulnerable groups.

(*b*) Achieve centralized collection and publication of data on the social situation on a regular basis; the minimal data set should be published in the national press and in any of the statistical offices' regular publications (such as Central Bank Reports).

(*c*) Give prominence to information on the situation of vulnerable groups as great as that given to economic data.

(*d*) Provide an incentive to search for and develop better data.

4 Country examples

The earlier discussion has focused on cases where data collection and dissemination are notably inadequate. Below examples are considered of countries where a well-defined system has been established for co-ordinating, analysing, and disseminating information.

(a) Botswana: nutritional surveillance for timely warning and intervention programmes Botswana instituted a comprehensive system for monitoring national developments to provide rapid and centralized information to support the Drought Relief Programmes (see vol. ii, ch. 1). Decisions on drought relief programmes are taken by an Inter-Ministerial Committee which reports directly to the Permanent Secretary of the Ministry of Finance and Development Planning, who in turn reports to the Vice-President (Fig. 14.1). Information and recommendations are fed to the Inter-Ministerial Committee by an Early Warning Technical Committee, which receives and processes information on nutritional status of children, rainfall, agricultural conditions, food supplies, and food reserves.

The National Nutrition Surveillance System reports on a monthly basis on the nutritional status of all under-5s attending health facilities throughout the country. There is very high attendance at health clinics in Botswana, so that near comprehensive data are collected. The information can be broken down by the 15 Health Regions in the country, and further by urban areas, villages, cattle posts, and even swamps and settlements. Nutritional surveillance of children is used to identify children in special need and take compensatory action as well as to generate statistics for use in monitoring national programmes.

Agro-meteorological information is collected through weekly radio reports on rainfall in 250 recording points around the country, from which a 'water-satisfaction' index is devised, and through monthly reports on agricultural conditions from 120 extension districts. In addition, Drought Assessment Tours supplement and confirm other data. All relevant data are reported to the Early Warning Technical Committee, which assesses the situation with respect to

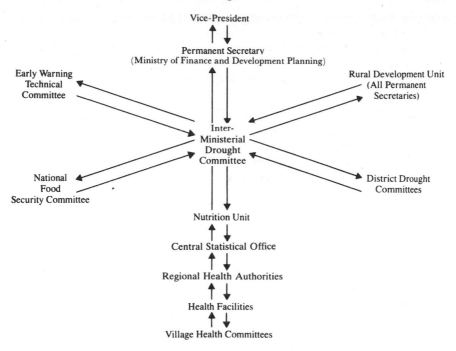

Fig. 14.1 Organization of Botswana's Nutritional Surveillance System: data flow and users

Source: UNICEF 1984.

drought, food supplies, and food needs, and makes recommendations to the Inter-Ministerial Drought Committee (IMDC) on the types and amount of drought recovery assistance needed in each administrative district.

Policy responds rapidly to changing indicators of nutritional status. For example, when underweight prevalence rates appeared to be escalating in 1984, supplementary feeding was increased. Again in 1985, evidence of higher levels of malnutrition led to restoration in full drought rations for the under-5s.

In the case of Botswana the close relationship between the collection of information and policy interventions has led to a system of information which is comprehensive, disaggregated, collected regularly with short intervals, and disseminated rapidly to a central point, ready to provide the basis for action.

(b) Indonesia Indonesia's National Family Nutritional Improvement Project focuses on action rather than data collection. The programme covers 30,000 villages and 70 per cent of Indonesian children. The focal point is the use of growth-monitoring combined with nutritional education, and some feeding supplementation for the malnourished. Information collected from the growth charts is relayed up from local to subdistrict regional and provincial levels on a monthly basis, and to the national level on a quarterly basis. While the information relayed is very simple—the proportion of children weighed each month and the proportion of those children that gain weight—this information itself would be enough to draw attention to serious deviations in progress. The information gathered is not related systematically to socio-economic descriptions of the families, nor to agricultural production or health conditions. However, in principle it is possible to analyse the data by *location* (even by village), thereby permitting programmes to be located in target areas. It would also be relatively simple to include some basic health data (on oral rehydration salts, health facilities, immunization, breast-feeding) in the charts and in the information transmitted.

(c) SIN in Costa Rica Costa Rica established a comprehensive information system, the Sistema de Información Nutricional (SIN) in 1978, with the aim of providing 'planners and administrators with adequate data on the nature and magnitude of the nutrition problem, and on the likely effect of their programmes on improving living conditions, and to enable them to monitor their activities, particularly in poor groups' (see Valverde *et al*. 1981). The system is designed to collect data over time, in a systematic way, by socio-economic and regional grouping, especially among deprived groups. It is a very good example of the sort of data collection processing and dissemination that we have described above, though more suitable for a middle-income country with considerable statistical resources.

Initially, 27 socio-economic groups were defined. The groups include agricultural labourers in different types of farm, farmers of different scale, professionals and wage-earners, the unemployed and the underemployed, by location. SIN's efforts are aimed at assisting evaluation of the impact of major policies related to nutrition, including policies towards agricultural prices, agricultural inputs, marketing, incomes of the poor, and direct food interventions.

SIN does not collect data directly itself but co-ordinates and analyses data collected by others, including:

1. Data on nutritional status of 6–9 year olds, which had been collected by teachers periodically for three decades but had never been used for evaluation. A data flow system has now been organized and used to produce a regional map of malnutrition. This is to be repeated every two years.

2. A 1978 National Nutrition Survey.

3. Biannual data on the nutrition of children of 6–59 months and socio-economic status of families, collected by the Rural Health Programme and the Community Health Programme.

4. Information on agriculture, demography, and other social and economic questions collected once every 10 years through the censuses.

5. Surveys of occupations, incomes, and employment, conducted three times a year by the Ministry of Labour and Social Security.

SIN's role has been to review existing data systems, provide technical support to improve the efficiency of data collection and processing, improve co-ordination, and identify needs. It produces monthly bulletins describing the data available and their potential usefulness and distributes them to the various government offices. It also issues periodic reports on socio-economic groups and changes in their social, economic, and nutritional conditions. It works closely with the Secretariat of National Food and Nutrition Policy which co-ordinates programmes on nutrition.

(d) Some lessons from the successful examples These three examples show that improved monitoring *is* possible, even in largely rural environments and in poor countries (as in Botswana and Indonesia). They also indicate the close connection between good monitoring and high commitment to protecting the vulnerable: all three countries instituted the information systems because they were needed to support policies to protect the vulnerable. Without that prior commitment, the system of monitoring would almost certainly not have been instituted, and if instituted would not have been devised to report to a central decision-making unit.

From these examples, it becomes clear that there are *two approaches to data collection:*

(*a*) Using survey techniques to acquire data.

(*b*) Getting data as a by-product of programmes (as in the Indonesian case, Catholic Relief Services data in Africa, data from hospitals or clinics which are collected as part of their routine procedures), or of routine administrative records of the Ministries of Health, Education, Social Welfare, and in a few countries (such as Brazil, for instance) of the vital registration system.

The survey technique approach is more likely to lend itself to 'representative' samples, and cover areas where no programmes are in existence and so may identify programme needs. It tends to be more subject to delay, and to be extremely costly. The programe approach usually involves more urgency (since the data is action-oriented), but is very often criticized for lack of representativeness, since those participating in a programme are by definition a special group. The programme approach is only possible, of course, where and when programmes exist; data collection stops when the programmes stop. Where there is a national programme in existence, as in Indonesia, it is the obvious source of data, although even in Indonesia about 30 per cent of the population are not covered. But where programmes are limited in coverage, it is essential to supplement the data. The major advantage of the programme approach is that there is generally an automatic link to action, completely absent in the survey approach. At the very least, the people who first look at the data are people whose business it is to take action.

In every country, a prime need is to centralize and co-ordinate all available data, whatever its origin. This normally involves using both survey and pro-gramme data (as in Costa Rica, for example). The urgency of data needs in work on adjustment means that it is essential to make maximum use of existing sources. The second step is to supplement this with new data sources which can be instituted quickly, either making use of existing programmes which may generate such data but do not transmit them (e.g. low-birth weight information from hospitals) or can readily collect them during their usual functions, or by small surveys. Large surveys usually involve long delays both before they are set up and in processing; so unless they are already well into the planning stage, they are not suitable for work on adjustment.

IV National and international action

1 National action

Action is needed to establish an institutional network which will ensure that the data are collected, co-ordinated, and disseminated as an intrinsic part of day-to-day government operations. This requires:

1. *Establishment of a central technical unit* for co-ordinating data on all status, process, and input indicators.

2. *Establishing a clear line of responsibility/reporting* from this unit to high-level bureaucrats and from there to political decision-makers. One approach is for the statistical unit to report to an Inter-Ministerial Committee which then reports to top political leaders (e.g. the President); another is for reporting to be channelled through a powerful ministry (preferably the Ministry of Finance or Planning). It is important that responsibility and accountability should be shared with ministers responsible for the major economic decisions and for negotiations with IMF and the World Bank, and only not with Ministries responsible for the social sectors.

3. *Rapid stock-taking of all available sources of data* on status, processes, and inputs. This should permit a preliminary identification of data suitable to be leading indicators of social stress.

4. *Publication of the forward indicators* over the radio and in the newspapers, and in a government statistical publication which deals with the major aspects of economic performance of the country and comes out regularly—in many countries, the Central Bank Reports would be a suitable venue.

5. *Identification of major gaps* in up-to-date knowledge, and formulation of recommendations on quick action to be taken to fill these gaps. For example, in some countries there may be no up-to-date information on nutrition or regional data may be absent or knowledge may be very deficient about incomes and expenditure in the informal sector. In the short run, these gaps may be filled by rapid assessment surveys; in the medium to long run, the unit could institute more extended surveys.

6. *Transmission of findings* to the appropriate ministry, and their use in dialogue with international institutions.

Restructuring is required—in statistical efforts as in other areas—to ensure that, given limited resources, the right priorities are selected. It appears that in many countries, statistical institutions and activities have developed in an unplanned way, in reaction to various historical pressures, some national, some international. Few countries consider carefully whether the outcome accords with priority needs. There is therefore potential for reallocating resources within the statistical service to improve statistics for the human dimension.

2 International action

The aim of international action should be: (*a*) to encourage national governments to collect, disseminate, and use appropriate statistics; (*b*) to publish comparable statistics on the human dimension across countries so as to permit comparisons and analysis; (*e*) to *use* indicators in country assessments, resource allocation, and national policy dialogues; and (*d*) to provide early warnings internationally.

A number of international institutions have concerns in this area, and have taken some action:

1. The *World Health Organization* attempts to monitor the achievements of 'Health for All by 2000'. Their major focus is on health (process and impact), of which nutrition is one element. Their focus is therefore narrower than the area covered here.

2. The *Pan-American Health Organization* is now compiling a regional publication on comparable data, including data on low birth weight for Latin America.

3. The *United Nations Research Institute on Social Development* has covered many of the issues discussed here, in a series of studies.

4. The *United Nations Statistical Office* is involved both in assisting the development of survey capacity and in publishing cross-country data.

5. The *International Labour Office* is involved in the area of employment, wages, and basic needs.

6. The *World Bank's World Development Report Annex on world development indicators* has brought together large quantities of data from various secondary sources. The Bank also assists countries to improve their information base, and has recently helped institute 'levels of living' surveys, which are household surveys giving detailed socio-economic information on different income groups, as well as occasionally, some anthropometric data (see Grootaert 1986).

7. The *Food and Agriculture Organization* has instituted a Global Information and Early Warning System related to problems of food supplies and famine, and also actively assists a number of countries in developing national early warning systems. The FAO system relates almost exclusively to problems arising from lack of availability of food supplies. It is mainly based on agro-metereological information, with some data on markets, food prices, distress sales, and migration, and sometimes includes nutritional and socio-economic information (see FAO 1985). Extension of the FAO system to economic crises,

with greater use of data on the human dimension, could provide the basis for both national and international early warnings of social stress.

Substantial international activity is therefore already underway, especially in terms of the first two objectives described above—encouragement of national governments, and publication of country statistics. Despite these efforts there nevertheless remain major national statistical deficiencies, deficiencies which are powerfully supported by the WHO findings in their attempt to monitor Health for All by 2000 (see WHO/HS/NAT. COM/83. 383). The major problems are the *sporadic* and *non-systematic* nature of much data collection in this area, and the lack of urgency in collection, processing, and analysis.

In the light of this, it seems that it is not *more* but *different* international action that is necessary to impart some urgency into the situation.

Emphasis should be put on the third objective, viz. greater use of these statistics in country assessment, resource allocation, and policy dialogue. This is not only critically important in itself, but would also be a powerful lever to encourage national governments to collect and disseminate the statistics systematically and urgently. Institutions which control financial flows are most powerful in this respect: this includes the international institutions, both private (the International Financial Institute, for example) and public (the IMF and the World Bank, especially), bilateral aid donors, and even commercial banks. Those institutions concerned with adjustment policies should have the greatest concern with the human consequences of these policies, as well as having the greatest short-term leverage. The most effective international action, in the short term, therefore would be for the human dimension of adjustment to be incorporated as an intrinsic aspect into policy dialogue and policy requirements of the IMF and of the World Bank, with appropriate statistics being a requirement for the identification of appropriate policies and for programme monitoring. As a short-term financing institution it is most appropriate for the Fund to include indicators of short-term change in the human dimension and in social stress as part of its monitoring of adjustment. The World Bank is more concerned with establishing statistical systems in the longer term. In this, in its own policy dialogue, and in project development, data on the conditions of vulnerable groups should be an integral element of World Bank activity.

From an international perspective, the statistical requirements of adjustment with a human face will be effectively promoted only when the need for this type of adjustment strategy is fully incorporated into the activities of the major international financial institutions.

15

The International System and the Protection of the Vulnerable

Gerald Helleiner and Frances Stewart

I Introduction

A new global economy has developed in recent decades, with manifold interconnections between national economies. These interconnections take the form
of increasing flows of goods, of workers and managers, technology, information,
and capital across national boundaries. Consequently, the 'domestic' economic
problems of particular countries cannot be analysed in isolation from the
international element of their origins, nor from their international implications.
'National' economic policies are, in fact, necessarily and increasingly international in their content. Electorates and policy-makers therefore now look
with far greater interest and concern at the economic policies of other nations
as they formulate their own positions, and make their own 'rational' decisions.
The new interconnections extend to the relationships between the developing
countries and the more industrialized economies. Whereas it has long been
assumed that the economic performance of the former is substantially dependent upon economic events and policies in the latter, there is now growing
realization that these are two-way relationships. Developing countries' earnings from primary commodity exports are significant elements in global
demand. Their success in penetrating Northern markets for industrial products
profoundly influences the emerging structure of industry and employment
there. Their capacity to service external debt is a key element in the stability
of the international financial system. These South–North 'feedbacks' are not yet
fully understood but their increased importance is now widely acknowledged.

This increasing interconnectedness in terms of economic relations has helped
to generate a quite dramatic rise in international or global consciousness,
partly the result of the vivid images presented world-wide on television, partly
following from the fact that such a large proportion of people's lives is directly
affected by developments outside their own national boundaries. This new
international consciousness extends to matters of social as well as more narrowly
economic policies. Governments are increasingly being held individually and
collectively responsible for social and economic successes and failures all over
the global village. The influence and immediacy of global communication

has enormously expanded the number of persons in all countries aware of developments in other countries, often thousands of miles away. This rise in the sense of global consciousness and responsibility has rarely been more clearly shown than in the public reaction in Europe and North America to the famine in Africa in the early 1980s. In this respect individuals' feelings of responsibility for 'the poorest he', wherever located, seems to run well ahead of the policies of many governments.

The global economy has been performing somewhat imperfectly in the 1970s and 1980s—achieving slower overall rates of growth and experiencing more severe shocks and instabilities than during the previous two decades. The implications have been disastrous for the poorest developing countries and vulnerable groups everywhere. The economic crises which occurred among so many developing countries in the first half of the 1980s were in large part the outcome of international developments—the trends and/or cycles in world output and trade, in commodity prices and international capital movements, and in interest rates that were described in Chapter 1. They illustrate graphically some of the implications of the rising international interdependence and indicate how seriously things can go wrong—in economic and social terms—when international conditions are unfavourable. The experience within the international economy also showed the transmission mechanisms whereby global economic events led to severe deterioration in particularly weak national economies and in the conditions of the poor.

Until now, this book has focused on identifying alternative adjustment policies in the context of a given international environment. Such an approach may seem to make little sense, given the international origins of such a large part of the problem. But as argued in earlier chapters, even in difficult international circumstances, national action can do much to protect the vulnerable. In any case, it represents the only way of protecting the vulnerable so long as the international environment does not improve; such national action would be even more essential if, as is quite possible, the international environment worsens further; and it would be generally desirable, indeed usually necessary, even with improvement in international conditions.

For some countries, however, national action alone cannot be sufficient, even with the most heroic economic and political efforts. For most, further worsening of international conditions will undermine national efforts to protect the vulnerable. In every case, an improved international environment would greatly ease adjustment problems, and consequently facilitate the protection of the vulnerable. Yet the prospect is for continued slow growth and increased susceptibility to short and medium-term instability and shocks in the global economy. If the unfortunate recent experience is not to repeat itself in the 1990s, international as well as national action will be required. This chapter therefore looks at changes in the international system which would help to protect those falling below an international poverty line, particularly those resident in the lowest income countries.

The changes discussed are organized into three categories:

(*a*)　Changes in the international environment which would permanently reduce the size of the adjustments needed, and facilitate their realization.

(*b*)　Buffer mechanisms to protect poor countries during economic fluctuations by providing bridging facilities of finance, or price support.

(*c*)　Changes in the treatment of individual countries undergoing adjustment to encourage and support efforts to adopt adjustment with a human face.

The next three sections discuss these three types of changes.

II Global conditions

Adverse changes in global conditions in the last decade and especially in the 1980s were largely responsible for the emergence of the acute and often intractable economic problems shared by so many poor countries in recent years. These adverse developments were recorded in Chapter 1. They include:

(*a*)　World recession and subsequently a marked slow-down in the growth of world output.

(*b*)　Reduced growth in world trade, partly because of the deceleration of world output, but accentuated by rising protectionism.

(*c*)　Very weak performance of primary commodity prices, which have fallen in real terms to their lowest levels since the Second World War, posing a critical problem for those countries most dependent on commodity exports— including most of the poorest countries, and all Sub-Saharan African countries.

(*d*)　On the capital account, the collapse of private voluntary lending in the 1980s.

(*e*)　Sluggish aid flows, which in aggregate have changed very little during the 1980s.

(*f*)　High international rates of interest which, together with shorter-term debt and the introduction of floating interest rates, have led to very high debt servicing obligations for developing countries, most of which had borrowed heavily in the 1970s; although nominal interest rates have fallen substantially since their peak in the early 1980s, in real terms they still are well above normal longer-term levels.

In consequence, both in Latin America as a whole and in Africa as a whole, as well as for most individual countries in these continents, outflows of interest and amortization now greatly exceed inflows in new capital. Not only does this represent a reversal of the normal and appropriate order—with resources flowing from poor countries to rich countries, rather than the other way round—but it also represents a massive change compared with the 1970s, forcing very great adjustments to achieve it. The requirements imposed by the change in capital account have come at a time when conditions, as just noted, were highly unfavourable from the perspective of the trade account, with sluggish markets and falling commodity prices. Together these conditions have made it extremely difficult to achieve expansionary adjustment of the sort recommended earlier as one important aspect of adjustment with a human face. In the absence of adequate offsetting finance, they have forced most countries into otherwise undesirable deflationary adjustments, with an excessive emphasis on austerity.

Unless there is a reversal of some of these adverse developments, Third World countries will continue to suffer intolerable adjustment pressures. These pressures will probably drive them to further deflationary adjustments, which are likely to worsen the conditions of vulnerable groups (as they have in the past), making it impossible for protective domestic policies to succeed fully in sustaining basic needs of the vulnerable. Current levels of net finance available for imports are in many cases already insufficient to pay for essential inputs or new investments. More generous and more appropriate financial flows are therefore essential in many countries from the perspective of securing adjustment and growth in the medium term, and ensuring regular debt servicing and growing markets for developed country products, even without considering the effects of financial strangulation on the conditions of the poor and the lives of their children. What is needed is a reversal of each of the adverse trends noted above. The changes needed have been well rehearsed elsewhere (see Brandt Commission Reports 1980, 1983; North–South Roundtable 1985). Here, therefore, no details will be discussed, but the major changes required will simply be noted.

1. *A steady expansion of world output, and improved macro-economic policy co-ordination among the industrialized countries to help achieve it.* Some important steps towards consultation and co-ordination on exchange rates and interest rate policies have been taken, but so far there is little evidence that the countries enjoying large current account surpluses (notably Japan and the Federal Republic of Germany) have accepted sufficient responsibility for sustaining world demand as US fiscal and current account deficits decline. *An expanding world economy would constitute the single most important element in the improvement of the external conditions within which the Third World countries seek to adjust.*

2. *A halt to threatened further protectionism,* which still appears to be escalating, and a roll-back of existing protectionist interventions. The agreement to initiate a new GATT round is an important step in this direction. It is essential that unravelling protectionist measures should encompass—and, indeed, give prime attention to—non-tariff barriers, including those against imports of primary commodities as well as manufactures. These are now of far greater importance than tariffs. Particular attention must be devoted to the trade barriers inhibiting export expansion in the poorest countries and those countries experiencing the most severe debt servicing and adjustment difficulties. Dismantling protectionism must also include the elimination of subsidies for primary exports by 'industrialized' countries.

3. *Support of poor countries' real earnings for primary commodity exports* in periods of

severe and/or prolonged slump, through international commodity agreements involving both producers and consumers, or through equivalent financing mechanisms.

4. *Restoration of stable longer-term positive net resource flows* (both public and private) to developing countries. Although public resource flows have been rising a little, in net terms there is now *negative* resource transfer from the major international financial institutions to developing countries. Both the IMF and the World Bank—on current policies—are expected to be net recipients of resources from Latin America and Sub-Saharan Africa over most of the rest of this decade.

5. *Reduction in real international interest rates* to more normal levels.

6. *Debt restructuring and/or relief* for developing countries for which current servicing obligations cut severely into prospects for appropriate adjustment.

To sum up, the changes in the general international environment to be achieved by the cluster of mechanisms just noted are intended (*a*) to improve growth prospects and the trading environment so that sustained expansion in export earnings becomes possible for the Third World as a whole, and especially for the worst-affected countries, i.e. those mainly dependent on primary commodities; and (*b*) to transform the capital account, stopping the negative resource transfer and reinstating a positive transfer, especially to the poorest countries. Together these changes would greatly reduce the extent of immediate deflationary adjustment needed, and greatly facilitate more orderly and more equitable adjustment with growth.

III Buffering and trigger mechanisms

In recent world economic experience, the poorest countries have suffered disproportionately from the weakness of international buffering mechanisms. These mechanisms should moderate short-term consequences of fluctuations in world conditions, enabling countries to ride out temporary crises and to adjust in orderly fashion to longer-term changes. This has not been achieved because these countries have typically suffered the most severe external shocks, have had the least access to offsetting finance, and the least basic capacity to readjust their economies in response to external changes.

Some international buffering mechanisms do exist, but they are generally inadequate in magnitude, unreliable in their availability, and inequitable in their intercountry distribution; and they have been seriously weakened in recent years. In no way do they adequately counterbalance other pro-cyclical mechanisms which act to multiply rather than moderate the effects of world fluctuations. Existing buffering mechanisms include commercial bank finance for countries in temporary balance of payments difficulties. This has only been available to countries considered commercially credit-worthy by the banks; even for these, bank finance has proven highly unstable and unreliable.

As far as intergovernmental buffer arrangements are concerned, the IMF is the central institutional instrument. Its credit facilities are made available for the explicit purpose of preventing member governments from 'resorting to measures destructive of national or international prosperity' (Article I*e*). Largely because of the perception that short-term balance of payments finance could be provided from alternative (commercial) sources, the resources of the IMF, and thus member governments' borrowing rights, have not expanded at a rate remotely approaching the rate at which the need for such finance has expanded. The IMF's special 'Oil Facility' played an important stop-gap role in the mid-1970s but has since been phased out. The Compensatory Financing Facility (CFF), which formerly providing balance of payments finance with few conditions to developing countries experiencing temporary difficulties in consequence of external shocks, still exists, but funds are now provided only on a highly conditional basis, and the amounts available have in any case fallen far short of recent needs. The automaticity and rapid disbursement necessary in an effective buffer system are obviously also missing from the IMF's 'upper credit tranche' (highly conditional) programmes which account for the bulk of its lending activity. The EEC's STABEX scheme for associated developing countries is another governmental buffering mechanism. It has the advantage of offering grants rather than loans to the poorest of these countries, but here too funding has been grossly inadequate.

So long as world economic fluctuations continue, there is an urgent need to improve buffering mechanisms for developing countries, and particularly for the poorest among them, so that short-term deflationary adjustment requirements are less, and policies may be directed to a much larger extent to medium-term and expansionary adjustment.

Buffering mechanisms for poor countries need to be greatly increased in their dimensions so that they can begin to meet already evident needs. Rather than be subject to prolonged and often unsuccessful negotiation, they also need to be virtually automatic in their functioning. To secure a more satisfactory system of buffering mechanisms for poor countries, it is necessary first to find further resources and appropriate institutions for intergovernmental buffer arrangements, and then to devise 'triggers' which would automatically activate buffer mechanisms and which would not be subject to abuse or manipulation.

1   Buffering mechanisms

There are a great number of institutional mechanisms already in existence which could readily be extended to increase buffering support. The most obvious are existing arrangements in respect of loans from the IMF or programme (sectoral or structural adjustment) loans from the World Bank. In each case existing facilities would need to be greatly expanded and conditionality reduced. Not only does high conditionality make buffering finance dependent on sometimes controversial domestic policy changes, but it also generally causes considerable delay, and often involves interruption even after the loans have been agreed. Low conditionality is appropriate for buffering finance, especially where the fluctuations leading to the need for such finance are expected to be short-lived. Where these flows are formula and trigger-based, potential problems of moral hazard are minimized.

In general, the IMF would seem to be the most appropriate institution for buffering finance since it is broadly designed for this purpose, although there is no reason why the World Bank could not do similar lending. Finance for expanded buffering could be obtained via enlarging IMF quotas, or by issuing additional SDRs for this purpose. Interest subsidies or grants associated with such enlargement would require further sources of financial support. Increased funding for the International Development Association (IDA) is an obvious prerequisite for an expanded World Bank role in buffering activities for low-income countries.

Experience with past low-conditionality facilities (including the CFF) and low interest credit has shown that it is quite feasible for the IMF to extend in these directions. The CFF was designed to meet a situation which was expected to be reversed quite rapidly. However, there is also a need for finance to permit more gradual adjustment to non-reversible exogenous changes. This need has, of course, become particularly apparent in recent years. As at present constituted, the IMF is less suitable to meet this need because of the short time perspective of most of its facilities. The World Bank's Structural Adjustment Loans are more suitable in this respect, but they have proved very slow to negotiate, and have involved extensive conditions. Its Sectoral Adjustment Loans are less complex and less intrusive, but still far from automatic. There is a need, therefore, for some amendment—either more long-term, low-conditional finance from the IMF, or a reduction in conditionality and more automaticity in World Bank programme finance—if appropriate buffers against irreversible changes are to be made available. Fund–Bank cooperation, perhaps on the model of the new Structural Adjustment Facility, is likely to be necessary as these buffers are developed.

Bilateral Overseas Development Assistance (ODA) may also be used countercyclically. For the most part, it has been less suitable than multilateral finance for this purpose, because it frequently consists of project finance rather than programme finance, and because single donors do not feel they can make a sufficient impact. However, bilateral donors can be highly significant in particular cases, as well as supporting appropriate multilateral action. OECD aid donors have committed themselves to important changes in the modalities of their assistance to Sub-Saharan Africa in response to the severe balance of payments pressures experienced in that continent in recent years.

While new finance provides one sort of bridge over temporary problems, another sort, often easier to organize, is delayed payments or relief on existing debt. Some countries are already using this as a source of bridging finance, some by agreement with creditors, others unilaterally. Unilateral action is not likely to be fruitful for those countries still in receipt of net flows or in a weak bargaining position for other reasons. It would in any case, generally be preferable to have international agreements to orderly rescheduling or forgiveness of payments in agreed circumstances. An international 'framework' agreement on what constitutes such circumstances, and on the type of rescheduling or relief acceptable in different circumstances, could then inform all debt negotiations, whether in the Paris or London clubs or elsewhere. The gearing of debt service payments to the varying capacity of debtor countries to pay over time is a particularly promising area for possible international agreements. Debt relief, as an alternative to debt rescheduling, is obviously particularly appropriate for the poorest countries. There are already many very poor countries for which an overall projection of resource requirements and availabilities can only lead to the conclusion that bilateral debts should now be written off in the interest of adjustment efforts.

Commodity price stabilization schemes and buffer stocks may help support poor countries' earning during slumps in world prices. The schemes are likely to be most successful if the price fluctuations are temporary, and if the interventions stabilize, rather than support, international prices. International agreements have tended to break down during prolonged periods of unusually low (or high) prices of the sort we are now witnessing. Although there are plentiful examples of failures in this area, their potential positive impact should not be underestimated. The schemes can be highly successful in both stabilization and support, given the necessary political determination and financial commitment, as evidenced by the EEC's interventions in support of domestic food producers.

This example also suggests that political support is more likely when those financing the scheme are in the same nation as those benefiting from it. It also shows, this time by its own failures, the importance of avoiding excessive production as a result of effective price support. While commodity price stabilization (and other ways of supporting) export earnings appear to be more difficult to achieve than bridging finance, the potential gains to producing countries are likely to be greater since credit only offers temporary relief. If confined to the poorest countries, international price or earnings support programmes need not be very expensive.

2 Trigger mechanisms

The appropriate trigger mechanisms for the provision of automatic buffering finance depends on a number of factors, including the rationale for and the nature of the particular buffer mechanism being triggered. Broadly, there are two approaches. The first is to trigger a buffer mechanism when there are adverse measured effects on vulnerable groups. With this approach, for example, evidence of nutritional deterioration, and/or rising infant mortality, would automatically trigger certain buffer mechanisms. The buffer would be triggered irrespective of the cause of the problem (which might not be international at all, but could for instance, be drought or domestic policies). The major advantage would be that this would be the most reliable way of ensuring that any deterioration in the condition of vulnerable groups was recorded, and that it did trigger compensatory action. The major disadvantages are that, like famine relief, it would inevitably work too slowly— coming into play only after much damage has been done—and that some new conditionality might be needed to ensure that the extra buffer resources were actually used to meet the needs of the vulnerable.

The second approach is to trigger compensation when some major deterioration is recorded in economic conditions. For example, the CFF and STABEX are triggered by 'shortfalls' in export earnings. Similarly, some countries have 'triggered' delays in debt service payments, limiting total payments so that they do not exceed some proportion of export earnings. These trigger mechanisms have the advantage of relating the buffer directly to the change in economic circumstances, and thus increasing the probability that resource flows will arrive in time. However, the changes may be quite remote from the conditions of vulnerable groups, and some conditionality as to the use of the resources may still be necessary.

3 Summary

A combination of the two approaches would be best. First, the conditions of the most vulnerable should be carefully monitored, and any deterioration should trigger compensatory international action. Secondly, there should also be monitoring of major economic events, particularly in the poorest countries where the largest numbers of vulnerable people are to be found. Buffers should also respond to deterioration in these major elements since they are likely to be followed by deterioration in human conditions, and by taking early action such adverse changes in the human condition may be avoided. The appropriate buffering mechanism would depend both on the particular country and on the nature of the adverse changes in economic circumstance. The object should be to provide early warning and compensatory action with respect to the overall welfare of the most vulnerable, as the FAO attempts to do with its early-warning systems for agricilatural output in famine-prone countries.

While it is not possible at this stage to lay down specific characteristics of buffering and trigger mechanisms, the following principles should be accepted, and buffer mechanisms devised accordingly: (*a*) Poor countries need buffer mechanisms to help avoid excessively deflationary adjustments and permit more gradual adjustments. (*b*) Existing buffer mechanisms are grossly inadequate. (*c*) Many of the existing mechanisms, if significantly extended, could provide the basis for a more adequate system. (*d*) It is essential to develop trigger mechanisms which would establish the need to activate automatic buffer mechanisms. (*e*) The condition of vulnerable groups must be monitored and any significant deterioration should provide a trigger. (*f*) Other exogenously determined economic conditions should also be monitored, in order to trigger automatic buffer mechanisms at an early enough stage and of an appropriate type.

The 1986 IMF agreement with Mexico provides a precedent and an example of a country programme involving triggers and buffers, albeit rather conservative ones. The agreement will increase financial flows to Mexico if the oil price falls below (and reduce them if it rises above) some agreed level; it will also increase finance if the growth rate falls below an agreed rate. If it were extended to generate extra financial support if aspects of the human condition (e.g. child malnutrition) deteriorated, then it would provide a full example of the sort of combination of triggers and buffers proposed here. In this case, the agreement is *ad hoc*, specific to Mexico. Each country is of course unique in circumstance, but it is certainly time for the principles to be agreed on an international basis, while their application would differ according to country circumstances.

IV International policies towards individual countries during adjustment

The previous sections have discussed reforms needed in the international context in which country adjustment takes place. This section is concerned with the treatment of individual countries during the adjustment process. How can external support best be designed so as to support countries undertaking a human face approach, and to encourage others to adopt such an approach? These changes needed fall into three areas (*a*) finance; (*b*) programme design and monitoring; (*c*) the modalities of international negotiations. In each area, the changes identified derive from the requirements of a growth-oriented approach to adjustment which protects the human dimension, as described in previous chapters.

1   Finance

In general, the approach would be assisted if there were more finance, and different forms of finance, than have typically been available in recent years.

It is generally agreed that a growth-oriented approach to adjustment requires more finance than is at present available. This indeed constituted an important aspect of the Baker initiative. More finance is needed to permit countries to maintain investment and basic needs expenditures, and avoid excessive deflation. The amount of extra finance needed will vary according to country circumstances. Some countries (e.g. the middle-income countries) can more readily protect their vulnerable groups in the short run with domestic resources than others, but still need further finance if they are to be able at the same time to sustain growth. Others (e.g. many African countries) find it impossible to support essential services for low-income groups without additional financial support. The needs of those in the latter category, although very great in relation to their resources, are quite small in relation to world magnitudes. The additional current financial needs in order at least to arrest declines in basic needs and investment in Sub-Saharan Africa, for example, are no greater for that whole continent (and according to many estimates substantially less—e.g. World Bank 1986*e*) than those now deemed necessary for Mexico.

Precise additional financial needs cannot be estimated in the aggregate, but need to be calculated country by country. It may not be plausible to expect enough extra finance to be forthcoming to fulfil the human face adjustment needs for all countries simultaneously. But at present only a minority of countries are pursuing such human face policies. A determined international effort could readily find the extra official finance at least for these countries, in one way or another, e.g. by permitting delayed debt payments, providing debt relief and temporarily ballooning new finance to countries which are following this approach. The international community—including bilateral donors and multilateral institutions providing finance and commodity aid, and major creditors—already supportive, in principle, of growth-oriented adjustment, should together aim to ensure adequate resources for countries following growth-oriented adjustment with a human face.

The quality of finance is at least as important as the quantity. It is important that programme commitments should be medium term, not short term (i.e. at least for three years, and preferably five), and that the finance available, where offered in the form of credits, be repayable over sufficiently long periods—corresponding to the objective of securing adjustment over the medium term. In current circumstances, external finance also needs, to a considerable extent, to be in programme, not project, form, and to be usable for the finance of recurrent costs (including salaries), and not only capital costs. In many countries, new projects may be of lesser priority than efficient and full operation of existing projects, while often new projects can find finance for recurrent costs. In such situations, finance for growth and protection of the vulnerable can be found by switching aid away from new project commitments. The human face approach to adjustment requires that governments allocate resources according to clear priorities, switching from low-priority uses to those that directly protect the vulnerable and contribute to growth. The same prioritization is essential for aid finance.

Tied and project aid, which dominates bilateral aid, can be counter productive in times of crisis—building and equipping new hospitals, for example, when priorities require a switch to basic health interventions. Among multilateral aid institutions, project aid still dominates. There has been some useful switch towards financing programmes and sectoral rehabilitation, but the pattern of aid is still, from a human face perspective, very far from the desirable one.

2   *Programme design and monitoring*

Programme design naturally closely relates to the dominant approach to adjustment. With a change in the approach, there will need to be a corresponding change in programme design, and perhaps also in the conditions attached to finance from the major agencies involved (viz. IMF and the World Bank). As described in Chapter 2, conditionality in the early 1980s has involved a mixture of demand, supply, and some general reforms, with the requirement for short-term demand restraint being a universal feature of supported adjustment programmes. Monetary variables have been used for programme monitoring by the IMF, and other macro-economic variables by the World Bank in its programme lending. The programmes were initially little concerned with distributional features of adjustment, nor with the incomes of the poor, and consequently human indicators have not featured in programme design or monitoring.

Recently, the IMF has let it be known that it will consider distributional implications of alternative programmes, at the request of governments (de Larosière's speech, July 1986). World Bank conditionality—associated with SALs—has recently begun to incorporate a poverty element, along with other conditions, although this element has not apparently been a very important feature of SAL conditions so far. These positive developments can now be built upon. Adjustment with a human face has a new legitimacy in the international financial institutions.

The human face approach to adjustment requires that the protection of vulnerable groups and the promotion of growth be integral aspect of adjustment programmes. The need to secure internal and external balance remains, of course, but as argued above a more gradual approach to adjustment may frequently be called for. In this case, demand conditions and the corresponding performance criteria and monitoring variables would be less strict in the short term. Programme monitoring could incorporate the major elements affecting the conditions of the most vulnerable, and those related to maintaining growth. Monitoring of performance must include human indicators on the condition of the most vulnerable (for discussion of relevant variables see Ch. 14). The level of investment and the growth of GNP could be added as indicators of growth orientation.

The aim is to change programme design and monitoring to incorporate the short and medium-term well-being of the most vulnerable as integral elements of programmes and monitoring, in contrast to the present system where they are ignored altogether or hurriedly tacked on at the end. Such changes need not increase the total extent and severity of performance monitoring: some relaxation of the more conventional monetary targets, both in number and in content, would roughly offset the proposed increase in the breadth of monitoring.

3 Modalities

The change in programme design, and possibly in the content of conditionality has implications for the modalities by which it is realized. At present, both at international and national levels, discussions and negotiations are dominated (often monopolized) by the financial agencies and ministries, whose outlook is normally both narrow in scope and short-term. The broader approach suggested here requires that those concerned with the well-being of the poor (social ministries and international agencies) and with long-term development (planning ministries) be involved as well. This will require major changes in the conduct of negotiations, both from the point of view of the international financial institutions and the UN system, and that of individual governments. The challenge will be to combine representation of major areas of concern with efficient and rapid decision-making.

There are already major problems associated with the present system—in addition to the narrowness of the concerns typically represented. On the one hand, there is strong resentment on the part of developing countries of excessive interventionism by external agencies, which often leads to complete breakdown in discussions. On the other, countries are subject to too many separate missions from overseas, which take up much too much time of very scarce administrative personnel. Particularly in Africa, the opportunity cost of their time is unacceptably high. On the face of it, there is a danger that adding the human dimension to conditionality and incorporating more decision-makers could add to both these problems.

More fundamentally, there is a need to change towards less confrontational modes in which programmes and conditions are truly mutually agreed by national governments and international agencies rather than seemingly being imposed from outside by the latter. Especially with the widening of conditions proposed, it will be important to change the system of negotiations towards a more co-operative partnership in defining objectives, designing programmes, and establishing conditions and performance criteria. Various ways of achieving this are possible. Most obviously one can work at reducing the number of separate foreign missions and strengthening national capacities. Others have proposed the introduction of independent commissions, at the request of governments, to help arrive at agreed programmes and financial commitments, particularly for small countries which have limited administrative capacity and weak bargaining power (Ranis 1984).

Such approaches require further investigation, and experimentation. Some reform of the modalities of negotiation is essential to ensure country commitment to adjustment programmes and international commitment to provide sufficient finance, and to widen the discussions to incorporate the concerns of adjustment with a human face.

V Conclusions

The 'adjustment' problem of individual countries cannot be understood independently of the international environment in which it developed. For many countries the adjustment problem of the 1980s arose from the deterioration in the international economic environment; and the extent and speed of adjustment needed over the next few years will depend on future developments in the international context—especially with respect to world growth of output, commodity prices, protectionism, and international money markets. Policy changes in these areas could radically change the nature of required adjustments, and could eliminate the necessity of deflationary adjustment in many countries. From the perspective of international policy making, then, the highest priority should be given to improving the international environment, thus preventing the continuation or recurrence of the debilitating effects on vulnerable groups that have resulted from past world economic developments.

In summary, international action for the protection of the vulnerable needs to operate at three levels: in the medium to long term, to improve the operations of the world economy so as to reduce the extent of short-term adjustment required and facilitate country adjustment; for the short to medium term, to introduce buffer mechanisms to protect vulnerable countries during economic fluctuations, reducing the need for excessive short-term adjustments; and finally in the short term, to improve the treatment of individual countries undergoing adjustment so as to give special support to those countries adopting adjustment with a human face, and to encourage others to adopt such an approach—by changes in finance, in conditionality, and in the modalities of negotiations.

Changes in domestic conditions can do much to protect the vulnerable. But the persistence of adverse changes in international conditions will ultimately undermine most national efforts. The increased sense of international responsibility and commitment must therefore be translated into policy changes, if recurrent and enlarged human crises, giving rise to malnutrition and ultimately starvation, are to be avoided.

16

Summary and Conclusions

Giovanni Andrea Cornia, Richard Jolly, and Frances Stewart

I 1981–86: The most severe economic downturn of the developing world since the 1930s

Between 1981 and 1986 the world economy, and particularly the developing market economies as a whole, experienced the most severe and prolonged recession since the 1930s. While most countries in South and East Asia managed to maintain satisfactory rates of growth over the period, 70 per cent of countries in Africa, the Middle East, and Latin America experienced negative cumulative growth rates in GDP per capita. Although the situation in OECD countries somewhat improved in 1984–86, the majority of the developing nations outside Asia continue to be affected by an unfavourable world environment, characterized by low commodity prices, negligible voluntary capital flows, a large accumulation of debt, and high real interest rates. In 1984–85, drought was a serious contributory factor, particularly in Africa. *Negative or slow growth is expected for the rest of the decade and beyond* for the group of developing economies outside Asia, unless radical policy changes are introduced in the areas of debt and capital flows, or a strong recovery in the industrial market economies revitalizes world trade and, with it, commodity prices, while special efforts are needed in African countries to raise agricultural productivity and food production.

II Widespread deterioration in child welfare

There is widespread and growing evidence that in the early 1980s these economic changes, compounded in some areas, especially Africa, by adverse climatic conditions, triggered a sharp reversal in the trend towards improvement in health, nutrition and education standards of children. Deterioration in child welfare has been documented in at least 8 countries in Latin America, 16 in Sub-Saharan Africa, 3 in North Africa and the Middle East, and 4 in South and East Asia (in most countries in Asia the situation of children continued to improve). In many more countries, social progress has been negligible or slowed considerably. Nutrition and education seem to be the area where deterioration is most evident and pronounced, an alarming sign in view of the permanent damage caused by malnutrition at an early age, and in view of the negative long-term implications of declining literacy. The mental and physical capacity of the future labour force is thus being undermined. With continuing poor economic performance and further declines in child welfare, it will become increasingly difficult and costly to offset the accumulated damage, especially in nutrition, education, and social infrastructure, and to resume improvement according to the previous trend.

III An unsatisfactory approach to the adjustment problem

The growing imbalances and stagnation of the 1980s have led many developing countries to introduce adjustment policies aimed at re-establishing equilibrium in the external accounts and controlling inflation while creating the conditions for resumed growth. Between 1980 and 1985 there were each year an average of 47 countries with an IMF adjustment programme (as compared to about 10 to 15 during the 1970s), while many others adjusted on their own account. Most of these adjustment programmes did not reverse the adverse developments in the conditions of children, nor, in many cases, did they lead to resumed economic growth. Conditions of children continued to worsen in many countries. While there are many causes of the deteriorating conditions—including the adverse course of the world economy and many weaknesses in national policies—it appears that the type of adjustment policies adopted have been an important contributory element in many cases. Certainly many of the adjustment programmes made no explicit effort to prevent further deterioration of the human situation in the short run—and usually relied on trickle–down from growth to improve the situation in the longer term.

Two main effects of the adjustment programmes adopted were responsible for this failure to sustain growth and child welfare. First, the predominantly deflationary character of most programmes which led to growing poverty through depressed employment and real incomes; secondly, the direct negative effects of certain macro-economic policies on the welfare of particular socio-economic groups. Direct negative effects on some vulnerable groups arose from policies toward the exchange rate and producer prices, associated with rising urban food prices, cuts in food subsidies (which were an element in one-third of the adjustment packages), and cuts in social expenditure per capita which occurred in over half the Third World countries between 1980 and 1984. Broadly, these negative effects on the poor can be traced to four major features of the traditional approach to adjustment; (*a*) a short-time horizon, (*b*) insufficient finance, which forces the adoption of abrupt demand contraction to achieve external balance; (*c*) the predominance of macro-economic as opposed to sectoral and targeted policies directed towards supporting groups and sectors particularly in need, and; (*d*) the lack of explicit consideration, in most cases, of the effects of such programmes on income distribution, on the incidence of poverty, or on the nutritional and health status of particular groups.

IV Adjustment lessons

Several lessons can be learned from the adjustment experience of the 10 countries covered by this study:

1. *Adjustment is clearly necessary.* Countries have to adapt to a changing world environment, and failure to do so entails huge losses of output and human welfare. The experience of Ghana over the years 1974–82 is a clear illustration of such a process of involution. The problem is not whether to adjust or not, but *how.*

2. *Growth is necessary, but growth-oriented adjustment is not enough* to ensure the protection of vulnerable groups either in the short or the medium term. In Brazil from 1981–85, successful efforts at adjusting with growth and at restructuring the productive base were accompanied by a nation-wide increase in infant mortality rate, low birth weight, and school drop-outs. This was because of the lack of a deliberate and coherent attempt to offset, at least partially, the effects on the poor of declining employment and wages and rising food prices, and to sustain and restructure public expenditure in crucial areas such as health care, immunization, feeding programmes, and primary education.

3. *The most vulnerable can be protected during adjustment, even in the absence of economic growth, by the adoption of targeted programmes. However, there are limits to what this approach can achieve over the medium run when growth becomes essential.* For example, by highly targeted programmes in the area of child health and nutrition throughout the 1970s and early 1980s, Chile succeeded in achieving a continuous decline in infant and child mortality despite severe economic fluctuations, high unemployment, and deteriorating income distribution. Jamaica maintained and even expanded social programmes during a period of economic decline in the 1970s. Yet, in both cases, the 1980s has seen a reversal. In Jamaica, this was associated with major political changes, but would probably have occurred in any political system, if economic decline continued. In Chile in the last couple of years malnutrition has started to rise, while the trend toward declining child mortality has been partially reversed as targeted interventions have no longer been sufficient to offset the collapse of entitlements among the low-income as a result of macro-economic developments.

4. *There are successful examples of alternative approaches* both in the area of adjustment with economic growth and in that of protection of the welfare of the most vulnerable. In South Korea, for instance, a current account deficit of over $4 billion was transformed into one of $1.3 billion, and a budget deficit of 5.6 per cent of GDP into one of 1.5 per cent during the 1980s. Economic growth was maintained on average at over 7 per cent a year over this period while all indicators—nutrition, infant mortality, and incomes of the low income groups—improved.

At the sectoral and micro level, there are many examples of successful attempts at extending programmes in favour of the vulnerable, both in the area of income and nutrition support and provision of services. In Zimbabwe for instance, basic health programmes in favour of children—immunization and control of diarrhoea, most notably—and an effective drought relief programme were sustained and even expanded during 1982–84, a period of severe adjustment and drought and overall budgetary restraint. Malnutrition did not increase, while infant mortality continued to decline. Other examples of successful sectoral programmes during adjustment are the drought relief programme in Botswana, the Livelihood Protection Programme in South Korea, and child feeding in Chile.

These examples are not odd exceptions. Some 80 countries have over the last year or two adopted expansion programmes for immunization towards the goal of immunizing *all* children under one year old against measles, polio, whooping cough, tetanus, diphtheria, and tuberculosis. These six vaccine-preventable diseases accounted for some 4.5 million deaths among under-5s in the early 1980s. Following a threefold increase in immunization from 1983–85, this total had already been reduced by a million by 1986. Similarly, over the period 1983–86, world use of oral rehydration salts (ORS) also increased three times. The fact that threefold increases in the use of vaccine and ORS were possible in spite of the severe economic setbacks show the gains that are feasible for social progress in the presence of serious economic constraints.

5. *A strategy which protects the vulnerable during adjustment not only raises human welfare but is also economically efficient.* Many studies have shown that investment in human resources is at least as vital for economic growth, and exhibits as high returns, as physical investment. All the main elements of the strategy have been shown to yield positive economic returns—for example, worker productivity rises with improved nutrition; small-scale producers in both agriculture and industry have been shown to be as efficient, and often more efficient, than large producers. The most important factor explaining the great economic success of the East Asian countries is agreed to be the very high levels of human capital, resulting from comprehensive education and health systems.

The experience of the country studies shows therefore that *there are examples of alternative adjustment approaches both at macro and micro levels. The conditions of children need not worsen during the adjustment process.*

V   The elements of adjustment with a human face

The inadequacy of the prevailing approach to adjustment calls for a broader approach, one which combines adjustment with protection of the vulnerable and the restoration of economic growth. Such an approach—termed here adjustment with a human face—has been shown to consist of six main policy components:

1. *More expansionary macro-economic policies,* aiming at sustaining levels of output, investment, and human need satisfaction over the adjustment period.

Structural adjustment of an economy normally takes much longer than conventional stabilization. A more gradual timing of adjustment and larger amounts of medium-term external finance will therefore be necessary.

2. *The use of meso policies*—within any given frame of macro policy—to reinforce the more expansionary macro approach and to secure the priority use of resources to fulfill the needs of the vulnerable. Meso policies determine the impact of policies towards taxation, government expenditure, foreign exchange, and credit (among others) on the distribution of income and resources. Essential aspects of meso policies for adjustment with a human face are using such policy instruments selectively for prioritizing and the restructuring of resources and activities in favour of the poor; for protecting the basic needs of the vulnerable; and in support of economic growth.

3. *Sectoral policies aiming at restructuring within the productive sector* to strengthen employment and income generating activities and raise productivity in low-income activities, focusing in particular on small farmers and informal sector producers in industry and services.

4. *Improving the equity and efficiency of the social sector* by restructuring public expenditure both between and within sectors (in particular away from high-cost areas and toward low-cost basic services), by improving the targeting of interventions and their cost-effectiveness.

5. *Compensatory programmes* (often of limited duration) to protect basic health and nutrition of the low-income during adjustment before growth resumption enables them to meet their minimum needs independently. Two major elements of such policies are public works employment schemes and nutrition interventions, encompassing targeted food subsidies and direct feeding for the most vulnerable.

6. *Monitoring* of the human situation, especially of living standards, health, and nutrition of low-income groups during the adjustment process, so that needs may be identified and the effectiveness of adjustment programmes assessed and modified accordingly. Monitoring of human conditions—especially the health and nutritional status of the population, particularly that of vulnerable groups—should be given as much weight in monitoring adjustment as monetary variables have in the conventional approach.

VI The new approach is a realistic proposition

It should be clear that *adjustment with a human face is a realistic proposition*. Each of the six policy components described above has been successfully adopted by some countries in recent years, while there are some examples of countries having followed an overall approach similar to the one proposed, as will be clear from the discussion below.

1 Macro policies

As noted above, South Korea adopted macro policies which combined adjustment with growth, and protection of human needs in the 1980s. South Korea was in some sense a 'special' case, because of the strong manufacturing base, highly qualified manpower, and skilled administration. More international support would be needed for other countries in a less favourable position.

Brazil and Zimbabwe also succeeded in resuming economic growth, after only a short recession, in large part because of the structural adjustment and expansionary macro policies adopted. These examples clearly demonstrate that the prolonged stagnation and recession experienced by Jamaica, Chile, and other countries are not *necessary* features of the environment of the 1980s, but may be modified by appropriate policies.

2 Meso policies

After years of decline, in mid-1985 the new Peruvian government introduced an adjustment programme aimed at reducing inflation while stimulating the demand for basic goods and services. A major feature of this package is the high selectivity attached to the use of scarce resources such as credit, key inputs, foreign exchange, and budgetary resources. In the area of credit, for instance, special credit lines have been opened (at market rates) for informal sector producers as well as for the agricultural, fishing, and non-traditional export sectors. In addition, credit on soft terms has been allocated to depressed areas with the purpose of increasing the productivity of poor farmers. In the area of currency exchange, a more favourable rate is applied for the import of priority inputs and debt servicing, while non-priority imports and other transactions (including exports) are carried out at market exchange rates. Considerable budgetary resources which would otherwise have been spent on military expenditures and debt servicing have been transferred to sustaining priority domestic production and extending crucial services in health and education. In all these areas, therefore, the incentive system has been geared to the satisfaction of the basic needs of the population and to encouraging efficient small-scale producers.

In Zimbabwe, policies towards both credit and government expenditure were used to support human face priorities. The share of credit going to small farmers in communal areas from the Agricultural Finance Corporation rose from 17 to 35 per cent between 1982/83 and 1985/86, while the value of marketed maize and cotton rose from $17 million in 1980 to $218 million in 1985, with their share rising from 10 per cent to 38 per cent. The share of defence and administration in current government expenditure fell from 44 per cent in 1980 to 28 per cent in 1984, while the share of education and health rose from 22 per cent to 27 per cent. The share of primary education in total educational expenditure rose from 32 per cent (1980) to 58 per cent (1984), and real expenditures per capita on primary education doubled during the adjustment period.

3 Policies to support productivity of small-scale producers and low-income activities

In the Jahaly Pacharr Smallholder project for irrigating rice in The Gambia, explicit efforts were made to help small farmers, and especially to incorporate women. Of the 3,000 beneficiaries 95 per cent were women, with credit and inputs provided directly to them and extension workers using women's groups. Over 1982–84, rice yields of six tonnes per hectare were achieved.

The Grameen Bank for the landless in rural Bangladesh has branches in 3,600 villages with 171,000 members, 70 per cent women. It has extended loans to the very poor and landless, for projects which have shown a potential positive return. The default rate has been almost negligible, and group solidarity has greatly increased. Other examples of successful projects, to support the productivity of the poor can be found in Chapters 9 and 10.

4 Improving the equity and efficiency of social services

Governments can greatly improve basic social services even at times of great financial stringency by restructuring government expenditures away from costly services mainly servicing the élite towards low-cost interventions such as primary health care, basic education, and self-help housing, and by better targeting and better management. In this respect, policies required for adjustment with a human face can be seen as a generalization of the approach UNICEF has adopted to interventions in health and education.

In Tanzania a comprehensive basic drugs scheme was introduced at a cost of barely 30 cents per head. In Burkina Faso, 70 per cent of the target population were immunized against major diseases at a cost of $4 per head, making use of volunteers. At the peak of the drought in 1983/84, the drought relief programme in Zimbabwe absorbed about 2.3 per cent of total government expenditure or about $5–7 per person/year. In Indonesia the cost of a highly successful integrated programme including nutritional surveillance, child feeding, immunization, and other activities never exceeded $5–6 per under-5 a year.

5 Compensatory policies: public works and nutrition support

The Maharashtra Employment Guarantee scheme provides employment on public works—mainly to develop economic infrastructure, such as irrigation and roads—to all who want employment. It provided employment for 800,000 workers in 1978–79, most of whom were landless or marginal farmers. Earnings from the scheme provided nearly 70 per cent of total earnings of the landless labourers. Public works schemes to provide work to the unemployed during adjustment were implemented in South Korea, Peru, and Chile, among others.

In Botswana, supplementary feeding programmes cover all primary school children, under-5s in rural areas and the malnourished in urban areas, pregnant and lactating women, and tuberculosis patients. Despite drought which has lasted more than five years and a fall in food production of famine proportions, malnutrition has been contained in Botswana. Jamaica also has a targeted food-aid scheme, designed to help meet nutritional needs of one-half of the population, following the introduction of a rigorous adjustment programme. Sri Lanka has a food stamp scheme aimed at half the population. In both cases, the schemes are not as generous as the subsidies replaced, and have been eroded by inflation, but they make some contribution to maintaining nutrition.

6 Monitoring

Botswana has the most comprehensive system of monitoring nutritional status at a national level, using the information to make decisions on programmes to protect people during drought. Data on the nutritional status of pre-school children are collected monthly at clinics. The information forms an important element in a system of early warning at a national level, as well as being used to identify children especially at risk and to provide special feeding for them.

In Chile, too, child nutritional monitoring has played an important role in identifying the malnourished and mounting programmes accordingly. More recently, Thailand has developed a national nutritional monitoring scheme, based on child weighing in primary health care centres throughout the country. And Indonesia since the mid-1970s has had a national system which now covers some two-thirds of the 64,000 villages of the country, involving monthly weighing of children.

VII Adjustment with a human face is conducive to long-term growth and equity

Adjustment with a human face is fully consistent with strategies aiming at promoting long-term growth while satisfying the basic needs of the population. Given the growing need faced by most countries in the 1980s for adjusting economic structures to a changing world environment *adjustment with a human face is a precondition for long-term growth*. Contrary to the conventional approach— by which reduction of external and internal imbalances is achieved by demand and import restraints, often entailing a decline in GDP as well as in investment in physical and human capital—adjustment with a human face involves a restructuring of the economy so that major imbalances are eliminated at a satisfactory level of output and investment while human capacities are maintained and developed. In this way the strategy lays the essential foundations for sustained development. Adjustment with a human face is thus an efficient strategy from the point of view of sustaining economic growth and meeting basic needs.

VIII   Adjustment with a human face: political administrative and financial feasibility

The strong emphasis placed on reallocating resources to priority needs, on restructuring government expenditure towards low-cost, wide-coverage action, and on improving the targeting of government interventions, requires a clear political commitment and leadership on the part of national authorities. There is also need for increased longer-term financial flows from abroad and changes in the world economic environment.

Domestically, some resistance will often be met from those groups who may not be the primary beneficiaries. However, adjustment which protects human conditions can also be an 'efficient' form of adjustment from a political point of view. In the short term, it can help to/reduce social tensions (food riots, for example) and reduce the probability of breakdown in the socio-political fabric by minimizing the human costs of adjustment. In the medium term, most parts of society will gain as economic growth is resumed. Political stability is therefore more likely as a result of this broader approach to adjustment.

The scope for improving domestic resource allocation has been shown to vary substantially from place to place. In certain countries only modest improvements in resource allocation are possible. Even in these cases, however, there is scope for introducing some of the elements of the new adjustment approach. Indeed, several of the policies aimed at supporting the productivity of small producers, or at extending basic health programmes in specific areas have *relatively modest financial and allocative implications*. In Pakistan, for instance, the extension of immunization services to almost all the country's children has required only a five-year postponement in the construction of one urban-hospital.

Community participation is an essential ingredient of adjustment with a human face. On the one hand it can help generating the political support needed to overcome short-term political and bureaucratic opposition. On the other, it is essential for the planning, implementing, and success of the approaches devised, as well as for keeping the cost of programmes down by means of community contributions.

IX   Changes are required on the international scene

During the early 1980s the international economic environment has exerted a negative influence on the character of adjustment policies. Stagnating world trade and growing protectionism have been a major hindrance to expansionary adjustment, while because of the collapse of voluntary lending and high debt servicing obligations almost no resources were left for restructuring, investment, and growth. This situation requires important changes.

1. *The main industrialized countries should promote the creation of a world environment more friendly to developing countries*, reducing the extent of the adjustment efforts the latter have to undertake. Policies should aim at reinvigorating and sustaining the currently anaemic levels of world demand; at allowing developing countries greater access to the agricultural and manufacturing markets of the industrialized countries; at reducing interest rates; and at increasing net resource flows to developing countries. For the most part, it is programme rather than project money which is required, with long repayment periods. Significant debt rescheduling and some debt write-offs can help achieve an improved net resource transfer.

2. *Buffer mechanisms for low-income countries* have to be put into place to compensate them for some of the adverse effects of recession. Existing facilities like the Compensatory Financing Facility and the STABEX could be developed so as to provide more adequate buffering by increasing their size, extending their coverage to include international shocks other than shortfalls in international commodity prices (interest rate rises, for instance) and reducing their conditionality. New types of buffers should also be considered. Additional financial support (in the form of automatic debt relief, increased allocations of SDRs, increased World Bank long-term soft loans, etc.) should be extended to countries experiencing worsening human indicators (such as increasing child malnutrition) following from international developments.

3. *Special support is needed for countries following human face policies*, including the provision of extra finance, and the substitution of programme for project finance. Human concerns should be explicitly integrated into all negotiations about adjustment, and the modalities of negotiations adapted to facilitate this. This is unfortunately not the case nowadays. Discussions about adjustment packages are generally conducted between the Ministry of Finance and the IMF and World Bank. Ministries and international organizations concerned with nutrition and the social sectors are for the most part left out of discussions on macro-economic policies, and have eventually to develop their policies within a given macro-economic adjustment framework which is often adverse to the poor.

Ways must be found to involve those responsible for health, nutrition, and human resource development in planning adjustment. This means that ministers of health and education should be brought into discussions of adjustment policy, especially into designing measures to maintain basic health and ·ducation services, and to protect vulnerable groups. International institutions involved in nutrition, health, and education also need to be brought into the formulation, execution, and monitoring of adjustment.

X   In conclusion

Policies for the protection of the vulnerable and the promotion of growth are urgently needed and form a viable and efficient strategy. While the policies described have been applied in places, in part or as a whole, with considerable success in the 1980s, it is now essential to spread their adoption more widely, and to ensure that adequate support is provided internationally. In most middle-income countries, there is substantial scope for protecting the vulnerable during adjustment by restructuring domestic resources, even in the absence of growth and without additional financial support from outside. Political leadership and community participation are the requirements for success in overcoming the unavoidable opposition such policies will encounter.

In low-income countries where the resource base and administrative capacity is less developed, more external resources will be needed. The external support, however, although critical for these countries, is very small in relation to the total financial resources of the donor community.

In the longer term, resumed economic growth is essential to permit continued protection and improvements in human conditions in both middle- and low-income countries. Improved external conditions—especially a reversal of the negative resource flows to the Third World now occurring—will be essential. A lasting solution to the problems of the vulnerable will also require sustained growth in the industrialized countries and improved trading conditions for Third World countries. But while these changes are crucial for the longer term, there is substantial potential for immediate action, both nationally and internationally, which would greatly improve the position of the vulnerable in the near future.

References

Addison, T., and L. Demery (1985), *Macro-economic Stabilisation, Income Distribution and Poverty: A Preliminary Survey*. Working Paper 15. London: Overseas Development Institute.

Ahmed, R. (1979), *Foodgrain Supply, Distribution and Consumption Policies Within a Dual Pricing Mechanism: A Case Study of Bangladesh*. Research Report 8. Washington, DC: IFPRI.

—— (1987). 'The Structure, Costs, and Benefits of the Food Subsidies in Bangladesh', in Pinstrup-Andersen P., ed. (1987).

Alderman, H., and J. von Braun (1986), 'Egypt's Food Subsidy Policy: Lessons from the Past and Options for the Future', *Food Policy*, 11/3: 223–7.

—— —— and S. Ahmed Sakr (1982), *Egypt's Food Subsidy and Rationing System: A Description*. Research Report 34. Washington, DC: IFPRI.

Allison, C. (1985), 'Women, Land, Labour and Survival: Getting Some Basic Facts Straight', in Allison, C., and R. Green, eds., *Sub-Saharan Africa: Getting the Facts Straight*. IDS Bulletin, 16/3: 24–30.

Altimir, O. (1984), 'Poverty, Income Distribution and Child Welfare in Latin America: A Comparison of Pre- and Post-recession Data', in Jolly, R., and G. A. Cornia, eds. (1984), 91–112.

Anderson, D. (1982), 'Small Industry in Developing Countries: Discussion of the Issues', *World Development*, 10/11: 913–48.

Anderson, D., and F. Khambata (1981), *Small Enterprises and Development Policy in the Philippines: A Case Study*. World Bank Staff Working Paper 468. Washington, DC: World Bank.

Arles, J. P. (1974), 'Emergency Employment Schemes', *International Labour Review*, 109/1: 69–78.

Ashe, J. (1985), *The PISCES II Experience: Local Efforts in Micro-enterprise Development*, vol. 1. Washington, DC: USAID.

Bacha, E. L. (1985), 'The Future Role of the International Monetary Fund in Latin America: Issues and Proposals'. Mimeographed. Catholic University, Rio de Janeiro.

Barerra, A. (1986), 'Maternal Schooling and Child Health'. Mimeographed. Yale University, Department of Economics.

Barker, R., and R. Herdt (1984), 'Who Benefits from the New Technology' in *The Rice Economy of Asia*. Washington, DC: Resources for the Future.

Beaton, G. H., and H. Ghassemi (1979), *Supplementary Feeding Programmes for Young Children in Developing Countries*. New York: UNICEF.

Becker, R. A., and A. Lechtig (1986a), 'Increasing Poverty and Infant Mortality in the North East of Brazil', *Journal of Tropical Pediatrics*, forthcoming.

—— —— (1986*b*), '*Brasil: evolução da mortalidade infantil no perodo 1977–1984*. Brasìlia: Centro de Documentação do Ministério da Saúde.

Behrman, J. R. (1986), 'The Impact of Economic Adjustment Programmes on Health and Nutrition in Developing Countries'. Mimeographed. University of Pennsylvania.

—— and A. Deolalikar (1986), 'Is Variety the Spice of Life? Implications for Nutrient Responses to Development'. Mimeographed. University of Pennsylvania.

Berry, A. R. (1972), 'The Relevance and Prospects of Small-scale Industry in Colombia'. Yale Economic Growth Center Discussion Paper, No. 142.

—— and W. R. Cline (1979), *Agrarian Structure and Productivity in Developing Countries*. Baltimore: John Hopkins University Press.

—— and A. Pinell-Siles (1979), *Small-scale Enterprise in Colombia: A Case Study*. Studies in Employment and Rural Development 56. Washington, DC: World Bank.

Bertholot, J. (1979), 'Food Aid through the World Food Aid Programme in Tunisia: How to Carry Out a Counter-Agrarian Reform'. Rome Declaration Group.

Brandt Commission (1980), *North–South: A Programme for Survival*. London: Pan Books.

—— (1983) *Common Crisis, North–South: Co-operation for Recovery*. London: Pan Books.

Bratton, M. (1986), 'Farmer Organisations and Food Production in Zimbabwe', *World Development*, 14/3: 367–84.

Brenner, M. H. (1973), 'Fetal, Infant, and Maternal Mortality during Periods of Economic Instability', *International Journal of Health Services*, 3/2: 45–59.

Burki, S. J., D. J. Davies, R. H. Hook, and J. W. Thomas (1976), *Public Works Programmes in Developing Countries: A Comparative Analysis*. World Bank Staff Working Paper 224. Washington, DC: World Bank.

Byerlee, D., C. Eicher, C. Liedholm, and D. Spencer (1979), 'Employment Output Conflicts, Factor Price Distortions and Choice of Technique: Empirical Results from Sierra Leone'. African Rural Economy Working Paper 26. Michigan State University.

Caldwell, J. C. (1981), 'Maternal Education as a Factor in Child Mortality', *World Health Forum*, 2/1: 75–8.

Chambers, R. (1979), 'Health, Agriculture and Rural Poverty: Why Seasons matter'. IDS Discussion Paper 149, Institute of Development Studies, University of Sussex.

—— and H. Singer (1981), 'Poverty, Malnutrition and Food Insecurity in Zambia', in Clay, E., R. Chambers, H. Singer, and M. Lipton, *Food Policy Issues in Low Income Countries*. World Bank Staff Working Paper 473. Washington, DC: World Bank.

—— R. Longhurst, and A. Pacey, eds. (1981), *Seasonal Dimensions to Rural Poverty*. London: Frances Pinter.

Chana, T., and H. Morrison (1975), 'Nairobi's Informal Economic Sector', *Ekistics*, 40/237: 120–30.

Chen, L. C., E. Hug, and S. D'Soura (1981*a*), 'Sex Bias in the Family Allocation of Food and Health Care in Rural Bangladesh', *Population and Development Review*, 7/1: 55–70.

—— J. Chakraborty, A. M. Sardar, and M. Yunus (1981*b*), 'Estimating and Partitioning the Mortality Impact of Several Modern Medical Technologies in Basic Health Services', *International Population Conference, Manila, 1981*, 2: 113–42. Liège: International Union for the Scientific Study of Population (IUSSP).

Child, F. (1977), 'Small-scale Rural Industry in Kenya'. African Studies Center, Occasional Paper 17, University of California, Los Angeles.

Clavano, N. R. (1981), 'The Results of a Change in Hospital Practices', *Assignment Children*, 55/6: 139–65.

——(1985), 'International Debt: Analysis, Experience and Prospects', *Journal of Development Planning*, 16: 25–56. New York: United Nations.

Coeytax, X. F. (1984), *The Role of the Family in Health: Appropriate Research Methods.* Geneva: WHO.

Collier, P. (1983), 'Oil and Inequality in Rural Nigeria', in Ghai, D., and S. Radwan, eds., *Agrarian Policies and Rural Poverty in Africa.* Geneva: ILO.

Collis, W. R. F. (1962), 'In the Ecology of Child Health and Nutrition in Nigerian Villages', *Tropical and Geographical Medicine*, 14: 140–63, 201–28.

Conti, A. (1983), 'Women in Rice Farming Systems in Madagascar and Zanzibar'. Mimeographed. Rome: FAO.

Cornia, G. A. (1984*a*), 'A Survey of Cross-sectional and Time-series Literature on Factors Affecting Child Welfare', in Jolly, R., and G. A. Cornia, eds. (1984).

——(1984*b*), 'A Cost Analysis of the Indonesian Experience with GOBI–FF, 1979–82'. Mimeographed. New York: UNICEF.

——(1985), 'Farm Size, Land Yields and Agricultural Production Functions: An Analysis for Fifteen Developing Countries', *World Development*, 13/4: 513–34.

Costa, E. (1974), 'Planning and Organisation of the "Frentes de Trabalho" in Northeast Brazil'. ILO/WEP 2-24.

——(1978), 'An Assessment of the Flows of Benefits Generated by Public Investment in the Employment Guarantee Scheme of Maharashtra'. ILO/WEP 2-24/WP 12.

Cousins, W. J., and G. Goydre (1979), *Changing Slum Communities*, New Delhi: Manohar.

Cumper, G. (1983), 'Economic Development, Health Services, and Health', in Lee, K., and A. Mills, eds. (1983), pp. 23–42.

Cutler, P. (1984), 'Famine Forecasting: Prices and Peasant Behaviour in Northern Ethiopia', *Disasters*, 8 Jan. 1984.

Daniel, P., R. Green, and M. Lipton (1984), 'Towards a Strategy for the Rural Poor in Sub-Saharan Africa'. IDS Discussion Paper 193, Institute of Development Studies, University of Sussex.

Darrow, K. (1985), 'Irrigation in Bangladesh: Appropriate Technology Case Studies'. Mimeographed. Washington, DC: ATI.

de Ferranti, D. (1984), 'Strategies for Paying for Health Services in Developing Countries', *World Health Statistics*, 37/4.

de Larosière, J. (1986), 'Address Before the Economic and Social Council of the United Nations'. Washington, DC: IMF.

Dell, S. (1983), 'Stabilization: The Political Economy of Overkill', in Williamson, J., ed. (1983) 7–46.

——(1986), 'The World Debt Problem: A Diagnosis'. Report to the Group of Twenty-Four. Mimeographed. New York: United Nations Institute for Training and Research.

Dey, J. (1982), 'Development Planning in The Gambia: The Gap Between Planners' and Farmers' Perceptions, Expectations and Objectives', *World Development*, 10: 377–96.

——(1984), 'Women Rice Farming Systems. Focus: Sub-Saharan Africa', *Women in Agriculture*, 2. Rome: FAO.

Dias, L., R. Camarano, and A. Lechtig (1986), 'Drought, Recession and Prevalence of Low Birth Weight Babies in Poor Urban Populations of the North East of Brazil', Letter to the editor in *Journal of Tropical Pediatrics*.

Dieguez (1985), 'Social Consequences of the Economic Crisis: Mexico 1982–1985'. Mimeographed.

Donovan, D. (1982), 'Macroeconomic Performance and Adjustment under Fund-supported Programmes: The Experience of the Seventies', *IMF Staff Papers*, 29: 171–203. Washington, DC: IMF.

Duque, J., and M. Pastrana (1973), 'Las estrategias de supervivencia economica de las unidades familiares del sector popular urbano'. Santiago: CELADE-PROELCE.

ECLA—Economic Commission for Latin America (1985), 'Balance preliminar de la economía latinoamericana durante 1985'. Documento Informative, 19 Dec.

Edirisinghe, N. (1986), *The Food Stamp Program in Sri Lanka: Costs, Benefits, and Policy Options*. Forthcoming research report. Washington, DC: IFPRI.

Feachem, R. G. (1986), 'Preventing Diarrhoea: What Are the Policy Options?', *Health Policy and Planning*, 1: 109–17.

Fei, J., G. Ranis, and S. Kuo (1979), *Growth and Equity: The Taiwan Case*. Oxford University Press.

Fisseha, Y., and J. Milimo (1985), 'Small Enterprises in Zambia: Summary of Survey Results'. Paper presented to African Studies Association Meeting, New Orleans.

Fleuret, A. (1979), 'The Role of Wild Foliage Plants in the Diet: A Case Study from Lushoto, Tanzania', *Economy of Food and Nutrition*, 8: 87–93.

—— and A. Fleuret (1980), 'Nutrition, Consumption and Agricultural Change', *Human Organisation*, 39: 250–60.

FAO—Food and Agriculture Organization (1984), *Integrating Nutrition into Agriculture and Rural Development Projects: Six Case Studies*. Nutrition in Agriculture 2. Rome: FAO.

—— (1985), *Review of the Purposes and Operational Modalities of the Global Information and Early Warning Systems on Food and Agriculture*. CFS 85/5. Rome: FAO.

—— (1986), *Food Outlook 1985: Statistical Supplement*. Rome: FAO.

Foxley, A. (1981), 'Stabilisation Policies and their Effects on Employment and Income Distribution: A Latin American Perspective', in Cline, W. R., and S. Weintraub, eds., *Economic Stabilization in Developing Countries*, 191–225. Washington, DC: Brookings Institute.

—— and D. Raczynski (1984), 'Vulnerable Groups in Recessionary Situations: The Case of Children and the Young in Chile', in Jolly, R., and G. A. Cornia, eds. (1984).

Franklin, D. L., and I. V. de Valdés (1985), 'Estrategias nutritionales de los hogares pobres', *Cuaderuos de economia*, 66: 247–65.

Freeman, H. E., R. E. Klein, J. W. Townsend, and A. Lechtig (1980), 'Nutrition and Cognitive Development among Rural Guatemalan Children', *American Journal of Public Health*, 70: 1277–85.

Garcia, M., and P. Pinstrup-Andersen (1986), *Pilot Food Subsidy Scheme in the Philippines: Impact on Poverty, Food Consumption and Nutritional Status*. Report prepared for UNDP. Washington, DC: IFPRI.

Gaude, J., N. Phan-Thuy, and G. Van Keupen (1984), 'Evaluation of Public Works Programmes: Policy Conclusions', *International Labour Review*, 123: 2.

Gavan, J. D., and I. S. Chandrasekera (1979), *The Impact of Public Foodgrain Distribution on Food Consumption and Welfare in Sri Lanka*. Research Report 13. Washington, DC: IFPRI.

George, P. S. (1985), 'Some Aspects of Procurement and Distribution of Foodgrains in India'. Working Paper on Food Subsidies, 1. Washington, DC: IFPRI.

Girling, R., and S. Keith (1977), 'Jamaica's Employment Crisis: A Political Economic Evaluation of the Jamaican Special Employment Programme'. ILO/WEP 2-24/WP 8.

Godfrey, M. (1985), 'Trade and Exchange Rate Policy: A Further Contribution to the Debate', in Rose, T., ed., *Crisis and Recovery in Sub-Saharan Africa*, 168–79. Paris: OECD.

Goldstein, M. (1986), *The Global Effects of Fund-supported Adjustment Programmes.* Occasional Paper 42. Washington, DC: IMF.

—— and M. S. Khan (1982), *Effects of Slowdown in Industrial Countries in Non-oil Developing Countries.* Occasional Paper 12. Washington, DC: IMF.

Gopaldas, T., N. Scrinivasan, I. Veraderejen, A. G. Shingwetar, R. Seth, R. S. Mathur, and B. Bharjava (1975), *Project Poshak*, vol. 1. New Delhi: CARE.

Gozo, K. M., and A. A. Aboagye (1985), 'Impact of the Recession in African Countries: Effects on the Poor'. Mimeographed. Geneva: ILO.

Green, R. H. (1986), 'Sub-Saharan Africa: Poverty of Development, Development of Poverty'. IDS Discussion Paper 218, Institute of Development Studies, University of Sussex.

—— and H. Singer (1984), 'Sub-Saharan Africa in Depression: the Impact on the Welfare of Children', in Jolly and Cornia, eds. (1984).

Griffin, K. and A. Ghose (1978), 'Growth and Impoverishment in the Rural Areas of Asia'. Mimeographed. Geneva: ILO.

Grootaert, C. (1986), 'Measuring and Analysing Levels of Living in Developing Countries'. Living Standards Measurement Studies 24. Washington, DC: World Bank.

Grosse, R. N., and D. J. Plessas (1984), 'Counting the Cost of Primary Health Care', *World Health Forum*, 15/3: 226–30.

Ground, R. (1985), 'A Survey and Critique of Adjustment Programmes in Latin America', in Devlin, R. *et al.*, *Adjustment and Debt Renegotiation in Latin America: Orthodox and Alternative Approaches.* Boulder: Lynner Rienner Publishers.

Guha, S. (1975a), 'Organisation, Planning and Administration of the Drought-prone Areas Programme in Admednagar and Sholapur Districts of Maharashtra State of India'. ILO/WEP 2-24/WP 4.

—— (1975b), 'Planning, Organisation and Administration of the Rural Employment Guarantee Scheme'. ILO/WEP 2-24/WP 2.

—— (1979), 'Policies to Enhance Income Redistributive Potential and Participatory Character of Labour-intensive Rural Works Programmes: Some Lessons from the Maharashtra Employment Guarantee Scheme'. ILO/WEP 2-24/WP 16.

—— (1981), 'Income Redistribution through Labour-intensive Public Works: Some Policy Issues', *International Labour Review*, 120/1: 67–82.

Haggblade, S. (1984), 'Private Sector Assessment: Synthesis Report for Burkina Faso'. Ouagadougou: USAID.

—— (1985), 'Home vs. Factory Brewing: The Impact of Shifting Markets Shares in Africa's Indigenous Beer Industry'. Paper for African Studies Association Meeting, New Orleans.

—— C. Liedholm, and D. Mead (1986), 'The Effect of Policy and Policy Reforms on Non-agricultural Enterprises and Employment in Developing Countries: A Review of Past Experiences'. Employment and Enterprise Policy Analysis Discussion Paper 1. Washington, DC: USAID.

Halstead, S. A., J. A. Walsh, and K. S. Warren, eds. (1985), *Good Health at Low Cost.* New York: Rockefeller Foundation.

Haque, W., *et al.* (1975), 'Towards a Theory of Rural Development'. Bangkok: UN Asian Development Institute.

Hart, K. (1970), 'Small-scale Entrepreneurs in Ghana and Development Planning', *Journal of Development Studies*, 6/4: 104–20.

—— (1973), 'Informal Income Opportunities and Urban Examples in Ghana', *Journal of Modern African Studies*, 11/1: 61–89.

Harvey, C., J. Jacob, G. Lamb, and B. Schaffer (1979), *Rural Employment and Administration in the Third World: Development Methods and Alternative Strategies.* Farnborough: ILO Saxon House.

Haswell, M. (1981), *Energy for Subsistence.* London: Macmillan.

Hayami, Y. (1981), 'Induced Innovation, Green Revolution and Income Distribution: Comment', *Economic Developmer' ınd Cultural Change*, 30/1: 169–76.

Helleiner, G. K. (1985a), 'Stab. ation Policies and the Poor'. Mimeographed. University of Toronto.

—— (1985b), 'Stabilization and Adjustment Policies and Global Poverty: Agenda for Changes'. Paper prepared for the ILO Geneva, Jan. 1986. Mimeographed. University of Toronto, Department of Economics.

Hicks, N., and A. Kubisch (1983), 'The Effects of Expenditure Reduction in Developing Countries'. Mimeographed. Washington, DC: World Bank.

—— —— (1984), 'Cutting Government Expenditures in LDCs', *Finance and Development*, 21/3: 37–9.

Hill, P. (1972), '*Rural Hausa: A Village and A Setting*'. Cambridge University Press.

Ho, S. (1976), *The Rural Non-farm Sector in Taiwan.* World Bank Studies in Employment and Rural Development 32. Washington, DC: IMF.

Hornik, R. C. (1985), *Nutrition Education: A State-of-the-Art Review.* Nutrition Policy Discussion Paper 1. United Nations: ACC/SCN.

Hossain, M. (1984), 'Impact of the Grameen Bank on Women's Involvement in Productive Activities'. Paper presented at UN/ESCAP workshop on Bank Credit for the Landless Women: A Case Study Tour of the Grameen Bank, Dhaka.

Huaman, J., 'Comedores populares y estrategia de sobrevivencia'. Mimeographed. Pontificia Universidad Católica del Peru, Lima.

Inter-American Development Bank (1985), *Annual Report, 1985.* Washington, DC: IBD.

IAI—International African Institute (1982), *Village Food Systems in West Africa.* London: IAI.

IFAD—International Fund for Agricultural Development (1985), *Annual Report 1985.* Rome: IFAD.

ILO—International Labour office (1972), *Employment, Incomes and Equality: A Strategy for Increasing Productive Employment in Kenya.* Geneva: ILO.

—— ILO/JASPA (1981), 'First Things First: Meeting the Basic Needs of the People in Nigeria'. Addis Ababa: ILO.

—— (1982), 'Basic Needs in Danger: A Basic Needs Oriented Development Strategy for Tanzania'. Addis Ababa: ILO.

—— (1984), 'The Informal Sector in Africa: Synthesis and Country Summaries'. Addis Ababa: ILO.

ILO/WEP (1977), 'Guidelines for the Organisation of Special Labour-intensive Works Programmes', E. Costa, S. Guha, M. Hussain, N. T. B. Thuy, and A. Fardet. Geneva: ILO.

IMF—International Monetary Fund *Annual Reports*. Washington, DC: IMF.

—— (1985), *Government Finance Statistics*, 9. Washington, DC: IMF.

—— (1986*a*), *Primary Commodities, Market Developments and Outlook*. World Economic and Financial Surveys. Washington, DC: IMF.

—— (1986*b*), *Fund-supported Programs, Fiscal Policy, and Income Distribution*. Occasional Paper 46. Washington, DC: IMF.

—— (1986*c*), *International Financial Statistics Yearbook, 1985*. Washington, DC: IMF.

—— (1986*d*), *World Economic Outlook, April 1986*. World Economic and Financial Surveys. Washington, DC: IMF.

—— (1986*e*) *Government Finance Statistics*. Washington, DC: IMF.

IRRI—International Rice Research Institute (1978), 'The Technical and Economic Characteristics of Rice Post-production Systems in the Bicol River Basin'. Los Baños, Philippines.

Islam Rahman, R. (1986), 'The Impact of Grameen Bank on the Situation of Poor Rural Women'. Working Paper 1, Grameen Evaluation Project, Bangladesh Institute of Development Studies.

Johnson, O., and J. Salop (1980), 'Distributional Aspects of Stabilisation Programmes in Developing Countries', IMF Staff Papers, 27/1: 1–23. Washington, DC: IMF.

Johnston, B., and W. Clark (1982), *Redesigning Rural Development: A Strategic Perspective*. Baltimore: John Hopkins University Press.

Jolly, R. (1977), 'The Provision of Education and its Costs', in *7th Commonwealth Conference Report*. London: Commonwealth Secretariat.

—— (1985), *Adjustment with a Human Face*. New York: UNICEF.

—— and G. A. Cornia (1984), *The Impact of World Recession on Children*. Oxford: Pergamon Press.

Joshi, H., H. Lubell, and J. Mouly (1976), *Abidjan: Urban Development and Employment in the Ivory Coast*. Geneva: ILO.

Kaplinsky, R. (1983), *Sugar Processing: The Development of a Third World Technology*. London: Intermediate Technology Publications.

Karim, R., M. Majid, and J. F. Levinson (1980), 'The Bangladesh Sorghum Experiment', *Food Policy* 5: 61–3.

Karp-Toledo, E. (October 1983), 'Situacion alimentaria-nutricional en la sierra sud del Peru'. Raleigh NC: AID-Lima/Sigma One Corporation.

Kaufman, D., and L. Lindauer (1984), *Income Transfers within Extended Families to Meet Basic Needs. The Evidence from El Salvador*. World Bank Staff Working Paper 644. Washington, DC: World Bank.

Kennedy, E. (1987), 'Alternatives to Consumer-oriented Food Subsidies as a Means of Achieving Nutrition Objectives', in Pinstrup-Andersen, P., ed. (1987), 4–6.

—— and P. Pinstrup-Andersen (1983), *Nutrition-related Policies and Programmes: Past Performances and Research Needs*. Washington, DC: IFPRI.

Kennedy, J. (1979), 'Making Manioc Starch in Sri Lanka: A Rural Industrial Enterprise', *Appropriate Technology*, 6/3.

Keynes, J. M. (1936), *General Theory of Employment, Interest and Money*. London: Macmillan.

Khan, M. S., and M. D. Knight (1985), *Fund-supported Adjustment Programmes and Economic Growth*. Occasional Paper 41. Washington, DC: IMF.

Khan, R. A. (1982), 'Issues of Food Distribution in Pakistan'. Staff Paper AE-101. Islamabad: Pakistan Agricultural Research Council.

Kielmann, A., *et al.* (1983), *Child and Maternal Health Services in Rural India: The Narangwal Experiment*. Baltimore and London: Johns Hopkins University Press.

Killick, T., ed. (1984), *The Quest for Economic Stabilisation: The IMF and the Third World*. London: Heinemann.

—— (1985), 'Developing Countries and the Changing International Financial Environment'. Paper prepared for ILO meeting, Jan. 1986.

Kumar, S. K. (1979), *Impact of Subsidized Rice on Food Consumption and Nutrition in Kerala*. Research Report 5. Washington, DC: IFPRI.

—— (1987), 'The Design, Income Distribution, and Consumption Effects of Maize Pricing Policies in Zambia', in Pinstrup-Andersen, P., ed. (1987).

Lafosse, V. S. (1984), 'Comedores comunales: la mujer frente a la crisis'. Grupo de Trabajo, Servicios Urbanos y Mujeres de Bajos Ingresos, Lima, Peru.

Lechtig, A., M. Irwin, and R. E. Klein (1980), *Societal Implications of Early Protein Energy Malnutrition: Prevention in Childhood of Specific Adult Health Problems*. Geneva: WHO.

Lee, K., and A. Mills, eds. (1983), *The Economics of Health in Developing Countries*. Oxford University Press.

Leslie, J., M. Lycette, and M. Buvinic (1986). *Weathering Economic Crises: The Crucial Role of Women in Health*. Washington, DC: The International Center for Research on Women.

Levinson, F. (1982), 'Towards Success in Combating Malnutrition: An Assessment of What Works' *Food and Nutrition Bulletin*, 4/3: 23–44.

Liedholm, C. (1973), 'Research on Employment in the Rural Non-farm Sector in Africa'. African Rural Employment Paper 5, Michigan State University.

—— and D. Mead (1985), 'Small-scale Industry in Africa'. Paper for African Studies Association Meeting, New Orleans.

Lipton, M. (1983*a*), *Poverty, Undernutrition, and Hunger*. World Bank Staff Working Paper 597. Washington, DC: World Bank.

—— (1983*b*) *Labour and Productivity*. World Bank Staff Working Paper 616. Washington, DC: World Bank.

—— (1985), *Land Assets and Rural Poverty*. World Bank Staff Working Paper 744. Washington, DC: World Bank.

—— with R. Longhurst (1985), *Modern Varieties, International Agricultural Research and the Poor*. Impact Study 2, Washington, DC: Consultative Group on International Agricultural Research (CGIAR).

Longhurst, R. (1981), 'Research Methodology and Rural Economy in Northern Nigeria' in *Rapid Rural Appraisal*, IDS Bulletin, 12/4.

—— (1986*a*), 'Farm-level Decision Making, Social Structure and an Agricultural Development Project in a Northern Nigerian Village'. Samaru Miscellaneous Paper 106, Ahmadu Bello University, Zaria.

—— (1986*b*), 'Agricultural Strategies, Food and Nutrition: Issues and Opportunities', *Nutrition and Health* 4/2: 83–94.

—— and M. Lipton (1985), 'Secondary Food Crops and the Reduction of Seasonal Food Insecurity: The Role of Agricultural Research'. Paper presented at the Annapolis IFPRI/FAO/AID Workshop on Seasonal Causes of Household Food Insecurity: Policy Implications and Research Needs.

Lustig, N. (1986), *Food Subsidy Programmes in Mexico*. Food Subsidies Working Paper 3. Washington, DC: IFPRI.

Manoff, R. K. (1985). *Social Marketing*. New York: Praeger.

Mateus, A. (1983), *Targeting Food Subsidies for the Needy: The Use of Cost–Benefit Analysis and Institutional Design*. World Bank Staff Working Paper 617. Washington, DC: World Bank.

May, M. J., and S. Stichter, eds. (1984), *African Women South of the Sahara*. London: Longman.

Mazumdar, D. (1976), 'The Urban Informal Sector', *World Development*, 4/8: 655–79.

McCord, C. W. *et al.* (1980), 'Death Rate, Land and the Price of Rice '75–78'. Evaluation Unit Report 4. Mimeographed. Christian Commission for Bangladesh.

McGranahan, D., E. Pizarro, and C. Richard (1985), *Measurement and Analysis of Socio-economic Development*. Geneva: United Nations Research Institute for Social Development.

Meerman, J. (1979), *Public Expenditure in Malaysia: Who Benefits and Why*. World Bank. Oxford University Press.

Mies, M. (1984), 'Capitalism and Subsistence: Rural Women in India', *Development: Seeds of Change* 4.

Ministry of Health, Republic of Malawi (1984), 'A Survey of Health Sector Costs and Financing in Malawi', *World Health Statistics*, 37/4: 375–86.

Ministry of Labour and Community Development, Barbados (1985), *Selected Data, 1985*. Kingston.

Mohan, R., and N. Hartline (1984), *The Poor of Bogota*. World Bank Staff Working Paper 635. Washington, DC: World Bank.

Morales-Anaya, R. (1985), 'Poverty, Infant Mortality and Economic Crisis in Bolivia'. Bolivia: UNICEF.

Morawetz, D. (1974), 'Employment Implications of Industrialisation in Developing Countries, *Economic Journal*, 84:491–542.

Moser, C. O. N. (1978), 'Informal Sector or Petty Production: Dualism or Dependence in Urban Development?', *The Urban Informal Sector: Critical Perspectives in World Developments*.

Mosley, W. H. (1985), 'Will Primary Health Care Reduce Infant and Child Mortality? A Critique of Some Current Strategies, with special reference to Africa and Asia', in J. Vallin and A. D. Lopez, eds. *Health Policy, Social Policy and Mortality Prospects*, pp. 108–38. Liège: International Union for the Scientific Study of Population (IUSSP).

—— and L. C. Chen (1984), 'An Analytical Framework for the Study of Child Survival in Developing Countries', *Population and Development Review*, 10, Supplement, 25–45.

Mridha, A. (1984), 'Country Paper on the Role of the Central Bank in the Development of Bank Credit for the Rural Poor'. Paper presented at UN/ESCAP workshop on Bank Credit for the Landless Women: A Case Study Tour of the Grameen Bank, Dhaka.

New, R. (1985), 'Sago Product Development in Papua New Guinea', *Appropriate Technology*, 12/2: 20–3.

Nihan, G., E. Demol, and C. Jondoh (1979), 'The Modern Informal Sector in Lomé', *International Labour Review*, 118/5: 630–44.

North–South Roundtable on Money and Finance (1985), 'Statement of the Round-table on Money and Finance, New York, 13–14 Dec. 1985'. Pakistan: North–South Roundtable Publications.

Nurkse, R. (1955), *Problems of Capital Formation in Underdeveloped Countries*. Oxford: Blackwell.

Ochoa, M. (1987), 'The Colombian Food Stamp Program', in Pinstrup-Andersen, P., ed. (1987).

OECD—Organisation for Economic Co-operation and Development (1985), *Twenty-five Years of Development Co-operation: A Review*. Paris: OECD.

—— (1986), *Economic Survey (May)*. Paris: OECD.

Oshima, H. T. (1971), 'Labour Force Explosion and the Labour Intensive Sector in Asian Growth', *Economic Development and Cultural Change*, 19/2: 161–83.

Pack, H. (1982), 'Aggregate Implications of Factor Substitution in Industrial Processes', *Journal of Development Economics*, 11: 1–37.

PAHO/WHO—Pan-American Health Organization (1983), *Oral Rehydration Therapy: An Annotated Bibliography*. Scientific Publications 445, 2nd edn. Washington, DC: PAHO.

Pastor, M. (1986), 'The Effects of IMF Programmes in the Third World: Debate and Evidence from Latin America', *World Development*, forthcoming.

Payne, P. (1986), 'Appropriate Indicators for Project Design and Evaluation', in UNICEF/WFP, *Food Aid and the Well-being of Children in the Developing World*. New York: UNICEF.

Perrin, R. K., and G. Scobie (1981), 'Market Intervention Policies for Increasing the Consumption of Nutrients by Low Income Households'. *American Journal of Agricultural Economics*, 63/1: 75–82.

Phan-Thuy, N. (1978), 'Cost–Benefit Analysis of Labour-intensive Public Works Programmes: A Case Study of the Pilot Intensive Rural Employment Project (PIREP) in Mangalur Block of Tamil Nadu in India'. ILO/WEP 2-24/WP 10.

Pinstrup-Andersen, P., (1983), 'Export Crop Production and Malnutrition', *Food and Nutrition*, 9: 6–14.

—— (1984), 'The Nutritional Impact of the Colombian Food and Nutrition Programme in the State of Cauca, Colombia'. Report to Colombian Government. Mimeographed. Washington, DC: IFPRI.

—— (1985), 'Food Prices and the Poor in Developing Countries', *European Review of Agricultural Economics*, 12: 1–2.

—— (1986a), 'Macroeconomic Adjustment Policies and Human Nutrition: Available Evidence and Research Needs'. Paper presented at the 12th Session of the UNACC/SCN, Tokyo.

—— (1986b), 'Assuring Food Security and Adequate Nutrition for the Poor during Periods of Economic Crises and Macroeconomic Adjustments: Policy Options and Experience with Food Subsidies and Transfer Programmes'. Paper presented at the 2nd Takemi Symposium on International Health, Harvard University.

—— ed. (1987), *Consumer-oriented Food Subsidies: Costs, Benefits, and Policy Options for Developing Countries*. Baltimore: Johns Hopkins University Press.

Popkin, B. (1980), 'Time Allocation of the Mother and Child and Nutrition', *Ecology of Food and Nutrition*, 9: 1–14.

PREALC—Program Regional de Empleo en América Latina y el Caribe (1985a), 'Mas allá de la crisis: Trabajos presentados a la IV Conferencia del PREALC'. Santiago: PREALC.

PREALC (1985*b*), 'Household Behaviour and Economic Crisis: Costa Rica 1979–1982'. Santiago: PREALC.

Preston, S. H. (1978), 'Morbidity and Development', *Population Bulletin of the UNECWA,* 15: 63–78.

—— (1980), 'Causes and Consequences of Mortality Declines in Less Developed Countries during the Twentieth Century', in Easterlin, R. A. ed., *Population and Economic Change in Developing Countries.* Washington, DC: National Bureau of Economic Research.

Psacharapolous, G. (1985), *Returns to Education: A Further International Update and Implications.* Washington, DC: World Bank. Education and Training Department.

Raczynski, D. and C. Serrano (1985), 'Vivir la pobreza: testimonio de mujeres'. Santiago: Corporacion Investigacciones Economicas Latino America (PISPAL–CIEPLAN).

Rahman, A. (1986), *The Demand and Marketing Aspects of Grameen Bank: A Closer Look.* Dakar: University Press.

Raj, K. N. (1984), 'The Causes and Consequences of World Recession', in Jolly, R., and G. A. Cornia, eds. (1984).

Ranis, G. (1984), 'Needed: Commitment to Structural Change', *Challenge,* 27/3: 21–6.

—— and F. Stewart (1987), 'Macro Policies for Appropriate Technology: Rural Linkages in the Philippines and Taiwan', in F. Stewart, ed. *Macro Policies for Appropriate Technology in Developing Countries.* Boulder, Col.: Westview.

Rao Maturu, N. (1979), 'Nutrition and Labour Productivity', *International Labour Review,* 118: 1/1 12.

Reichman, T. M., and R. Stillson (1978), 'Experience with Programs of Balance of Payments Adjustment: Stand-by Arrangements in the Higher Credit Tranches', *IMF Staff Papers,* 25/2. Washington, DC: IMF.

Richards, P. (1985), *Indigenous Agricultural Revolution.* London: Hutchinson.

Rios, A. R. (1984), 'The Invisible Economy of Poverty: The Case of Brazil', *La Pauvreté, mondes en developpement* 12/45: 1–191.

Robertson, L., J. H. Davis, and K. Jobe (1984), 'Service Volume and Other Factors Affecting the Costs of Immunizations in the Gambia', *Bulletin of World Health Organization,* 62/5: 729–36.

Robertson, R. *et al.* (1984), 'Service Volume and Other Factors Affecting the Cost of Immunization in The Gambia', *Bulletin of the WHO,* 62/5: 729–36.

Rogers, B. L. (1987), 'Design and Implementation Considerations for Consumer Food Price Subsidies', in Pinstrup-Andersen, P., ed. (1987).

—— and J. F. Levinson (1976), 'Subsidized Food Consumption Systems in Low-income Countries: The Pakistan Experience'. MIT International Nutrition Planning Programme Discussion Paper 6, Massachusetts Institute of Technology.

Rosero-Bixby, L. (1985), 'Infant Mortality Decline in Costa Rica', in Halstead, S. A. *et al.* (1985), 125–38.

Roy, D. K. (1986), 'Employment and Growth': A Strategy for Employment-oriented Industrialisation in Bangladesh. An Empirical Investigation'. Mimeographed. University of Antwerp.

Rudra, A., and A. K. Sen (1980), 'Farm Size and Labour Use: Analysis and Policy', *Economic and Political Weekly,* 15/5–7: 391–4.

Rutishauser, I. H. E., and R. Whitehead (1972), 'Energy Intake and Expenditure in

1- to 3-year-old Ugandan Children Living in a Rural Environment', *British Journal of Nutrition*, 28: 145–52.

Sáenz, A., and J. Di Paula (1981), 'Precisiones teórico-metodológicas sobre la noción de estrategias de existencias', *Demografía y economía*, 15/2: 46. (Mexico).

Safilios-Rothschild, C. (1980), *The Role of the Family: A Neglected Aspect of Poverty*. World Bank Staff Working Paper 403, Washington, DC: World Bank.

Scandizzo, P. L. (1984), 'Aggregate Supply Response: Empirical Evidence on Key Issues'. Mimeographed.

Schofield, S. (1974), 'Seasonal Factors Affecting Nutrition in Different Age Groups', *Journal of Development Studies*, 11: 24–47.

Scrimshaw, N. (1986), 'Nutritional and Health Consequence of Economic Adjustment Policies that Increase Poverty'. Paper for North–South Roundtable on Development: The Human Dimension. Saltburg, Sept.

Sebstad, J. (1982), *Struggle and Development among Self-employed Women*. Washington, DC: USAID.

Selowsky, M. (1979), *Who Benefits from Government Expenditure? A Case Study of Colombia*. World Bank, Oxford University Press.

Sethuraman, S. V. (1976), 'The Urban Informal Sector. Concept, Measurement, and Policy', *International Labour Review*, 14/1: 69–81.

—— ed. (1981), *The Urban Informal Sector in Developing Countries: Employment, Poverty, and Environment*. Geneva: ILO.

—— (1986), *Malnutrition and Food Consumption in Sri Lanka: An Analysis of Changes during the Past Decade*. Washington, DC: IFPRI.

Sharpley, J. (1984), 'The Potential of Domestic Stabilisation Measures', in Killick, T., ed. (1984).

Shetty, M. S. (1963), *Small-scale and Household Industries in a Developing Economy: A Study of Their Rationale, Structure and Operating Conditions*. New York: Asia Publishing House.

Singer, H. W. (1983), 'North–South Multipliers', *World Development*, 11/5: 451–4.

Solter, S., A. Hasibaun, and B. Yusuf (1986), 'An Epidemiological Approach to Health Planning and Problem-solving in Indonesia', *Health Policy and Planning*, 1:99–108.

Steel. W. (1977), *Small-scale Employment and Production in Developing Countries: Evidence from Ghana*. New York: Praeger.

Stinson, W. (1982), *Community Financing of Primary Health Care*. Washington, DC: American Public Health Association.

Sukhatme, P. V., ed. (1982), 'Newer Concepts in Nutrition and their Implication for Policy'. Pune, India: Maharashtra Association for the Cultivation of Science Research Institute.

Swenson, G. (1973), 'The Effects of Increase in Rice Production on Employment and Income Distribution in Thanjavur District, South India'. Ph.D. thesis, Michigan State University.

Taucher, E. (1983), 'Fertility and Mortality in Latin America', *Populi*, 10/3: 31–40.

Taylor, L. (1986), 'Developing Countries in the World Economy: Macro Effects of Myriad Shocks'. Paper for the Second Takemi Symposium on International Health, Harvard School of Public Health. Mimeographed. Massachusetts Institute of Technology.

Terra, J. P., and M. Hopenhaym (1986), 'Recesión políticas de ajuste y sus efectos sobre la situación de la infancia en el Uruguay, 1973–84'. Montevideo: Centro Latino-Americano Economía Humana (CLAEH).

Thomas, J. W., and R. M. Hook (1977), *Creating Rural Employment: A Manual for Organizing Rural Works Programmes*. Washington, DC: USAID.

—— S. J. Burki, P. C. Davies, and R. M. Hook (1975), 'Employment and Development: A Comparative Analysis of the Role of Public Works Programmes'. Harvard Institute for International Development.

Tienda, M. (1978), 'Dependency, Extension and the Family Life-cycle Squeeze in Peru'. University of Wisconsin, Center for Demography and Ecology, Paper 78-28.

Timberlake, L. (1985), *Africa in Crisis: The Cures of Environmental Bankruptcy*. London and Washington, DC: International Institute for Environment and Development, (Earthscan paperback).

Todd, J. (1971), 'Size of Firm and Efficiency in Colombian Manufacturing'. Economics Research Memorandum 41, Williams College Center for Development.

Tokman, V. E. (1978). 'An Exploration into the Nature of Formal–Informal Sector Relationships'. *World Development*, 6/9–10: 1065–75.

—— (1986), 'Ajuste y empleo: Los desafios del presente'. Oficina Internacional del Trabajo. Santiago: PREALC.

Tripp, R. (1981), 'Farmers and Traders: Some Economic Determinants of Nutritional Status in Northern Ghana', *Journal of Tropical Pediatrics*, 27: 15–21.

UN-DIESA (1983), 'Findings of the World Fertility Survey on Trends, Differentials and Discriminants of Mortality in Developing Countries'. Paper for the International Conference on Population, 1984, Export Group on Mortality and Health Policy. Rome: UN-DIESA.

—— (1985), *Demographic Yearbook 1984*. New York: UN.

—— (1986), *World Economic Survey 1986*. New York: UN.

UNDP/ILO (1986), Eighth Joint Meeting for Support to Special Public Works Programmes: Paper for the Agenda, New York: UN.

UNICEF (1981), *Report on Tanzania, 1980–81*. New York: UNICEF.

—— (1982), 'The UNICEF Home Gardens Handbook for People Promoting Mixed Gardening in the Humid Tropics'. New York: UNICEF.

—— (1983), *The State of the World's Children 1984*. Oxford University Press.

—— (1985a), *Within Human Reach: A Future for Africa's Children*. New York: UNICEF.

—— (1985b), *State of the World's Children 1985*. New York: Oxford University Press.

—— (1986), *Statistics on Children in UNICEF-assisted Countries*. New York: UNICEF.

UNICEF-Brazil (1984). *Annual Report for Brazil*. Mimeographed. Brasilia: UNICEF.

UNICEF-Burkina Faso (1986), 'The Situation Analysis of Children and Women in Burkina Faso'. Mimeographed. Ouagadougou: UNICEF.

UNICEF-Burma (1986), 'Children and Women in Burma: A Situation Analysis Report'. Mimeographed. Rangoon: Government of the Socialist Republic of the Union of Burma and UNICEF,

UNICEF-New Delhi (1986), 'Establishing a Child Monitoring System in India'. Paper for UNICEF Workshop on Establishing a Monitoring System for Child Survival and Development in India, Jan., New Delhi.

UNICEF-Ghana (July 1984), 'The Situation Analysis of Children and Women'. Mimeographed. Accra: UNICEF.

UNICEF-Kenya (1984), 'Situation Analysis of Children and Women in Kenya: Section 4, The Well-being of Children'. Mimeographed. Nairobi: Republic of Kenya, Central Bureau of Statistics, Ministry of Finance and Planning and UNICEF.

UNICEF-Peru (1985), 'Comedores Multifamiliares'. Mimeographed. Lima: UNICEF.

UNICEF-Philippines (1985), 'A Report on the Situation of Children in Negros Occidental'. Mimeographed. Manila: UNICEF.

UNICEF-Tanzania (1985), 'Analysis of the Situation of Children and Women'. Mimeographed. Dar es Salaam. Government of the United Republic of Tanzania and UNICEF.

UNICEF-The Gambia (1985), '1985 Annual Report'. Mimeographed, Banjul: UNICEF.

UNICEF-Sri Lanka (1985), 'Sri Lanka: The Social Impact of Economic Policies during the Last Decade'. Mimeographed. Colombo: UNICEF.

UNICEF-UDD (1986), 'Progress Report April–Dec. 1985'. Mimeographed. Amman: Urban Development Department.

UNICEF-Zambia (1986), 'Situation Analysis of Children and Women in Zambia'. Government of the Republic of Zambia and UNICEF. Mimeographed.

Valverde, V., Z. Rojas, P. Vinocus, and A. Thomson (1981), 'Organisation of an Information System for Food and Nutrition Programmes in Costa Rica', *Food and Nutrition*, 7/1: 32–40. Rome: FAO.

Van der Linde, M. (1984), 'Sistematización de la experiencia de los comedores familiares y/o populares al nivel de Lima Metropolitana'. Mimeographed. Lima.

Waife, R. S., and M. C. Burkhart, eds. (1981), *The Nonphysician and Family Health in Sub-Sahara Africa*. Boston: The Pathfinder Fund.

Walsh, J. A. (1985), 'Immunisation: A Question of Priorities'. Mimeographed. New York: UNICEF.

Wellings, P., and M. Sutcliffe (1984), 'Developing the Urban Informal Sector in South Africa: The Reformist Paradigm and its Fallacies'. *Development and Change*, 15: 517–50.

Wickramaarachchi, S. P. (1984), 'Keeping the People's Surplus in People's Hands', *Development: Seeds of Change*, 2.

Williamson, J., ed. (1983), *IMF Conditionality*. Washington, DC: Institute of International Economics.

Williamson-Gray, C. (1982), *Food Consumption Parameters for Brazil and Their Application to Food Policy*. Research Report 32. Washington, DC: IFPRI.

World Bank (1980), *World Development Report, 1980*. New York: Oxford University Press.

—— (1984), 'Alternative Financing Mechanisms for Education in Developing Countries'. Mimeographed. Washington, DC: World Bank.

—— (1986a), *World Development Report 1986*. New York: Oxford University Press.

—— (1986b), *Poverty and Hunger: Issues and Options for Food Security in Developing Countries*. World Bank Policy Study. Washington, DC: World Bank.

—— (1986c), *Poverty in Latin America: The Impact of Depression*. Report 6369, Latin America and the Caribbean Regional Office. Washington, DC: World Bank.

—— (1986d), *Commodity Trade and Price Trends*. Washington, DC: World Bank.

—— (1986e), *Financing Adjustment with Growth in Sub-Saharan Africa, 1986–90*. Washington, DC: World Bank.

—— (1986f), *Bangladesh: Recent Economic Developments and Medium-term Prospects*. South Asia Programs Department Report 6049, vol. 1. Washington, DC: World Bank.

WHO—World Health Organization (1978), 'Alma Ata 1978: Primary Health Care', Alma Ata, USSR 6–12 Sept. 1978. *Health for All* 1. Geneva: WHO.

—— (1985), *The Use of Essential Drugs*. Technical Report 722. Geneva: WHO.

—— (1986), 'Repercussions of the World Economic Situation'. Provisional Report by the Director-general, 39th World Health Assembly, A39/4.

WHO/UNICEF (1985), *Gardening for Food in the Semi-arid Tropics: A Handbook for Programme Planners*. New York: UNICEF.

Youssef, N. H., and C. B. Hetler (1984), 'Rural Households Headed by Women: Priority Concern for Development', World Employment Programme Research, Working Paper 31, Geneva: WEP.

Yunus, M. (1982), 'Grameen Bank Project in Bangladesh: A Poverty Focussed Rural Development Programme'. Grameen Bank Paper 19. Dhaka.

—— (1984), 'Introduction to the Grameen Bank'. Paper presented to the UN/ESCAP Workshop on Bank Credit for Landless Women: A Study Tour of the Grameen Bank, Dhaka.

Zerilin, M., and M. Manzoor (1985), 'Positive Deviance in Child Nutrition: With Emphasis on Psycho-social and Behavioural Aspects and Implications for Development'. Prepared for the WHO/UNICEF Joint Nutrition Support Programme, Tufts University School of Nutrition, Medford.

Zulu, J. B., and S. M. Nsouli (1985), *Adjustment Programs in Africa: The Recent Experience*. Occasional Paper 34, Washington, DC: IMF.

Index